MODERN SYRIA
From Ottoman Rule to Pivotal Role in the Middle East

Modern Syria

From Ottoman Rule to Pivotal Role in the Middle East

EDITED BY

Moshe Ma'oz

Joseph Ginat, and

Onn Winckler

SUSSEX
ACADEMIC
PRESS

BRIGHTON • PORTLAND

2 4 6 8 10 9 7 5 3 1
First published 1999 in Great Britain by
SUSSEX ACADEMIC PRESS
Box 2950
Brighton BN2 5SP

and in the United States of America by
'SUSSEX ACADEMIC PRESS
5804 N.E. Hassalo St.
Portland, Oregon 97213-3644

British Library Cataloguing in Publication Data
A CIP catalogue record for this book is available from the British Library.

Library of Congress Cataloging-in-Publication Data
Modern Syria : from Ottoman rule to pivotal role in the Middle East / edited by Moshe Ma'oz, Joseph Ginat, Onn Winckler.
p. cm
Includes bibliographical references and index.
ISBN 1-898723-83-4 (hc : alk. paper). — ISBN 1-902210-32-8 (pbk. : alk paper)
1. Syria—History—1971– 2. Syria—Foreign relations—1971–
3. Syria—Social conditions—1971– 4. Syria—Economic conditions—1971–
I. Ma'oz, Moshe. II. Ginat, J. III. Winckler, Onn.
DS98.4.M63 1999
956.91—dc21 99-29246
CIP

Printed by Bookcraft, Midsomer Norton, Bath
This book is printed on acid-free paper

Contents

Preface vii
Acknowledgments xix
List of Abbreviations xx

1 Introduction: The Emergence of Modern Syria 1
Moshe Ma'oz, Joseph Ginat, and Onn Winckler

Part I The Political System under Asad 15

2 In Search of Legitimacy: Asad's Islamic Image in the Syrian Official Press
Mordechai Kedar 17

3 Syria: The Renewed Struggle for Power
Eyal Zisser 33

Part II Economic Developments and Structural Changes 55

4 History and Political Culture in Syria: Obstacles to Integration in the Global Economy After the Gulf War
David W. Lesch 57

5 Syria: Economic Development, Achievements, Problems and Prospects
Moshe Efrat 79

6 The Syrian Road to the Middle East Peace Process: The Socioeconomic Perspective
Onn Winckler 109

Part III Socio-Demographic Aspects 133

7 The Question of Citizenship of the Algerian Immigrants in Syria, 1847–1900
Ş. Tufan Buzpınar 135

8 European Foreigners in Damascus and Aleppo During the Late Ottoman Period
Yoram Shalit 150

9 Betwixt and Between: The Arab Al-'Aramshah Tribe of Southern Lebanon
Joseph Ginat 170

Part IV Regional Relations 189

10 The Franco-Syrian Treaty Negotiations and the Question of Lebanon, 1936–1939
Meir Zamir 191

11 Syrian–Iraqi Relations: Iraq as a Factor in the Syrian Foreign Policy
Michael Eppel 210

12 Turkish–Syrian Relations: An Update
David Kushner 228

Part V Strategy toward Israel 243

13 Syria's Struggle over Water with Israel, 1959–1967
Moshe Shemesh 245

14 Changes in Syria's Regional Strategic Position *vis-à-vis* Israel
Moshe Ma'oz 257

15 Asad's Art of the Double Game
Daniel Pipes 272

The Contributors 293
Index 297

Preface

This volume is the outcome of the conference: Modern Syria (19th and 20th Centuries): Social, Economic and Political Issues, held on December 17–18, 1996 by the Jewish–Arab Center at the University of Haifa, Israel. The Berta Von Suttner Research Program of Germany provided financial assistance for the conference, for which we express our profound thanks. The fifteen chapters included in this volume are based on lectures of the participants at the conference on a wide range of issues covering the political, social and economic history of Syria from the late Ottoman period until the present day. The chapters present different aspects of the changes and processes occurring in Syria during the period under discussion. The views expressed are those of the authors themselves and do not necessarily represent those of the Jewish–Arab Center or the editors.

The Introduction of the volume, "The Emergence of Modern Syria," by the editors, contains two sections. The first section traces the development of Syria from a part of the large Ottoman Empire (1516–1917), with the central authority in Istanbul, through the French Mandate period (1920–46) into an independent state (1946) and the emergence of a national and territorial identity. The second section analyzes the tools and methods enabling Hafiz al-Asad and the Ba'th party to achieve political stability in Syria during the past three decades. However, it must be emphasized, according to the authors, that this stability "depends to a large degree on Asad's personality and political skills, rather than on deep-rooted political traditions and institutions."

Part I, The Political System Under Asad, contains two chapters dealing with crucial issues in the continuous political stability of Syria. Chapter 2, Mordechai Kedar's "In Search of Legitimacy: Asad's Islamic Image in the Syrian Official Press," analyzes Asad's attempts to achieve a wide religious legitimacy for his leadership in a country with more than three-quarters of its citizens comprised by Sunni-Muslims. Rightly, the author opens the chapter by saying that: "The Muslim religion presents the most serious ideological challenge to the legitimacy of Hafiz al-Asad's regime." During the years 1976–82, the "Muslim Brotherhood" constituted the most serious threat to the very existence of the Syrian 'Alawi–Ba'thi regime, led by Asad.

Kedar notes that in order to achieve religious legitimacy, "Asad spares no efforts to gain Islamic 'imprimatur' to himself as a Muslim and to his being a president as a Muslim leader." These efforts encompass many aspects, including the restoration to the Syrian Constitution of the previous formulation of the presidential oath: "I swear by Allah Akbar." Thus, from time to time, Asad makes sure to obtain the authorization that he is Muslim from various religious figures, among them the *Mufti* of Damascus and the Lebanese Shi'i *Imam*, Musa al-Sadr. This chapter, however, concentrates on one particular aspect of these efforts – the Islamic messages of the Syrian government in the local press, entirely state-controlled, during Asad's era, especially in the months of *Ramadan*.

Throughout the chapter, Kedar offers many examples in which Asad appears in the Syrian press as a legitimate Muslim leader, including Asad's participation in public prayers, particularly during the month of *Ramadan*; the announcement of *Ramadan* and *'Id al-Fitr*; holiday greetings sent to Asad from foreign leaders and Syrian notables, particularly religious figures; publication of the Qur'an; and reports of Asad's activities within the international Islamic framework. The major conclusion of the chapter is that while the religious factor continues to play an important role in Syrian internal politics, "it is by no means clear that one may still speak of a viable threat directed at the Asad regime from extreme Islamic elements."

Chapter 3, Eyal Zisser's "Syria: The Renewed Struggle for Power," probes one of the most, if not the most, important questions in Syria – the successor of Asad. Zisser's basic assumption is: "It would therefore appear that the challenges and difficulties – from within and from without – that confront the Syrian regime today do not pose even a potential threat to the stability or continued existence of the regime." However, at the same time, it must be taken into account that the current Syrian regime is, first and foremost, of a personal nature, centered around Asad himself. While this is a clear advantage to Asad as the current ruler, it also raises some questions regarding the future regime in the post-Asad era. Such questions arose in full force during 1983–84, following Asad's heart attack, when his brother Rif'at tried to promote himself to the position of Asad's successor.

After this episode, the succession question lost its urgency for almost a decade. However, in the early 1990s, Asad decided that the time had come to again confront the succession question. The only candidate was his eldest and favorite son, Basil, who followed in Asad's footsteps and embarked on a military career in preparation for entering politics. At the same time, he enjoyed considerable popular support, even outside the 'Alawi community and the Ba'th party, as the successor of choice. However, the death of Basil in a car accident in January 1994 reopened the succession question, this time without a broad consensus regarding the appropriate nominee.

The new candidate as Asad's successor was his second son, Bashar. However, according to Zisser, it seems that Asad's step to establish Bashar as his successor "has already aroused some tension and unrest among the ranks, thus revealing the extent to which the succession issue is sensitive and complicated." The key question is: Can Asad succeed in passing the reins of power to Bashar while he is still alive? It seems that the answer to this crucial question depends to a large extent on the support of the commanders of the army and the security forces, which hold the practical reins of power, particularly in light of the fissures that have appeared in the highest echelons. At the moment, Asad's succession remains an open question.

Part II, Economic Developments and Structural Changes, contains three chapters providing a broad overview of the various economic structural changes and developments occurring in Syria under Asad's regime. Chapter 4, David W. Lesch's "History and Political Culture in Syria: Obstacles to Integration in the Global Economy After the Gulf War," examines the obstacles of Western companies to penetration into the Syrian market during the 1990s, following Law No. 10 of May 1991, due mainly to decades of state-dominated economy. Lesch's chapter is unique in that he gives the readers simultaneously an academic and a business perspective by virtue of the fact that in addition to his academic position, the author is also the manager of the MEIBA company, which promotes business of Western companies in the Middle East.

In the second section of the chapter, Lesch analyzes the process of transferring the Syrian economy into a state domain and reviews the economic developments in Syria during the Asad era. He also addresses the succession question and the peace negotiations with Israel beginning in the Madrid Conference of 1991. Lesch concludes his chapter by stating that: "Finding the 'magic pace' of reform that will indeed contribute to economic growth while not undermining his [Asad's] support base is the key, and his 'zigzag' approach has been fairly effective. But time is not on his side, and the hard economic realities will most likely require a watershed change of policy in the not-too-distant future, regardless of progress on the peace front, if the regime is to survive." However, he added that: "Syria's history, political culture, business environment, and regional setting are working against him, but Asad has been extremely adept at managing through crisis periods before; regional circumstances may again allow him room to wade through the mess intact." The harsh economic situation in Syria in 1997–98, due both to the continued low oil prices and the severe drought, only emphasize the need for reforms in the Syrian economy in order to revive economic expansion.

Chapter 5, Moshe Efrat's "Syria: Economic Development, Achievements, Problems and Prospects," considers the economic developments in Syria during the period of 1980–94 in relation to a wide variety of issues, including: changes in the economic growth rates; investments and domestic savings; progress in the economic liberalization process, due mainly to Law No. 10 (May 1991); the employment structure and increase in available job opportunities; the oil sector; the balance of payments; foreign trade composition and developments; and most importantly, the import of arms and the defense burden of the 1980s, when military expenditures constituted more than half of the governmental budget and approximately 20 percent of the GDP.

Regarding future Syrian economic developments, Efrat argues that: "In the foreseeable future, it is unlikely that any major new liberalization measures will be promulgated. As far as the Syrian regime is concerned, the public sector is not only instrumental in controlling the economy, it is also – and perhaps even more importantly – a medium for securing the ascent and predominance of the 'Alawi community." Thus, the author does not project rapid economic development in Syria in the foreseeable future. However, Efrat does argue that through the implementation of some key measures, including deepening the liberalization process, simplifying the exchange rate structure, and establishing a private banking system, the Syrian authorities have the potential to alleviate at least some of the current economic and social difficulties.

Chapter 6, Onn Winckler's "The Syrian Road to the Middle East Peace Process: The Socioeconomic Perspective," investigates the socioeconomic factors which encouraged Asad in the late 1980s to abandon the "strategic balance" policy and to enter into peace negotiations with Israel following the 1990–91 Gulf crisis. Winckler claims that the Syrian authorities were able to allocate huge financial and manpower resources to military and security purposes and at the same time to achieve high rates of economic growth as long as the oil prices were high during the 1970s and early 1980s. However, with the end of the bonanza time of very high oil prices at the end of the "oil decade" in 1982, in parallel to the refusal of the Soviets to continue supplying arms to Syria on open credit, as well as the prolonged negative consequences of the high natural increase rates, the Syrian economy could no longer sustain the economic costs of the "strategic balance" policy and entered into a deep recession during the latter part of the 1980s, forcing a withdrawal from that policy.

According to the author, one of the major reasons that Syria joined the anti-Iraqi coalition during the 1990–91 Gulf crisis was to gain economic benefits from both the capital-rich Gulf countries and the West. Indeed, this calculated move paid off and Syria won significant economic benefits and, at the same time, considerable political advantage, both in the international arena and in the Arab world. Combined with the sharp rise in oil revenues and increasing agricultural production due to good weather, Syria achieved high economic growth rates of 7 percent annually on average, in real terms, during the first half of the 1990s. Its improved economic situation, according to the author, also affected the Syrian-Israeli peace negotiations. Whereas Egypt, the Palestinians, and Jordan all entered into peace negotiations with Israel when their economies were in such a grim state as to constitute a real threat to the continuation of the existing regimes, Syria, in contrast, was able to manage slow negotiations with Israel and to insist on all its basic demands. However, during the last two years (1997–98), the rate of economic growth in Syria has markedly slowed down to less than 2 percent annually on average and the question remains as to how the current economic recession in Syria will affect the process of Syrian–Israeli peace negotiations.

Part III, Socio-Demographic Aspects, contains three chapters highlighting new information regarding some of the various socio-demographic issues of the Syrian region. Chapter 7, Ş. Tufan Buzpınar's "The Question of Citizenship of the Algerian Immigrants in Syria, 1847–1900," deals with the issue of the immigration of Algerians into the Syrian region following the French occupation of Algiers in July 1830. In addition to examining the process of migration itself and the absorption of the Algerian immigrants in Syria, the chapter analyzes the relationship between the French and the Ottoman authorities, both in Syria and in Istanbul, regarding the immigrants' identity and their naturalization as Ottoman citizens.

While the number of Algerian immigrants arriving to Syria through 1882 was quite considerable, no major problems emerged between the Ottoman regime and the French, or between the immigrants and the local authorities in Syria. However, from 1882 onward, a substantial change in the attitudes of the Ottoman authorities *vis-à-vis* the Algerian immigrants emerged. The immediate reason was the claim of the Syrian Wali that Amir 'Abd al-Qader (the leader of the Algerian immigrants) was protecting certain Algerian immigrants who had committed crimes. However, the Ottoman authorities were mainly disturbed by the French attitude toward the immigrants, who had begun to emphasize their traditional links to Syria within the framework of the competition with

England for overseas possessions. As the author writes: "Their [the French] goal was to increase the number of Algerians who had French citizenship or at least French protectorship." In 1889, the Ottoman authorities finally achieved their objective to make the Algerian immigrants Ottoman citizens. The issue of the Algerian immigrants in Syria is only one example of how the struggle between the European powers for control and influence over Ottoman territories started already in the nineteenth century. It also contributes to a better understanding of the French position regarding the division of the Mandates for the former Ottoman territories between France and Britain following World War I.

Chapter 8, Yoram Shalit's "European Foreigners in Damascus and Aleppo During the Late Ottoman Period," provides us with inside observations on the day-to-day life of foreigners in Aleppo and Damascus during the late Ottoman period. The main aim of this chapter is to reexamine the widespread assumption that the absence of Europeans in Damascus during the seventeenth and eighteenth centuries, in contrast to Aleppo, was due to the intolerant attitude of the Damascus Muslim inhabitants towards foreigners.

Shalit argues that the real reason for the absence of foreigners was a purely economic one. In eighteenth century Damascus, the higher strata of society was primarily comprised of the 'ulama, whose economic base was the purchase of real estate and therefore did not necessitate close ties with foreign traders. In Aleppo, on the other hand, the vested economic and commercial interests of the upper strata dictated their close ties with foreign traders. On the part of the foreign traders as well, their varied economic interests in Aleppo forced them to locate their trade stations in the city. However, on the contrary, while Damascus was a potential market for European consumer goods, it had no attractive product, like silks, to offer in return. Moreover, the Damascene trade was connected to a large degree with the *Hajj* caravan, which, for religious reasons, was limited to participation by Muslims. Lacking economic interests, there was no reason for the Europeans to locate their trading stations in Damascus. In any case, Shalit writes: "They [the lower strata] did not have the potential to trade with foreigners and were therefore also not accustomed to their presence, if any." This fact provides some explanation for their attitude toward foreigners in both of the cities during the eighteenth century. Only in the early nineteenth century is a change evident, with consuls residing in Damascus as well.

Chapter 9, Joseph Ginat's "Betwixt and Between: The Arab al-'Aramshah Tribe of Southern Lebanon," describes and analyzes the history and socio-political developments of a Bedouin tribe located on both sides of the Lebanese–Israeli border. The first section of the chapter traces the two different assumptions regarding the origin of the tribe. This is followed by an account of the difficulties of the tribe arising from the establishment of borders in the early 1920s between the French and the British Mandates, which divided the tribe, for the first time in its history, between two different political entities. The second section delineates the social changes which the tribe has undergone during the last two generations, including the sedentarization process and the women's tribal position, which, according to Ginat, "is much higher than in other Bedouin tribes in the region and elsewhere."

The latter part of the chapter deals with the complications emerging from the division of the tribe between two hostile countries, particularly following the Israeli invasion of Lebanon in June 1982. Whereas in the past, the two parts of the tribe kept in close contact in spite of the border, the establishment of the security zone by Israel in south Lebanon in 1985, maneuvered the Lebanese part of the tribe into a position of betwixt and between the IDF and the SLA, on the one hand, and Hizballah and the LNA, on the other. Ginat concludes by stating that: "The situation in south Lebanon is, of course, not an easy one for the 150,000 people who live there. But the al-ʻAramshah case is much more complicated than for any other ethnic group . . . They are aware of the fact that they will face many difficulties when Israel finally withdraws. At the present time, they are trying to find any kind of safety valve in order to protect themselves from known as well as unknown dangers."

Part IV, Regional Relations, contains three chapters each of which addresses Syria's relations with one of its three neighboring countries – Lebanon, Iraq and Turkey. Chapter 10, Meir Zamir's "The Franco-Syrian Treaty Negotiations and the Question of Lebanon, 1936–1939," discusses the Franco–Lebanese–Syrian triangle in terms of the final borders and relations between Syria and Lebanon. During the negotiations on both treaties (the Franco–Syrian and the Franco–Lebanese) during 1936, the Syrians demanded "either to link Lebanon politically and economically to Syria or to revise Lebanon's border," particularly in regard to two areas: the Biqaʻ valley and Tripoli.

The return of these two areas to Syria was opposed by the Maronite Church, by French military circles, and by officials in the Quai d'Orsay, as well as by French companies with economic interests in Beirut. Thus, in order to achieve their demands, the Syrian National Bloc operated a massive campaign among the Muslim population in Lebanon and among leading Christian Lebanese political and clerical figures, urging them to support Lebanese unity with Syria and to oppose Lebanon's alliance with France. The French, on the other hand, repeatedly warned them that collaboration with the Syrians would be "endangering Lebanon's very existence." Finally, in the Franco–Syrian Treaty (September 1939), in return for the French agreement to grant Syria independence, the Syrian delegation was obliged to renounce its territorial claims in Lebanon, and the Biqa' valley and Tripoli were incorporated into Lebanese territory. In addition, the 1939 Franco–Turkish agreement accorded the province of Alexandretta (Iskenderun) to Turkey.

However, France's refusal to ratify both of the treaties left open the issue of Syrio–Lebanon relations. Referring to Syria's stance on Lebanon, Jamil Mardam wrote in September 1939 as follows: "In the littoral we have recognized a separate but not a foreign state. Lebanon will always be part of us, despite itself and despite ourselves." Zamir concludes his chapter by stating that: "This statement was to accurately describe relations between Syria and Lebanon after independence. Syria's ambitions in Lebanon, which had eluded the National Bloc between the two World Wars, were finally realized by President Hafiz al-Asad in the May 1991 Treaty of Brotherhood Cooperation and Coordination, which effectively subjugated Lebanon to Syria."

Chapter 11, Michael Eppel's "Syrian–Iraqi Relations: Iraq as a Factor in the Syrian Foreign Policy," explores the changes in the relations between Syria and Iraq since their establishment until the present day. The main thesis is that during the period under discussion, the relations between the two countries have undergone four main phases. In the first phase, lasting from the early 1920s until the ascendancy of the Ba'th party in both countries, in 1963, relations between Syria and Iraq "were characterized by asymmetry and an unequal balance of power," due to the Iraqi intervention in Syrian domestic politics. The second phase, beginning with the ascendancy of the Ba'th regime (with the Arab unity ideology) in both countries, was characterized by a rift between the two Ba'th parties that created hostility between the countries themselves. This trend was strengthened when Syria, in contrast to most other Arab states, supported Iran during the 1980–88 Iran–Iraq war.

The 1990–91 Gulf crisis and the sanctions imposed on Iraq by the UN created a new phase in the balance of power between Syria and Iraq – for the first time, in favor of the former. Thus, during the 1990s, according to the author, "the Iraqi threat against Syria . . . disappeared, at least in the short term." In the spring of 1997, the fourth phase began with an improvement in the relations between the two countries. Regarding the future relations between Syria and Iraq, Eppel projects that: "the personal mistrust and hostility between the two leaders [Asad and Saddam Husayn] reduces the chances for rapprochement and long-standing alliance between their countries, but does not negate tactical cooperation . . . Continued stagnation of the peace process, combined with the rapprochement between Israel and Turkey, and the continuation of the Turkish threat to the Euphrates waters . . . constitute grounds for a thaw in Syrian relations with Iraq in order to demonstrate Syria's dissatisfaction and to exert pressure on the West."

Chapter 12, David Kushner's "Turkish–Syrian Relations: An Update," surveys and analyzes the relations between Turkey and Syria from the early 1980s onward. The main thesis is that since Syria's independence, the relations between the two countries can be divided into two main phases. In the first phase, lasting until after the collapse of the UAR in September 1961, their relations "moved from a rather chilly beginning toward a state confrontation." The second phase has been characterized by improved relations, due to the adoption of a more realistic and flexible approach by both of the countries. However, in spite of the improved relations, "important 'irritants' continued to cast a shadow over the nature of relations," the most important of which are the disagreement over the proper distribution of the Euphrates River's water and the alleged support given by Syria to terrorist organizations operating in Turkish territories.

Thus, in spite of the various agreements that have been signed between Turkey and Syria since the mid-1980s, the state of relations between the two countries deteriorated again in the mid-1990s, deriving primarily from the expansion of Turkish irrigation projects with no agreement about the water distribution issue, on the one hand, and increasing cases of infiltration from Syria into Turkey, on the other. During recent years, in addition to the "traditional" factors that have hindered Turkish–Syrian relations, a new one has emerged, namely, the Turkish–Israeli military cooperation, which is viewed by Syria as a threat. In October 1998, the Turkish government decided to force Syria to withdraw once and for all from supporting the PKK "by bringing matters to the brink of war." Eventually, the crisis was ended by an agreement signed in Ankara later that year. As a result, Abdullah Öcalan (the PKK leader) was forced out of Syria and was extradited to the Turkish authorities. It remains to be seen how long the new understanding between Turkey and Syria will last.

Part V, Strategy toward Israel, contains three chapters providing a broad overview on the Syrian strategy toward Israel from the 1950s until the present. Chapter 13, Moshe Shemesh's "Syria's Struggle over Water with Israel, 1959–1967," focuses on the conflict over the diversion of the Jordan River's water, which was one of the major catalysts leading to the June 1967 war. In the first section of the chapter, Shemesh describes the firm objection of the Syrian Ba'th leaders to the Israeli Jordan River's water diversion scheme. While they advocated taking military action in order to prevent the completion of the Israeli scheme, the UAR president,

'Abd al-Nasser, preferred to deal with the issue through the Mixed Armistice Commission. This controversy, however, contributed to the resignation of the Ba'th ministers from the UAR government in late 1959.

In response to the completion of the Israeli Water Carrier, the Second Arab Summit (September 1964) decided to conduct a diversion scheme of the Jordan's tributaries. Syria was the first country to begin operation in her own territory in November 1964. The Israeli reaction was almost immediate, and in November 1964 armed clashes erupted, making it clear that Israel was determined to prevent Syria from completing its diversion scheme at all costs. However, the clashes with the IDF, which continued until July 1966, did not prevent the Syrians from continuing the diversion work in spite of the absence of commitment from the other Arab countries, especially Egypt, to provide military support to Syria in case of an all-out war with Israel. The author concludes the chapter by saying that in the final analysis, "Syria had to admit that it could not fight alone against Israel . . . The need to compensate itself for this failure and bolster its shattered prestige led Syria to support the Fatah organization's guerrilla attacks against Israel."

Chapter 14, Moshe Ma'oz's "Changes in Syria's Regional Strategic Position *vis-à-vis* Israel," deals with Syria's attitude toward Israel from its independence onward. The author opens the chapter by stating that: "One of the main characteristics of the Syrian quest for pan-Arab and anti-Israeli leadership was the dichotomy between the grand design and the ability to carry it out." While Syria's ongoing internal problems during the 1950s and 1960s prevented it from fulfilling this leading role, the ascendancy of Asad in late 1970 changed this state of affairs, and for the first time, Syria had a powerful leader with ambitions to gain pan-Arab influence. The thesis is that under Asad, the Syrian policy *vis-à-vis* Israel can be divided into four main phases: The first was characterized by "all-Arab solidarity" in order to promote a coordinated struggle against Israel. The second phase consisted of Asad's efforts toward establishing the "Fertile Crescent" with Iraq, as an alternative to Egypt, while at the same time trying to forge a "Greater Syria" union with Lebanon, Jordan and the Palestinians. The third stage of "strategic balance" was adopted following the Egyptian–Israeli peace treaty (March 1979), on the one hand, and failure to establish either the "Fertile Crescent" or "Greater Syria," on the other. However, by the late 1980s, Asad was forced to withdraw from this policy and to adopt a new policy of the "two-track strategy."

Ma'oz claims that "by late 1995 or early 1996, Syria and Israel became rather close to concluding a peace agreement," as they reached a mutual understanding on many issues, including Israeli withdrawal from the

Golan Heights. However, the suspension of the bilateral talks by the new Israeli Prime Minister, Shimon Peres, as a result of Damascus' refusal to condemn the bloody terrorist attacks by the Hamas in Israel, and the negative attitude of the new Netanyahu government elected in late May 1996 regarding the Golan Heights, halted the Israeli–Syrian peace negotiations. Ma'oz concludes the chapter by arguing that: "following the election of Ehud Barak as Israel's Prime Minister in May 1999, the prospects for Syrian–Israeli peacemaking have once again become promising."

Chapter 15, Daniel Pipes' "Asad's Art of the Double Game," represents a different approach to Syria's aims and policies toward Israel. The main thesis is that the unwillingness of Asad's regime to take a stand may be its most characteristic feature. Instead, Asad prefers to juggle several policies at the same time – what Pipes refers to as "the art of the double game," that is, taking two contrary steps or initiating two contradictory policies at the same time. Although the chapter concentrates on Syria's foreign affairs, the author claims that the double game is played in the domestic arena as well.

In order to support his thesis, Pipes indicates that Asad simultaneously maintains good and bad relations with other Middle Eastern governments and leaders. The clearest example of Asad's double game is in the Hizballah's operation. While Syria creates the illusion that Hizballah is an independent Lebanese organization aiming to liberate south Lebanon from Israeli occupation, in reality, according to Pipes, "the Hizballah not only receives Syrian funding, equipment, logistics, and information, but Damascus must approve all Iranian aid." Also in the case of the peace negotiations with Israel, between July 1991 and May 1996, the author claims that Asad took "a flurry of contradictory steps, moving toward and away from Israel."

Pipes traces both the roots and the motivations behind Asad's double game. He notes that: "In part, it may result from Asad's 'Alawi origins . . . 'Alawis have a long tradition of religious dissimulation (*taqiyya*), honed over the centuries by the need to pretend to be Muslim . . . In part too, the double game reflects Asad's cautious personality. He avoids risk whenever possible and it [the double game] allows him to take the fewest chances." Moreover, the double game brings a number of benefits, mainly an air of mystery, time to move slowly in making major shifts in policy, and greater flexibility of action.

Despite the diverse approaches among the various contributors to this volume on many issues, primarily regarding Asad's intentions *vis-à-vis* Israel, the degree of changes which have occurred in the Syrian economy and its future prospects, there is a consensus that during the last generation, under Asad and the Ba'th regime, Syria has undergone fundamental changes in a wide variety of aspects. It seems that the most important of these changes is that within only one generation, Syria has become a pivotal factor in Middle Eastern politics, with broad recognition of its military strength and powerful political position. Moreover, whereas during the 1940s and 1950s Syria was subject to annexation attempts, mainly by the Hashemites, and during the period February 1958–September 1961 the country was under direct Egyptian control, it is now itself in a position of control over another Middle Eastern country, namely, Lebanon.

In the field of economic structure and policies, the changes made have been substantial as well. Although Syria continues to be a low-middle income country with per capita GDP less than $1,400, a closer examination of the changes occurring in the Syrian economy since the late 1980s reveals the high potential that exists in many sectors. Now, it remains to be seen whether the Syrian regime will be able to utilize that potential in the coming years, and how the current economic recession in Syria will affect both the shape and the pace of the future Syrian–Israeli peace negotiations.

Moshe Ma'oz
Joseph Ginat
Onn Winckler
August 1999

Acknowledgments

The Berta Von Suttner Research Program of Germany provided the financial assistance for the conference, as well as for publication of this volume, for which we express our profound thanks. We would like to take this opportunity to extend a special thanks to Dr. Karlheinz Koppe from the Berta Von Suttner Research Program for the personal interest and involvement that he has shown in this publication. We would like also to express our profound thanks to those who helped in both conducting the conference and producing this volume. First and foremost, we would like to express our gratitude to the authors of this volume for their contributions and cooperation during the production process. Also our heartfelt gratitude goes to Dr. Ibrahim Geries, the head of the Jewish–Arab Center, Ms. Zvia Haimovitz, the administrator of the Center, and Ms. Rivka Fedder, the secretary, who were responsible for the smooth operation of both the conference and the production of the volume. We would also like to thank Ms. Sharon Woodrow for editing, Ms. Hana Katz for typing, Mr. Eyal Ari for proofing the manuscripts, and Mr. Joshua Rubin for arranging the figures and tables.

Abbreviations

b/d	Barrel per day.
DoP	Declaration of Principles (The Israeli-Palestinian agreement – September 1993).
EU	European Union.
GCC	Gulf Cooperation Council.
GDP	Gross Domestic Product.
GFCF	Gross Fixed Capital Formation.
GNP	Gross National Product.
IBRD	International Bank for Reconstruction and Development.
IDF	The Israeli Defense Forces.
IJMES	*International Journal of Middle East Studies.*
ISI	Import-Substituting Industrialization.
LNA	Lebanese National Army.
IMF	International Monetary Fund.
LS	Syrian Pound.
MEI	*Middle East International.*
MER	*Middle East Record.*
MES	*Middle Eastern Studies.*
PKK	Partiya Kerkeran-i Kurdistan.
PLO	Palestinian Liberation Organization.
SIPRI	Stockholm International Peace Research Institute.
SLA	South Lebanese Army.
UAE	United Arab Emirates.
UAR	United Arab Republic.
UN	United Nations.
UNDP	United Nations Development Programme.
UNICEF	United Nations Children's Fund.
UN ECWA/ ESCWA	United Nations Economic (and Social) Commission for Western Asia.
USACDA	US Arms Control and Disarmament Agency

1

Introduction: The Emergence of Modern Syria

Moshe Ma'oz, Joseph Ginat, and Onn Winckler

Historical Background

During its long history, stretching back to about 2,500 BC[1] and until independence in 1946, Syria had never constituted a unified and separate state. Rather, it was part of large empires or controlled by external rulers, such as the Persians, the Greeks and the Romans, and from 1516 until the end of World War I, it was part of the Ottoman Empire.[2] Even the term "Syria" is a Greek word. The Arabs, who conquered the region in the seventh century, used the name *Bilad al-Sham* (the country in the north or the northern region). Only during the mid-nineteenth century did the Arabs adopt the term *Suriyya* ("Syria") as a reflection of local patriotism.[3]

Syria under Ottoman Rule (1516–1917)

Under Ottoman rule, Syria was not a separate political entity, but was divided into several *Wilayets* (provinces) with the central authority in Istanbul. Although for centuries the basic allegiance of the majority Sunni-Muslim population was to the Ottoman-Islamic state, several groups or regions developed into socio-political autonomies and/or maintained their communal-religious identities, notably 'Alawis, Druze, and Christians. Indeed, an important identity of the vast majority of the Syrian population was with the tribe, the religious sect, or the place of residence, rather than with the country. In addition, among the Sunni-Muslim majority there existed a socioeconomic gap between a small urban oligarchy – landlords and 'ulama – and many small and landless peasants in the rural areas and lower stratums in the urban centers. Since the economic structure of the

Syrian region at that time was based primarily on agriculture, the middle class was rather very small. In addition, the absence of a central educational system contributed to the diversification of the Syrian population during most of the Ottoman period.

Only during the 1830s, under the regime of the Egyptian ruler Ibrahim Pasha, was the local power structure destroyed and a central authority imposed. However, the Ottoman *Tanzimat* regime that followed[4] was too weak to pursue the Egyptian reforms in the Syrian region and thus needed the assistance of indigenous notables and tribal *Shaykhs* in order to enforce its authority. Nevertheless, toward the end of the century Ottoman authority gradually extended, while since the 1860s there emerged for the first time among Christian intellectuals notions of Syrian territorial identity and Arab cultural consciousness. These notions subsequently merged into a Syrian–Arab national ideology, notably under the rule of Amir (later king) Faysal in Syria (1918–20).

Syria under the French Mandate: Combating Syrian Nationalism

At the San-Remo Conference (1920), the Mandate[5] for Syria and Lebanon was allocated to France,[6] which ousted Faysal from Syria in July 1920. The French authorities discouraged the development of a Syrian national community, while adopting two major methods by which to control Syria and Lebanon. The first was to achieve cooperation with the traditional élite, mainly the Sunni-Muslim urban upper class, which consisted of a few hundred families and constituted the political, as well as the socio-economic, élite. They owned the vast majority of the agricultural land, being the chief economic sector in Syria,[7] and dominated the commercial and industrial activities in the major urban centers.

The second method was to "divide and rule" – the aim being to weaken the Syrian–Arab national movement. In order to achieve this aim, the Mandate authorities divided Syria into several administrative and political units, notably the Territories of the 'Alawis and the Druze, as well as the region of Alexandretta and the Jazira. The official French explanation for the establishment of these units was that it was "due to the separatist feelings of various sections of the population and their different levels of development."[8]

In addition to encouraging separate 'Alawi and Druze autonomies, the French also recruited many members of these sects to the "Troupes Spéciales du Levant,"[9] all of which contributed to the fostering of communal separatism and to the widening of the gap between the Sunni-Muslim majority and the various minorities.[10] Moreover, the absence of a national ideological consensus and of a prominent leader with the necessary prestige and political skills to lead a nationalist movement, also contributed to maintaining the sectarian and class division among Syrian society throughout the Mandatory period.

Independent Syria: Attempts at National Integration

Following World War II,[11] even though Syria gained its independence, it lacked any exclusive central authority capable of serving as a focus of identity and loyalty for the whole population. In fact, it was a political entity without a national community.[12] In order to achieve Syrian national integration following independence, the new authorities endeavored to weaken the autonomous status of the various minorities. Under Adib Shishakli's regime, minority representation in the Syrian People's Assembly was completely abolished (in 1953), while measures were adopted to Arabize and Islamize public life and institutions. Simultaneously, the Syrian regime attempted to overcome the military strength of the Druze and the 'Alawis and to impose central authority. However, only after smashing the 1954 Druze revolt[13] did the central government achieve military superiority throughout the country. From then on, members of the minorities became more involved in Syrian political life, mainly through the army and the Ba'th party,[14] while the traditional parties primarily consisted of upper-class urban Sunni-Muslims.[15]

The new political parties, notably the Ba'th and the Communists, utilized the socioeconomic unrest in Syria at that time – due mainly to the unequal distribution of the means of production in both the urban centers and the countryside – as well as the political instability and the aspirations of the middle class to increase their political participation. As Raymond Hinnebusch noted: "The Ba'th recruited all those who were outside the system of connections, patronage and kin on which the old regime was built."[16] Many of the disaffected, particularly among the rural lower-middle class and young members of the minorities (including Hafiz al-Asad himself),[17] were recruited by the party. However, for the young members of the minorities, the army continued to be the major avenue for socioeconomic mobility. Many of them were promoted in rank, mainly by senior Ba'th officers who strove to increase their influence in the army. Over time, the new recruits rose through the ranks of the military hierarchy.

By the mid-1950s, Syria's political parties, particularly the new parties, the Ba'th party, the Syrian National party and the Communist party,[18] had come to the conclusion that the parliamentary system and the political structure could not help them to gain power in the country. Indeed, following the Shishakli's disposition in February 1954 and the parliamentary elections in September of that year,[19] the former oligarchy of the conservative parties succeeded again to gain political power and to form a new government. However, by that time, the influence of the young radical army officers in the political system was irreversible and the struggle for power was practically conducted amongst their respective factions, with the Ba'th military faction gaining an upper hand by 1957.

The Creation of the UAR (February 1958–September 1961)

The ascendancy of the young radical army officers coincided, on the one hand, with the rise of anti-Western feelings among the civilian population, particularly following the signing of the Baghdad Pact in February 1955.[20] On the other hand, the leaders of the Ba'th party, both civilian and military, became increasingly concerned about the alleged threats of Communist elements in Syria and of political and/or military pressures from neighboring countries (Israel, Turkey, and Iraq). These concerns led the pro-Ba'th army officers and the civilian leaders of Syria to initiate a union with Egypt in February 1958, known as the UAR (United Arab Republic).[21]

The union with Egypt constituted a major turning point in Syrian political and socioeconomic history. Under the UAR regime, the activities of all the political parties were banned, while a comprehensive Agrarian Reform Law (Law No. 161/1958) was introduced in September 1958. Other socialist reforms were also initiated, such as the nationalization of major private assets and establishments. The socialist trend in Syria was strengthened further with the July 1961 Socialist Decrees.[22] Many young educated Syrians were integrated into the public sector, while young army officers were rapidly promoted to key positions, replacing the veteran officers of the former oligarchy. Many of these young officers were of Druze and 'Alawi origin.

Syria under the Ba'th Regime (1963–1970)

These young officers, including Asad, played a prominent role in the March 1963 Ba'th revolution.[23] While these officers exploited the party and its old civilian leaders for their purposes,[24] in practice they adopted the party's ideology, mainly in the socioeconomic arena. The major socioeconomic changes which began during the union with Egypt were further reinforced under the Ba'th rule and the neo-Ba'th regime that followed (February 1966–November 1970).[25]

At that juncture, following the February 1966 *coup d'état,* the temporary and unprecedented cooperation between the Ba'th officers from the various religious sects was terminated. The 'Alawi officers, led by Salah Jadid and Asad, enjoyed superiority in both the army and the party commands, and eventually overcame the Druze officers. Yet, during the neo-Ba'th period, the sectarian factor was not the only reason for the struggle among the new Syrian leaders. Other factors, such as a personal rivalry and different approaches in foreign and socioeconomic policies,[26] also played a major role in the struggle for power between Asad and Jadid. This struggle, which began in February 1966, surfaced in February 1969 and ended in November 1970 with the victory of Asad, who became the supreme Syrian leader.

Syria under Asad: Integrated and Stable Nation State

Asad has ruled Syria longer than any previous leader and has, for the first time, made Syria a stable polity and a regional power. How has Asad succeeded where all his predecessors failed? What are the reasons for this unique phenomenon in modern Syrian political history?

One explanation attributes this success to Asad's personal qualities, combined with his deep understanding of the internal Syrian political scene and its various forces and groups. Also, in contrast to his predecessors, from the beginning of his rule, Asad was not inclined to share political power with his comrades within a collective leadership. By early 1971, Asad had formed a new presidential system granting him extensive political, military and legislative authority, and the Permanent Constitution (1973) has rendered the president almost unlimited control over the country in these various arenas. Asad has exercised his control over the country through both formal institutions and informal channels. The formal institutions include the Constitution, the government, the People's Assembly, and the Ba'th Party. In Asad's perception, his regime is based on institutions rather than the sole power of one man or a group of military officers. As Patrick Seale states: "When I last had an extended interview with him, in March 1988, I was struck by one of his remarks: 'I have always been a man of institutions'." Seale also noted that: "In his own perception – if not in that of many others – he rules by consent through institutions in which the people participate. Even in inner party counsels, he [Asad] insists, the exercise of power is collective."[27]

The unofficial channels include the team of advisers in the al-Mujahidin Palace (the presidential palace) and some ten intelligence and security organizations, assigned to combat any sign of opposition to the regime and to the president himself. Still the most important unofficial channel is the *Jama'a* (company), which includes the powerful and influential figures in Asad's regime among the military, the security forces and the political élite. They assist Asad to safeguard the regime, to exercise effective control over the country, and to advise him in both domestic and international affairs.[28]

Another important instrument of Asad's control is the system of appointments to the key positions in the army, the security forces, and the government bureaucracy. A major criterion for appointment to these bodies is the degree of loyalty to Asad himself. Thus, in the top levels of the army and the security forces, one can find relatively large numbers of 'Alawi relatives and comrades. Yet, many in top positions are Sunni-Muslims, such as Mustafa Talas, the Minister of Defense, and the Vice President, 'Abd al-Halim Khaddam, whose personal loyalty to Asad is beyond reproach. The appointment of many Sunni-Muslims to government bureaucracy in all ranks, including the top positions, has contributed to enhancing the legitimacy of the central authority among both government employees and the public.

Asad has also tried to consolidate his regime via a broad-based consensus and legitimization among the various stratums of Syrian society, and he presents himself as a popular national leader. Thus, he described his coup against Jadid as *al-Harakat al-Tashihiyya* ("The Corrective Movement"), and, from the beginning of his rule, he has emphasized the participation of the citizens in the process of decision-making through elections to the People's Assembly and to other representative organizations. Although the Ba'th is the "leading party" in the country, six other Socialist parties have participated in the elections to the People's Assembly within the National Progressive Front, formed in 1972. However, as Patrick Seale noted:

> Such gestures toward political pluralism are of limited significance. Even accredited members of the National Progressive Front are not allowed to recruit followers in the army or at the universities, both of which are exclusive preserves of the Ba'th. Nor do they have nationwide organizations to compare with that of the Ba'th . . . Remnants of past political battles, these groups have more to do with Syria's political archeology than with its current concerns.[29]

Indeed, Asad has endeavored to expand the ranks of the Ba'th party with Sunni-Muslim members, lower urban stratums and peasants in order to portray the party as popular and representative of the entire Syrian society. In fact, this process has enabled the newly recruited members of these groups to participate in discussions within the party and to feel like an integral part of the political system.[30] In particular, through the Agricultural Cooperatives, the professional unions, women's unions and youth organizations, Asad has managed to increase the political participation of many groups that serve as "channels" between the regime and the masses.[31]

In order to gain wide public support, Asad has markedly improved the standard of living of the population, particularly that of the peasants and the lower stratums of urban society. Thus, massive development programs have been created in a wide variety of socioeconomic areas and public services greatly expanded in rural provinces. In the field of education, the achievements have been impressive. For example, the illiteracy rate among the Syrian population (10 years and over) was down to 20.6 percent by 1993, compared with 53.4 percent in 1960. Significant progress has been made in the countryside and the remote provinces. While in 1970 the illiteracy rate in the rural areas was 65.5 percent, this rate sharply declined to 28.4 percent by 1989.[32] During the years 1990–95, the primary school enrollment ratio in Syria reached 100 percent for males and 91 percent for females.[33] Due to the wide base of the age pyramid of the Syrian population, more than 80 percent of the total population was under the age of 40 by 1996.[34] This means that they have received their education, from elementary school through the university level, under Ba'th rule with emphasis on the party's ideology and identification with the regime.[35] There is no doubt that the expansion of educational facilities has contributed to a great extent to the integration of Syrian society. In addition to the improvement of educational services, the standard of living has also sharply improved in the rural areas. According to UNDP figures, by the late 1980s, 99 percent of the Syrian rural population had access to health services, as compared with 80 percent in Tunisia and only 30 percent in Morocco, for example.[36] Another field of improvement in public services in the rural areas is the expansion of the electricity network.[37]

In order to appease the traditional urban middle and upper classes, which had been affected by the socialist measures of the Ba'th regime during the 1960s,[38] Asad modified the socialist measures of his predecessors, mainly by encouraging the activity of the private sector and by lifting restrictions on the import of consumer goods. During the 1980s, and particularly during the first half of the 1990s, privatization measures were considerably enhanced following Law No. 10 (May 1991), aimed at encouraging private investments in the Syrian economy.[39] The main reason for the recent liberalization policy, in addition to the collapse of Communism in eastern Europe, emerged from the need to repair the severe economic recession that the Syrian economy underwent during the latter part of the 1980s. The opening of the economy to large-scale investments by the private sector serves the economic interests of the urban middle and upper classes, which belong primarily to the Sunni-Muslim majority.

Economic improvements notwithstanding, the major challenge to Asad's regime remains the Islamic opposition among large segments of the Sunni-Muslim population, who reject the secular ideology of the Ba'th and 'Alawi military rule. Islamic opposition to the Ba'th regime started shortly after the March 1963 revolution, and during the years 1963–70 many clashes occurred between the regime and conservative Islamic elements, turning into large-scale violence and the killing of dozens of protesters.[40]

From his early days as ruler of Syria, Asad was aware of the dangers of large-scale Islamic opposition. Thus, in June 1971, in order to appease the conservative Sunni-Muslim circles, particularly the religious leadership, Asad restored to the Syrian Constitution the previous formulation of the presidential oath: "I swear by Allah Akbar," which had been removed from the Constitution in 1969 (under Jadid's regime). In addition, in the Permanent Constitution of March 1973, Asad reinstated the article establishing Islam as the religion of the President, which also had previously been removed from the 1969 Constitution. Simultaneously in 1973, Asad encouraged the Shi'i Imam of Lebanon, Musa al-Sadr, to certify that the 'Alawis are Shi'i-Muslims. Asad also performed the small *Hajj* (*'Umra*) during a visit to Saudi Arabia in February 1974, and made numerous other gestures to the Sunni-Muslim majority, such as publicly participating in prayers on many occasions, raising the rank of many religious leaders in the government bureaucracy and increasing their salaries as well.[41]

However, these gestures did not eradicate the Islamic opposition to the Ba'th or to Asad. During the late 1970s and early 1980s, the Islamic opposition stepped up its activities, including assassinations of 'Alawi military officers, high-ranking government employees and Ba'thist leaders. These guerrilla operations were intensified during the early 1980s and culminated in February 1982, when a large group of Muslim Brotherhood initiated an armed rebellion in the city of Hama. In reaction, the Syrian army shelled the city, destroying large parts of it and killing an estimated 10,000 to 30,000 inhabitants.[42]

It would appear in retrospect that this brutal massacre constituted a "deadly blow" to the Islamic opposition in Syria. Yet, since the early

1990s, Asad has resumed his efforts to appease the Sunni-Muslim conservative elements by granting amnesty and releasing from jail thousands of "Muslim Brothers," as well as permitting the construction of hundreds of mosques and the opening of Qur'anic schools. Alongside the notions of Arab nationalism and Syrian patriotism, he also promotes moderate Islamic tenets as essential components of the Syrian-Arab national community.

Syria: Dilemmas and Prospects

Apart from the Islamic challenge, it would appear that one of the major dilemmas facing the Syrian leadership since the late 1980s has been how to adjust economic growth and privatization with the authoritarian characteristics of the political regime. Is it possible to advance economic liberalization, including opening the country to millions of tourists, and at the same time sustain the autocratic features of the regime and prevent more political freedom and democratization?[43] This has been the Chinese model, whereas in the Egyptian case economic liberalization has required taking some steps toward democratization. Asad has apparently preferred to take slow steps toward economic reform because a rapid pace might have social consequences that could threaten the stability of the regime. Similarly, while maintaining strong authoritarian control, Asad has tried to make his regime look as democratic and pluralistic as possible by creating various social and political institutions and conducting elections to bodies such as the People's Assembly.

Finally, regarding the crucial issue of socio-national integration, despite all actions and measures taken by Asad and his significant achievements, Syria is still far from being a cohesive national community. In fact, many in Syria still consider Asad's regime as a military-'Alawi system. Yet, many other Syrians have developed a different attitude. Large segments of the Syrian population have benefited from the regime and its socio-economic policies, among them Sunni-Muslim peasants, the new middle class, "blue collar" workers, and residents of the remote provinces. To those one should add the hundreds of thousands of Ba'th members and their families who also back the regime and its policies. All these groups constitute the support base of the regime.

But, it must be emphasized that political stability in Syria depends to a large degree on Asad's personality and political skills, rather than on deep-rooted political traditions and institutions. Consequently, the end of Asad's era may bring about serious repercussions on Syria's regime and stability; only the continued alliance of common interests among the

'Alawi-Sunni élite under an acceptable leader may prevent political upheavals or strife, and sustain the Ba'th rule in Syria.

Notes

1 On the ancient history of the Syrian region, see: Albert H. Hourani, *Syria and Lebanon* (Oxford, 1954), pp. 6–40 [hereafter: Hourani, *Syria and Lebanon*].

2 See, e.g., Derek Hopwood, *Syria 1945–1986: Politics and Society* (London, 1988), pp. 13–30.

3 On the early development of Syrian local nationality during the nineteenth century, see: Fruma Schreier-Zachs, *From Communal to Territorial Identity: The Emergence of "The Concept of Syria," 1831–1881* (Unpublished Ph.D. thesis, University of Haifa, 1997).

4 See: Moshe Ma'oz, *Ottoman Reform in Syria and Palestine* (Oxford, 1968).

5 On the principles of the Mandate system, see: Hourani, *Syria and Lebanon*, pp. 163–66.

6 The major studies on Syria under the French Mandatory government included: Hourani, *Syria and Lebanon*; Stephen H. Longrigg, *Syria and Lebanon Under the French Mandate* (Oxford and New York, 1958); Philip S. Khoury, *Syria and the French Mandate: The Politics of Arab Nationalism* (Princeton, 1987) [hereafter: Khoury, *Syria and the French Mandate*]. Regarding the French interests in the Syrian–Lebanese region prior to World War I, see: William I. Shorrock, "The Origin of the French Mandate in Syria and Lebanon," *IJMES*, Vol. 1 (1970), pp. 133–53.

7 On the distribution of the agricultural lands in Syria prior to the Agrarian Reform Law of September 1958, see: Raymond A. Hinnebusch, *Peasant and Bureaucracy in Ba'thist Syria: The Political Economy of Rural Development* (Boulder, 1989), p. 88, table 5.1; IBRAD (International Bank for Reconstruction and development), *The Economic Development of Syria* (Baltimore, 1955), pp. 354–55; Ziad Keilany, "Land Reform in Syria," *Middle Eastern Studies*, Vol. 16, No. 3 (October 1980), pp. 209–10.

8 Hourani, *Syria and Lebanon*, p. 172.

9 The Syrian army from the beginning was composed by a large number of Druze and especially 'Alawi soldiers. This was one of the major reasons for the prominent role of both 'Alawi and Druze officers in the various *coup d'états* during the years 1949–70.

10 See also: Itamar Rabinovich, "The Compact Minorities and the Syrian State," *Journal of Contemporary History*, Vol. 14 (1979), pp. 693–712.

11 On the developments in Syria during World War II which led to the independence in 1946, see: George Kirk, *The Middle East in the War* (London and New York, 1952), pp. 78–129; Hourani, *Syria and Lebanon*, pp. 230–58; 279–307.

12 This fact, more than any others, constituted the major reason for the political instability in Syria until late 1970, with the ascendancy of Hafiz al-Asad as the Syrian leader.

13 See: Joshua Landis, "Shishakli and the Druzes: Integration and Intransigence," in Thomas Philipp and Birgit Schaebler (eds), *The Syrian*

Land: Processes of Integration and Fragmentation (Stuttgart, 1998), pp. 369–95.

14 On the development of the Ba'th party and its ideology, see: Kamal Abu-Jaber, *The Arab Ba'th Socialist Party: History, Ideology, and Organization* (New York, 1966); John F. Devlin, *The Ba'th Party: A History from its Origins to 1966* (Stanford, 1979).

15 See, e.g., Khoury, *Syria and the French Mandate*, pp. 254–61, table 10.2.

16 Raymond A. Hinnebusch, "Party and Peasant in Syria," *Cairo Papers in Social Science*, Vol. 3, Monograph 1 (November 1979), p. 17 [hereafter: Hinnebusch, "Party and Peasant"].

17 On the enlistment of Asad to the Ba'th Party in 1946, see: Moshe Ma'oz, *Asad-The Sphinx of Damascus: A Political Biography* (London, 1988), pp. 25–27 [hereafter: Ma'oz, *Asad*]; Patrick Seale, *Asad of Syria: The Struggle for the Middle East* (London, 1988), pp. 35–37 [hereafter: Seale, *Asad*].

18 On the new political parties in Syria during the 1940s and the 1950s, see: Seale, *The Struggle for Syria* (London and New York, 1965),pp. 64–72; 159–63 [hereafter: Seale, *The Struggle for Syria*].

19 On the September 1954 parliamentary elections, see: *Ibid.*, pp.164–85.

20 On the Baghdad Pact, see: Elie Podeh, *The Quest for Hegemony in the Arab World: The Struggle over the Baghdad Pact* (Leiden, 1995); Seale, *The Struggle for Syria*, pp. 186–237.

21 On the circumstances and rationale which led to the Syrian–Egyptian union, see: Elie Podeh, *The Rise and Fall of the United Arab Republic, 1958–1961* (Brighton and Portland, 1999); Malcolm Kerr, *The Arab Cold War, 1957–1967*, 2nd edn (London and New York, 1967), pp. 14–34.

22 On the July 1961 Decrees, see: Tabitha Petran, *Syria* (London, 1972), pp. 139–40; John Waterbury, *The Egypt of Nasser and Sadat: The Political Economy of Two Regimes* (Princeton, 1983), pp. 73–79.

23 On the integration of Syrian minorities, particularly the 'Alawis, in the political life, see, e.g., Mahmud A. Faksh, "The 'Alawi Community of Syria: A New Dominent Political Force," *Middle Eastern Studies*, Vol. 20, No. 2 (April 1984), pp. 133–53; Daniel Pipes, "The 'Alawi Capture of Power in Syria," *Middle Eastern Studies*, Vol. 25, No. 4 (October 1989), pp. 429–50.

24 In 1964, Salah al-Din al-Bitar was removed from the position of the Prime Minister, and Michel Aflaq went into exile voluntarily.

25 On the *coup d'état* of the neo-Ba'th in February 1966 and the socioeconomic roots of its leaders, see: Itamar Rabinovich, *Syria Under the Ba'th Regime, 1963–66: The Army-Party Symbiosis* (Jerusalem, 1972), pp. 181–218 [hereafter: Rabinovich, *Syria Under the Ba'th*]; Abraham Ben-Zur, "The Neo-Ba'th Party of Syria," *New Outlook*, Vol. 12 (1969), pp. 21–37; Alasdair Drysdale, "The Syrian Political Elite, 1966–1976: A Spatial and Social Analysis," *Middle Eastern Studies*, Vol. 17, No. 1 (1981), pp. 3–30.

26 See: Ma'oz, *Asad*, pp. 35–40; Seale, *Asad*, pp. 35–37.

27 Patrick Seale, "Asad: Between Institutions and Autocracy," in Richard T. Antoun and Donald Quataert (eds), *Syria: Society, Culture, and Policy* (New York, 1991), p. 98.

28 On the relations between Asad and his ministers and military chiefs, see: Seale, *ibid.*, pp. 105–10.

29 *Ibid.*, p. 103.

30 See, e. g., Yehya M. Sadowski, "Cadres, Guns, and Money: the Eighth

Regional congress of the Syrian Ba'th," *Merip Reports* (July/August 1985), pp. 3–8.

31 See also: Moshe Ma'oz, "Hafiz al-Asad: A Political Profile," *Jerusalem Quarterly*, No. 8 (Summer 1978), pp. 16–31; Majid Khadduri, *Arab Personalities in Politics* (Washington, 1981), pp. 181–238.

32 Syrian Arab Republic, Office of the Prime Minister, Central Bureau of Statistics, *Statistical Abstract – 1995* (Damascus, 1996), p. 64, table 12/2; Syrian Arab Republic, Office of the Prime Minister, Central Bureau of Statistics, *Composition and Growth of Population in the Syrian Arab Republic* (Damascus, September 1979), p. 11, table 1.9.

33 UNICEF, *The State of the World's Children – 1997* (New York and London, 1998), p. 87, table 4.

34 ESCWA, *Demographic and Related Socio-Economic Data Sheets for Countries of the Economic and Social Commission for Western Asia*, No. 9 (1997), p. 108, table 1.

35 See: Roy Delwin and Thomas Naff, "Ba'thist Ideology, Economic Development and Educational Strategy," *Middle Eastern Studies*, Vol. 25, No. 4 (October 1989), pp. 451–79.

36 UNDP (United Nations Development Programme), *Human Development Report – 1994* (Oxford, 1995), p. 148, table 10.

37 On the improvement of the Syrian electricity network during the 1980s and the early 1990s, see: Onn Winckler, *Demographic Developments and Population Policies in Ba'thist Syria* (Brighton and Portland, 1999), pp. 133–35. On the economic development in Syria under Asad regime, see: Volker Perthes, *The Political Economy of Syria under Asad* (London and New York, 1995); Kais Firro, "The Syrian Economy under the Assad Regime," in Moshe Ma'oz and Avner Yaniv (eds), *Syria under Assad: Domestic Constraints and Regional Risk*s (London and Sidney, 1986), pp. 36–68; Syed Aziz al-Ahsan, "Economic Policy and Class Structure in Syria: 1958–1980," *IJMES*, Vol. 16 (1984), pp. 315–21.

38 See: Ziad Kelaney, "Socialism and Economic Change in Syria," *Middle Eastern Studies*, Vol. 9 (1973), pp. 61–72.

39 On Law No. 10 from May 1991 and its implications, see, e.g., Sylvia Pölling, "Investment Law No. 10: Which Future for the Private Sector?" in Kienle (ed.), *Contemporary Syria*, pp. 14–25.

40 See: Rabinovich, *Syria Under the Ba'th*, pp. 109–26; Raymond A. Hinnebusch, *Authoritarian Power and State Formation in Ba'thist Syria* (Boulder, 1990), p. 291 [hereafter: Hinnebusch, *Authoritarian Power and State Formation*].

41 Thomas Mayer, "The Islamic Opposition in Syria, 1961–1982,"*Orient*, Vol. 9 (1983), p. 593. See also Kedar's chapter in this volume.

42 Ma'oz, *Asad*, pp. 159–63. On the development of the Muslim Brotherhood movement in Syria and the Islamic opposition to the Ba'th regime, see: Hanna Batatu, "Syrian Muslim Brethren," *Merip Reports*, Vol. 9, No. 12 (November/December 1982), pp. 12–20; F. H. Lawson, "Social Bases for the Hama Revolt," *Merip Reports*, Vol. 9, No. 12 (November/December 1982), pp. 24–28; Raymond A. Hinnebusch, "The Islamic Movement in Syria," in Ali Hilal Dessuoki (ed.), *Islamic Resurgence in the Arab World* (New York, 1982), pp. 138–69; Raymond A. Hinnebusch, *Authoritarian Power and State Formation*, pp. 276–300; Umar F. Abdallah, *The Islamic Struggle in*

Syria (Berkeley, 1983); Eyal Zisser, "The Muslim Brotherhood Movement in Syria: Between Completion and Struggle," in Meir Litvak (ed.), *Islam and Democracy in the Arab World* (Tel Aviv, 1997), pp. 96–122 (in Hebrew); Hans Günter Lobmeyer, "Islamic Ideology and Secular Discourse: The Islamists of Syria," *Orient*, Vol. 32, No. 3 (1991), pp. 395–418.

43 For an interesting discussion on the connection between economic liberalization and structural political changes in Syria under Asad, see: Volker Perthes, *The Political Economy of Syria under Asad* (London and New York, 1995), pp. 257–62; see also: idem, "The Private Sector, Economic liberalization, and the Prospects of Democratization: the Case of Syria and some other Arab Countries," in Ghassan Salamé (ed.), *Democracy Without Democrats? The Renewal of Politics in the Muslim World* (London and New York, 1994), pp. 243–67.

Part I

The Political System under Asad

2

In Search of Legitimacy: Asad's Islamic Image in the Syrian Official Press

Mordechai Kedar

The Muslim religion presents the most serious ideological challenge to the legitimacy of Hafiz al-Asad regime, and the extremist adherents of Islam have been, and are likely to remain in the foreseeable future, the "hardest nut to crack" among the ideological opposition to Asad and his regime. During the late 1970s and early 1980s, Islamic extremists – the Muslim Brotherhood movement – constituted the most serious threat to the very existence of Asad's regime in Syria and were thus accorded the most "special treatment" on his part. This treatment reached its peak with the events of Hama in February 1982, including the death of thousands of Syrian citizens. While the inter-religious tension has abated in recent years, the Islamic threat posed by the majority Sunni-Muslim community is still the most serious potential threat facing the dominance of Asad's 'Alawi-Ba'th regime in Syria. Nevertheless, with the passage of time, the seriousness of the threat is diminishing, and it is by no means clear that one may still speak of a viable threat directed at the Asad regime from extreme Islamic elements.

Since personal commitment and loyalty to the leader is a well-established need in Arab societies, Asad spares no effort to gain Islamic "imprimatur" to himself as a Muslim and to his being a president as a Muslim leader. Under such circumstances, the Islamic component in the political message is particularly problematic and complex and is therefore the subject of this chapter. The complex and multi-sided platform of the Ba'th regime, run by 'Alawis in a country with a Sunni-Muslim majority, dictates that it integrate its "information" in the state media into an overall set of government messages. While this study makes no attempt to survey the totality of the Syrian government's relations with Islam, its beliefs and institutions, it does present some of the manifestations of this relationship in the government's message that appears in the local, entirely state-controlled, press, particularly during the month of *Ramadan* and close to the holidays. Such a discussion must be preceded by a general remark: Religious matters – whether relating to the Sunni-Muslims, 'Alawis, Druze, or Christians – are not generally dealt with in Syrian newspapers, and this limited occupation with religious subjects enables the government to circumvent the problem surrounding beliefs and opinions.

Historical Background

Writing in 1956, Michel 'Aflaq, the Ba'th theoretician, associated religion with the old corrupt social order, oppressing and exploiting the weak:

> Those that are unaware of a system which they must penetrate and who do not respond to the legitimate yearning rising up in the heart of the oppressed, who, at the time, saw in religion the weapon relied upon by the oppressors . . . those who were not aware of this yearning, did not fathom its depth so as to overcome it by means of positive, optimal means in the belief that the faith can be revived by the removal of oppression and corruption and that a thousand excuses justifying the religion would not make a bit of difference compared with a single act of abolishing a single manifestation of oppression: they are the real enemies of religion. There is no use in preaching, time and again, that religion is good and is the pinnacle of perfection . . . all this is without consequence except for abuse and exploitation, intentional or unintentional; for those who do exploit the corrupt status utilize this status to numb the people in order to keep them from rebelling against those who would oppress and enslave them.[1]

In its Declaration of Principles, the Ba'th party, which assumed power in Syria in early March 1963, makes no explicit reference to religion or to the party's attitude toward it. However, the section dealing with "the Party's policy in regard to education and learning" stated:

> The educational policy of the party strives to create a new generation of Arabs that believes in the unity of the nation and the eternity of its mission, that is committed to scientific thought freed from the shackles of superstition and backward customs.[2]

Although the nature of the "shackles of superstition" is not explicitly defined, it is fair to assume that the term refers to religious dogma, while "backward customs" are indicative of religious commandments and practices. Moreover, this brief section makes profane use of religious terminology: *khalq* – create; *mu'min* – believe; *risalah* – mission – as an expression of the idea that Ba'th socialism is heir to the place once occupied by religion in the Arab nation. In the same vein, but in much sharper language, a junior morale guidance officer of the Syrian Army named Ibrahim Khalas wrote an article in the Army journal of April 1967, entitled "The Path Toward the Creation of Our New Arab Man" (implying that it is man who performs the act of creation, rather than the Deity!). In this article he wrote:

> those who rebel against the moribund and debased values of their society which are merely the outcome of feudalism and imperialism, values which have turned Arab man into a degraded, submissive human being, a fatalistic person resigned to his fate who knows nothing better than to exclaim "there is no power, no strength but that of the supreme and great God." But the new values which will create the new Arab man are such as emerge from the afflicted man who rebels, that burst forth from the heart of the starved man, break out of the new socialist revolutionary man who believes in man and man only; and the only way to establish the culture of the Arabs and to build Arab society is to create the new Socialist Arab man who believes that God, the religions, feudalism, imperialism, the fat cats and all the values that dominated the former society are nothing but mummies embalmed in the museums of history.[3]

This article caused violent uprisings throughout Syria, and in order to appease the enraged public, Khalas was discharged from office. It is also possible that the escalation in incidents at the border with Israel in April 1967 motivated the Syrian regime to deflect public opinion away from internal problems – of which the offending article represents one manifestation – to external threats which presented a national duty to rally behind the leadership and to support it. Asad, who, at that time, was the Minister of Defense and a senior member of the national leadership, was impelled to deal with demonstrations and disturbances of public order, and the Khalas article certainly had an effect on Asad's mode of behavior and his pronouncements in the religious-sectarian sphere.

Daniel Pipes noted in this regard that:

> Contrary to the impression Asad fosters, few of the world's almost billion Muslims consider him a fellow believer. Rather, they see him as an 'Alawi, an adherent of a small, secretive post-Islamic religion restricted almost exclusively to Syria. This fact makes Asad an outsider in his own country, with profound implications for his regime and his goals.[4]

Since assuming the presidency in November 1970, Asad has been treading on very thin ice in dealing with religious issues, which, for him, are fraught with serious problems in view of the following factors:

1. The traditional political culture among Arabs identifies – or at least strives to identify – the *de facto* ruler as the head of the religious community. This is the ideal situation according to Islam; however, there is no Arab state where it actually prevails.
2. The political leadership in Syria is under no illusion that the Sunni majority accepts as self-evident the Islamic "imprimatur" of religious purity which has been bestowed upon the ʻAlawi sect. Martin Kramer notes that: "according to most Sunni believers, the article of faith of the ʻAlawis can not be accommodated within Islam. Life under an ʻAlawi political leadership is tantamount to being subjected to domination by heretics,"[5] whose worship, in their view, incorporates pagan elements. Thus, according to orthodox Sunni-Islam, not only has the ʻAlawi sect no right to rule, it is indeed doubtful whether it has the right to live![6] As a result, "the ʻAlawis have always been a rural, impoverished and subjugated population of landless, oppressed peasants . . . The majority Sunni Muslim population generally despise and hate the ʻAlawis for their religious heresies and their social and economic backwardness."[7]
3. The integration of the various ethnic groups in Syria into a single Syrian people – a basic message in the Syrian press – may be damaged by dealing with factors, and especially religious matters, that make each group unique. This is especially true with regard to the Druze and ʻAlawi sects, whose esoteric beliefs are supposed to be secret. Dealing with religion – especially beliefs and ideas that tend to be ultimate – may highlight the differences that distinguish and separate the various religious sects among the Syrian society.
4. The Baʻth's secular ideology and attitude toward religion, as evident in the words of ʻAflaq, are inconsistent with intense religious involvement, including the various revelations, rituals, and institutions.
5. The impossibility of ignoring the external expressions of the religious events which surround most of the Sunni-Muslim population throughout the month of *Ramadan* and *ʻId al-Fitr* at the end of it, as well as *ʻId al-Adha*,[8] has implications on many aspects of the country's life. The government must publicly relate to the fast and its impact on the ability to work, especially when *Ramadan* falls in summer, on consumption habits in general and food consumption in particular, on holiday ceremonies, and on public prayer. Ignoring these things totally might convey to the Sunni-Muslim majority a

message of alienation, which the government has no desire whatsoever to do.

6 In contrast to other political messages, most of which do not have to compete with opposing sets of messages, the regime's political message on religious conflicts with an orderly, well-established set of authentic religious messages, whose institutions – the mosques dispersed throughout the country – the government cannot eliminate, even if it wanted to. The most it can do is to censor and supervise whatever is going on in the mosques and what the figures who operate through them are doing, though too tight supervision may lead to conflict, which the government would prefer to avoid.

These political-religious difficulties form a permanent background against which most of the internal events in Syria take place. Between 1979 and 1982, they even erupted in a bloodbath, when the Muslim Brotherhood rebelled against the government, only to be suppressed with an iron fist in Hama in February 1982.[9] On the legislative level, we may note the twisting and turning which arose from the clause in the constitution stipulating that the president must be a Muslim. Moshe Ma'oz's description of Asad's approach to this issue is informative:

> The special measures that Asad took since his rise were designed to appease or neutralize the conservative Sunni-Muslim groups and especially its religious leadership.[10]

However, Asad's statements and actions on behalf of Islam and his being a Muslim did not impress Islam's extremists. The newspaper *al-Nadhir*, as the organ of the Muslim Brotherhood, did not spare Asad and his regime its scathing criticism and variously calls Asad a "tyrant," a "criminal," "Satan," "the butcher of Syria," and the "shah[11] of Syria." Asad's regime is called a "government of crime and aggression," a "criminal government," the "enemy of Islam and the Muslims," "the sectarian agent regime (of the Soviet Union)," and other names in this spirit.[12] The Muslim Brotherhood's stand on Asad and his government, which purports to represent the stand of Islam, necessitates a special media response parallel to an operational response.

It should be noted that Asad tried his best behind the scenes to recruit the Shi'i Supreme Council in Lebanon to support its head, Imam Musa al-Sadr, in his 1973 attempt to bring about the election of a Lebanese 'Alawi representative to the council. Such an appointment would mean Shi'i recognition of the 'Alawi sect as a legitimate Shi'i faction. Sadr's actions raised great opposition, and since his disappearance in 1979, there has been no further activity in this direction.[13] The question of whether the 'Alawis (and thereby Asad himself) are Muslims consists of three sub-questions:

1 *What is the status in Islamic law of the 'Alawi sect to which he belongs?* The Muslim Brotherhood's answer to this question is treated at length by Martin Kramer,[14] who notes, among other things, the above-mentioned excoriation in *al-Nadhir*. The following excerpt discusses the status of this sect as viewed through the writings of prominent figures of the Twelfth Shi'a, the Shi'i faction to which Iran belongs and from whose leaders in Qom the 'Alawi sect has sought authorization for the past hundred years:

> The Nusayris [the former name of the 'Alawis] regard themselves associated with Muhammad, the son of Nusayr al-Numayri, who was active around 270 *Hijra* [900 AD]. They also have other local names which they are called in the places where they reside, such as al-Takhtajiyah and al-Hattaboun in West Anatolia, and al-'Ali Ilahiyah [those who believe that 'Ali is a god] in Iran. After the French conquered Syria, they were given the name "'Alawis," because they raised the Imam 'Ali, may he rest in peace, to a god. This name stuck, which pleases them, since it frees them from the humiliation, the hatred, and the heresy that was associated throughout history with the name "the Nusayris." This name also opens up horizons for them to get closer to Shi'a, which supports them . . . In his book Beliefs and Factions, Sa'ad al-Din al-Qomi (died 301/932) provides detailed information about the principles of Shi'a and the Imami and Zaydi Shi'a factions and their opponents, and expands at length on the "ghulat" [those who exaggerate in 'Ali's degree] and their factions . . . and this is what he says about the Nusayris: 'a group which believes that 'Ali, the son of Muhammad, may he rest in peace, was an Imam in his life.' This group became a deviant group, believing that a man named Muhammad b. Nusayr al-Numayri claimed that he was a prophet and messenger and that 'Ali b. Muhammad al-'Askari appointed him as a messenger. He believed in reincarnation and exaggerated the status of Abu al-Hasan ('Ali the fourth Khalif), believing in his divinity. He lifted the prohibitions and permitted sodomy, claiming that this was a type of modesty . . . [15]

2 *To what extent does the Syrian public accept Asad as a Muslim?* An answer to this question would require conducting a field study in Syria, which cannot be done under the current political conditions.

3 *How does Asad present himself and how do the media present him?* In answer to this question, Moshe Ma'oz quotes the Beirut newspaper *al-Nahar*, which quotes Asad:

> I believe in Allah and in the spiritual legacy of our nation. I regard Islam as a faith of love and justice and thus a socialist religion. I pray, fast during the month of fasting, and hope that the day will come when I can make the pilgrimage to Mecca.[16]

Up to the time of this writing (January 1999), Asad has not been privileged to make the *Hajj* pilgrimage to Mecca. He did, however, make the little pilgrimage, or *'Umra*, in February 1974. This event was covered in a full-page illustrated article in the official Syrian newspaper *al-Thawra* of February 5, 1974.

From time to time, Asad makes sure to have the authorization that he is a believer renewed by obtaining the authorization of his belonging to Islam from various religious sages, among them the *Mufti* of Damascus, *Shaykh* Ahmad Kaftaru. Another example of this can be found in the closing words of the *Imam* of the al-Murabit Mosque in Damascus during the 1995 *'Id al-Fitr* prayers: "We pray to Allah, ask his aid, and supplicate him, please God send success to the believer, President Hafiz al-Asad."[17] The words are spoken within hearing of Asad, who is photographed at the head of the people in prayer – the traditional place of the leader of the Islamic community. Under the entry "Allah" in *Hafiz al-Asad – a Lexicon of Political and Social Thought*, Asad is quoted as saying:

> Even if we disagree about the road that leads to God, the important thing is that this is God, and we all worship Him. No one has the right to force on others their way to God . . . God belongs to everyone, and He regards all people as equal. It is hard to accept that he adopts a particular class of his sons and that the others are lower, that is, that they were created only to be inferior . . . Every man is free to decide how he will pray, how he will worship God, and how he sees God."[18]

Here Asad is portrayed to regard Islam as a religion of love and justice, and to believe in a God that considers all the creatures of the world as equal and all religions as legitimate. Clearly, this syncretistic opinion is by no means compatible with the attitude of "correct Islam" toward other religions. However, in the newspaper documentation of his actions, Asad appears as a leader who carries on the tradition of the earliest Islamic rulers. Moreover, near the holidays, the Syrian newspapers usually carry announcements whose essential message is that Asad is a bona fide Muslim, who, as the political ruler, is also responsible, in accordance with the Islamic ideal, for the religious institutions and the persons who run them. Below are a number of examples of subjects in the press where Asad appears as a legitimate Muslim leader: public prayer; announcement of *Ramadan*, *'Id al-Fitr*, and other holiday rituals; holiday greetings sent to

Asad from foreign leaders and Syrian notables; mourning ceremonies for Asad's son; the Islamic declaration of allegiance, the *Bay'ah*; publication of the Qur'an; and reports of Asad's activities within the international Islamic framework.

(1) *Asad in public prayer*. Asad participates in public prayer on the last Friday of *Ramadan* and on the *'Id al-Fitr* and *'Id al-Adha* holidays. His participation is generally reported in the lead article, under very large headlines,[19] and with a photo spreading over the entire width of the page and showing him in the center of the first row of devotees, which is the traditional place of the ruler in Islam. On the occasion of *'Id al-Adha* of 1987, for example, in addition to the lead article, the giant headline, and a photograph spanning the width of the first page, the daily newspaper *al-Thawra* presented its readers with an inside page consisting entirely of photos of Asad kneeling and shaking hands with those greeting him in the mosque. The only text on the page, at its center, read: "President Asad Prays the Prayer of the Blessed Holiday of the Sacrifice in the Umayya Mosque in Damascus."[20]

It should be noted, however, that in the papers surveyed, there was no photo showing Asad in "*sujud*" – prostration – with his face touching the carpet. It may be that he and his media associates believe that showing him in prostration, which is described "as close as can be to the Blessed Allah,"[21] might be viewed as an exaggeration in the intensity of the message that they want to relay and thus counter to the desired result. Another possible reason for not showing Asad in prostration is to avoid portraying him as supplicant to anyone or anything, since total submission, even to God, might tarnish his presidential image. Asad evidently regards the act of standing on the place where the Umayya *Khalifas* once stood and praying in their mosque as highly symbolic. At less important religious events, such as the *al-Qadr* night prayers[22] and the *Hijri* new year, official prayers are held, generally conducted by the Minister of the *Waqfs* (endowments). The newspapers report – always on the first page – that the prayers were conducted "under the auspices of President Asad," even if he does not attend them.[23]

(2) *Announcement of Ramadan and 'Id al-Fitr*. The media's preoccupation with the month of *Ramadan* begins the day before through an announcement in which the chief *Shari'a Qadi* of Damascus invites the citizens to look out for the birth of the new moon and calls upon anyone who sights it to bring his testimony to the *Shari'a* court. The next day, in a front page announcement of the first day of *Ramadan*, there is a notice whose wording is almost invariable: The headline, "Today, the First Day of *Ramadan*, President Asad Receives Blessings for the Honorable Month," is followed by the text:

> It is clear on the basis of the *Shari'a* that the first day of the honorable month of *Ramadan* of 1414 Hijri is Friday, February 11, 1994 of the Christian calendar. Mr. President Hafiz al-Asad received a telegram from Mr. Ahmad al-Hal, the Chief Judge of the Damascus *Shari'a* court, stating that the first day of the honorable month of Ramadan of 1414 *Hijri* is Friday, February 11, 1994 of the Christian calendar, and wishing the President and his honorable family, Arabs, Muslims, and everyone together, all the best, health and blessings, and that God will make the blessed month one in which hopes for glory and victory are fulfilled.[24]

The announcement to the President is repeated in almost identical words at the end of *Ramadan*, on the first of the month that opens *'Id al-Fitr*. Again, after the court determines that the new moon has been born, it reports its birth in a telegram to Asad, and only then is the information released to the newspapers. This process preserves the president's pre-eminence over the *Shari'a* court and its religious affairs, and thus implicitly depicts Asad as following the path of the Islamic ruler's mastery over religious matters in his country.

It should be pointed out that Asad adopted this stance somewhat late. The above announcement was not placed in the newspapers on the eve of *Ramadan* 1971, and appeared for the first time only on the eve of *Ramadan* 1972, and even then without any mention of Asad himself, but only of the Chief Judge of the Damascus *Shari'a* court. The determination of the beginning of the month is a particularly well-suited occasion for depicting Asad as an authentic Muslim leader, for Islam does not have a single uniform calendar; rather, the date is set monthly, in accordance with the testimony of witnesses of the new moon, by the *Shari'a* court of every Islamic country. The local independence of the religious court in Syria thus provides a source of Asad's ability to prove himself as an overseer of religious matters in its jurisdiction.

(3) *Holiday Rituals*. In mosques throughout Syria, the *Imams* refer to Asad in their holiday sermons. For example, a notice on the fourth page of *al-Thawra* on *'Id al-Adha* in 1987 bears the headline: "Mosque Speeches Extol President Asad for his Support in the Problems of the Arabs and Islam." The notice reads: "The honorable *Shaykh* Tawfiq al-Sayyid, the *Mufti* of Tartus, made the holiday speech. In the name of the people of Tartus, he blessed the leader of the nation and the symbol of its struggle, President Hafiz al-Asad, who has devoted his life to the struggle for his nation, people, and birthland . . . "[25] It should be noted, however, that in the headline, the word 'Arabs' precedes 'Islam', thereby indicating that the *Mufti* follows Asad's scale of priorities, as shown in the next paragraph.

(4) *Holiday Blessings from Foreign Leaders*. During the holidays, the

newspapers publish holiday greetings which the president receives from leaders and other figures of the Arab, Islamic, and Western world by telegram and telephone, as well as the greetings that he sends back to these leaders. On *'Id al-Fitr* of March 1995, for example, the first page of *al-Thawra* carries a list of 25 heads of state who exchanged holiday greetings with Asad. At the head of the list is King Fahd of the Saudi Arab Kingdom, Servant of the Holy Places, followed by 15 heads of Arab states, seven heads of Islamic states, and, at the end, presidents Clinton and Mandela. This is followed by another list of no less than 57 personages of lower rank from Arab and Islamic countries.[26] With minor modifications, such lists are published on most holidays.

The leaders on the list are named by their full names and official titles (i.e., King Husayn b. Talal), as are their countries (i.e., the Hashemite Kingdom of Jordan). Moreover, the list is not presented in one continuum, but rather each leader receives a separate paragraph. The full names and titles are aimed at giving the holiday greetings an official aura so as to convey the message that Asad is officially acknowledged as a legitimate Muslim leader by the heads of Arab states, the heads of Islamic states, and the leaders of the world.[27]

(5) *Holiday Greetings from Prominent Syrian Figures.* A telegram bearing a *Ramadan* greeting to Asad from the Syrian Minister of the *Waqfs* contains the following paragraph:

> Your pioneering attitudes, your honest ways, and your heroic principles, and the wisdom that is clear to all eyes, reflect a figure of a believing Muslim, who does not accept the denigration and humiliation of his people and his nation . . . The most exalted greetings to the President, the leader Hafiz al-Asad, who loves his God and his people, and believes in the holiness of the *Jihad* for God and for the return of the rights and liberation of the land and the holy places till the word of God will reign supreme and the words of the heretics [will be] at the bottom . . . [28]

The purpose of phrases like "a believing Muslim" and "believes in the holiness of the *Jihad* for God" is to bestow Islamic validation upon Asad as a leader of Islamic country in order to counter the known doubts about it, of which the Minister was well aware.

(6) *Ramadan 1994 in the Shadow of Asad's Mourning.* The official Syrian press is generally careful to maintain a modern, secular character and has a tendency to ignore matters relating to Islam during *Ramadan*. However, during *Ramadan* 1994, the Syrian press behaved differently from every previous *Ramadan*. The death of Basil, Asad's first-born son, on January 23, 1994, about two weeks before *Ramadan*, brought about a temporary change in the press treatment of Islam, though unrelated to

Ramadan. Giant condolence notices (of up to a page) were published by personages and institutions in Syria, and generally opened with the traditional headline, "In the Name of Allah, Most Gracious, Ever Merciful," followed by a passage from the Qur'an. Official mourning ceremonies bore a conspicuous Islamic tone, and one could find headlines like: "Bashar al-Asad was Present at the Reading of the Qur'an in Memory of the Soul of the Deceased," as well as announcements like: "The captain, the parachutist Bashar al-Asad was present at the ceremony of the holy Qur'an and the prayers that were held yesterday . . . "[29]

About three years after Basil's death, on January 26, 1997, the daily newspaper *al-Ba'th* reported on its first page that a delegation of Arab pharmacists visited the memorial to Basil, laid a wreath of flowers in his memory, and "read the [*Surat al-*] *Fatiha* in memory of his pure soul." It is not at all clear if mourning customs like the reading of *Surat al-Fatiha* are part of the usual mourning practices of the 'Alawi sect. The Islamic nature of the mourning for Basil may have stemmed from the absence of any official, secular mourning ceremony, on the one hand, and Asad's unwillingness to give an 'Alawi coloring to the public expressions of mourning, on the other hand. In this connection, it may be pointed out that many condolence telegrams noted the renewal of the *Bay'ah* (the traditional oath of allegiance to a new caliph) for Asad after the death of his son. The main headline of *al-Thawra* quotes the People's Council declaration: "The great tragedy has become a renewed oath of allegiance from the masses of the people and nation to the leader Asad."[30]

(7) *Publication of the Qur'an*. The writing and publication of the Qur'an in Arab countries has never been like the publication of an ordinary book. While the latter is initiated by professional publishers, the former is a state matter because of the politico-religious conflict with the Shi'a on the accepted canonical version. The process involves the authorization of a given version, the editing of the text, the selection of the lettering style, and, at the end of the process, the official approval by the highest religious authority of the entire enterprise and his signature on all the copies. All of these steps require active involvement and sometimes even funding by the state's official religious authorities. The publication of a Qur'an without state authorization and supervision is perceived as a conspiracy against the government.

The eve of November 1, 1972 (the 27th of *Ramadan* and the night of *al-Qadr*), two weeks before the second anniversary of the "Corrections Movement," a delegation of Islamic religious figures, headed by the Minister of *Waqfs*, the scholar 'Abd al-Sattar al-Sayyed, presented Asad with the first copy of the Qur'an which was published in Syria at his initiative. In his speech, the Minister of *Waqfs* says: "I am honored, along with the members of the delegation, to present you [Asad] with this copy of the honorable book, planted by your hand and the fruit of your instructions."[31] These words by the minister credit Asad with being the one who initiated and ordered the publication of the new edition of the Qur'an. Since the long process involved – writing by a calligrapher, proofreading, correcting, and printing – could take up to a year, Asad evidently set the wheels in motion about a year after his assumption of the presidency. By doing so, he had hoped to acquire legitimacy as an equal among equals with the current leaders of the Islamic states.

(8) *The Bay'ah (Oath of Allegiance) to Asad.* This custom derives from the depths of Arab Islamic political culture, which considers the *Bay'ah* an obligatory act whenever there is any kind of crisis in the leadership, such as a new leader's assumption of power or the leader's recovery from a serious illness or any serious personal calamity that may threaten his authority or the continuation of his rule. The repeated use of the *Bay'ah* adds a historio-linguistic note to the Arab-Islamic authenticity of Asad's leadership. The "renewal of the *Bay'ah*" motif appeared in the main headline of *al-Thawra* on the occasion of Asad's election as Secretary General of the Central Committee of the Ba'th party: "The Masses of our Syrian People and Arabic Nation Renew the *Bay'ah* to the Leader Asad."[32] Similar announcements have been made upon the anniversary of the founding of the Ba'th party, following the coup attempt by the president's brother Rif'at al-Asad; on the occasion of the referendum regarding Asad's continuation as president; and on the eve of the *Ramadan* feast that Asad held as a sign of respect for the religious sages and heads of the religious sects. The message of Islamic allegiance to the president, delivered by religious figures, has great public relations value against the background of the bloody conflict between the government and the Muslim Brotherhood two years earlier. The motif of the renewal of the *Bay'ah* is also sounded by the Druze population. The banner head of *al-Thawra*, March 12, 1987, four days after the Holiday of the Revolution, reads: "Telegram to the Leader Asad from the People of Buq'ata in the Occupied Golan," and this is followed by the headline: "We Renew Our Oath of Absolute Allegiance to the Leader Asad and we are Sure of the Victory Under his Courageous Leadership." Even though they have several synonymous terms (i.e., "loyalty," "allegiance"), the Buq'ata Druze chose the motif of the *Bay'ah*, evidently adopting the political lexicon of Asad's Syria on the Holiday of the Revolution. The message of this headline presentation of the Druze *Bay'ah* is: If the residents of Buq'ata, who suffer under the occupation, retain their loyalty to Asad, then the residents of Syria – free of foreign occupation – should certainly be loyal to him.

(9) *Asad's Activities within the International Islamic Framework.* Asad utilizes the conferences of Islamic Countries in order to gain legitimacy from this politico-religious sphere as well. For example, in reporting on the Conference of Islamic States held in Kuwait on January 27, 1987, the main headline in *al-Thawra* reads: "The Presence of the Leader al-Asad Arouses Great Interest, Gives Support to the Conference and Grants It International Significance." The message accords great importance to Asad's participation in the conference, even before he has uttered a single word. Two days later, on 29 January, the same newspaper reported in its main headline: "The Leader al-Asad is Engaged in Intensive Activity at the Conference; His Historic Speech is Widely Echoed." Thus, it is affirmed that Asad is not a passive participant; rather, he is very active and his words are widely disseminated.

Reports of his meetings with other Islamic heads-of-state strengthen Asad's pretensions of being an Islamic leader of international significance, implying that they recognize him as a Muslim and a legitimate Islamic leader. On February 1, 1987, *al-Thawra*'s main headline reads: "You are the Pride of the Nation and the Speaker of the Truth." Above the main headline it was written: "The Leader al-Asad Receives Many Congratulatory Telegrams and Letters Praising Him for the Historical Speech at the Islamic Conference." Thus, we see that during the conference the message was one of Islamic legitimacy; after it was over the paper translates Asad's success at the conference into leadership of the Arab Nation. The message which unifies the recognition of Asad as a legitimate Muslim ruler with his being the leader of the Arab nation is aimed at depicting him as following in the footsteps of the leaders of the Muslims and the Arabs at a time when the two were still united, at the dawn of Islam.

Conclusion

Islam has two functions in the Syrian state-controlled press: First, to provide ideas that will strengthen the recognition granted the 'Alawis as Muslims. This function can be discerned in the ideas, supposedly taken from Islam, about the equality of men, that no man is superior to any other except through his contribution to society, the people and the land. This is a humanistic idea, which places man at the center of the world and subordinates the entire universe, including God Himself, to man's wishes and goals. This is the antithesis of Islam, which demands that man's every wish and drive be subordinated to God's will as expressed by His commandments. The idea of the equality of all men and all religions – a humanistic and anti-Islamic idea in its very essence – is the basis of the goods which the officials of Islam are compelled to provide to the atheistic Ba'th regime in Syria so that the regime will be able to create "equality" among the various religious denominations in the country. Within the framework of this new social equality, the population will then be able to accept the idea of being ruled by an 'Alawi.

The second function of Islam is to provide Asad with events and opportunities that will enable him to appear in the media sitting or, even better, standing among the *Khalifs* of yore. The Umayya Mosque in Damascus – in which Asad appears at the head of the worshippers on holidays – is a fitting background for the performance which he produces and in which he stars, a performance whose other participants carry the titles of *Shaykh*, *Mufti*, etc., and whose audience is the Sunni-Muslim majority of Syria. The actors mouth a text whose ideas – and perhaps the wording as well – are predetermined.

Public prayer, the announcement of the commencement of *Ramadan* and *'Id al-Fitr*, holiday greetings from leaders abroad and senior officials in Syria, publication of the Qur'an, receiving the oath of allegiance, and participating in international Islamic forums – all these are concrete expressions of Asad's following the historical path taken by the *Khalifs* of Islam. Presenting this image to the mass media is a strategy fueled by Asad's wish to receive historico-religious legitimization as a Muslim who is fit to rule over the community of believers, or at least those living in Syria.

Notes

This chapter is based on the author's Ph.D. dissertation submitted to the Senate of Bar-Ilan University (Israel) in 1997. The dissertation was written under the supervision of Professor Michael Winter from Tel Aviv University.

1 Michel 'Aflaq, *Fi Sabil al-Ba'th* [In the Path of Ba'th] (Beirut, 1978, 20th Printing), p. 207.

2 Hizb al-Ba'th al-Arabi, *Harakat Qawmiyya Sha'biyya Inqilabiyya Tunadhil fi Sabil al-Wahda al-Arabiya wal-Huriyya wal-Ishtirakiyya – Al-Dustur* [Arab Ba'th Party, Revolutionary Popular National Movement Struggling for the Arab Unity, Freedom and Socialism – The Constitution] (Damascus, 1947).

3 Ibrahim Khalas, al-Tariq li-Khalq 'Insanina al-'Arabi al-Jadid, [the Path Toward the Creation of Our New Arab Man], *Jaysh al-Sha'b*, No. 749, April 25, 1967.

4 Daniel Pipes, *Syria Beyond the Peace Process* (Washington, D.C.: Washington Institute for Near East Policy, Policy Paper, No. 40, 1996), p. 9.

5 Martin Kramer, "The 'Alawites and Shi'ite Islam," in Avner Yaniv, Moshe Ma'oz, and Avi Kober (eds), *Syria and Israel's Security* (Tel Aviv, 1991), p. 171 (in Hebrew); see also: Moshe Ma'oz, *Asad – The Sphinx of Damascus: A Political Biography* (Tel Aviv, 1988) pp. 13, 31 (in Hebrew) [hereafter: Ma'oz, *Asad*].

6 On the position of the Muslim Brotherhood on "sectarian rule" and its program for restoring Syria to reconciliation with the Kingdom of Heaven, see: Qiyadat al-Thawra al-Islamiyya fi Suriyya, *Bayan al-Thawra al-Islamiyya fi Suriyya wa-Minhajuha* [Leadership of Islamic Revolution in Syria, "Manifesto of the Islamic Revolution in Syria and its Charter"], published on behalf of the Islamic revolution in Syria in Damascus on November 9, 1980.

7 Ma'oz, *Asad*, p. 30.

8 Holiday of the Sacrifice.

9 For an exhaustive summary of the Muslim Brotherhood revolt, see: Ma'oz, *Asad*, p. 52; see also: Tomi Meir, "The Muslim Brotherhood and the Islamic Opposition in Syria," (in Hebrew), *Monthly Review* (Tel Aviv, Ministry of Defense), No. 9 (September 1982), pp. 43–47; and the Introduction and Lesch's chapter.

10 Moshe Ma'oz, "The Growth of Modern Syria," in Avner Yaniv, Moshe Ma'oz, and Avi Kober (eds), *Syria and Israel's Security* (Tel Aviv, 1991), pp. 50–51 (in Hebrew).

11 Including the absence of legitimacy from which he suffered, the style of his rule, and the end of his rule a year before the publication.

12 See, e. g., *al-Nadhir*, No. 24, October 22, 1980, pp. 12, 19 [Information Bulletin, published by the Fighters of the Holy War (the *Mujahidin*) in Syria]. In this newspaper, the name of the president was constantly written without the definite article "al" in order to denigrate him.

13 Martin Kramer, *Arab Awakening and Islamic Revival – The Politics of Ideology in the Middle East* (New Brunswick, 1996), p. 200.

14 *Ibid.*, p. 172, and p. 183, note 3.

15 *Al-Nadhir*, No. 24, October 22, 1980, pp. 35–37.

16 *Al-Nahar* (Beirut), March 17, 1971; quoted by Ma'oz, *Asad*, p. 62.

17 *Al-Thawra* (Damascus), March 4, 1995.

18 Iskandar Louka, *Hafiz al-Asad – Mu'jam fi al-Fikr al-Siyasi wal-Ijtima'i*, (Damascus, 1995), pp. 105–7.

19 See, e.g., *al-Thawra*, June 30, 1984; March 4, 1995.

20 *Al-Thawra*, August 5, 1987. See also: Moshe Ma'oz, "The Emergence of Modern Syria," in Moshe Ma'oz and Avner Yaniv (eds), *Syria under Assad: Domestic Constraints and Regional Risks* (London and Sydney, 1986), p. 30.

21 As described in an Arabic poster titled "The Prayer" brought out by Dar al-Shimal in Tripoli, Lebanon, in 1987.

22 *Ramadan* 27–28, the night in which according the Islamic faith the Qur'an was brought down.

23 See, e.g., *al-Thawra*, June 22, 1979; February 27, 1995; *al-Ba'th*, June 12, 1994.

24 *Al-Thawra*, February 11, 1994. This version is a change from the accepted version: "God will endow on you goodness, happiness, and blessings."

25 *Al-Thawra*, August 5, 1987.
26 *Al-Thawra*, March 3, 1995.
27 The order of appearance of the leaders on the list, with the absence of several leaders – such as the presidents of Iran, Libya, and Tunisia – and the appearance of ʻArafat with the heads of states, even though it is noted that he is head of the PLO and the Palestinian Authority, has political significance which deserves a separate discussion.
28 *Al-Baʻth* (Damascus), January 31, 1995.
29 *Al-Thawra*, February 12, 1994. On the political significance of Bashar's participation in the ceremonies and of the front-page announcements of this participation, see Eyal Zisser, "Syria – The Renewed Struggle for the Inheritance," *Data and Analysis* (The Dayan Center, Tel Aviv University), February 1994, p. 29 (in Hebrew).
30 *Al-Thawra*, February 16, 1994.
31 *Al-Baʻth*, November 3, 1972.
32 *Al-Thawra*, January 24, 1985.

3

Syria: The Renewed Struggle for Power

Eyal Zisser

In February 1996, Syrian President Hafiz al-Asad met with Muslim clerics on the occasion of the Fast of *Ramadan*. In his address to this gathering, Asad credited himself with being responsible for the healthy domestic state in Syria. He declared that Syria's situation was at its best, and that comparing the country's condition at the time when he rose to power with its present condition would enable one to appreciate the extent of progress made since then.[1] Several months later, in early May 1996, Damascus and other cities in Syria were rocked by a series of powerful explosions.[2] According to various reports, some of the explosions in Damascus were aimed at President Asad as he made his way to the military cemetery at Najha to participate in the annual memorial services of Martyr's Day on May 6.[3]

The wave of explosions evoked fears of a renewal of the Islamic Movement's anti-regime activities, or at least the end of the period of domestic stability that the country had been enjoying.[4] However, these assessments proved to be hasty and unfounded. It quickly became clear, with a high degree of probability, that these bombs had been placed in Syrian cities by Turkish intelligence agents, as part of the Turkish government's struggle against the Syrian government in the first half of 1996. Such actions were meant to make the latter withdraw its support of the PKK Kurdish underground movement that operated against Turkish targets in southern Turkey and other parts of the country.[5]

However, this revelation was not enough to calm the Syrian regime's fears. The explosions in Damascus and other Syrian cities came at an inconvenient time for the regime, which had been faced with a long series of regional and international challenges and, perhaps, even threats. Among them were concerns over the cooling of relations with the United

States, the further deterioration in relations with Jordan and the Palestinian Authority, and the change in administration in Israel with the rise of a hawkish government that might, in Syria's view, take military action against it.[6] It is therefore no wonder that the Syrian Minister of Information, Muhammad Salman, was quick to warn that Syria had become the victim of a conspiracy initiated and implemented by Israel and the West.[7] Importantly, however, Salman made sure to emphasize that despite the external challenges facing the Syrian regime, the domestic front in the country was calm and quiet and that his country served as a shining example of domestic tranquillity and sense of security.[8]

It would therefore appear that the challenges and difficulties – from within and from without – that confront the Syrian regime today do not pose even a potential threat to the stability or continued existence of the regime. In truth, the collapse of the Soviet Union, Syria's main ally during the 1970s and 1980s, created some fissures in the wall of the Syrian regime's stability. It robbed the regime of political, military, and economic support, and exposed it, at least in its own view, to a series of regional and international threats. In addition, it dealt a serious blow to the world concept still encapsulated in the Ba'th party's historical slogan: "Unity, Freedom and Socialism." This slogan, as we know, served as an important source of legitimacy for Ba'th rule and, thus, of the party's ability to mobilize support among broad sectors of Syrian society. Events in the Middle East did arouse a measure of domestic criticism of the regime's path, mainly increasing demands for greater democratization and the adoption of more liberal social and economic policies. The regime's bind was further exacerbated by a series of increasingly pressing domestic problems, of cumulative effect, such as a high birth rate, accelerated urbanization, and signs of impending shortages of land and water.

Of course, the Syrian regime was forced to act in response to this bind in which it found itself. It even enjoyed some success in several spheres, as in the improvement of its regional and international standing and the provision of political and economic stability at home. For these very reasons, it appears that the most daunting problem facing the Ba'th regime is not necessarily in external threats and constraints, or even in domestic social and economic challenges. While all of these problems, especially in the social and economic domains, may have some negative implications for the stability of the regime in Syria, they pertain more to threats in the interim and long-term, rather than the immediate term. The real threat to the stability or existence of the regime comes from within, that is, it is rooted in the regime's own ranks. Its main component is the threat to internal cohesion set against the background of the struggle for succession in the anticipation of Asad's departure from the political scene. Initial signs of this struggle, and thus the first cracks in the regime's stability, are already visible in the context of President Asad's attempts to promote his son Bashar as his successor.

This step, involving the infusion of fresh blood into the senior echelons of the military–defense establishment, has already aroused some tension and unrest among the ranks, thus revealing the extent to which the succession issue is sensitive and complicated. While the senior echelons of the regime, both military and civilian, will presumably want to resolve the succession issue peacefully, thus retaining their rule and ensuring continued political stability, their success cannot be taken for granted. Therefore, the issue continues to hover like a question mark above the future of the regime in Syria.

At the end of the 1980s, in the wake of the collapse of the Soviet Union, the Syrian regime found itself embroiled in one of the most serious crises in its history. For many years, the Soviet Union had been Syria's main source of political, economic, and military support *vis-à-vis* any threat to its existence, mainly, at least in Syria's view, from Israel and the United States. The Syrians considered this a very real threat in the late 1980s while the country was being accused of involvement in terrorist activities (for instance, the blowing-up of the Pan Am plane over Lockerbie, Scotland).[9] The collapse of this strategic supporter of the Syrian Ba'th regime not only threw the regime into dire international and regional straits, but also dealt a heavy blow to several basic concepts on which it drew its legitimacy, such as socialism, pan-Arabism, and the concepts of "eternal struggle" against Israel and Western imperialism. Indeed, the first signs of dissatisfaction and public criticism of the regime's path already began to emerge when, for example, leaflets distributed in Damascus following the overthrow of the Ceaucesçu regime in Romania in December 1989 read "Every Ceaucesçu will have his day."[10]

As soon as the Syrian regime realized the extent of its crisis at home and abroad, particularly the threat to its stability and its very existence, it took steps to improve the situation. These steps were manifested by a change in political orientation, foremost in attempts to draw closer to and improve relations with the United States. As part of this strategy, Syria joined the anti-Iraq coalition led by the United States during the Gulf crisis of 1990/91, and it joined the peace process with Israel in October 1991.[11]

Certain changes, albeit much more limited ones, were made in Syrian domestic affairs, mainly in the social and economic spheres. They included greater economic openness to the West and the beginnings of limited economic liberalization. These changes allowed the regime to achieve economic stability and to create relative prosperity. Notably, however, the main reason for the regime's success in gaining economic stability was a confluence of convenient economic and political conditions: increased Syrian oil revenues because of stepped-up production following the discovery of new oil fields in the 1980s, coupled with increased external aid and foreign investments, mainly from the Gulf oil-exporting countries.[12] Of course, these conditions may change, with attendant implications for the regime's ability to maintain economic stability in the future.

It is of note that the difficulties facing the regime may further escalate a demographic crisis that has already begun to surface. Syria's natural increase rate, albeit slightly reduced during the last decade, is still high, amounting to almost 3 percent annually.[13] Thus far, the country has been able to deal with its rapid population growth through its reserves of unexploited land and, as already mentioned, its increased oil revenues. However, signs of demographic pressure are beginning to emerge. Over the past several years, the regime has taken the initiative in placing the issue of natural increase on the public agenda.[14] However, the regime does not seem to have, for the time being, a clear plan of action for dealing with the issue. The danger to domestic stability is clear, albeit for the interim and, especially, the long-term.

Economic stability in the country has also contributed to enhancing political stability. Indeed, it is difficult today to point to any serious threat to the regime from within. The Muslim Brotherhood movement, which engulfed the regime in crisis in the early 1980s, was dealt a serious blow, and, for all intents and purposes, has ceased to exist as an organized movement. Moreover, for the past several years, its leaders, most of whom fled into exile, have been pursuing a process of reconciliation with the Ba‘thi regime. In this process, the regime has released thousands of imprisoned members of the movement from jails and allowed several prominent Islamic Movement leaders, such as ‘Adnan ‘Uqla and ‘Abd al-Fatah Abu-Ghudda, to return to Syria from exile and resume their religious activities there.[15]

The regime has also allowed other population groups to integrate into its ranks, especially businessmen in the economic élite, mostly urban Sunnis. This élite, identified as one of the sharpest critics of the Ba‘th party in its early stages, has benefited the most from the country's economic and political stability. Thus for example, the regime allotted about 40 percent of seats in the People's Assembly to independent candidates, including businessmen and, incidentally, religious clerics.[16] The rest of the seats were divided among the Ba‘th party and its satellite parties, all of which are organized under the National Progressive Front. It should be noted, however, that while the People's Assembly is an important body in day-to-day living, mainly within socioeconomic spheres, its influence on security affairs and foreign policy, not to mention the future of the regime, is marginal, if existent at all.

Thus, it must be emphasized that despite the limited changes taking place in Syria over the past several years, the regime has clearly refrained from introducing any real changes into the systems that affect life in the country, especially concerning the structure of the regime and its political apparatus, such as the introduction of greater democratization, reduction of the strength of the military–defense power foci, and the like. It would therefore appear that the regime's policy measures, both foreign and domestic, have been designed to allow it to maintain the status quo, that is, the political and socioeconomic order that have existed in the country since Asad rose to power in November 1970. In other words, their intent is to minimize the influence of changes in the international and regional arenas on Syrian society, mainly the influences of the growth and formulation of a New World order, or even a new Middle East order, under Western political, economic, and cultural dominance.

For the time being, the Syrian regime has succeeded in preserving the country's regional and international status, to no small degree thanks to its dialogue – albeit limited – with the United States. More important is its success in maintaining political and economic stability in Syria, thus keeping the entire country calm. Nevertheless, despite the regime's achievements, fissures have appeared in recent years in the cohesion of the senior echelons heading it, with implications for its future stability. These events reflect the resumption of the power struggles within the Syrian senior echelons, struggles that are still largely invisible to the spectator on the sidelines. These struggles are at least partially rooted in Asad's desire to entrench and strengthen the status of his son Bashar in the struggle for succession. Another factor behind the leadership struggles is the fact that in recent years, the present Syrian security–military leadership has changed from being an asset to a liability, that is, from the central prop of the regime on which it relied for its continued existence, to a source of possible instability and internal tension.

The Succession Struggle: Asad Throws his Full Weight Behind his Son Bashar

Researchers disagree on how to describe and characterize Asad's regime – as a communal, tribal or family regime, or perhaps as an ideological regime authentically representing a broad coalition of social forces anchored in the new order that arose in Syria following the Ba'th revolution of March 8, 1963.[17] Irrespective of the answer to this question, it is clear that the regime in Syria is first and foremost a personal regime centered around the image and figure of Asad. The President serves the regime as a nucleus or an adhesive binding that holds its various components together. The fear of Asad, but mainly the awe and respect in which he is held by the Syrian public for his proven achievements (preservation of domestic political stability and his record in the struggle against Israel), constitute the source of the Syrian regime's power.

This is a clear advantage for the regime established by Asad, which, as already mentioned, is focused exclusively on Asad the man, but this also seems to be its most obvious disadvantage. After all, under the present circumstances, much, perhaps too much, depends on Asad the man, and this raises questions regarding the future of the regime once Asad has departed the political scene in Syria.

Such questions arose in full force in 1983–84, after President Asad suffered a heart attack. While Asad did attempt to turn over the running of day-to-day affairs temporarily to a six-man committee, made up entirely of his Sunni friends and partners ('Abd al-Halim Khaddam, Hikmat Shihabi, 'Abdallah al-Ahmar, Mustafa Talas, Mahmud al-Zu'bi and Ra'uf al-Kasm), the attempt was opposed by the 'Alawi element in the Syrian leadership and Asad's brother Rif'at, who tried to exploit his brother's illness in order to promote his own status as the President's successor. Rif'at managed to impose himself on the committee, despite the fact that some members were his long-time rivals. He did so under pressure from, or at least with the support and assistance of the senior 'Alawi officers echelons in the army. However, Rif'at ran into broad opposition among his colleagues in the Syrian senior political and military echelons when President Asad recovered and sought to settle accounts with his disobedient brother, who had operated independently in opposition to his directives. Rif'at now found himself alone as his 'Alawi colleagues refused to support him against Asad and were quick to declare loyalty to the President.[18]

The resulting fraternal struggle threatened to bring the Syrian regime to the brink of civil war, which was thwarted by Asad's victory over his brother. He won the confrontation thanks to solid support from the entire military and political leadership, coupled with mediation and reconciliation efforts made by family members, headed by Asad's mother, Na'isa.[19] Rif'at was gradually removed from all of his power centers in Syria and quickly went into extended exile abroad.

Following this episode, the issue of succession and, in a more general sense, the question of the future of the regime after Asad's departure, lost some of its urgency. On the other hand, although Rif'at, the main and, in effect, the only claimant to the position, was removed from the Syrian political arena, the issue was not fully confronted and thus remained unresolved. It seems that President Asad purposefully refrained from dealing with this issue, preferring to postpone the moment of reckoning in choosing a successor because his sense that he still had more time;[20] because of his desire to prevent shock waves within the regime's senior echelons at all costs; and, perhaps, because of the paucity of choices for a fitting and willing successor.

In the early 1990s, President Asad apparently had a change of heart and decided that the time had come to pay renewed attention to succession question. A contributing factor, it seems, was the "maturing" of President Asad's eldest son, Basil, who had always appeared to be his father's talented favorite son. Basil had chosen to follow in his father's footsteps and embarked on a military career in preparation for a political career. Basil, born in March 1962, was active from a very early age in the Ba'th party youth movement. At the age of 18, he was accepted to the Syrian Army Officers' Academy, and after graduation he rose in the ranks for about a decade, gaining knowledge and professional experience and, especially, developing close relations with members of the senior echelons of the Syrian security-military establishment.[21]

In the early 1990s, Basil's rise accelerated and culminated in his appointment as the Commander of a brigade of the Republican Guards unit, whose task it is to protect the regime. This is a division-sized élite unit which had been established to replace Rif'at's Defense Companies Division and which, following his ouster, became a regular division in the Syrian army.[22] Concurrently, there was an escalation of signals from Damascus that President Asad intended to declare his son Basil as his successor.

These signals were designed to test, or perhaps to prepare, the ground in Syria and abroad for an official and binding announcement of Basil as successor. First, Basil began to receive increased exposure among the Syrian public, most of which had no personal knowledge of him. This exposure focused mainly on Basil's sports activities, as head of the Syrian Olympic equestrian team, and on his activities in promoting the use of computers in Syria.[23] Second, during the December 1991 referendum that approved Asad's candidacy for a fourth term as President, Basil's picture was circulated along with that of his father. Third, Asad began to be called Abu Basil, although in the past he had been called Abu-Sulayman, after his grandfather, Sulayman.[24] Fourth, the Arab press outside Syria carried a growing number of articles about Asad's intentions to appoint

Basil as his successor. Most of these reports apparently originated in intentional leaks from Damascus.[25]

Basil's undeclared candidacy for the successor's role managed to stave off the struggle for succession, as potential opponents preferred to avoid an open confrontation on this issue with President Asad and with Basil himself, whose position was growing stronger. Therefore, many in Syria, even outside the 'Alawi community to which Basil belonged, considered him to be a guarantee of continued political stability and economic prosperity, which the country had been enjoying following the Gulf crisis of 1990–91.[26]

Asad's decision to choose Basil as his successor, if he indeed had decided to do so, was anchored in the character and fabric of the Syrian regime. This regime is known to be not only ideological and military, but also ethnic and, even more so, tribal and familial in complexion (because many of its senior figures are members of Asad's Qalbiyya tribe of relatives). Some also claim that Asad was influenced by a number of Communist family dictatorships with which he maintained close ties, such as that of Kim Il Sung in North Korea and, especially, that of Nicolae Ceaucesçu in Romania. Aside from that, it bears reiterating that the Syrian regime is distinctly personal, that is, identified with the image and activities of President Asad, who established it and has been bolstering it for the past 29 years. It would appear that Asad views his role as president as a national and historic mission and takes the trouble to emphasize his personal contribution to Syria's consolidation. Therefore, he presumably fears that his achievements will dissipate if there is no fitting successor.[27]

On January 21, 1994, Basil was killed in an automobile accident at the age of 32. Basil's death shocked many people both inside and outside Syria. A five-day period of national mourning was declared all over Syria, and, according to foreign news reports, there was a feeling of genuine grief among much of the population, apparently because Basil had been so popular and had been considered as the guarantee of continued stability in the country.[28] One obvious result of Basil's death was the renewal of the succession struggle and the beginning of a period of nervousness and disquiet within the Syrian leadership.

The new candidate as Asad's successor was his second son, Bashar, who was born on September 11, 1965. At the time of Basil's death, Bashar was training in his specialty as an ophthalmologist in Britain. Ever since Bashar returned to Syria in the wake of his brother's death, Asad has been taking steps to push him along the military path, albeit a shorter one, that his elder brother had taken. Basil, as we shall recall, took a long series of courses during his military service in all branches of the Syrian army. Now Bashar followed a similar track, including a tank battalion commanders' course and a command and staff course, both of which are essential to the senior officers' echelon in the Syrian army. This program culminated in Bashar's appointment as Basil's replacement to be a brigade commander in the Republican Guards unit. Upon Bashar's return to Syria in 1994, he held the rank of a Captain (*Naqib*); he was later promoted to the rank of Lt. Col. (*Muqaddam*) in July 1997, and then became a Colonel (*Aqid*) in January 1999.[29]

Since his return to Syria, Bashar has been given broad media coverage. For instance, during the mourning ceremonies for his brother, he was presented as the person who would carry on as the torchbearer. This also held true concerning the various activities that Basil had sponsored, such as equestrian events and computer conferences (Bashar is now the chairman of the Syrian Computer Association).[30] Of special importance is the handling of the Lebanese issue, which President Asad placed in Bashar's hands. Bashar began to establish ties with various power sources in Lebanon, such as Sulayman Tony Faranjiyya, the grandson of former Lebanese President Sulayman Faranjiyya and a member of the Faranjiyya family, with which the Asad family has had close relations for many years. In late 1998, it became known in Damascus that the responsibility for the "Lebanese file" was transferred from Vice President 'Abd al-Halim Khaddam to Bashar.[31]

No less significant was the process of building a support base for Bashar within the Syrian military apparatus, a process that has gained momentum since mid-1994. Indeed, there have been broad and unprecedented changes taking place over the past few years in the Syrian army's chain of command, mainly at the intermediate level. In the course of these changes, a number of young 'Alawi officers were appointed, many of them unknown, apparently close to Bashar and counted among his supporters. These young officers may eventually grant him the support that he needs in the struggle for succession.

One of these officers was Lt. Gen. 'Ali Hasan, who was appointed commander of the Republican Guards unit in place of 'Adnan Makhluf, the cousin of the President's wife and commander of the unit from the time it was established. The background to Makhluf's dismissal and the appointment of 'Ali Hasan was an argument over authority between Bashar and Makhluf, in which Bashar emerged as the victor, presumably with his father's backing. Another appointment, made back in July 1994, was that of Bashir al-Najjar to the post of head of the General Security Directorate. Najjar had served as chief of the Customs Directorate, had been identified in the past as one of Basil's supporters, and had participated together with him in the struggle against smuggling and drug dealing that Basil had initiated and supervised. Najjar is of Sunni extraction, like all the past heads of this directorate, but the strong man in the directorate is his deputy, Muhammad Nasif Khayrbak, a member of the 'Alawi Khayrbak family. In July 1998, Najjar was replaced by 'Ali Khuri, but Khayrbak continued to play a key role in the directorate.[32]

Even with all the effort being invested in propping up Bashar, it is notable that, true to form, the manner in which Asad is dealing with the promotion of his son as his successor is characterized by extreme caution and a demonstrably slow pace. Asad, behaving like a man with time on his hands, has refrained from any expression, let alone public display, of his intention to promote his son as his heir. It is difficult to judge how much time Asad believes he has at his disposal. According to the Syrian constitution, the Syrian president must be at least 40 years old, and Bashar will be 40 in 2005, one year before the end of Asad's fifth term. Asad began his fifth seven-year term in March 11, 1999. As is known, the president is elected in a referendum after his candidacy has been approved by the Ba'th Party Regional Command and given official confirmation by the People's Assembly.

Nevertheless, it seems that the attempt to establish Bashar as the successor to Basil and thus to Asad has encountered some difficulties. The attitude in Syria and elsewhere to Bashar's candidacy is marked by some doubt because of his youth and, more importantly, his lack of practical experience in managing military and state affairs. In addition, the Syrian public has the impression that Bashar, in complete contrast to his elder brother, Basil, is lacking in such personal attributes as charisma, determination, and decisiveness, which are essential to anyone holding the reins of power in Syria.[33] Therefore, despite the respect and even awe with which the Syrian people hold President Asad, and their natural tendency to express faithful support of the President, there are still some signs of doubt about Bashar's candidacy. These reservations are expressed for now in statements, mostly off the record, by Syrians both inside and outside the ruling apparatus, to the effect that Syria is not a monarchy and that the Syrian public will not accept efforts to force an unfit successor upon it.[34]

Noteworthy in this context is the fact that in the past, two other figures were often mentioned as possible successors: Vice President 'Abd al-Halim Khaddam and former CGS (Chief of the General Staff) Hikmat Shihabi. The advantage of these two men was in their contribution to the regime's standing within the Sunni community, as well as its image in the Arab world. Nevertheless, Shihabi was forced to retire in July 1998 due to ill health and perhaps as a way to clear the road to Bashar, while Khaddam is also known to be ill. In addition, Khaddam's standing has been in a constant decline, and during 1997–98 he lost some of his power and authority to Bashar, such as his responsibility for the "Lebanese file."[35]

Rif'at Asad is also mentioned as a possible candidate. Rif'at returned to Syria in July 1992 from a prolonged exile abroad. According to reports from Damascus, his power is waning and he is in effect under house arrest. In February 1998, President Asad even ousted his brother from the post of Vice President for National Security, which Rif'at had held since 1984.[36] Nevertheless, he is still the best-known and highest-ranking 'Alawi personality in Syria after Hafiz al-Asad. This is an important point, as the list of contenders to the succession lacks, at least for the time being, any senior 'Alawi figures aside from Bashar. In the event of a crisis or a threat to 'Alawi control over the country, the 'Alawi senior military-security echelons may unite, for lack of choice, around Rif'at, as it did in 1983 when President Asad was thought to be on his deathbed.

In addition to Rif'at, there are several other senior 'Alawis worthy of mention as possible candidates, among them 'Ali Aslan, the current CGS; the Third and the Second Corps, Shafiq Fayyadh and Ibrahim Safi (former commanders of Divisions 3 and 1); and Muhammad al-Khuli, former commander of the Air Force. Alongside them are the heads of the various security apparatuses, including 'Ali Duba, Deputy CGS and head of the Military Security Department; and 'Adnan Badr Hasan, head of the Political Security Directorate. The younger generation of 'Alawi officers, who have been promoted to positions of command in the past few years, are not well-known enough, and one doubts whether they are ready to fulfill a leading role in the process of choosing a successor or even producing a candidate for this position themselves. As already mentioned, the conventional wisdom is that most of the younger officers are close to Bashar or owe their promotions to him, and when the day comes, as they will have established themselves and accumulated power, they will support him in the decisive battle for succession.

Therefore, the key question in the future of the succession struggle in Syria is: Will President Asad succeed in passing on the reins of power to his son Bashar while he is still alive – assuming that this is indeed his intention – or will he depart the political scene in Syria before then? In the first instance, Bashar ostensibly stands a good chance of consolidating his control over the regime. In the second instance, he will have to struggle for primacy against strong and influential rivals, who may refuse to genuflect to the young candidate who was foisted upon them, despite his pedigree.

In such a situation, the decision will be passed on, as was the case in the past, to the informal regime leadership, namely, the commanders of the army units and security forces, most of them 'Alawis, who hold the practical reins of power and ensure the stability and very existence of the regime. These figures comprise the hidden side of the Syrian ruling apparatus. Unlike institutions such as the People's Assembly and the government, their status is not anchored in the Syrian constitution. However, because they control the army units and the security agencies, they hold the key in deciding the country's fate and in choosing a successor. It was this group who, in the period 1976–82, determined the outcome of the Muslim Brotherhood rebellion against the regime, and it was they who gave Hafiz al-Asad the advantage over his brother Rif'at in the struggle between them in 1983–84.

It may also be assumed that this group of officers in the army and the security forces learned the lesson of Rif'at's rebellion in 1983–84 and will therefore try, at any price, to work out a consensus as to the identity of the successor. The choice may be, depending on circumstances, Bashar, Rif'at, a collective leadership from their own ranks, or one of the formerly mentioned Sunni candidates. However, it must be borne in mind that the question of the succession is inseparably connected with the personal fate of these officers and commanders, who are in control of the country's important power centers, which any successor may try to wrest from them. Therefore, one cannot rule out the possibility that the succession issue may develop into a violent power struggle. Indeed, the sensitivity of these officers and commanders to their status has already given rise to tensions within the Syrian regime, even before the signal has been given for the actual succession struggle to begin.

The Senior Military–Security Echelons: From an Asset to the Regime to a Liability

These senior officers of the military-security apparatus were at one time, as already mentioned, an unequivocal asset to the regime and a major element in ensuring its stability, if not its very existence. In the past several years, however, the people who comprise these echelons have gradually become a liability to the regime and an obstacle in its path. It should be emphasized that no change has taken place in the degree to which the regime needs these people or in its basic dependence on military and security institutions in order to preserve itself. The problem thus lies more with the particular figures heading these institutions at the present time.

Some of these personalities have controlled the major power centers in the Syrian army security apparatuses for about two decades, if not longer. 'Ali Duba, for example, has been the head of military security since 1974, and Ibrahim Safi and Shafiq Fayyadh served as divisional commanders for over a decade until recent promotions to corps commanders.[37] Thus, any attempt to make Bashar, who is a full generation their junior, President Asad's successor, may very well encounter opposition or strong doubts from this quarter. In any event, even if these figures support him, they will consider themselves as his equal, if not his superior, since they will take the credit for his rise to power. Due to their long-standing term of office in positions of power, this is an aging and even an ailing group of people. For instance, the commander of the special forces, 'Ali Haydar,[38] suffered, even before his ouster, from a blood clot and other health problems characteristic of other senior officers and commanders.[39] This state of affairs, besides detracting from their individual effectiveness, may breed inefficiency and encourage corruption.

Furthermore, some members of the security élite are identified with the brutal and dark side of the regime. For example, Muhammad al-Khuli, former commander of the Air Force, was accused of being responsible for the Hindawi affair (the attempt to blow up an El Al plane at Heathrow Airport in 1986). 'Ali Duba, head of the Military Security Department, was involved in putting down the Muslim Brotherhood rebellion in Hama in February 1982. Such affairs may create future difficulties for the regime in its efforts to improve Syria's image as a "law-abiding" country, a step essential in improving its relations with the United States and Western Europe.[40]

It is also claimed that the present senior military-security echelons may obstruct the regime in changing Syria's political, social, and economic orientation. These senior personalities may, ostensibly, fear a process of change that could vitiate their status and influence. According to one recent assessment, these groups might represent a possible source of opposition to a peace agreement with Israel, since such an accord could result in cutbacks in the Syrian army and security forces, thus weakening their clout in an "era of peace."[41]

However, this claim seems baseless because nothing in the change in Syria's political orientation, even in the possibility of establishing peaceful relations with Israel, would have any implications for the status of the army and security forces. These agencies will continue to serve the regime as a major source of support in preserving its stability and existence, in that the largest threat accounting for the regime's dependency on the services of the army and security forces lies within the domestic sphere (from Islamic and other elements). Since this threat will only grow and intensify, as has happened in other Arab countries, the regime will have to increasingly rely on the strength of its military and security forces. It is also noteworthy that Asad is not – and has never been – a reformer with a vision of change. Thus, there is little likelihood of the emergence of basic disagreements between him or, more precisely, between his world view and that of his colleagues in the leadership. Asad's recent approach to policy has been designed to preserve the status quo in Syria, including its existing political apparatus, rather than to change it.

Fissures have appeared in the cohesion of the Syrian leadership over the past several years, and occasional but significant signs of tension between Asad and the military-security leadership have begun to surface, especially among the senior echelons (the heads of directorates in the security services and the upper army ranks). These fissures apparently originate in the need, and perhaps even the desire, of the regime to inject new blood into the ranks in view of the challenges facing the Ba'th regime, not the least of which is the promotion of Bashar as Asad's successor. However, this "infusion of new blood" is to be carried out at the expense of the "old guard," which could arouse the latter's opposition to the regime.

One telling example of this struggle is that of Lt. Gen. 'Ali Haydar's dismissal as Commander of the Special Forces in July 1994. Press reports originating in Damascus indicated that his dismissal and arrest were due to his statements denouncing President Asad, his son, and his policies. Several other senior officers in the Special Forces, apparently Haydar's close associates and supporters, were also dismissed. Haydar was replaced by Lt. Gen. 'Ali Habib, who had headed the Syrian expeditionary force in the Gulf crisis of 1990–91.[42]

'Ali Haydar had been commander of the Special Forces for about two decades and was considered to be one of the mainstays of the regime. The forces under his command played an important role in putting down the Muslim Brotherhood rebellion in the period 1976–82, especially with respect to the uprising in Hama in February 1982. In the course of the conflict between Asad and his brother Rif'at in 1983–84, Haydar supported the president and, together with other senior army commanders, tipped the scale in the latter's favor.[43]

It is not sufficiently clear why Haydar turned against the president. It apparently had to do with his frustration at not being promoted in rank and function. While Haydar's colleagues and members of his generation, such as Shafiq Fayyadh and Ibrahim Safi, had been promoted to the post of corps commander, Haydar had been left behind.[44] His disloyalty may have also been a result of his "sensing" that his career was nearing its end. Thus, the Haydar affair may be viewed as a representative case reflecting a more comprehensive problem involving many high-ranking officials in the Syrian army and security forces, who, like him, are approaching the end of their careers and may work against the regime out of frustration and despair or out of hope of preserving their status. The very fact that Haydar dared to challenge the regime and the fact that he was ousted from the leadership may be indicative of the stability, or lack thereof, in the regime, at least insofar as the image it projects for external consumption. However, Haydar's case remains an isolated episode, and it seems that the regime did not face any difficulty in reshuffling the army's upper echelons since that time. Indeed, when it became known that the CGS, Hikmat Shihabi, retired on July 1, 1998, there were those who expected restlessness within the Syrian military leadership. This did not come to pass, however, mainly because Shihabi lacked any "divisions" of his own due to his Sunni origins and because he was widely regarded as an ailing old man who had been finding it difficult to function.[45]

The Appointment of Muhammad al-Khuli as Commander of the Air Force

In early 1994, press sources in Damascus reported that Muhammad al-Khuli had been appointed as commander of the Syrian Air Force.[46] Muhammad al-Khuli, a close associate of Asad, had served until 1987 as the head of the Security Directorate in the Air Force. In the wake of the Hindawi affair and in response to British and American pressure, Khuli was dismissed from his post and made deputy commander of the Air Force. His appointment to this post was considered to be symbolic and lacking in importance, regarded as a "kick upstairs" and an attempt by Asad to remove Khuli, who had fallen from grace, from the position of power that he had occupied. According to Patrick Seale, Asad's sympathetic biographer, Khuli had also acted in the Hindawi affair behind Asad's back.[47]

If this description is true, then Khuli's present appointment as commander of the Air Force was clearly a move contrary to the desires of the United States and Britain, at the very time when Syria aspired to improve its image in the West and its relations with these two countries. Why, then, was Asad prepared to endanger his relations with the West by appointing Khuli to his new post? Perhaps he felt the need to compensate and repay an old and loyal confidant and friend. He may even have hoped that this friend, who had proven his loyalty in the past, would strengthen the foundations of the regime at difficult moments, such as the one it is now experiencing. It also appears that Asad expected Khuli to support his son Bashar in the expected struggle for succession.[48] Khuli, however, retired in June 1999 in the age of 66.[49]

The Appointment of a New Chain of Command in the Syrian Army

It is important to emphasize that the Syrian army's senior echelons have undergone an overall face-lift with the replacement of most of its division commanders in recent years. This move was designed to fill a vacuum created by the promotion of some of the previous division commanders, such as Ibrahim Safi and Shafiq Fayyadh. In other cases, new commanders have been appointed to replace long-tenured commanders who were pensioned off or transferred to less important and influential administrative positions.[50] Since the process of raising a new generation of commanders is in full swing and most of the new faces are unfamiliar, it is difficult to draw any unequivocal conclusions about the future of the regime, or the succession. Nevertheless, this process, some of it set in motion by the regime itself, is also part of a more comprehensive process of infusing new blood into the senior Syrian military-security echelons, with the aim of enhancing their effectiveness in serving the regime and ensuring their support for Bashar as Asad's successor. However, the growth of a young officers' corps is being accomplished at the expense of veteran officers who have to step aside and may, at some stage, seek their revenge.

Indeed, under the surface the Syrian political apparatus is already busy preparing for the possibility of a renewed struggle over the succession. However, one cannot ignore the substantial difference between the struggle we see here and that characterizing Syria from the 1940s to the 1960s. First, at least for the time being, the present struggle lacks an ideological basis. It is not a struggle over Syria's path and its political and socioeconomic orientation, but rather a power struggle focused entirely on gaining political control over the country.

Second, the struggle observed today is being waged mostly within the 'Alawi community or, more precisely, within the community's leadership, which fills important functions in the military and security services. The role played by other power factors or elements in the regime, particularly by the members of other communities, is marginal.

Third, most of this struggle is subterranean. In the last quarter-century, unlike in the past, Syria has had a stable and centrist regime headed by an accepted, powerful leader whom everyone obeys. Therefore, as long as Asad remains in power, this struggle presumably will not be allowed to break out into the open and will be limited to silent strife within the corridors of the regime.

Fourth, the Syrian army's size and complexity, created by the military build-up that Syria has been undergoing ever since Asad rose to power, has made it almost impossible, or at least very complicated, to employ force in changing the face of the regime or in dictating the outcome of the succession. A move of this kind requires very precise planning and coordination, which may run into greater opposition by virtue of the size of the army. In any event, the implications of a forceful confrontation in such a situation could prove disastrous for those participating in it. This situation has created a mechanism for the desire and the will to solve problems by peaceful means.

Such motivation for a peaceful solution to the succession struggle also reflects the fact that all the power factions in Syria are acquainted with one another. After all, these are army officers and commanders who have been involved in the Asad regime for over two decades. They have been Asad's partners on this long path; they know each other very well, and some are even connected by family ties.

Fifth, the existence of the ruling apparatus in Asad's Syria makes it necessary to take into consideration, even if only for external consumption, the institutions on which Syria's ruling tradition have been based for the past quarter-century. This tradition derives its legitimacy from the Syrian constitution, but primarily reflects the political and socioeconomic order that has evolved in Syria since the Ba'th revolution of March 8, 1963. This socioeconomic order finds expression in the present ruling coalition in Syria, a coalition of minorities and marginal players in Syrian society – 'Alawis, rural Sunnis, Druze, Isma'ilis, and others – that holds the reins of both the formal and informal ruling institutions in the country. Therefore, this situation requires the commanders of the army and security units to act to ensure support for and, above all, legitimacy for any solution that they wish to dictate and implement in the matter of the succession.

Finally, the sensitive balancing mechanism in the military-security establishment may also make it difficult to let the succession confrontation escalate into violence. During his tenure in power, Asad has succeeded in taking most of the 'Alawis in power under his wing. Most members of the 'Alawi coalition surrounding Asad are bound by political or family alliances. However, his ability to control them is the result of his ability to exploit, and sometimes even to enflame, internecine struggles among the members of this coalition, based on tribal, family or even personal rivalries. The 'Alawi coalition is not as cohesive as is generally believed, and its ability to group together behind a single candidate should not be taken for granted.[51] On the other hand, the sensitive system of balances and restraints among the components of the 'Alawi coalition may induce it to function as a moderating element in the face of a hasty decision to mount an all-out battle for succession in which each contender is pitted against everyone else.

Conclusions

Over the past several years, fissures have begun to appear in the façade of stability and cohesion that the Syrian regime has been projecting for external consumption for nearly a decade.

First, the struggle for succession, swept under the rug in the mid-1980s, has begun to break out onto the surface and has slowly risen to the top of Syria's current political agenda. Jockeying for position in anticipation of Asad's departure from the political scene has given rise to tension and nervousness within the regime leadership that may potentially lead to self-destruction, as proven by the events of 1983–84 (the struggle between the brothers Hafiz and Rif'at al-Asad). While Asad aspires to promote his son Bashar as his successor, his desire to do so is significant only if it is implemented while Asad's position as ruler remains strong.

Second, the veteran and loyal senior security echelons are gradually becoming a burden on the regime because of their aging membership and negative image in the West. This element might even prove to be an obstacle in Asad's campaign to bequeath his rule to his son Bashar. The 'Ali Haydar case suggests that these senior personalities may not be prepared to sit idly by and allow themselves to be removed from the power centers that they control today.

It is true that the Syrian regime has succeeded in extricating itself, at least to some extent, from the crisis that beset it in the late 1980s. However, the regime still faces several serious challenges, mainly as the outcome of the adoption of a new path since the early 1990s, and some of which were directly, if belatedly, caused by the collapse of the Soviet Union.

The first of these challenges is the need to face up to the collapse of the Ba'th party's world view: the end of pan-Arabism, the end of the socialist era, and progress in the peace negotiations with Israel, which are aimed at ending the "eternal struggle" against this country. Since this world view has for years granted the regime its legitimacy, the danger involved in its collapse – anachronism and irrelevance – is clear.

Second, the implications of closer relations with the West, as expressed in increased economic and political openness, must be controlled. This openness, though limited as it has been, has the potential for encouraging a series of trends in Syrian society that the regime would like to restrain, particularly the demand for political and economic reforms. The regime's rapprochement with the West also limits its ability to act, as in the past, with toughness and brutality against opposition elements. Finally, economic openness to the West is making the regime increasingly dependent on its continued development of economic, as well as political, ties with the West, both of which form an important and essential element in improving the country's economy and, in turn, helping to preserve Syrian political stability and the very existence of the regime.

In this context, it is worth noting that the regime remains committed, at least for external consumption, to its world view, and has avoided any public ideological discussion of the need to modify it. For example, the Ba'th Party Conference, originally scheduled for 1989, did not convene in 1998, and there are only few indications that it will be convened in 1999. The Conference is the body that elects the party institutions, including such functions as the Regional Command and the Central Committee, which are responsible for choosing the President's successor.

While the regime is taking steps to give itself a democratic, or at least a more open, image, this is not enough to indicate any real change in the country's political structure or system, let alone introduction of genuine democracy. Economic liberalization in Syria is still in its early stages, and the economy is still, for the most part, run along socialist lines and controlled by the governmental.

Less than 40 years ago, the British journalist Patrick Seale, in his book *The Struggle for Syria,* described a weak and unstable country engaged in a constant struggle over its image, its path, and its very existence, and, therefore, over who would control it.[52] This struggle ostensibly ended for the good with the accession to rule of Hafiz al-Asad on November 16, 1970. Asad has indeed granted Syria a political stability, at least in relative terms, the likes of which the country had never known before. The sense of tranquillity that the Asad regime projected in all directions prompted Patrick Seale to call his second book on Syria, a biography of Asad published in 1988, *Asad of Syria: The Struggle for the Middle East.* This book portrays Syria as a regional power, an agent of status and influence, which seeks to gain control over the entire Middle East on the basis of its power.[53] However, this sense of tranquillity appears to have been premature because the struggle for Syria, this time in the sphere of political control – an issue that had seemed to be settled – is about to resume. In any event, the last word on the subject has yet to be spoken.

Notes

1 *Al-Thawra* (Damascus), February 22, 1996.
2 *Al-Hayat* (London), June 10, 1996; *New York Times*, June 10, 1996.
3 *Financial Times* (London), June 11, 1996.
4 *Ibid.*; *Ha'aretz* (Tel Aviv), June 11, 1996. See also: Allgemeiner Deutscher Nachrichtendienst (AND), May 11, 1996 – *DR* (Daily Report, US Foreign Broadcasting Information Service), May 13, 1996.
5 *Al-Sharq al-Awsat* (London, Jeddah and Riyadh), June 6, 1996, *Yedi'ot Aharonot* (Tel Aviv), June 16, 1996. In late December 1996, a bomb exploded in a bus in Damascus. This time the Syrian regime was forced to admit that such an incident happened. It is unclear whether Turkish agents are responsible for this bomb as well. It is noteworthy that a small and unknown Islamic group, "The Ja'far Shuwayhat Group," claimed responsibility for this bomb portraying it as a revenge for the arrest and the murder by the Syrian authorities of Shuwayhat who was one of its members and was arrested and killed by the Syrian authorities after being accused of being involved in terrorist actions against American targets in Saudi Arabia. See: BBC, Reuters, January 10, 1997.
6 See: *al-Hayat*, June 3, 1996. For the Syrian perspective, see: *Tishrin* (Damascus), June 21, 1996.
7 *Al-Sharq al-Awsat,* June 6, 1996.
8 *Ibid.*
9 See: Eyal Zisser, "Syria," *MECS* (Middle East Contemporary Survey), Vol. XV (1991), p. 673.
10 *Davar* (Tel Aviv), March 8, 1990.
11 See: Eyal Zisser, "Syria," *MECS*, Vol. XV (1991), pp. 665–89
12 For more, see, e.g., Eberhard Kienle (ed.), *Contemporary Syria: Liberalization Between Cold War and Cold Peace* (London, 1994); Volker Perthes, *The Political Economy of Syria Under Asad* (London, 1995).
13 See: Onn Winckler, *Demographic Developments and Population Policies in Ba'thist Syria* (Brighton and Portland, 1999), p. 26, table 2.1.
14 See: *al-Thawra*, July 13, 1993; April 3, 1994; April 21, 1994; October 21, 1994; October 23, 1994; *al-Ba'th* (Damascus), June 16, 1994; July 14, 1994; September 7, 1994.
15 Reuters, December 15, 1995; *al-Wasat* (London), May 13, 1996; June 3, 1996.
16 *Al-Wasat*, June 3, 1994; see also: Eyal Zisser, "Syria," *MECS,* Vol. XVIII (1994), pp. 615–17.
17 See: Raymond A. Hinnebusch, *Authoritarian Power and State Formation in Ba'thist Syria: Army, Party and Peasant* (Boulder, 1990). For a different perspective, see: Daniel Pipes, *Syria Beyond the Peace Process,* The Washington Institute, Policy Papers, No. 40 (Washington, 1996).
18 See: Patrick Seale, *Asad of Syria: The Struggle for the Middle East* (London, 1988), pp. 421–40 [hereafter: Seale, *Asad*].
19 *Ibid.*
20 Asad, born in October 1930, is not among the older Middle Eastern leaders.
21 *Libération* (Paris), January 23–24, 1993. See also: 'Izzat al-Sa'dani, *Basil fi 'Uyun al-Misriyyin* (Cairo, 1994).

22 *Financial Times* (London), March 18, 1992; *Ha'aretz*, July 24, 1992.
23 See, e.g., *al-Ba'th*, August 12, 1992; August 16, 1992.
24 *Financial Times,* March 18, 1992.
25 *al-Muharrir* (Paris), March 30, 1992; *Akhbar al-'Usbu'*, June 25, 1992.
26 On the recovery of the Syrian economy during the 1990s, see the chapters of Efrat, Lesch and Winckler in this volume.
27 See: Seale, *Asad,* pp. 441–60; idem, "Asad: Between Institutions and Autocracy," in Richard Antoun and Donald Quantaert (eds.) *Syria: Society, Culture and Polity* (New York, 1991). See also: Eyal Zisser, "Asad of Syria – The Leader and the Image," *Orient*, Vol. 35, No. 2 (1994), pp. 247–60.
28 *Tishrin, al-Thawra, al-Hayat*, January 22, 1994; *Yedi'ot Aharonot,* January 23, 1994.
29 *Al-Wasat,* November 17, 1994; May 7, 1995; *al-Sharq al-Awsat,* March 7, 1994; *New York Times*, January 10, 1997; *Ha'aretz*, January 5, 1998.
30 *Al-Ba'th*, April 15, 1994; May 10, 1994; *al-Thawra*, March 26, 1996.
31 *Al-Thawra*, February 10, 1994; April 15, 1994; *al-Ba'th*, May 10, 1994; Reuters, January 10, 1997. See also: *al-Watan al-'Arabi* (Paris), January 31, 1997; *Mideast Mirror* (London), December 11, 1998.
32 *Al-Muharrir*, September 26, 1994; *Yedi'ot Aharonot*, November 24, 1994. See also an interview by the author with Patrick Seale. London, September 25, 1995; *al-Hayat*, July 3, 1998. See also: Eyal Zisser, "Syria," *MECS*, Vol. XVIII (1994), pp. 613–15.
33 *Al-Wasat,* May 1, 1995; Interview of the author with Patrick Seale. London, September 25, 1995.
34 Interview by the author with Syrian Academic. Washington, June 23, 1996.
35 See: Alasdair Drysdale, "The Succession Question in Syria," *The Middle East Journal*, Vol. 39, No. 2 (Spring 1985), pp. 246–57; Eyal Zisser, "Decision Making in Asad's Syria" (Washington, D.C., Washington Institute for Near East Policy, 1998), pp. 8–12.
36 *New York Times*, January 28, 1997; *Ha'aretz*, February 10, 1998.
37 Seale, *Asad*, pp. 428–29; "Syria: Impact of Wielding Power on 'Alawi Cohesiveness," Paris, Monde Arabe: *Maghreb-Machrek* (January–February 1995), pp. 93–119 – *DR*, October 3, 1995.
38 'Ali Haydar, born in Jabla, in the 'Alawi region, belongs to one of the prominent families in the Haddadin tribe, one of the largest in the 'Alawi community, and his family thus far has ardently supported Asad and his regime.
39 *Yedi'ot Aharonot,* September 4, 1994; November 25, 1994.
40 Seale, *Asad,* pp. 475–82.
41 *Ha'aretz,* September 22, 1994; *Yedi'ot Aharonot*, November 25, 1994; *Jane's Defence Weekly*, November 26, 1994.
42 *Al-Hayat*, September 3, 1994; *al-Muharrir,* September 26, 1994; *Yedi'ot Aharonot,* November 28, 1994.
43 Seale, *Asad,* pp. 421–40.
44 See Israeli Prime Minister and Minister of Defense Yitzhak Rabin's interview to Yedi'ot Aharonot. *Yedi'ot Aharonot,* September 4, 1994.
45 *Al-Hayat*, *Ha'aretz,* July 3, 1998.
46 *Al-Hayat*, September 3, 1994.
47 Seale, *Asad,* pp. 475–85.
48 Interview by the author with Syrian Academic. Washington, June 23, 1996.

See also: "Syria: Impact of Wielding Power on 'Alawi Cohesiveness," Paris, Monde Arabe: *Maghreb-Machrek* (January–February 1995), pp. 93–119 – *DR*, October 3, 1995.

49 *Al-Hayat*, June 14, 1999.

50 R. Beirut, December 31,1994 – DR, January 4, 1995. See also an interview by the author with Patrick Seale, London, September 25, 1995.

51 See: "Syria: Wielding Power on 'Alawi Cohesiveness," Paris, Monde Arabe: *Maghreb-Machrek (*January–February 1995), pp. 93–119 – *DR*, October 3, 1995.

52 Patrick Seale, *The Struggle for Syria* (London, 1965).

53 Patrick Seale, *Asad of Syria: The Struggle for the Middle East* (London, 1988).

Part II

Economic Developments and Structural Changes

4

History and Political Culture in Syria: Obstacles to Integration in the Global Economy After the Gulf War

David W. Lesch

Good harvests in the early 1990s produced a tremendous grain (mostly wheat) surplus in Syria. When traveling around Syria during this time, one immediately noticed the mountains of sacks of grain sitting out in the open at depots across the country, often with lines of trucks over a mile long waiting to unload more sacks of grain at what are in essence government-subsidized prices. As such, one of the major business opportunities in Syria has been in grain silos. My company, Middle East International Business Associates, Inc. (MEIBA), which identifies market opportunities, arranges financing for, and represents (primarily) US companies interested in entering Middle East markets, established a relationship with a grain silo construction company in the US to bid on this publicly tendered opportunity in Syria. Although we made it to the final cut of three companies (the contract ultimately went to an Italian firm), the problems that we encountered during the course of this process, which lasted over two years, are symptomatic of the obstacles produced by decades of a state-dominated economy. Economic rationalization is here subordinated to regime survival and regional standing, inhibiting Syria's halting progression toward economic liberalization and global economic integration.

The first order of business, as in any business venture in Syria, is to choose the right local broker who: First, informs you in a timely fashion of the opportunity; and second, has additional local contacts and information in order to help facilitate the deal and make the bid more competitive. There are proscribed entrances into the Syrian economy, carefully controlled by the so-called "five-percenters," or in Arabic, *wasta* (literally, "mediation"). One cannot enter into a private or public sector business situation without a local mediator because the vertical patronage networks that exist in the country require it; indeed, the mediator provides access to decision-makers for those who would not otherwise have it. It really functions as an additional form of control by the state, fragmenting bourgeoisie and upper bourgeoisie classes who might in its absence coalesce into a recognizable opposition. In addition, it spreads the wealth to certain classes, supplements the income of government officials tied into the five-percenter organizations, and co-opts more into the idea of maintaining regime stability. Many would argue that this is a highly corrupt system; others, especially in the area itself, would say that it is just part of doing business in the Middle East.

The problem is finding the "right" five-percenter – for every legitimate group, there are at least ten others who are in effect hustlers and cannot even come close to providing the necessary services. We established a relationship with an influential group with whom we had not previously worked; the lack of trust emanating from this group, however, almost killed the deal on several occasions, creating bottlenecks of paperwork in order to assure and reassure them that, indeed, they would be properly compensated. We should have been moving forward and working synergistically to put together a professional proposal; as it turned out, we were just barely able to submit the proposal to the proper government ministry before the deadline. This paranoia is something that I have found to be pervasive in Syria in a number of different industry areas. It can, perhaps, be attributed to the reality of living in a security state, which tends to produce a very suspicious populace. This is, however, no way to do business, especially when time is of the essence; comfort zones and proper documentation are always desired, but obsessive concern over relatively trivial matters can often prove detrimental to ever getting a potential deal off the ground.

The next problem was the actual bid proposal itself. The tender called for constructing 200 grain silos with accompanying materials, including an advanced electrical system that would centrally control operations. A job of this magnitude, under normal American conditions, would cost approximately $18 million, which was about $9 million more than what the Syrian government was willing to pay! In other words, despite the professed expressions by the Syrian government about wanting high technology from the West in order to accelerate technology transfer as well as simply to acquire a higher quality product, most in the country are still wedded to the apparent axiom that cheaper is better. What is advertised is usually not what the government wants; typically, then, competitors from countries, such as Egypt, with their cheaper labor and transportation costs, make US firms non-competitive in most industry areas. In some cases, it is true, the money is just not there, but mostly it is an attitude bred by a generation of Soviet and East European barter deals involving inferior quality products and an authoritarian corporatist system unwilling to undermine its clientelist network through competition.

We were still "in the game" only because our US client was willing to strip its proposal down to the bare bones, admitting it could never even attempt to build in the US what it was proposing for Syria – it would be laughed out of the business. We needed to establish a joint venture with a local contractor who could also help bring down the price of our bid by providing cheap local labor and materials (which is actually a plus from the government's point of view, since we would be utilizing local resources). We, in fact, were successful in bringing the price of the bid down to a competitive level – but the end product will certainly not be of high quality, and economy in the long-term never entered the equation from the Syrian side.[1]

Another problem was dealing with the bid and performance bonds. Very few international companies are willing to put up any significant bond in Syria because of the lack of a sufficient regulatory regime, rule of law, and transparency; indeed, there have been some notorious incidents involving companies who were unable to recover bid or performance bonds (and Syria is not subject to World Bank, IMF, or any other outside regulatory agencies, since it does not participate in any of their directed programs). We overcame this obstacle by contacting a Syrian individual who is, of course, quite wealthy, but he is also politically powerful, and therefore not someone whom the Syrian government would "stiff." All of this, however, the five-percenter together with the "bonder," cuts into the US company's profits as well as our own; in addition, it drives the bottom line price upward.

Presumably, though, every international company has to go through the same process so that everyone is theoretically on a level playing field. Unfortunately, because of layers of groups receiving their "cut" in order to keep a bid price competitive, what suffers is the actual quality of the product. There is a great deal of economic potential in Syria, but the weight of an ossified business environment continues to prevent this potential from being realized. Historical momentum, regional adversity, and political culture cut into economic rationality, and these are difficult to overcome. This begs the question of whether or not Syria is ready to take on all of the challenges and opportunities that would result in the event of peace with Israel. That is, will Syria be overcome by or ride piggyback on the new wave of investors likely to invade the region – or is peace even necessary to achieve *sufficient* economic growth, which, in my view, is increasingly being thought of as a viable alternative, whether it is justifiable or not.

The State Becomes Dominant

Until the second half of the nineteenth century, Syria had for centuries been a largely self-sufficient agrarian and trade-based economy. The opening of the Suez Canal in 1869, as well as the continuing economic problems of the Ottoman Empire in general by the 1870s (climaxing with its bankruptcy in 1875), forced a downturn in the Syrian economy for the remainder of the century and into the early twentieth century.[2] Generally speaking, Syrians were (and continue to be) extremely adaptable to changing conditions, and they always find new markets and adopt new techniques when necessary.[3] This did not, however, overcome the general economic malaise in Syria caused by World War I. A pattern of dependence upon Europe emerged in which the rate of economic growth was, for the most part, determined by outside sources – a development that only deepened with the imposition of the French Mandate after the war.

As such, as early as World War I, there existed a strong feeling among high-placed Syrians that more state intervention was necessary in order to return economic prosperity to Syria. As Roger Owen noted:

> By 1914 there was fairly general agreement in such circles that political weakness was partly the result of over-dependence on agriculture (to the exclusion of industry) and on foreign financial institutions, and that the only satisfactory way ahead was to use the state apparatus to intervene more directly in pursuit of a more national economic policy.[4]

Because of the Mandate system, when the British and the French seemed to just trade places with the Ottomans with respect to economic decision-making, Syrians would have to wait until after World War II before they could actually begin to chart a new economic course and promote the state apparatus to a dominant position.[5] This, however, did not preclude change from occurring in other spheres. The older generation of Syrian leaders, primarily the landed aristocratic families of Damascus and Aleppo, who had held the predominant administrative positions (and thus also political power) under both the Ottomans and the French, had been largely discredited by World War II in the eyes of the younger Syrian generation. These younger activists had become politically aware during the Mandate period and saw their elders as corrupt and failing to deliver on their promise of real independence. The older generation of leaders were also seen to have been co-opted by the French and leading the nation economically toward what was termed as capitalist exhaustion.

What was rejected by this new generation of leaders, symbolized by such movements formed in the inter-war years as the Ba'th party in Syria and the Free Officers Movement in Egypt, was not only the ancien regimes in and of themselves, but also their ideologies based on such Western European imports as liberal constitutionalism. As someone once remarked, the leaders of the ancien regimes grew up quoting Voltaire, Locke, and Mill, while their sons and daughters quoted Marx and Lenin (and Hegel and Nietzsche for some until fascism became discredited with the fall of Nazi Germany). The final straw for the ancien regimes throughout much of the Middle East heartland was the humiliating defeat that led to the creation of Israel in 1948. Within ten years of this epic moment, all of the primary Arab combatants' regimes had been overthrown by movements professing a vehemently anti-imperialist, anti-Israeli, and Arab socialist doctrine. As Charles Issawi noted in the early 1960s:

> In the last forty years, and more particularly in the last ten, three main shifts of power have taken place in the Middle East: from foreigners to nationals; from the landed interest to the industrial, financial, commercial and managerial interests; and from the private sector to the state.[6]

It was, of course, a well-intentioned process aimed at redistributing wealth and political power more equitably, ending reliance on outside powers, eliminating corruption, and restoring justice. The path of state capitalism was chosen by a number of countries in the developing world at that time. One of the first official acts of these new regimes after they came to power was land reform in order to undercut the influence and wealth of the landed aristocracy/agrarian bourgeoisie.[7] These regimes established a social contract with the people, promising to institute adequate safety nets, to provide employment and social services, and to ensure political and economic equality.

As typically happened in many countries, Syria instead developed a bloated and inefficient public sector that has for over three decades (after the Ba'th party formally took power in 1963) provided the support base for the ruling regime. In the process, it has established a classic "bonapartist" state, where economic policy has been driven by regime survival, especially in a regional environment that was anything but a benevolent capitalist world order.[8] As time went on, the wealth funneled to the state as the capital accumulator became the source of patronage in erecting a pervasive clientelist network, primarily in the military, bureaucracy, and other elements of society tied to the state apparatus.

Asad's Correction

Hafiz al-Asad came to power in a late 1970 intra-Ba'th coup that cast out the radical left-wing of the party, which was ideologically committed to the destruction of Israel (and domestically to a more true socialist, rather than state capitalist, economic path). Contrary to popular belief, Asad's assumption of power signaled the departure of an ideologically-based foreign policy to a much more pragmatic one prepared to diplomatically resolve the Arab-Israeli conflict but wholeheartedly committed to a full return of the Golan Heights.[9] Thus, its primary intent in the area of foreign relations was to bring Syria back within accepted parameters inside the Arab fold, mainly by establishing a working relationship with Egypt and Saudi Arabia in order to coordinate policy toward Israel.

Domestically, it signaled a retreat from the radical economic policies of Salah Jadid's regime and the opening up of the economy to the private sector. Indeed, Asad's political program upon his ascension to power was called the Corrective Movement (*al-Harakat al-Tashihiyya*). This first opening, or *Infitah*, paralleled a similar process in Egypt under President Anwar Sadat, one that especially gained steam after the October 1973 War which resulted in a four-fold increase in the price per barrel of oil. While the profits largely accumulated in the pockets of the oil-exporting Persian/Arabian Gulf states, the non-oil Arab states bordering Israel (the "confrontation" states) also benefited enormously from the new economic realities in the Middle East. The only way that countries such as Saudi Arabia and Kuwait could fight the Arab-Israeli conflict and still maintain their "Arab" credentials was to provide healthy amounts of financial aid and grants to the confrontation states. Countries such as Egypt and Syria also reaped the rewards of remittances from its citizens who were arriving by the tens of thousands in the Gulf countries as laborers.

The 1970s thus resulted in impressive growth in the Syrian economy. In fact, Asad's decision to open up the economy to allow more flexibility for the private sector was not a reaction to the inability of the public sector to accumulate capital (as it would be with the second *Infitah* in the 1980s), but to find mechanisms to distribute the wealth that was suddenly pouring into the country. The growth was not structurally stimulated, but was due largely to Arab transfers.[10] In addition, during the "oil boom" years of the 1970s, few states (and certainly Syria and Egypt were not among them) did anything to accumulate foreign exchange reserves or direct remittances toward more productive activity. As such, changes in the regional and/or international economic environment could, and did, have deleterious repercussions for Syria, a country whose prosperity seemed to rely almost totally on the vagaries of the oil market and seasonal rainfalls.[11]

The Economic Crisis of the 1980s

The decade of the 1980s was as bad for Syria as the 1970s were good. Not only were the structural defects and inefficiencies of Syria's state capitalist economy becoming obvious, but the regional and international political and economic environments exacerbated already existing problems. Most damaging was the drop in oil prices by the mid-1980s due to the world oil glut. Not only did this adversely affect Syria's own oil export revenues, but it also reduced remittances from abroad as well as financial aid from the oil-rich Gulf countries, who were implementing belt-tightening measures for the first time since their rise to wealth.

Concurrent with this development was an unfortunate decade-long drought that devastated an agricultural sector which was already hurting and had been typically neglected for years in lieu of ISI (Import-Substituting Industrialization) policies (as in Egypt, Algeria, Tunisia, Morocco, etc.). In addition, the general Third World debt of the early 1980s reduced capital inflow, and the recession in the industrialized countries had negative runoff effects upon the developing nations. Finally, the winding down and eventual end of the Superpowers' Cold War deprived Syria of the military and economic aid that it had been receiving in large amounts from the former Soviet Union and the East European states.[12] This turn of events contributed in great measure to Syria's participation in the US-led anti-Iraqi coalition during the Gulf crisis of 1990–91 and in the ensuing Madrid peace process that began in October 1991.[13]

As a result, Syria developed in the early 1980s a severe balance of payments and foreign exchange crisis. By then it had become clear that the state could no longer be the engine of capital accumulation. Therefore, the regime decided that the private sector had to be given more leeway to fill the capital void and that the country as a whole had to create a more investor-friendly business environment in order to attract foreign investment and repatriate the billions of dollars of expatriate capital, which had fled the country in the mid-1960s during Syria's radical socialist stage (characterized by widespread nationalization). This second *Infitah* was brought on by economic crisis and not economic largesse. A series of decrees in 1985, 1986, and 1991 were designed to open the country to foreign investment, give the private sector more freedom and opportunity, create mixed-sector enterprises with some outright privatization, and clamp down on corruption.

Perforce, Asad embarked on what has been called a program of selective stabilization and selective liberalization.[14] It had to be "selective" because of the following dilemma: If Asad were to liberalize too much and/or too quickly, it could undercut the public sector patronage system that has maintained the regime in power. Asad has tried to insulate the public sector as much as possible from the effects of incremental liberalization, but ultimately it, too, has been adversely affected (such as a decrease in real wages from inflation due to currency devaluation, reduction of subsidies, and some privatization). This explains the "zigzag" approach that the regime has taken toward economic reform. It also explains the regime's schizophrenia at times, when outdated repressive laws, despite the fact that they are all but ignored by both the populace and the government, are still kept officially on the books just in case they are needed for the regime's self-interest. Arbitrariness is thus used by Asad as a method of control (the 1986 foreign currency law, ostensibly to crack down on black market foreign currency exchanges, is a case in point). Furthermore, there is no outside party looking over the shoulder of the regime and pressuring it to accelerate the reform process; indeed, Syria is remarkably independent of any external interference in its economic decision-making. This is the way that Asad wants it, for, as previously stated, economic decisions are based not on economic rationality alone, but also on political motives related to regime survival and regional standing.

The IMF and World Bank do not, at least on the surface, integrate these political motives into their structural adjustment plans. This independent posture on the part of the Asad regime does place it out on the proverbial limb at times, since there is no one else to blame for periods of economic lethargy. However, it is a willing trade-off for maintaining what Volker Perthes calls economic "ad-hocism" and for avoiding the perception of being beholden to outside (particularly Western) interests, a charge that has been particularly damaging to the Sadat and Mubarak regimes in Egypt since the 1979 Egyptian–Israeli peace treaty brokered by the United States.[15]

Syria's selective liberalization has been moderately successful. The Investment Law No. 10 (May 1991) set the standard for Syria's opening up to outside investment. This law offers the same incentives to local and foreign investors, meaning that companies which obtain licenses receive duty-free privileges for the import of capital goods and materials necessary for a project. At that time, this was hailed as an important step in the economic liberalization of Syria, and it was; however, it is a positive step only if followed up with other necessary reforms – to date, nothing really significant in terms of economic liberalization has occurred in Syria since the investment law was promulgated eight years ago. Yet again, much of Syria's economic upturn by the early 1990s was due not so much to an intrinsically strong economy as to the economic windfall of financing from the Gulf states for infrastructural projects as a kind of compensation for Syria's significant participation in the anti-Iraqi alliance during the 1990–91 Gulf crisis. At the same time, there was a modest increase in oil production and an end to the drought. These "soft" factors resemble the ones that led to the economic growth period of the 1970s, which may make Syria's economy as vulnerable now as it was in the early 1980s.

In addition to the continuing burden of an overly dominant public sector, there are a number of other problems inhibiting economic growth: no private banking system or stock market to organize capital; an inadequate regulatory regime and insufficient transparency; a private sector that may be too fragmented to lead the way in capital accumulation or to attain sufficient political power in order to accelerate reform; and an overall world capital shortage in which available capital has been directed more toward "safer" regions.[16] Rampant corruption continues, especially, as previously mentioned, with the ubiquitous "five-percenters," who, in connivance with government officials, have established proscribed entrances into the Syrian economy that require further investment of time, money, and energy on the part of foreign companies. The absence of a tradition of large-scale domestic capital investment, or as Raymond Hinnebusch noted, "to become too big is to invite trouble from the government," as well as intervention by the powerful labor union (a strong remnant of the socialist compact), have led to a proliferation of small-scale enterprises and investment in non-productive areas, such as commerce instead of manufacturing.[17]

Furthermore, economic growth is hindered by a widespread lack of professionalism within many government ministries, which are generally unaccustomed to providing the data and services commonly expected by leading multinational corporations; outdated technology and techniques that make equipment congruency with Western firms difficult; and an overall hesitancy to enact policies that could lead to unregulated foreign competition. As a latecomer, it is believed that Syrian firms would be at a disadvantage in such a competitive climate and that the petit bourgeoisie in particular could be overwhelmed by the multinationals.[18] This could then force important sectors in Syria to seek alternative leadership because the social contract made with the people by the state capitalist regime when it came to power would be broken, and there would be no legitimizing ideology that could soften the inevitable inequities and economic dislocation brought about by serious market-oriented reform.[19] Finally, and perhaps most importantly, in the long term, with an annual population growth rate of almost 3 percent, Syria's population could grow faster than the economy, with all the ensuing negative economic and social repercussions – a serious problem that many other Arab countries are now facing as well. Syria seems to be well-along the path of what has been called "second-rate modernization," a process that can actually retard economic growth by replacing traditional crafts and occupations, which do provide value, with "menial" production-line jobs, thus perpetually placing the economy at a comparative disadvantage to the West.[20]

Political Economy

Rather than an academic discipline that examines the interaction between politics and economics, when this term is applied to Syria it means the state's political control of the economy. The willing formation of the dominant state apparatus was deemed necessary in the 1950s in order to correct the pervasive economic, social, and political problems of the day as determined by a sector of the Syrian population that had been, for the most part, excluded from the decision-making process as well as the socioeconomic benefits that accrue from it. In alliance with the military, which also had its grievances against the ancien regime and provided the muscle for the Ba'thist ideologues, the government quickly became the arbiter of all things.

The transition to a patronage-based authoritarian state was all too easy and expected, especially when an 'Alawi minority sect within Syria, through its opportunistic ascension in the military during the French Mandate and its association with the Ba'th party in the late 1950s, had gained the reins of power by 1963. The 'Alawis would stubbornly hold onto those reins, for to lose power would mean an instant return to its traditionally deprived and oppressed existence. Asad is not only maintaining himself and his cronies in power, but his community as well.[21]

There are non-ʿAlawis in important positions within the Syrian regime, but there is no doubt within the country that this minority group dominates the state, despite the fact that most Muslims, whether Sunni or Shiʿite, do not consider the ʿAlawis to be Muslims at all.

As previously stated, Asad's is, in effect, a Bonapartist regime primarily interested in regime survival, and the social and economic well-being of Syria as a whole is not necessarily a goal in and of itself, but a means to an end.[22] Asad no doubt understands the relationship between economic prosperity and regime stability, but his regime's dominant posture, as expressed through the state security apparatus, the military, the perceived necessities of living in a dangerous regional environment, and the appropriation of the nation's political culture, has created too many clientelist networks to allow the implementation of change in anything but an incremental fashion.

Despite some macro-economic policy changes that have trimmed the public sector base to a certain extent, more effort has actually been exerted by the regime to co-opt important elements of the private sector, that is, the potential avenues of opposition, into the idea of regime maintenance. As a result, the private sector is still largely fragmented and too dependent upon the state to become a significant pressure group. The parallels to the Saudi monarchy are noteworthy, where the Saʿud Royal Family has managed over the years to successfully co-opt at the same time the young technocrats educated in the West, the tribal leaders, and the religious establishment. Together in the state political and economic apparatus, their well-being is directly tied to that of the monarchy's. Asad may actually turn out to be more successful at co-optation than the Saudis, since the gap between mobilization and assimilation is much less in Syria than it has been in recent years in Saudi Arabia, the latter having experienced some internal instability of late as a result (Asad has, for all intents and purposes, eliminated the religious opposition with the infamous 1982 crackdown of the Muslim Brotherhood rebellion at Hama, with various estimates putting the death toll at anywhere between 20,000 and 40,000).[23]

As such, Syria's selective liberalization has been as much directed by a desire to broaden the regime's support base during a time of change as the intrinsic need to improve its economic situation in general. Therefore, significant elements of the bourgeoisie have been brought – some would say forced – *de facto* and *de jure*, into a coalition of sorts with the state.[24] There are some, particularly young Sunni entrepreneurs (in their thirties and forties), who are possibly being driven out of the country by a security apparatus that views them as a primary threat to its position. It is this group of entrepreneurs, especially those who do not play by the rules of the business game in Syria, that generally most want peace and economic reform in order to enhance their business opportunities. While there are a number of examples of this happening in Syria over the past year, it is too early to make any sweeping conclusions. It could still be the result of cyclical crackdowns by the security services, especially during a period of heightened tension with both Israel and Turkey, or it could simply be a matter of personal vendettas. Yet, something resembling the capital (and personal) flight of market-oriented Syrians in the 1960s would not at all be inconsistent with the political interests of important and powerful groups within the Syrian government, however detrimental it would be to the economy in the long run.

There are even questions circulating as to whether Hafiz al-Asad is *really* in control of the country, and that the multi-faced security apparatus has gone off on its own in order to secure positions in the jockeying for succession and real power. Whether or not this is true, the fact that intelligent Syrians are even questioning the leadership capacities of Asad could be a telling sign. If it is true, this does not at all bode well for the Syrian–Israeli peace process, one that has depended on Asad's ability to deliver the country to the peace table. Figuratively speaking, the "state" bourgeoisie in Syria not only refers to the public sector, but also to important elements within the private sector. It is not surprising, then, especially with the end of the Cold War and new regional realities in the Middle East since the 1990–91 Gulf crisis, that the offspring of those in the bureaucracy, military, and state bourgeoisie (in its strictest sense) have been increasingly choosing private sector careers. On the one hand, this has led to enhanced access to political power for the private sector, with lucrative results; on the other hand, however, it has, as one scholar put it, "amalgamated" these societal elements together behind the regime, and it has not led to an acquisition of political power itself by the private sector.[25] Indeed, as Ghassan Salamé stated, this state of affairs can be described as "bourgeoisies leaving politics to their masters who secure the stability these bourgeoisies need to enrich themselves."[26] One thing that Asad has provided, which none of his modern predecessors have been able to do, is stability. For most Syrians accustomed to the pre-1970 frequency of military coups, this has been a willing trade-off for less political freedom.

In any event, many within the Syrian private sector are quite hesitant to embrace full-fledged market reform. They worry that large multinational corporations will do to, inter alia, the petit bourgeoisie (shopkeepers in the *suqs* for instance) what Wal-Mart has done to the family-owned business in Smalltown, USA.[27] Although not an obstacle to peace, the regime has some reservations about the repercussions of a peace accord that might lead to the virtual elimination of the petit bourgeoisie, who have been a bedrock of support for the regime over the years (and who could turn to an Islamic alternative to rectify their lot, especially if what is confronting them is perceived to be Western economic and cultural imperialism). Asad's incremental pace of reform is largely self-serving, but it might also be more prudent than foolish, for he does not want to follow the Egyptian example of the 1970s, when it was overwhelmed by internal economic change and foreign investment. Moreover, with severe economic problems in the export-led growth states of East and Southeast Asia and the virtual economic collapse of Russia, countries such as Syria, which have been either voluntarily or involuntarily adopting market economy strategies, increasingly have doubts about the direction and pace of economic reform and whether or not integration into the global economy is actually desirable. All of this only creates more obstacles to reform in Syria as the skeptics offer genuine fears and ex post facto rationalizations in order to increase the inertia and halt the already crawling pace of change. Asad's tightly knit system, which he has meticulously built in his nearly three decades in power, has only a limited carrying capacity for change.

Succession and Peace

The need for political control has been especially acute of late because of two factors: (1) the succession problem; and (2) the downturn in Syrian–Israeli peace negotiations since the June 1996 election of the *Likud* party leader, Benjamin Netanyahu, as the Prime Minister in Israel. The succession issue became a serious problem in 1994, when Asad's eldest son, Basil, who had been groomed to assume his father's post, died in a car accident.[28] He was very popular in the military, as well as with the populace, and was a charismatic figure. In the wake of his premature passing, Asad called back his other son, Bashar, from London, where he had been studying opthalmology. To say the least, he had not built up the loyalty within the military and the security apparatus that Basil enjoyed. Even as Asad's untested son is slowly being elevated within the country's propaganda, he is and will always be somewhat suspect by many. As such, Asad cannot totally alienate the support base that has kept him in power over the years, especially the Ba'th party, the military, and the bureaucracy, because he will need them when the time comes for Bashar to hopefully assume power. Indeed, there is a great deal of speculation in Syria about who will actually hold the reins of power, whether or not Bashar al-Asad becomes president; such discussions were not nearly as widespread when Basil was alive. Bashar al-Asad is genuinely liked by most Syrians. He is seen as gentle and compassionate; he is also forward-looking in terms of his ideas to bring Syria in line with the rest of the world in the realm of information technology. For all of these same reasons, however, he is also seen to be, at best, nothing more than a pawn in the hands of others, if in fact he has the opportunity to come to power at all. This situation limits the extent to which Hafiz al-Asad can implement economic reform that would further undercut and threaten these very same bases of support. To some degree, the succession question also limits Asad's maneuverability on the Israeli front as well, since the peace talks in general have been, at best, only modestly popular within the military, the bureaucracy, and the Ba'th party.

The potential instability of a succession dispute was made plainly clear to Asad in 1984, when, during the Lebanese imbroglio, he fell seriously ill. The resulting jockeying for position within the Syrian hierarchy was very disturbing to the Syrian president, especially since it was his brother, Rif'at, who, as commander of Asad's Praetorian Guard called the Defense Brigades, was at the root of the problem. It led to a major shake-up within the Syrian government, including Rif'at's exile until 1992. Asad does not want this to happen again, and in order to ensure that it does not, he needs the support of those who have been loyal to the regime.

Some speculate that he should just create new support groups, made up of those (especially the Sunni-Muslim business community) who will forward economic reform. But it is not that simple; one cannot just flip-flop patronage networks. Asad is not so dominant that he could just jettison his military and security apparatus – his is an authoritarian regime, not a totalitarian one. Besides, those who would accelerate economic reform have been so thoroughly integrated within the system (as Asad intended) that they are too fragmented and co-opted at the present time to form an effective support group in and of itself. If this were to happen, it would seem to some to be a reversion to the days when the wealthy land-owning families, that is, the large-scale capitalists, ran the country and, as such, would be vociferously opposed by many important segments of society simply on an ideological basis.

The peace process, or lack thereof, also limits the extent to which the government can implement economic reform within Syria. The Syrian–Israeli talks, beginning with the Madrid meeting in October 1991 and proceeding in fits and spurts since, were suspended indefinitely in February 1996 following the Hamas attacks in Israel. The Israeli Operation Grapes of Wrath, carried out in Lebanon in April 1996 in order to respond to Hizballah attacks emanating from south Lebanon against northern Israeli settlements, only exacerbated tensions between

Israel and Syria (US–Syrian relations, which had been steadily improving since the Gulf War, also took a definite turn for the worse during this episode). Finally, the election of Benjamin Netanyahu, who has publicly stated – contrary to what his immediate predecessors, Shimon Peres and Yitzhak Rabin, indicated – that he will not return the Golan Heights to Syria, dealt the coup de grâce to the Syrian–Israeli peace process for the time being. As a result, the vitriolic, and on several occasions belligerent, rhetoric between Jerusalem and Damascus since the May 1996 Israeli election has resembled pre-1990 discourse.[29]

What this means on the economic front is that, again, in a time of enhanced tension with Israel, Asad must rely more heavily on the support of those elements who least want market-oriented reform, leaving him with much less flexibility to implement dramatic new policies. Despite what in essence is a state of non-belligerency between Syria and Israel at the present juncture, one must remember that most Syrians genuinely fear Israeli expansionism as much as, if not more, than the obverse.[30]

In any event, it is clear that the simple signing of a peace treaty in and of itself will not provide the economic panacea that many Syrians expect. Egypt signed along the dotted line in 1979, and it is, in many ways, in worse economic shape today than it was then. Jordan, which signed a peace treaty with Israel in late October 1994, is also still waiting for its economic windfall. Indeed, with its dominant economy, Israel has benefited much more than its peace partners, something of which Asad is quite wary.[31] Peace with Israel will open up the Syrian economy to more private foreign investment, increase the inward flow of economic aid from international financial institutions, and allow the government to redirect some of its defense expenditures; nevertheless, as previously discussed, all of this can have negative consequences as well. What peace with Israel will do is to give Asad more flexibility to enact the only thing that will improve the Syrian economy: serious systemic economic reform (and not just tax holidays, selective waivers, inconsistent crackdowns on corruption, superficial foreign investment laws, etc.).

In a less tense atmosphere, with pressure building up on Damascus as a Middle East "common market" becomes much more of a possibility, Asad will not be as beholden to entrenched interests, and even they will see (as some have already) the necessity for an acceleration of the reform process. To some extent, this is exactly what was happening when the peace process was moving forward and had momentum in 1994–95, reflected on the economic front by two very ambitious (some would say wishful thinking) Middle East economic conferences held in Casablanca (1994) and Amman (1995), which most of the Arab states (including Syria) and Israel attended.

With the downward turn in the peace process since the Netanyahu election, the 1996 economic summit meeting in Cairo barely took place (Syria did not attend) and was full of political rhetoric with very little economic substance. Only a sprinkling of Arab government representatives (not including Egyptian, Syrian, or Saudi officials) attended the 1997 meeting in the capital city of Qatar, Doha; and the 1998 meeting was not even seriously planned. There is considerable doubt, in my mind at least, that one could today recreate in Syria the kind of positive and momentum-induced atmosphere for peace that was present from 1994 through early 1996. An important and possibly historic window of opportunity may have been missed beyond the ill-effects of the Rabin assassination. More importantly, the alignment forces of peace in Syria in a domestic, regional, and economic sense were real during this period of time.

Asad's ascension to power in late 1970 signaled a much more pragmatic policy *vis-à-vis* Israel, with a clear willingness for a negotiated settlement. However, he felt that the Arab world as a whole, and Syria in particular after Egypt made peace with Israel in 1979, must bargain from a position of strength rather than weakness in order to compel Israel to do what UN Security Council Resolution 242 (November 1967) enjoins all those who have accepted it to do: exchange captured territories for peace. For Syria, this means an unequivocal total Israeli withdrawal from the Golan Heights. He has definitely used the Arab-Israeli conflict at times to maintain power in a particular fashion, but getting back the Golan Heights would provide him with the "legitimacy momentum," if you will, that just may allow him to break the social and political contracts he has established with select groups, which currently inhibit his flexibility with regard to economic reform.

In any event, Asad has more grand strategies in mind and things to worry about in the Arab-Israeli and inter-Arab arenas than domestic economic reform policies. This is especially the case since mid-1996, for he suspects that Netanyahu has been attempting to isolate Syria through a pincer movement emanating from Israel, Lebanon, and Turkey – and backed, if not orchestrated, by the United States. Netanyahu's "Lebanon First" policy, that is, an Israeli withdrawal from south Lebanon not linked to the Golan Heights situation, seems to want to accomplish through withdrawal what former Israeli Prime Minister Menachem Begin tried to achieve through invasion in 1982.[32] The fact that it was the pro-peace Israeli Prime Minister Shimon Peres who launched the Grapes of Wrath bombardment of Lebanon in April 1996 was even more disillusioning and disheartening to Syrians in general (in addition to the perceived lack of a proper US response).

Asad is certainly committed to, but not desperate for, a peaceful resolution with Israel, but only if the conditions are satisfactory. Indeed, during the Madrid conference, Syria made some significant concessions that has shown it to be serious about peace.[33] The international and regional environment dictates this path, but Asad is quite willing and able to make it a long and winding one if he feels that he is being short-changed, pressured, and/or threatened.

His strategy in the peace process is the same as it would be (and has been) during the Arab-Israeli conflict, namely, to prevent Syria's isolation and not allow Israeli dominance in the region.[34] He takes an active stance *vis-à-vis* the peace process; he does not want it to be the result of a defensive position into which he has been forced. Israel, on the other hand, seems to also view the peace process as part of an offensive strategy, and it would like Syria to come to the peace table in a disadvantageous bargaining position as the result of having no other options available. Asad will go to great lengths to ensure that Syria is not placed in this position, even if it is in appearance only. How long he can maintain this posture in the face of what Damascus views as unrelenting pressure and/or whether or not he can outlast Israel's current political environment before some sort of domestic implosion occurs is the big question. Regardless of this, the Syrian–Israeli path was not given the opportunity to progress before events in late 1995 and early 1996 overtook it, which is always the vulnerability of protracted negotiations in the Middle East.

Conclusion

The heritage of obstacles in Syria to implementing widespread economic reform that would allow it to sustain economic growth and open new doors into the global economy are plenty. The inertia of the authoritarian bonapartist state based on a patrimonial clientelist system is extremely difficult to overcome, especially in what is perceived to be an unfriendly neighborhood that only further restricts the flexibility of the regime to maneuver through the political and economic morass. It has been said that the Soviet Union under Gorbachev was guilty of instituting *Glasnost* without *Perestroika*, while the Chinese leadership has been accused of implementing *Perestroika* without *Glasnost*. Asad can legitimately be accused of not doing either; yet Gorbachev, Yeltsin, Deng, and Jiang have probably envied the Syrian president's remarkable staying power and the regime's stability, control, and, at a certain level, even popularity.

Asad's luck, with timely oil price hikes and good harvests, far-sighted political choices, such as his decision to join the anti-Iraqi alliance during the1990–91 Gulf crisis, and selective stabilization and liberalization have allowed him to weather political and economic crises to date, and with a modicum of success. Finding the "magic pace" of reform that will indeed contribute to economic growth while not undermining his support base is the key, and his "zigzag" approach has been fairly effective. But time is not on his side, and the hard economic realities will most likely require a watershed change of policy in the not-too-distant future, regardless of progress on the peace front, if the regime is to survive. It is important to remember that the introduction of Investment Law No. 10 (1991), which was hailed at the time as the beginning of true economic liberalization in Syria, is already eight years old, and not much has happened since – it has not, thus far, inaugurated the opening up of the Syrian economy as many had envisioned. Syria's history, political culture, business environment, and regional setting are working against him, but Asad has been extremely adept at managing through crisis periods before; regional circumstances may again allow him room to wade through the mess intact. In the meantime, however, Western, especially American, companies continue to find little reason to enter the Syrian market in anything but exceptional circumstances.

Notes

1 On one bid proposal with a US cold storage group that we represented in Syria, the lack of equipment congruency developed into a serious problem. The Syrian government insisted on using an ammonia-based system, which is all but totally outdated in the US. We asked why it was insisting on ammonia-based when the US company's system would be much more durable and productive, thereby saving money in the long term. The response was that the workers wanted to be able to smell a leak when the system inevitably broke down; in other words, the natural expectation of inferior quality material seemed to cloud their judgement – a frustrating inability to conceptualize over the long rather than short term based on psychological as well as practical factors. Ultimately, the US company's bid came in twice as high as the winning bid, which was an outdated, used, East European ammonia-based cold storage system.

2 For a discussion of the Syrian economy during this period, see: Roger Owen, *The Middle East in the World Economy 1800–1914* (New York, 1981), pp. 76–82, 153–79, and 244–72.

3 *Ibid.*, p. 289.

4 *Ibid.*, p. 293.

5 For more on this transition, see the classic work on the subject by Philip S. Khoury, *Syria and the French Mandate: The Politics of Arab Nationalism, 1920–1945* (Princeton, 1987). Indeed, it was worse under the French because of the lack of resources that the French had in the country (as compared with

the Ottomans) to essentially buy political loyalty; the difference in cultural attitudes and practices from the Ottomans; and the French policy of divide and rule imported from the quite separate colonial environment of Morocco.

6 Charles Isaawi, *The Economic History of the Middle East 1800–1914* (Chicago, 1966), p. 505.

7 On this transformation, see: Hanna Batatu, "Some Observations on the Social Roots of Syria's Ruling Military Group and the Causes of its Dominance," *Middle East Journal*, Vol. 35 (Summer 1981), pp. 331–44.

8 On the threatening regional and international environment of the 1950s, which greatly contributed to the political and economic direction of Syrian regimes, see: David W. Lesch, *Syria and the United States: Eisenhower's Cold War in the Middle East* (Boulder, Colo., 1992).

9 Asad was Minister of Defense in the Syrian government at the time of the June 1967 War, so he feels a personal responsibility to regain in its entirety the land lost to Israel – Asad and the Syrian public are absolutely committed to this, and any thoughts that Syria will now or in the foreseeable future accept anything less than full Israeli withdrawal are unrealistic.

10 On this regard, see also Winckler's chapter in this volume.

11 Steven Heydemann, "The Political Logic of Economic Rationality: Selective Stabilization in Syria," in Henri Barkey (ed.), *The Politics of Economic Reform in the Middle East* (New York, 1992), p. 32.

12 Various estimates put the range of the Syrian debt to the USSR/Russia in the neighborhood of $10–12 billion. Russia obviously wants some or all of this amount eventually paid back; however, Asad firmly believes that the debt was erased when the Soviet Union ceased to exist, and in his view, it was not just a one-way street – Moscow received in kind the political and diplomatic influence it was seeking in the Middle East in large part through Damascus. Apparently, the debt issue was settled between the two countries in the fall of 1998 when a Russian Defense Ministry delegation visited Syria, the way largely being paved by the appointment of former Soviet Middle East advisor and Arabist Yvegeny Primakov as Russia's new Prime Minister. Damascus will repay at least part of the debt in return for a rekindling of the arms relationship with Moscow – another symptom of the fallout of the end of Syrian–Israeli negotiations and Israel's defense cooperation with Turkey. Other than this, Syria's debt is relatively modest as compared with other lower middle-income countries (although large when viewed per capita). Also, it should be noted at this time that I do not list "military burden" as one of the main reasons for the downturn of the Syrian economy in the 1980s. Certainly, some military spending could have been diverted toward more productive enterprises; however, most of the money spent toward Asad's goal of achieving at least a deterrent strategic parity against Israel in the 1980s (so that Syria could bargain from a position of strength and counter the isolation within the Middle East due to its unpopular support for Iran in the Iran–Iraq war and Egypt's signing a peace treaty with Israel in 1979) came from outside sources, particularly the Soviet bloc and the Gulf states. Indeed, if it were not for Syria's geographic and confrontational position in the Arab-Israeli arena, it would have received very little aid, whether economic or military, from outside sources (an environment that also had its political benefits in the domestic arena as well). There are a good many economists who debate the supposed debilitating effects of an overly large military; it

depends on the specific situation, but a large military can provide a measure of economic relief for the regime by employing thousands of young men who would otherwise be unemployed. Therefore, It can at least be said that Syria's military burden is actually not as overwhelming as it would appear or has been portrayed. For more on this question, see: Patrick Lawson, *Unaffordable Ambitions: Syria's Military Buildup and Economic Crisis* (Washington, D.C.: The Washington Institute for Near East Policy, 1989).

13 Syria's participation was, of course, also based on its enmity toward Iraq because of severe differences on a number of political, ideological, and geographical issues; it was similar to Asad's decision to support non-Arab Iran in the Iran–Iraq War, the only significant Arab country to do so.

14 See: Heydemann, "The Political Logic of Economic Rationality," pp. 11–39.

15 Volker Perthes, *The Political Economy of Syria under Asad* (London, 1995).

16 For example, only one-third of one percent of the $62 billion of equity flows to emerging markets last year went to the Middle East; in addition, only 3 percent of private capital flows went to the Middle East between the years 1980–1993. All this means that capital is going elsewhere because the Middle East business environment, for a host of reasons, is not viewed as particularly attractive. Henry T. Azzam, *Capital Markets in the Arab World* (Washington, D.C., 1995), p. 1.

17 Raymond A. Hinnebusch, "Syria," in Tim Niblock and Emma Murphy (eds), *Economic and Political Liberalization in the Middle East* (London, 1993), p. 194. If a company becomes too large, it will be "noticed" by the government, which means that it could become subject to the arbitrary crackdowns against black market activities in foreign currency and goods in which virtually all Syrian companies engage. The flip side of this is that in order to avoid arbitrary crackdowns, government officials must be paid off, and a company then becomes subject to the whim of others. With regard to the strong Syrian labor union (the General Federation of Trade Unions or GFTU), which is still one of the significant hallmarks of the Ba'th party, so many benefits and services need to be paid according to union strictures that many entrepreneurs cannot afford to hire more than the workers, all of which puts downward pressure on the size of private sector businesses and prevents the formation of a large-scale private manufacturing sector.

18 Miyoko Kuroda, "Economic Liberalization and the Suq in Syria," in Niblock and Murphy (eds), *Economic and Political Liberalization*, pp. 204–5.

19 Hinnebusch, "Syria," p. 178.

20 Rodney Wilson, *Economic Development in the Middle East* (London, 1995), p. 49. There are those who suggest that emerging market countries such as Syria could essentially skip altogether the industrial/manufacturing stage of economic development and move from a pre-industrial directly to a service-oriented economy, which has been a trend within the development economies. If Syria's tourism market ever reaches its full potential, this could be a viable alternative.

21 Although this has not stopped intra-'Alawi Ba'thist struggles from occurring, such as Asad's overthrow of the 'Alawi regime led by Salah Jadid in 1970.

22 As Wilson observed of similar type economies in Iran under the Shah, Turkey under Ataturk, and Egypt under Nasser, "industrialization has been pursued with a disregard for financial objectives because profit has not been a major

or even a significant motivation." Rodney Wilson, *Economic Development in the Middle East*, p. 39.

23 See also: the Introduction of this volume.

24 Perthes, *The Political Economy of Syria under Asad*, p. 254.

25 *Ibid.*

26 Ghassan Salamé, *al-Mujtama' wal-Dawla fil-Mashriq al-'Arabi* [Society and State in the Arab East] (Beirut, 1987), p. 206 (as quoted in Perthes, *The Political Economy of Syria under Asad*, p. 254). Perthes goes on to note that "the chambers as the official representatives of Syria's business community would not even, as one member of the Damascus chamber of Commerce executive sarcastically noted, submit a memorandum to the Prime Minister unless asked for it." (*Ibid.*).

27 David W. Lesch, "Damascus Won't Accept Peace at any Price," *The Christian Science Monitor*, December 6, 1995.

28 For a particularly interesting piece on the succession issue, see: Zisser's chapter in this volume and Douglas Jehl in *The New York Times*, January 28, 1997.

29 For example, see widely reported claims by Israeli "security chiefs" in October 1996 that Syria was preparing for the possibility of launching a limited war against Israel to regain the Golan and, as a result, the Israeli army was seeking an additional $1.1 billion to build-up its defense capability. Associated Press report, *San Antonio Express-News*, October 29, 1996; *The New York Times*, October 29, 1996. For a reaction casting in doubt Israeli claims, see: David W. Lesch, "Syrian Threat to Israel not as Reported," *San Antonio Express-News*, November 11, 1996.

30 For instance, Syrians are often taught that their homeland has been for millennia an object of desire to the Judaic, Turkish, and Persian civilizations, a situation that many feel still exists today. Indeed, Syria's being a crossroads of civilization may be good for tourism with the plethora of impressive archeological ruins from empires gone by, but it has not been particularly healthy for the nation's psyche.

31 Asad was quoted in *al-Ahram* (Cairo) in December 1995 as saying that Shimon Peres' vision of a Middle Eastern common market was ultimately an attempt to "eliminate the concept of Arabism, and by extension the Arabs . . . our inner feeling of being a nation, and our national and social identity . . . ." Quoted in Patrick Seale and Linda Butler, "Asad's Regional Strategy and the Challenge from Netanyahu," *Journal of Palestine Studies*, Vol. 26, No. 1 (Autumn 1996), p. 36 [hereafter: Seale and Butler, "Asad's Regional Strategy"].

32 Greatly exacerbating Syria's fear of being encircled was the deepening Israeli-Turkish military relationship, symbolized by a series of defense agreements in early 1996. Indeed, one could see the Hizballah rocket attacks into northern Israel that elicited the Israeli Grapes of Wrath as Asad's response to this development. The deterioration in Syrian–Turkish relations is reminiscent of the 1950s, when the US under the Eisenhower administration attempted to pressure, through Turkey, a Syria that, from Washington's point of view, was becoming a Soviet client-state (on this subject, see: Lesch, *Syria and the United States*); On Syrian–Hizballah relations, see: Graham Usher, "Hizballah, Syria, and the Lebanese Elections," *Journal of Palestine Studies*, Vol. 26, No. 2 (Winter 1997), pp. 59–67. One must also remember

that Iraq is viewed from Damascus as a potential threat, especially since Syria's participation in the anti-Iraqi coalition during the 1990–91 Gulf crisis (although there have been of late repeated reports of attempts by Damascus and Baghdad to improve relations, almost in direct proportion to the demise in Syrian–Israeli relations). Syria's continued alliance with Iran can be seen as Asad's attempt to prevent total isolation and to increase his leverage *vis-à-vis* Iraq as well as the peace process. The fact that Jordan and Egypt are at peace with Israel, that the PLO signed a DoP with Israel, and that current peace negotiations are focusing entirely on the Palestinian channel, only feeds into the fear of Syrian isolation and marginalization. A host of other issues also complicate Syria's relations with Iraq and Turkey, such as the Kurdish problem and the potentially explosive issue of water-sharing. See also in this regard: Kushner's chapter in this volume and Robert Olsen, "Turkey-Syria Relations: Kurds and Water," *Middle East Policy*, Vol. 5, No. 2 (May 1997), pp. 168–93.

33 See: Seale and Butler, "Asad's Regional Strategy," pp. 27–41; Raymond A. Hinnebusch, "Does Syria Want Peace? Syrian Policy in the Syrian–Israeli Peace Negotiations," *Journal of Palestine Studies*, Vol. 26, No. 1 (Autumn 1996), pp. 42–57; "Fresh Light on the Syrian–Israeli Peace Negotiations: An Interview with Ambassador Walid Moualem," *Journal of Palestine Studies*, Vol. 26, No. 2 (Winter 1997), pp. 81–94.

34 Seale and Butler, "Asad's Regional Strategy," pp. 36–37. Asad himself noted that, "our stance in the battle for peace will not be less courageous than our stances on the battlefield"; Shimon Peres observed that Asad "is conducting the peace process just as one conducts a military campaign – slowly, patiently, directed by strategic and tactical considerations." Both quotes in Hinnebusch, "Does Syria Want Peace?," pp. 44–45.

5

Syria: Economic Development, Achievements, Problems and Prospects

Moshe Efrat

Since the accession of Hafiz al-Asad to the Presidency in 1970, national defense has been the overriding concern of policy-making in Syria, mainly as the result of the combined effect of the Arab-Israeli conflict and the longstanding rivalry and tension with Iraq. Economic objectives derive from this overriding concern, and in general terms are intended to strengthen the economy for the achievement of these strategic and political objectives.

The Syrian government has advocated the pursuit of policies designed to achieve rapid economic and social development through public ownership of the major means of production, in order to forestall social injustices (unemployment, inequitable distribution of income, etc.). These objectives have been pursued with some minor shifts in emphasis, within the constraints imposed by external circumstances.

The Syrian economy has a relatively diversified agricultural and industrial base, a large service sector, and an important oil sector. However, the actual performance of the economy has been thus far greatly influenced – if not determined – mainly by the following exogenous factors: weather conditions; fluctuations of oil prices; political and economic developments in the Middle East which significantly affect the arms race, export earnings, workers' remittances and the level of Arab financial grants; and, finally, the financial terms of the defense imports supplied predominantly by Moscow.

Economic Background

The Syrian economy is in a transition process. Therefore, it is important to place the recent economic developments and policies within a longer-term context. For more than two decades, most aspects of the Syrian economy were dominated by the public sector, including production and pricing, internal distribution of investments and foreign trade. By contrast, the activities of the private sector were constrained by various rules and regulations.

These policies allowed progress in building a modern infrastructure and improving income distribution, but at the same time created widespread disincentives and distortions, holding back economic development and deepening Syria's financial imbalances. During the second half of the 1980s, the impact of economic distortions was confounded by the loss of traditional trade and most favored military links with the former Soviet Block, as well as by the decline in external financial support from the Arab Gulf oil-exporting countries. Economic growth slowed, pressures on prices and exchange rates intensified, and external payment problems began to emerge. Moreover, with private sector imports constrained by the lack of foreign currency, widespread shortages of imports appeared in the market.

Economic Liberalization in Progress

In a major shift in the early 1990s, the Syrian authorities embarked on a strategy of gradual adjustment aimed at revitalizing growth through a more realistic exchange rate, relaxation of import controls, and an increased role for market forces in price determination. While maintaining a significant dominant role for the public sector, the new strategy improved incentives for private export and investments. The implementation of this strategy was facilitated by an increase in available external resources as domestic oil production and exports rose, in addition to the significant financial aid which Syria received from Saudi Arabia and its allies as payment for joining the anti-Iraqi coalition in the 1990–91 Gulf crisis.

Economic Growth in Perspective

During the second half of the 1980s, the annual economic growth rate in real terms hardly averaged one percent, while the annual population growth rate at that time amounted to 3 percent. This performance was in clear contrast to the much higher economic growth rates of the 1970s, amounting to more than 8 percent a year on average. During the early 1980s, the economic growth rates sharply declined to an average of only 4 percent a year in real terms during the period of 1980–84. During the early 1990s, however, the Syrian economy grew at high rates of 6–7 percent a year on average in real terms. This performance was induced by gradual decontrol of the economy, improvements in the incentive systems, and higher agricultural production, despite the adverse effects of deceleration of oil production and a very low growth rate (3 percent annually) of the manufacturing sector.

In essence, the only salient structural change that affected the Syrian economy during the period 1980–94 was centered in the rapid expansion of the mining sector (mostly oil). This sector constituted about 22 percent of the GDP during the period of 1990–94, compared with less than 8 percent in the early 1980s. By contrast, the contributions of the agricultural and the manufacturing sectors remained stagnant – roughly one-fifth and approximately 6 percent, respectively (see table 5.1 and figure 5.1).

Table 5.1 GDP by type of activity, 1980–94
(percentages of total – annual average)

Sector	1980–84	1985–89	1990–94
Agriculture	22.8	21.1	20.7
Mining	7.4	11.6	21.6
Manufacturing	4.8	7.0	5.8
Electricity, gas and water	0.2	0.4	0.8
Construction	5.9	4.5	2.5
Trade	23.6	23.1	19.2
Transport and communications	8.7	10.5	10.3
Finance and insurance	6.3	4.9	4.6
Government services	18.2	14.9	12.9
Community, social and personal services	2.1	2.0	1.6
Total	100.0	100.0	100.0

Sources: UN, *National Accounts Statistics: Main Aggregates and Detailed Tables*, various issues; Syrian Arab Republic, Office of the Prime Minister, Central Bureau of Statistics, *Statistical Abstract*, various issues (Damascus: Government Printing Press).

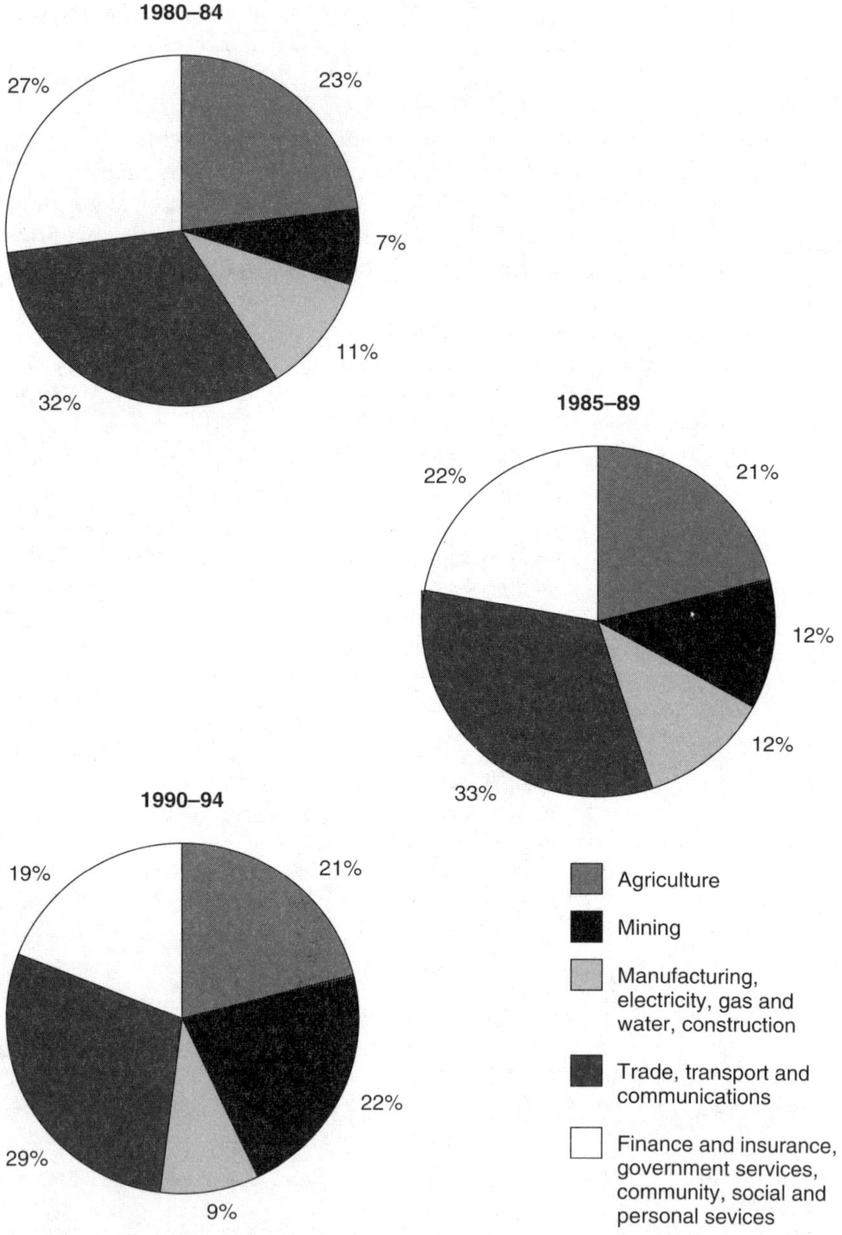

Figure 5.1 GDP by type of activity, 1980–94

Investments and Domestic Savings

During the years 1990–94, GFCF (Gross Fixed Capital Formation) accounted on average for about 23 percent of the GDP, a much higher rate than in the period 1985–89, but equivalent to the rate achieved in the period 1980–84 (19 percent and 24 percent, respectively). Domestic savings rose to almost 14 percent of the GDP during the years 1990–94, in comparison with an average of only 11 percent in the 1980s (see table 5.2 and figure 5.2).

However, without underestimating the importance and impact of higher rates of investment and domestic savings on the Syrian economy in 1990–94, it is essential not to overlook – as Syrian officials often do – the special conditions which largely contributed to achieving those rates. In fact, the additional resources needed to actually attain higher rates in investment and domestic savings were, to a large extent, drawn from the capital "saved" through Syria's reluctance to honor overdue external debts. Syrian official foreign debt arrears (excluding military debts) amounted to at least $1.8–$2.0 billion, equivalent to about 3 percent of Syria's total GDP in the first half of the 1990s. In other words, the relatively high level of investment and domestic savings in 1990–94 cannot be repeated as long as Syria is unable to finance its objectives with its own limited resources or reach a settlement with its foreign creditors.

While about two-thirds of total investment was contributed by the

Table 5.2 Investment and savings, 1980–94

		Percentage of GDP				
		Gross fixed capital formation				
Period	GDP growth (real terms)	Public	Private	Total	Domestic savings	Savings: investment gap
		(annual average)				
1980–84	4.6	15.5	8.8	24.3	10.9	–13.5
1985–89	0.9	10.6	8.3	18.9	10.9	–8.0
1990–94	7.6	9.1	13.7	22.8	13.6	–9.2

Source: UN *National Accounts Statistics: Main Aggregates and Detailed Tables*, various issues; Syria, *Statistical Abstract*, various issues.

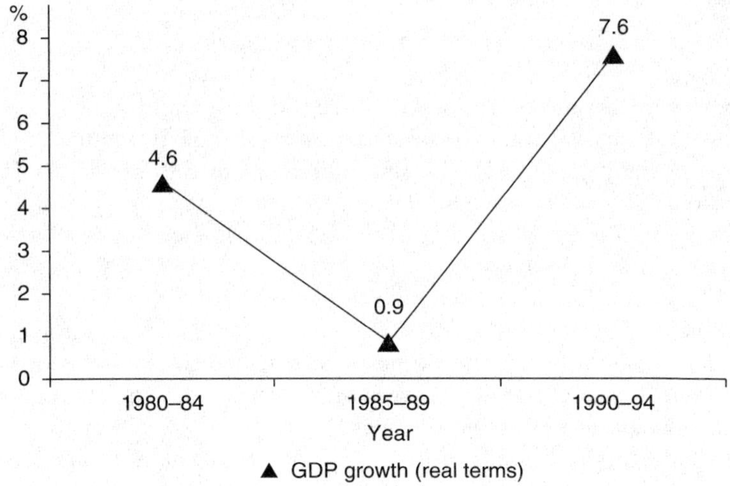

Figure 5.2 GDP growth (real terms), 1980–94

Table 5.3 Distribution of public investments, by sectors, 1980–94 (percentages of total – annual average)

Sector	1981–85	1986–90	1991–94
Agriculture and fisheries	13.4	24.7	27.6
Mining and quarrying	7.0	10.3	7.2
Manufacturing	10.7	3.7	9.2
Electricity, gas and water	12.9	16.4	15.4
Construction	2.0	1.5	0.9
Transport, communications and storage	15.3	10.1	12.1
Social Services	31.8	28.3	23.8
Others	6.9	5.0	3.8
Total	100	100	100
Total ($US billion)	2.8	2.7	3.1

Sources: Syria, *Statistical Abstract*, various issues; *Central Bank of Syria*, Quarterly Bulletin, various issues; *Syrie et Monde Arabe*, various issues.

public sector in 1980–84, its share declined gradually to 40 percent in the period 1990–94. By contrast, the private sector steadily increased its share from one-third in the first half of the 1980s to 60 percent of total investment in the period 1990–94. The impressive rise in importance of the private sector in total investment reflects the improvement of private sector confidence following various liberalization measures introduced in the first half of the 1990s.

The Structure of Public Investments

Public sector investment amounted to $3.1 billion a year on average in 1990–94, roughly 13 percent higher than its annual investment in the 1980s. In the period 1990–94, more than one-quarter of the total annual investment was allocated to the agricultural sector, 15 percent to the development of utilities (electricity, gas, and water), 12 percent to transport and communication, and 9 percent to the manufacturing sector (see table 5.3). In essence, the priorities given to the various sectors in the period 1990–94 were actually similar to those allocated during the second half of the 1980s.

The Limited Impact of the New Investment Law

The private sector is estimated to have contributed to about one-half of the GDP in the first half of the 1990s.[1] While mining (petroleum and phosphate), utilities, the communication network, and the financial sector are either public sector monopolies or are heavily dominated by the public sector, agriculture and most services fall almost entirely in the private domain, as does a large share of manufacturing and trade.

In order to induce private investment, the new economic strategy contributed to the adoption of Investment Law No. 10 in May 1991. This law provided the first important opening of traditional industries to private and foreign participation, and was aimed to serve mainly as a channel for attracting resources held by Syrians abroad. The accumulated private expatriate holdings abroad are estimated at $26 billion by the World Bank, and not two to three times higher as claimed by Syrian officials.[2]

Law No. 10 offers private investors a range of incentives, such as reduced trade restrictions, the repatriation of foreign capital and profits, and a ten-year tax-free holiday. However, the major deterrent to private foreign capital is an article of this law, according to which any approved

Table 5.4 Investment projects approved under law No. 10 (May 1991), 1991–95 ($US million)

Period	No. of projects	No. of workers	Capital investment		
			Total	Foreign exchange component	Imported inputs
June 1992	428	35,860	1,655	1,304	957
April 1993	738	56,400	2,225	1,715	1,340
August 1993	908	na	3,100	na	na
September 1994	1,047	86,000	3,710	2,750	1,725
September 1995	1,349	147,200	6,075	4,640	2,230

na = No data available

Sources: Syria, *Statistical Abstract*, various issues; EIU, *Country Report – Syria*, various issues; *Syrie et Monde Arabe*, No. 467 (Janvier 1993), p. 13; No. 474 (August 1993), p. 1; *al-Hayat* (London), March 16; April 12, 1994.

Table 5.5 Employment and GDP by sectors, 1981–94 (in percentages)

Sector	Employment			GDP		
	1981	1990	1994	1981	1990	1994
Agriculture	23	25	29	19	20	21
Mining	1	1	1	11	23	21
Manufacturing	15	15	15	8	6	6
Electricity, gas and water	1	1	1	1	1	1
Construction	16	10	11	6	3	3
Trade	9	11	12	25	18	20
Transport, communication and storage	6	6	6	7	11	11
Finance and insurance	1	1	1	6	4	5
Social and community services	29*	30	24	17	14	12
Total	100	100	100	100	100	100

Note: * including not stated.

Sources: Syria, *Stasticial Abstract*, various issues; UN, *National Accounts Statistics: Main Aggregates and Detailed Tables*, various issues.

project must have a minimum of 25 percent state ownership in the capital of joint venture companies to be established. By September 1995, a total of 1,349 projects had been approved by the Supreme Council of Investment (SCI), with a total capital of more than $6 billion (of which more than $4.6 billion is hard currency) generating 147,200 new jobs (see table 5.4). About two-thirds of the total investment of the approved projects is allocated to the manufacturing sector and the rest mainly to the services sector (e.g., transportation).

Despite the boom in new projects submitted to and approved by the SIC, the success of the new investment law has thus far been limited. By the end of 1995, only $352 million had actually been invested in various projects, that is, less than 6 percent of the total investment approved by the SIC.[3] This is in clear contrast to the overinflated investment alleged by Syrian officials, such as the Minister of Economy and Foreign Trade and the Director of SIC, who claim that the total investment in fact amounted to $4.6 or $5.5 billion, respectively.[4] In essence, the main achievement is in the very return of the limited inflow of direct foreign investment in Syria to the prevailing level during the period 1982–86 (on average, more than $100 million a year), thereby ending the net outflow of foreign private capital which characterized the period from 1987 to 1990.

Employment and Output

According to official Syrian data, overall employment rose by 7 percent a year in the period 1990–94, in comparison with 5 percent a year in the 1980s. However, the main costs of job creation is still borne by the agricultural sector, which has absorbed roughly more than one-third of the total additional annual jobs since the early 1980s. The manufacturing sector absorbed only 15 percent from 1980 to 1994. In fact, the manufacturing sector is still composed mostly of small and medium-sized plants related to import substitution of consumer goods (e.g., textiles and light consumer durables) and intermediate goods for construction and agricultural development. Only a modest part of the manufacturing sector is comprised of export-oriented industries, in both the public and the private sectors.

Even with the accumulated investment over the years, the manufacturing sector remains over-manned and inefficient. During the period 1980–94, despite absorbing 15 percent of total employment, the manufacturing sector was still contributing between only 6 to 8 percent of the GNP. Syrian development strategy has thus far failed to shift the costs of job creation to the manufacturing sector, as its emphasis has been primarily centered on intensive capital investments (see table 5.5).

The Oil Sector: In Search of New Foreign Investors

Oil output in Syria, which has grown rapidly since the mid-1980s, appears to have peaked now at about 30 million tons a year, contributing to more than 50 percent of total Syrian annual exports. The Syrian authorities expect to maintain the level of current production until the year 2000 and even beyond. Syria's total proven recoverable oil reserves are estimated at 1.7 billion barrels.[5] However, as oil fields are reaching their maturity, it is doubtful whether Syria will succeed in fulfilling its goal. Since 1990, Syria has estimated a reduction in the development of existing oil fields, and new oil fields are not commercially exploitable.

Moreover, foreign companies are losing interest in the development and exploration of oil in Syria. By 1995, only five of the 22 foreign companies prospecting oil in 1990 were still active in the country. Syria is now ranked as no. 101 in the world in terms of profitability of oil exploration in its territory. Western oil groups have criticized the new and improved terms offered in 1994 and 1995 by Syrian oil officials, and thus far Syria has not been able to attract additional foreign partners to engage in new exploitation or to raise output from existing fields. Increased investment is required in 1996 and 1997 in order to maintain current production levels of crude oil and to modernize the distribution and processing infrastructure. As a result, oil output may decline for a few years,[6] considering the substantial time lags involved in expanding production.

Defense Costs and Defense Burden

Defense expenditure reports by Syria consist mainly of recurring expenditures and omit all or most capital purchases. No less controversial are the assessments of the magnitude of arms transfer deliveries.[7] In order to accurately assess the real magnitude of total Syrian defense costs, our methodology used a two-stage procedure in our aggregate estimation. This procedure took into account the official Syrian figures on budgeted defense outlays and added in the estimates of arms transfers to Syria according to the most important Western sources: the US Arms Control and Disarmament Agency (ACDA) and the Stockholm Peace Research Institute (SIPRI).[8] The massive arms imports transferred to Syria over the

Table 5.6 Arms transfers to Syria: Western assessments, 1980–94 ($US million)

	ACDA (a)		SIPRI (b)	
Year	(Current prices)	(Constant 1990 prices)	(Current prices)	(Constant 1990 prices)
1980	3,300	5,348	1,172	1,900
1985	1,500	1,671	1,779	1,982
1990	950	881	30	28
1991	650	580	155	138
1992	525	456	394	342
1993	220	187	221	188
1994	10	9	65	55

Notes: (a) ACDA data represent the transfer of *all* military equipment under terms of grant, credit, barter or cash. The military equipment includes major weapons systems (aircraft, armored vehicles, artillery, guidance and radar systems, missiles and warships) as well as parts thereof, ammunition, other equipment and commodities designed for military use.

(b) SIPRI data cover *only* six categories of major weapons systems (aircraft, armored vehicles, artillery, guidance and radar systems, missiles and warships) but exclude all other equipment and commodities for military use.

Sources: US, Arms Control and Disarmament Agency (ACDA), *World Military Expenditures and Arms Transfers*, various issues; *Stockholm International Peace Research Institute* (SIPRI), letters to the author, 24 and 27 March 1996.

period 1980–94 amounted to between $15,220 to $23,555 million, according to SIPRI and ACDA, respectively (see tables 5.6 and 5.7).

This can be further broken down as follows:

1 During the 1980s, in the aftermath of the peace treaty between Egypt and Israel, the total of Syrian arms imports amounted to between $14.3 billion and $21.2 billion, according to SIPRI and ACDA, respectively. Therefore, annual arms imports averaged between $1,430 million and $2,120 million during the period, according to these estimates. That is to say, the average annual Syrian arms imports were equivalent to between 45 and 66 percent of annual civilian imports.
2 In the period 1990–94, Syrian total arms imports amounted to between $865 million and $2,355 million, according to SIPRI and ACDA, respectively. Thus, on average, Syrian annual arms imports

Table 5.7 Budgeted defense expenditures and total defence costs, 1980–94 (millions of LS)

Year	Budgeted defense expenditures	Arms transfers				In percent of GDP		
	Official version (1)	ACDA version* (2)	SIPRI version* (3)	Total defense costs based on ACDA version (1+2 = 4)	Total defense costs based on SIPRI version (1–3 = 5)	Budgeted defense expenditures official version (6)	Total defense costs based on ACDA version (7)	Total defense costs based on SIPRI version (8)
1980	8,000	13,035	4,629	21,035	12,629	15.6	41.0	24.6
1981	8,800	10,850	3,672	19,650	12,472	13.4	29.9	19.0
1982	9,200	10,894	8,548	20,094	17,748	13.4	29.2	25.9
1983	10,050	14,402	8,847	24,452	18,897	13.7	33.3	25.8
1984	12,600	9,271	7,627	21,871	20,227	16.7	29.0	26.8
1985	13,000	7,050	8,361	20,050	21,361	15.6	24.1	25.6
1986	13,600	7,744	9,856	21,344	23,456	13.6	21.3	23.5
1987	13,200	20,300	13,357	33,500	26,557	10.3	26.1	20.7
1988	13,300	27,300	29,400	40,600	42,700	7.2	22.0	23.1
1989	15,300	23,320	8,650	38,620	23,950	7.3	18.4	11.4
1990	15,300	20,710	654	36,010	15,954	5.7	13.5	5.9
1991	14,600	17,420	4,154	42,020	28,754	7.9	13.4	9.2
1992	24,600	15,698	11,780	40,298	36,380	6.6	10.8	9.8
1993	25,000	6,974	7,006	31,974	32,006	6.0	7.7	7.7
1994	32,700	339	2,203	33,039	34,903	6.6	6.7	7.0

Note: * ACDA and SIPRI estimates converted at the effective exchange rate.

Source: Syria, *Statistical Abstract*, various issues; ACDA, *World Military Expenditures and Arms Transfers*, various issues; *SIPRI*, letters to the author, 24 and 27 March 1996.

were estimated at between \$170 and \$470 million a year. In other terms, the arms transferred to Syria in the period 1990–94 were equivalent to between 6 and 15 percent of the total annual civilian imports for this period.

In order to assess the real value of Syrian defense costs for the period 1980–94, we based our calculation on the effective exchange rate of Syrian currency and converted the Western assessments of Syrian arms imports (quoted in US dollars) into LS (Syrian pound):

1 *Effective exchange rate.* It is noteworthy that Syria has a highly complex and non-transparent exchange and trade system with a multiple exchange rate. As a result, the official exchange rate does not reflect the real exchange rate of Syrian currency. Moreover, the official exchange rate has been further appreciated due to Syria's high inflation rate. Thus, in order to properly reflect the value of Syrian arms imports in Syrian currency, our assessment is based on the effective exchange rate, as estimated by the IMF's Information Notification System.
2 *Conversion of arms imports to LS.* Syria, as other countries, has published data on defense expenditures and the GDP quoted in Syrian currency. Scholars commonly use the official exchange rate in order to convert data on defense expenditures and the GDP in dollar terms for international comparisons and otherwise. While such a practice is appropriate for a country with a single and realistic official exchange rate, this is not the case for countries such as Syria, which maintain complex, multiple, and unrealistic official exchange rates. Consequently, the use of official Syrian exchange rates for assessing total defense costs in general, and regarding arms imports in particular, is both misleading and distorting. Instead, the use of the effective exchange rate is clearly less complex than the almost impossible task of converting the Syrian GDP (quoted in LS) into US dollars by using a methodology that will accurately reflect the various sectors of the Syrian economy.

   Therefore, in order to accurately assess Syrian arms imports in real terms, we have converted Western estimates from US dollars into LS, calculated on the basis of the effective exchange rate during the surveyed period. Our empirical analysis distinguishes between two main definitions: "defense costs" and "defense burden." In our view, total "defense costs" include the officially budgeted defense outlays, as well as the real value of arms imports – either financed by grants, credits or Syrian-pledged payments. The "defense burden"

Table 5.8 Defense costs: official and alternative assessments, 1980–94

Period	Percentage of current budget			Percentage of GDP				
	Budgeted defense expenditures	Education	Health	Budgeted defense expenditures – official version	Total defense costs based on ACDA version*	Total defense costs based on SIPRI version*	Education	Health
1980–84	54.0	12.1	0.9	14.6	32.5	24.4	3.3	0.9
1985–89	50.6	14.6	1.1	10.8	22.4	20.9	3.1	1.1
1990–94	42.0	13.9	1.9	6.6	8.4	7.9	2.1	1.9
1980–89	52.3	13.3	1.0	12.7	27.5	22.6	3.2	1.0
1980–94	48.9	13.5	1.3	10.6	21.1	17.7	2.8	1.3

Note: * Includes budgeted defense expenditures and arms imports.

Sources: Syria, *Statistical Abstract*, various issues; ACDA, *World Military Expenditures and Army Transfers*, various issues; SIPRI, letters to the author, 24 and 27 March 1996.

includes the officially budgeted defense expenditures, as well as Syrian actual payments for arms imports, if any. We compared three versions of the defense costs in Syria: the officially budgeted defense expenditures, which exclude arms imports, and two other more realistic versions, ACDA and SIPRI, which do include Syrian arms imports (see tables 5.7 and 5.8).

As shown in tables 5.7 and 5.8, the Syrian defense costs fluctuated sharply over the surveyed period, mainly as a result of political developments in the international or regional arenas. Total defense costs in the 1980s accounted for between 22 and 27 percent of the GDP a year on average, according to SIPRI or ACDA versions, respectively, in comparison with less than 13 percent of the GDP as reported by official Syrian sources. However, the highest level was reached during the period from 1980 to 1984 in the wake of the peace agreement between Israel and Egypt: 14.6 percent of the GDP, according to the official Syrian version, versus 32.5 percent or 24.4 percent of the GDP as quoted by ACDA and SIPRI, respectively. The lowest level of defense costs was found in the period from 1990 to 1994, due to the dramatic and substantial cuts in arms imports following the disintegration of the Soviet Union. During that period, defense costs accounted for 6.6 percent of the GDP, according to the official Syrian version, and roughly 8 percent according to both ACDA and SIPRI.

In order to put our findings into a proper perspective, it is noteworthy to mention that the world defense burden accounted on average for less than 5.5 percent of the GDP in the 1980s and less than 4 percent over the period 1990–94, in both the developed and developing countries.[9] In other words, the Syrian real defense costs were four to five times higher than the average world defense burden during the 1980s and two times higher than in the first half of the 1990s. However, despite massive Syrian arms acquisitions over the years (more than 90 percent of which was supplied by the Soviet Union), President Asad succeeded in extracting invaluable concessions by exploiting Syria's status as prime ally in the region in order to defer the repayment of military debts due, or even to obtain Soviet consent to write off part of those debts.[10]

According to Russian sources, Syria was compelled to settle some of its military debts. As a result, Syria tremendously increased its exports to Moscow and settled in kind more than $2.2 billion out of its total military debts in 1989–91.[11] Those repayments, however, barely amounted to 10–15 percent of the total value of the military equipment supplied to Syria by Moscow over the period 1980–94. By the end of 1994, Syria's foreign debt amounted to approximately $16 billion,[12] of which more than 80 percent was owed to the former Soviet Union.[13] While in the past Syria benefited from "most-favored nation" status in purchasing arms equipment,[14] the radical political changes in Moscow have imposed new terms for arms imports to Syria, based mainly on commercial considerations. Thus, from the late 1980s onward, for the first time since the October 1973 war, Syria has actually been bearing the heavy financial costs of arms acquisitions from its own limited resources. In order to comply with its financial obligation to Moscow, Syria had to postpone settling its overdue debts of approximately $2 billion to the World Bank and Western countries, thereby severely affecting its creditworthiness in international financial markets in general, and in Western financial markets in particular.

In fact, as a result of the special political relationship between Damascus and Moscow, the latter bore a substantial share of the total Syrian defense costs over the period 1980–94, though decreasing over time as follows:

1 From 1980 to 1988, Damascus and Moscow equally shared the burden of Syria's total defense costs. While Syria was bearing only the budgeted defense expenditures, Moscow made its massive arms supplies without any Syrian payments for those arms imports or for previous military debts.
2 Syria was bearing 75 percent of its total defense costs during the period 1992–94, while Moscow was bearing only 25 percent as a result of limited unpaid arms supplies.
3 During the years 1989 to 1991 did Syria bear its total defense costs; Syria was compelled to pay Moscow for the current supply of spare parts and to repay some of its military debts.

In the past, as the result of Soviet political and strategic conditions, Syria benefited from massive military equipment deliveries without having to bear the financial costs deriving from such acquisitions. More recently, the radical political changes in Moscow have imposed new terms on Syria as far as defense imports are concerned, based mainly on commercial conditions. That is to say, defense acquisitions are now conditional on Syria's ability to finance these imports from its own resources. By contrast, in the past Syria has never been able to pay for arms imports despite its receipt of massive Arab financial grants. The prospects for the foreseeable future are certainly no brighter.

Therefore, hard choices need to be made in Syria regarding the distribution of available resources between the defense sector and socioeconomic development. Even if the costs of defense imports are overlooked, the fact is that the heavy costs of the budgeted defense expenditures (which exclude arms imports) prevented Syria from giving higher priority to the education and health sectors throughout the period 1980–94. This was the case in spite of the massive financial grants received during the surveyed period, officially estimated at $12.6 billion. While over the years the budgeted defense outlays absorbed 50 percent of the annual Syrian budgetary expenditures, or 10.6 percent of the GDP, education and health were hardly allocated 15 percent of the total current annual budgetary spending, or 4 percent of the GDP (see table 5.8).

The Balance of Payments Performance and Implications

During the years 1989–92, for the first time since 1980, the status of Syria's external payments improved radically, with the current account (excluding foreign grants) showing a surplus of more than $0.8 billion a year on average, in clear contrast to the $1 to $2 billion deficit a year during the period 1980–88 (see tables 5.9 and 5.10). This exceptional performance was generated by the combined effect of the following main factors: First, a three-fold increase in oil receipts to almost $1.8 billion a year due to a substantial rise in quantity as well as in price (see table 5.12). Second, an impressive three-fold increase in non-oil exports to more than $1.6 billion a year on average, mainly as the result of in-kind repayment of $2.2 billion of military debts to Moscow. Third, a marginal increase in civilian imports averaging $2.3 billion a year, roughly at the same level as in the preceding years (see tables 5.9 and 5.10).

Notwithstanding Syria's achievements over the period 1989–92 in terms of its external payments position, the country reverted back in to its longstanding normative payments deficit in 1993–94, with the annual current account generating a deficit of $0.6 billion annually on average, while the foreign grants were declined sharply to $100 million annually. This deficit resulted mainly from the two following factors: First, the stagnation in total annual exports mainly due to the loss of Syria's traditional markets in the former Soviet block in general, and the Russian Federation in particular. Second, the impressive rise in civilian imports to $4 billion a year on average (two times higher than the level of imports during the period 1986–92), which was generated primarily by the sharp increase in private sector imports due to trade liberalization.

It is noteworthy that during the period 1980–88, Syrian annual current account deficits (excluding foreign grants) amounted on average to more than $1.6 billion and were covered to a large extent – up to 71 percent – by foreign grants (averaging $1.2 billion a year). As a result of the Syrian

Table 5.9 Balance of payment developments by main sub-periods, 1980–94 ($US million – annual average)

Period	Exports	Imports*	Balance of trade	Net services & income	Private transfers	Balance (excluding official grants)	Official grants	Current account
1980–85	1,989	–3,951	–1,962	–387	446	–1,903	1,419	–484
1986–88	1,247	–2,192	–945	–398	339	–1,004	686	–586
1989–92	3,427	–2,295	1,132	–721	400	811	456	1,267
1993–94	3,479	–4,022	–543	–542	462	–623	97	–526

Notes: * Excludes defense imports.

Sources: IMF, *Balance of Payments Yearbook*, various issues.

Table 5.10 Balance of payments: selected indicators, 1980–94 ($US million)

Year	Exports		Imports*	Balance of trade	Net services and income	Unrequited transfers			Current account
	Total	of which oil				Private transfers**	Official grants	Total	
1980	2,112	1,662	–4,010	–1,898	–144	774	1,520	2,294	251
1981	2,212	1,657	–4,404	–2,192	–400	436	1,848	2,284	–308
1982	2,002	1,523	–3,636	–1,634	–427	411	1,400	1,811	–250
1983	1,917	1,332	–4,023	–2,106	–428	386	1,304	1,690	–844
1984	1,834	1,176	–3,687	–1,853	–493	321	1,231	1,552	–794
1985	1,856	1,220	–3,946	–2,090	–430	350	1,212	1,562	–958
1986	1,037	561	–2,363	–1,326	–260	323	759	1,082	–504
1987	1,357	703	–2,226	–869	–525	334	762	1,096	–298
1988	1,347	591	–1,986	–639	–409	360	537	897	–151
1989	3,013	1,182	–1,821	1,192	–627	430	227	657	1,222
1990	4,156	1,907	–2,062	2,094	–804	385	88	473	1,763
1991	3,438	1,836	–2,354	1,084	–698	350	926	1,276	1,662
1992	3,100	2,157	–2,941	159	–754	433	584	1,017	422
1993	3,203	1,939	–3,476	–273	–706	426	60	486	–493
1994	3,755	1,983	–4,569	–814	–377	498	133	631	–560

Notes: * Excludes defense imports.
** Includes workers' remittance transfers from abroad as well as remittances made to finance some private sector imports.

Sources: IMF, *Balance of Payments Yearbook*, various issues.

current account surpluses during the period 1989–92 – and for the first time in more than 20 years – Arab financial grants ($0.5 billion a year) did not contribute to covering the traditional deficits, but rather served to further ameliorate the already improved balance of payments position reflected in surpluses. However, the balance of payments performance in 1993–94 put an end to the exceptional surpluses in the current account position again deteriorated and suffered from its traditional negative position. Of the $0.6 billion current account deficit, only 15 percent was covered by foreign grants, which declined significantly to $100 million a year (see table 5.11).[15]

Capital Movement and Foreign Debt in Perspective

In stark contrast to the period 1980–84, capital receipts from the mid-

Table 5.11 Drawing and repayments of external civilian loans and credits, 1980–94 ($US million)

Period	Long-term capital			Short-term capital			Total capital flows		
	Receipts	Repayments	Total, Net	Receipts	Repayments	Total, Net	Receipts	Repayments	Total, Net
1980–84	2,776	–2,462	314	913	–708	205	3,689	–3,170	519
1985–89	1,624	–1,556	68	2,448	–1,928	520	4,072	–3,484	588
1990–94	2,652	–3,404	–752	6,022	–3,615	2,407	8,674	–7,019	1,655
				(Annual average)					
1980–84	555	–492	63	152	–142	10	707	–634	73
1985–89	325	–311	14	489	–386	103	814	–697	117
1990–94	528	–681	–153	1,204	–723	481	1,732	–1,404	328

Source: IMF, *Balance of Payments Statistics Yearbook*, various issues.

1980s onward consisted largely of short-term capital rising from 25 percent to 60–70 percent, respectively. Concessional long-term capital receipts from other countries and international/regional agencies for financing capital expenditures steadily declined from 75 percent of total receipts in the period 1980–84 ($555 million out of $707 million a year) to 30 percent in 1990–94 ($528 million out of $1.732 billion a year – see table 5.11).

The sharp decrease in importance of concessional long-term receipts since the mid-1980s resulted from both political and financial factors:

1 Since 1986 Syria has failed to clear financial debt arrears to the World Bank amounting to more than $0.5 billion in 1995. As a result, new loans were not allocated or disbursed.
2 The EU imposed sanctions on Syria during the period 1986–90 as a result of its involvement in a plot to blow up an Israeli airline in 1986. Even though sanctions were lifted in 1990, disbursements of new loans have been practically suspended again, as Syria has repeatedly failed to settle its accumulated debt arrears amounting to $1 billion by the end of 1995.

Consequently, and despite Syria's failure to honor its external financial commitments of $2 billion, including $1.5 billion to the World Bank and the EU, the still-heavy costs of long-term loans over the period 1990–94 were not offset by long-term capital receipts. During this period, long-term net capital balance amounted to a deficit of more than $150 million a year on average. Increased reliance was placed on short-term capital receipts amounting on average to $1.7 billion a year, two times higher than during the 1980s. Moreover, the short-term capital inflow financed not only short-term repayment commitments, but also was essential to offset long-term capital net deficit. In fact, the net balance of short-term capital resulted more from the combined impact of public sector borrowing abroad and foreign exchange used by the private sector to import goods and finance than through letters of credit obtained abroad and through their own resources abroad.

Against this background, Syria faces a net external financing need that is expected to rise in the foreseeable future. In fact, its balance of payments outlook is even more complicated by three downside risks:

1 International oil prices are volatile and may weaken in the coming years, particularly if and when Iraq resumes oil exports.
2 Delaying the settlement of Syria's payment arrears would significantly aggravate its already damaged creditworthiness and further

reduce foreign capital inflow.

3 Moreover, this weakened creditworthiness would have a negative impact on Syrian and foreign private sector confidence, which has improved only in recent years.

Foreign Trade Developments

The Syrian balance of trade was dominated and determined in the fluctuations of oil trade during the period 1980–94. While oil exports constituted more than 50 percent of its total annual exports, the share of oil in total civilian imports declined steadily from 35 percent during the years 1980–85 to less than 5 percent over the period 1989–94 (see table 5.12 and figure 5.3). Due to the sizeable oil imports during the period 1980–88, the balance of oil trade made a partial contribution to reducing the non-oil trade deficit. However, over the years 1989–92, the average annual surplus in oil trade ($1,741 million a year) enabled Syria, for the first time, to more than offset its large deficit in non-oil trade ($609 million a year). Notwithstanding the increase in oil trade surplus in 1993–94 (on average $1.8 billion a year), the substantial rise in non-oil imports contributed to enormous growth in the non-oil trade deficit (about $2.5 billion a year). As a result, the balance of trade registered a deficit of more than $0.5 billion a year during the period 1993–94, in clear contrast to a surplus of more than $1.1 billion a year over the years 1989–92.

Composition of Syrian Foreign Trade. During the period 1990–94 non-oil exports constituted more than 40 percent of total annual exports. This included 20 percent of manufactured goods, almost equally divided between textiles and other industrial products, and 20 percent of agri-

Table 5.12 Oil and non-oil balance of trade, 1980–94 (annual average)

Period	Oil trade (percentage of total)		Oil trade, balance ($US million)	Non-oil trade balance ($US million)	Balance of trade ($US million)
	Exports	Imports			
1980–85	72	35	60	–2,022	–1,962
1986–88	50	17	236	–1,181	–945
1989–92	52	1	1,741	–609	1,132
1993–94	56	4	1,809	–2,452	–543

Sources: Syria, *Statistical Abstract*, various issues; *Central Bank of Syria*, Quarterly Bulletin, various issues.

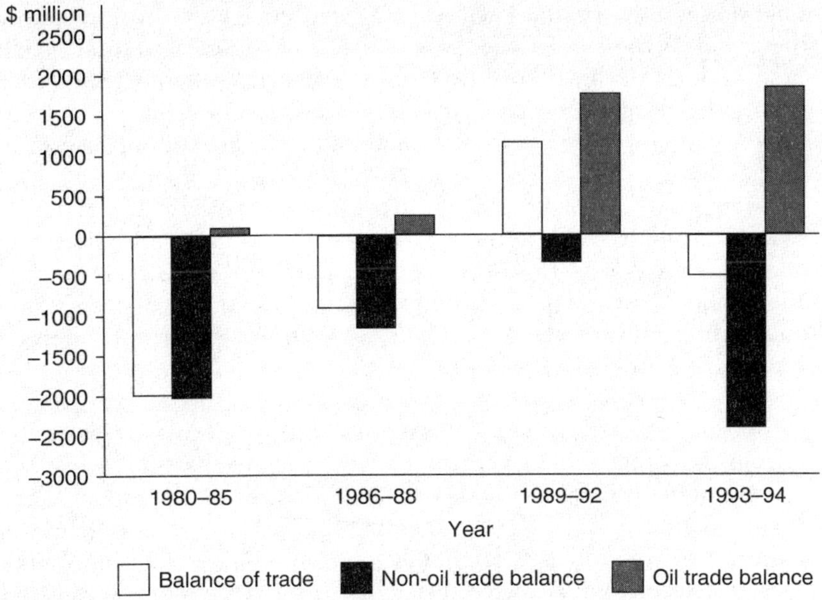

Figure 5.3 Oil and non-oil balance of trade, 1980–94

cultural products, including roughly 8 percent of fruits and vegetables and 5 percent of raw cotton. The increase in the domestic production of light crude oil during these years resulted in a sharp reduction in petroleum imports to only 3 percent of total annual imports. Each group of machinery and equipment, as well as foodstuffs, accounted for 20 percent of total annual imports, 15 percent for metal products, 10 percent for transport equipment, and about 8 percent for textiles.[16]

Geographical Distribution of Syrian Foreign Trade. In the period 1990–94, the European Union served as Syria's major export market, accounting for about 55 percent of total Syrian annual exports, a much higher rate than in the 1980s. The share of exports to the former Soviet block countries declined to only 16 percent from almost 40 percent during the 1980s. The Arab markets absorbed about one-quarter of the total Syrian annual exports, two times higher than in the 1980s. However, the share of the Arab markets in Syria's annual non-oil exports was actually much higher: 55 percent during the period 1990–94, in comparison with about 30 percent on average in the 1980s. The European Union supplied more than 36 percent of total civilian annual imports during the period 1990–94, slightly higher than its average annual share in the 1980s. The former Soviet Block continued to supply 15 percent as in the 1980s. The share of the Arab countries in total Syrian annual imports declined steadily from the first half of the 1980s as a result of the drop in Syrian petroleum imports. Over the years from 1990–94, only 6 percent of total annual imports were supplied by Arab countries.[17]

Foreign Trade by Sectors. The distribution of Syrian foreign trade between the public sector and the private sector was substantially transformed over the period 1980–94 in both exports and imports. However, as the public sector monopolized oil trade, the actual role of each sector should be more accurately assessed in examining the Syrian non-oil trade (see table 5.13 and figure 5.4).

1 *Non-oil exports*: The share of the public sector decreased gradually from 67 percent to 23 percent over the period 1980–94, while the share of the private sector rose from 33 percent to 77 percent in the same period. In fact, the rapid expansion of Syrian non-oil exports during this period was facilitated only by the contribution of the private sector, which succeeded in increasing its exports seven-fold to $1.2 billion a year on average over the years 1990–94. In contrast, public sector non-oil exports remained stagnant, amounting to $365 million a year, at the very most.
2 *Non-oil imports*: During the years 1990–94, the private sector's share in total non-oil imports accounted for 60 percent, two times higher than its share in the 1980s. While the public sector's annual non-oil imports amounted to about $1.2 billion a year during the period 1990–94 (one-third lower than in 1980–84), private imports amounted to $1.8 billion a year, almost three times higher than in the 1980s.[18]

Table 5.13 Syrian foreign trade by sectors,* 1980–94 (percentages of total – annual average)

Period	Exports			Imports (civilian)		
	Public sector	Private sector	Total	Public sector	Private sector	Total
1980–84	90	10	100	83	17	100
1985–89	71	29	100	74	26	100
1990–94	69	31	100	43	57	100

Notes: * Including oil trade.

Sources: Syria, *Central Bank of Syria, Quarterly Bulletin*, various issues; idem, *Statistical Abstract*, various issues.

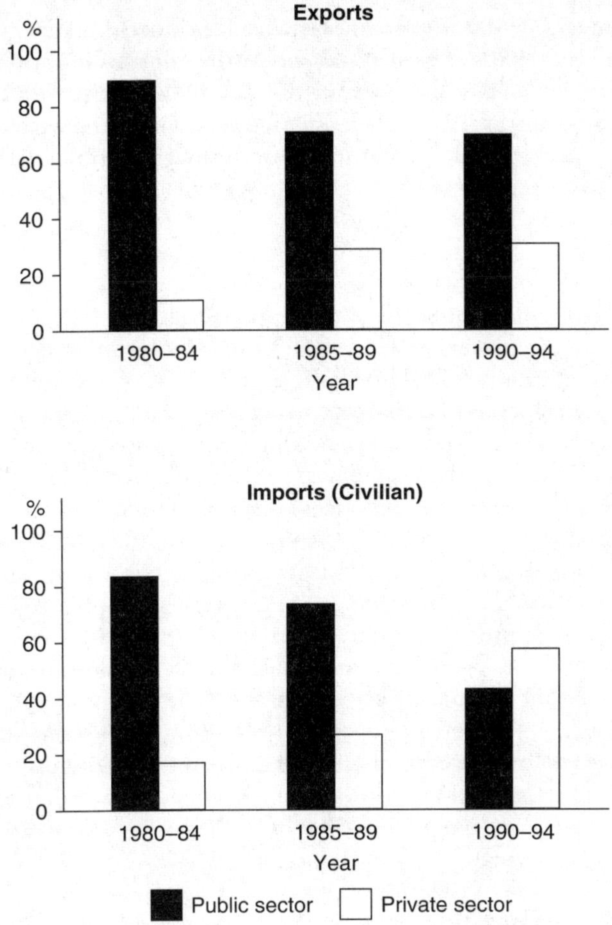

Figure 5.4 Syrian foreign trade by sectors,* 1980–94
Note: * including oil trade.

The increasing role of the private sector in Syrian foreign trade, both in exports and imports alike, during the period 1990–94, was the result of the combined effect of trade liberalization measures, investment incentives offered to the private sector, and appreciation of the real exchange rate. However, it is necessary to emphasize the fact that, in practice, the Syrian authorities have refused to allocate foreign exchange from their resources in order to finance private imports. Therefore, the private sector has been forced to rely on its own resources to finance its imports, giving private exporters a strong interest in inflating the supposed value of their exchange so as to secure higher actual imports.[19] Basically, the private sector is an important factor contributing to a potentially substantial increase in Syrian non-oil exports. However, considering the multiple exchange rates and inflated value of non-oil exports, actual private exports are at least 20 percent lower than the official figures. Consequently, the real prospects of increasing non-oil exports are significantly more limited than officially touted.

Conclusions and Projections

The success of any fundamental liberalization in Syria is critically dependent on three main factors: First, decreasing, or at least maintaining, the present level of defense expenditures, which almost exclude any arms imports. Second, reducing the dominance of the public sector and thereby expanding the sphere of activity open to the dynamic private sector. Third, increasing the total amount of external economic and financial assistance (including grants) to a significantly higher level than that provided in the first half of the 1990s.

In the foreseeable future, it is unlikely that any major new liberalization measures will be promulgated. As far as the Syrian regime is concerned, the public sector is not only instrumental in controlling the economy, it is also – and perhaps even more importantly – a medium for securing the ascent and predominance of the 'Alawi community. The public sector is in fact deeply infiltrated by 'Alawis; as a result, they not only politically support the regime, but also benefit from a relatively higher standard of living.[20] In fact, there are no plans to sell off public enterprises or scale down the public sector for the time being.

However, the Syrian authorities are likely to considerably reduce a variety of existing restrictive measures related to foreign trade and price controls. Such measures would induce private sector activity, but still would not significantly stimulate the repatriation of Syrian private holdings abroad. Foreign private investment (Syrian or otherwise) is unlikely to increase substantially above the level already reached in the first half of the 1990s, and in fact is expected to be marginal when compared with official projections or optimistic statements. Despite the large foreign payment arrears accumulated by the end of 1995, actual Syrian external debt servicing constituted a heavy, if not unbearable, burden on the balance of payments position in the first half of the 1990s. Servicing Syrian foreign debts increased steadily to 50 percent of total annual exports in the period 1990–94, from less than one-third in the period 1980–84. The persistence of large external arrears will continue to deeply harm Syria's creditworthiness in the international financial markets, reducing the availability of long-term loans and credit and increasing the cost of borrowing. Thus far, the Syrian authorities have favored the bilateral-creditors approach to arrears and debt rescheduling. While such an approach may be politically preferred, it has not proved to be rewarding insofar as it has already delayed the vital settlement of those arrears for many years.

During the years 1990–94, the flow of foreign loans for development and financial grants was a direct consequence of Syria's rehabilitation in the eyes of the outside world following the 1990–91 Gulf crisis. Even Arab funding, which has served as the primary source of backing for Syrian development projects since the end of the Gulf crisis, is diminishing as the Gulf oil-exporting countries struggle to deal with their own domestic financial problems.[21]

In order to secure an amelioration of the standard of living of the population and to induce economic development through implementation of a high rate of investment, Syria needs to attain at least a moderate rate of growth, namely 5–6 percent annually in real terms. However, achieving such a critical national objective is unrealistic if Syria must continue to rely primarily on its own resources. Syria is in fact expected to face considerable financial gaps over the next few years, resulting from the following three main factors:

1 It seems that Syria will be unable to increase its total annual exports on average by 50 percent from 1996 to 2000 in comparison with the period 1990–94. Syrian oil exports and receipts are likely to fall initially as the result of higher domestic consumption, and then to fall even further when Iraq resumes its oil exports. Consequently, it will be necessary to vastly increase non-oil exports, which are predominately controlled by the private sector. Such targets could be reached, at least partly, only if new liberalizing measures were to be implemented together with the unification of the exchange rate.
2 Annual civilian imports should be two times higher in comparison with the actual level of imports in the period 1990–94.
3 The current account is expected to again generate at least an annual deficit of $1 to $2 billion, as in the period 1980–88 when the economy was affected by a slow rate of economic growth.

Since Syrian domestic savings could finance, at the very best, only 50 percent of total annual investment, the reliance on considerable external economic aid is both imperative and vital. Therefore, in addition to the financial requirements deriving from the rescheduling of overdue civilian external debt arrears, securing the expansion of the Syrian economy during the period 1996–2000 would entail the net flow of between $13 to $18 billion of foreign financial aid in order to cover annual current account deficits and service current foreign debt obligations. However, the magnitude of foreign financial aid required would be at least 50 percent higher if the Syrian leadership were to decide to modernize and re-equip the Syrian armed forces with Western military equipment.

Under an unchanged policy stance, Syria's economy is expected to remain weak and macroeconomic disequilibrium to become more pronounced over the period 1996–2000, with adverse implications for economic growth. Even if the external current account deficits were to be smaller than projected, the financing requirements would still be larger than those of the 1980s. Moreover, the increased dependence on short-term private capital inflow to finance current account imbalances, the low level of reserves, and the lingering external arrears have exacerbated the underlying imbalances which reflect a number of deeply-rooted and interrelated institutional and structural impediments.

In realpolitik perspective, the Syrian economy must implement two complex but fundamental strategic changes at the same time:

1 Accelerate the move away from an economy still dominated and controlled by the public sector in order to firmly establish an outward-oriented market-based economy.
2 Give an impetus to the transition from a period of belligerency and war to an era of non-belligerency and peace, with all the implications involved. This will entail granting higher priority to the social and economic sectors at the expense of the defense sector, meaning cuts in defense spending, demobilization, etc.

The success of any fundamental economic reform in general, and the move to a peace-oriented economy in particular, is critically dependent on the continuation of substantial external financial support. Syria is in fact unable, at least in the foreseeable future, to bear the heavy economic and social costs generated by the complex structural difficulties involved. Without considerable foreign economic aid, such profound and multi-faceted difficulties would most likely lead to social unrest and economic stagnation or decline.

However, the Syrian authorities could contribute to alleviating the economic and social difficulties deriving from the required fundamental changes through the implementation of various key measures, including:

1 Deepening and accelerating the liberalization process in order to bring all the reform elements into a comprehensive and consistent framework. More rapid liberalization would achieve a substantial and durable improvement in the external payments position.
2 Simplifying the exchange rate structure by unifying the multiple exchange rates at a market-based level as soon as possible. This would also eliminate subsidies and improve resource allocation by setting more realistic prices.
3 Granting equal footing in the banking sector to the private and public sectors only on the basis of financial and economic considerations. The financial sector is currently operating in a non-competitive environment, namely, accommodating public sector needs while constraining private sector activity at a time of large expansion in private investment and trade. Financial savings are low and real interest rates are negative. If a new policy were to be implemented, it would contribute to reversing the performance of the banking sector and inducing substantially higher domestic savings, as well as eliminating (or at least sharply reducing) the costly and considerable subsidies to the public sector. Moreover, it would facilitate an increase in competitiveness and autonomy among public enterprises, while enhancing efficiency and profitability as well.

The implementation of the various macroeconomic adjustment policies (exchange rates, decontrol prices, establishment of real interest rates, etc.), together with an early normalization of financial relations with external creditors, will go a long way toward strengthening private sector confidence. The increased activity of the private sector in trade and investment during the first half of the 1990s indicates that this growth momentum can be sustained and enhanced in the period ahead. Moreover, the new opportunities will allow private sector investment to reach its real potential and to devote higher priority to export-oriented projects in the agricultural and manufacturing sectors, which have been so far been basically neglected. In the long-term perspective, the expansion of the agricultural and manufacturing private sectors through the promotion of export-oriented endeavors will reduce dependency on the oil sector and contribute to a sound and more balanced economy.

Notes

1 *Al-Iqtisad Wal-Naft*, No. 143 (October–November 1995), p. 47; *Syria et Monde Arabe*, No. 467 (Janvier 1993), p. 8; *al-Thawra* (Damascus), June 16, 1996.

2 Ishak Diwan-Lyn Squire, *Economic Development and Cooperation in the Middle East and North Africa*, World Bank, Discussion Paper Series, No. 9 (Washington, D.C., November 1993), p. 23; *Syrie et Monde Arabe*, No. 467 (Janvier 1993), p. 42; *MEED*, May 24, 1991, p. 28.
3 *MEES* (Middle East Economic Survey), September 30, 1996, p. B4, quoting UNCTAD, World Investment Report, 1996.
4 *Al-Hayat* (London), February 11, 1995; EIU, *Country Profile – Syria, 1995–96*, p. 31.
5 *Jordan Times* (Amman), June 9–10, 1994; EIU, *Syria – Country Report*, No. 2 (1995), p. 12.
6 *Al-Hayat*, February 7, 1994; February 11, 1995; *Arab News* (Jidda) February 2, 1995; EIU, *Syria – Country Report*, No. 2 (1995), pp. 6, 13; *International Herald Tribune* (Paris and Zurich), Syria Supplement, November 16–17, 1991.
7 US, Arms Control and Disarmament Agency (ACDA), *Military Expenditures and Arms Transfer – 1991/1992* (Washington, D.C., 1994), p. 150; Nancy Happe and John Wakeman-Lim, *Military Expenditure and Arms Trade: Alternative Data Sources*, IMF, Working Papers, (Washington, D.C., June 1994), pp. 4–5.
8 Arms trade data are excluded from Syrian foreign trade and balance of payments data.
9 ACDA, *Military Expenditures and Arms Transfers*, various issues; Moshe Efrat, "The Soviet Union and the Syrian Military-Economic Dimension," in M. Efrat and J. Bercovitch (eds), *Superpowers and Client States in the Middle East* (London and New York, 1991), pp. 253–57.
10 Efraim Karsh, *The Soviet Union and Syria: the Assad Years* (London and New York, 1988), pp. 17, 49, 292.
11 *Finansovye Izvestiia* (Moscow), August 8, 1996, as quoted by *Commonwealth of Independent States and the Middle East*, Vol. XXI, No. 7–8 (1996), p. 75.
12 *MEED*, September 29, 1995, p. 10.
13 *The Middle East* (February 1995), pp. 28–29. See also Lesch's and Winckler's chapters in this volume.
14 Moshe Efrat, "The Economics of Soviet Arms Transfers to the Third World," in Peter Wiles and Moshe Efrat, *The Economics of Soviet Arms* (Suntory-Toyota International Center for Economics & Related Disciplines, London School of Economics, 1985), pp. 7–8.
15 See also: IMF, *Balance of Payments Statistics Yearbook*, various issues.
16 Syria, *Statistical Abstract,* various issues; UN, *International Trade Statistics,* Yearbook, various issues.
17 *Ibid.*
18 Syria, *Statistical Abstract,* various issues; Central Bank of Syria, *Quarterly Bulletin*, various issues.
19 *MEED*, April 12, 1991, p. 5; September 27, 1991, p. 5.
20 Alain Chanet, "L'espace Tribal Alaouite à l'épreuve du Pouvoir – la Désintégration par la Politique," *Maghreb-Machrek*, No. 147 (Janvier–Mars 1995), pp. 103–4.
21 *MEED*, September 27, 1991, p. 4; EIU, *Country Report – Syria*, No. 4 (1995), p. 14.

6

The Syrian Road to the Middle East Peace Process: The Socioeconomic Perspective

Onn Winckler

The peace agreement between Egypt and Israel, in March 1979, left Syria alone in the armed struggle against Israel. After the Camp David accord in August 1978, the Syrian President, Hafiz al-Asad, imposed on the Syrian society and economy a high-priority mission: To achieve a strategic balance with Israel, meaning that Syria by itself, without any other Arab countries, would succeed in conducting a military confrontation against Israel. One of the most important questions is: Why did the Syrian authorities, with their limited resources, adopt this "strategic balance" policy? Rizkallah Hilan provides us with one set of factors that explains what led Asad to adopt such a policy:

> As is well known, Syria was the birthplace of Arab-Islamic civilization, and since the nineteenth century has been the principal source of Arab nationalism and the anti-imperialist struggle. Because of this, the Syrians see themselves charged with a historic mission of Arab nationalism, which is always evident in their discourse.[1]

Beyond the historical explanations, there were also some practical factors which led Asad to adopt the strategic balance policy. The first, and perhaps the most important, factor was the Egyptian-Israeli peace treaty of March 1979, which removed Egypt from the war circle against Israel, at least for the time being. The second factor was the Iran–Iraq war, which began in 1980. The Syrian support of the Irani side, and the tension between Asad and the Iraqi President, Saddam Husayn, turned Iraq into an impossible partner in any future military confrontation between Syria and Israel. The third factor, it seems, was the close relationship between Jordan and Israel, which brought Asad to assume that in any future Syrian–Israeli military confrontation, Jordan would not support him. The token participation of Jordan in the October 1973 war only strengthened this basic assumption. Thus, the option for establishing the "East Front" against Israel was no longer relevant.

In order to achieve a strategic balance with Israel, the Syrian authorities allocated substantial resources – in fact one of the highest among the non-oil Middle Eastern countries – for military purposes. During the late 1970s and the first half of the 1980s, military expenditures constituted approximately 20 percent of the total Syrian GDP.[2] The import of arms to Syria totaled $2 billion in 1979 and increased to $2.7 billion in 1980, as compared with $650 million only three years earlier, in 1977, the last year before the adaptation of the strategic balance policy.[3] By the mid-1980s, according to foreign sources, military expenditures were running between 50 and 60 percent of the total Syrian governmental budget.[4] According to one source, defense spending accounted for 58 percent of the total governmental budget in 1985.[5] One year later, in 1986, Syrian military expenditures were reported to constitute 55 percent of the total governmental outlay.[6] In that particular year, Syrian military expenditures amounted to $3.6 billion and increased to almost $4 billion one year later, in 1987.[7] Indeed, within only a few years, from the late 1970s until the mid-1980s, it seems that the Syrian army achieved a balance with the Israeli army in terms of quantity. By 1986, the Syrian army had half a million soldiers in the regular service, with approximately 4,100 tanks and 650 aircraft.[8] In addition, considerable financial resources were allocated to the various Syrian intelligence units, employing approximately 200,000 men by the mid-1980s.[9]

At the same time, during the 1970s and until the late 1980s, the high natural increase rates, which amounted to an average of 3.5 percent annually (see table 6.1) – one of the highest not only in the Middle East, but worldwide – had a variety of negative socioeconomic consequences. The first and foremost was the creation of a wide base of the age pyramid, with almost half the population in the mid-1980s under the age of 15,[10] making them consumers rather than producers. The direct result of the disproportionately high percentage of the young population was a very low rate of labor force participation: approximately 23 percent,[11] as compared with 50 percent and even higher in the industrialized countries,[12] due to their lower percentages of the young population in addition to higher rates of labor force participation among women. Thus, the ratio between breadwinners and dependents in Syria was 1:4.5, as compared with 1:2 or even less in the industrialized countries during the 1980s.

Table 6.1 Syrian demographic characteristics, 1960–96

Year	Total population (in thousands)	CBR	CDR	NI (%)	TFR
1960	4,565	47.9	17.7	3.0	7.3
1970	6,305	47.8	13.5	3.4	7.6
1980	8,704	45.8	8.3	3.8	7.3
1990	12,116	44.0	7.0	3.7	6.4
1994	13,812	28.0	5.4	2.3	4.7
1996	14,620	29.3	4.9	2.4	4.0

CBR = crude birth rate; **CDR** = crude death rate; **NI** = natural increase; **TFR** = total fertility rate.

Sources: Syria, Office of Prime Minister, Central Bureau of Statistics, *Statistical Abstract*, various issues, 1973–96 (Damascus: Government Printing press); ECWA/ESCWA, *Demographic and Related Socio-Economic Data Sheets for Countries of the Economic (and Social) Commission for Western Asia*, various issues (Beirut, Baghdad, and Amman); The World Bank, *World Tables*, various issues (Baltimore and London); The World Bank, *World Development Report*, various issues (Oxford and New York); Syrian Arab Republic, Office of the Prime Minister, Central Bureau of statistics, *Composition and Growth of Population in the Syrian Arab Republic* (Damascus, September 1979).

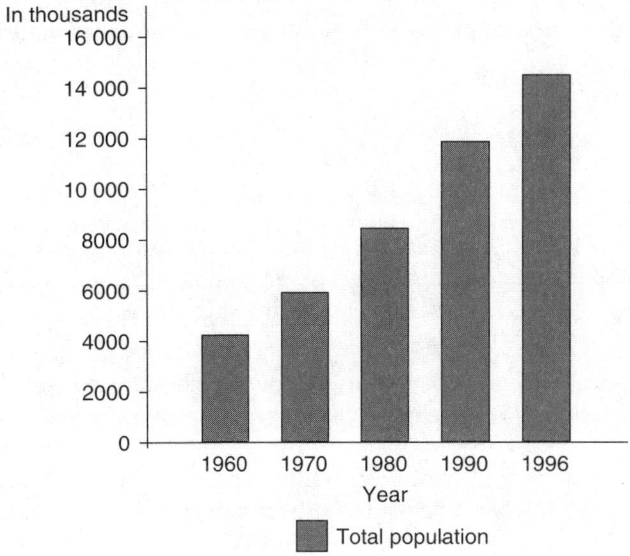

Figure 6.1 Syrian total population, 1960–96

Moreover, children and teenagers are large consumers of public services, such as health care and education, while their productive contribution is marginal, if any, particularly in the urban areas. In a country such as Syria, where public services are largely free of charge or are heavily subsidized, in addition to the heavy subsidies on basic food items, the large proportion of the young population has far-reaching consequences, including a substantial negative impact on the rate of economic growth.

Another major devastating result of the rapid population growth in Syria, especially in the rural areas, has been the steady decline of the per capita agricultural land under cultivation. While during the years 1960–94, the cropped area in Syria increased by approximately 40 percent,[13] at the same time the population size more than tripled, increasing from 4.565 million to 13.812 million (see table 6.1). The imbalance between the rate of population growth, on the one hand, and the cultivated agricultural land, on the other, caused a substantial net reduction in the per capita cropped area. This is extremely important in a country such as Syria where, even in the mid-1990s, the rural population constitutes almost half of the total population.[14]

However, in spite of these adverse effects of the rapid population growth, until the early 1980s the Syrian government was simultaneously able to allocate huge resources for military and security purposes and to

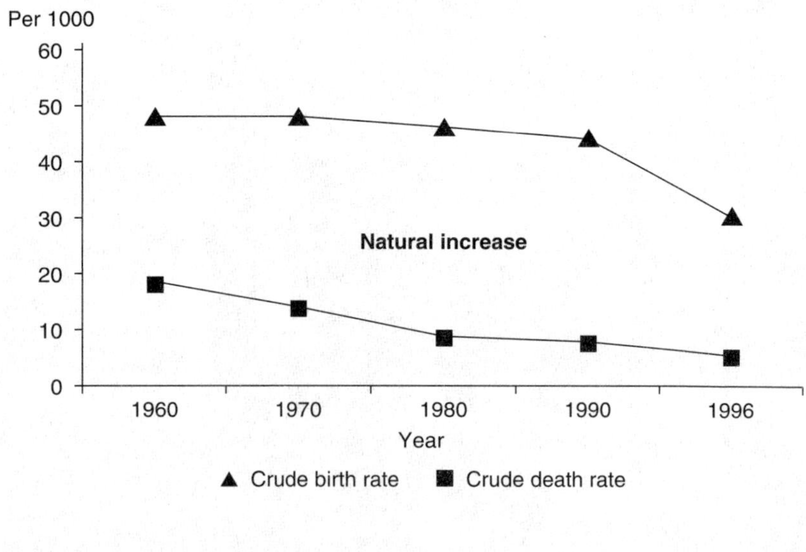

Figure 6.2 Syrian natural increase rates, 1960–96

achieve a rapid increase in the standard of living, due to high rates of economic growth. During the 1970s and the early 1980s, the Syrian economy enjoyed prosperity and achieved high rates of economic growth, amounting to approximately 10 percent annually. This was primarily due to high investment rates, which were equal to approximately 25–30 percent of the GDP during that period.[15] Such prosperity was the outcome of a combination of several factors, the first and foremost being the sharp rise in oil prices during the "oil decade" (1973–82). In addition to the steady capital inflow to Syria from the Soviet Union, the increasing oil prices caused a sharp increase in the capital inflow to Syria from the rich Arab oil-exporting countries in the form of soft loans to finance investments in socioeconomic development plans, as well as large-scale grants. Arab aid to Syria amounted to $500–600 million annually by the mid-1970s and increased to $1.6 billion in 1979, following the resolution of the Arab Summit Conference, held in Baghdad in November 1978, to increase the aid to the "confrontation states" with Israel.[16] Moreover, until 1976, Syria also benefited from $136 million annually in oil transit dues paid by Iraq.[17] No less important were the remittances sent home by the Syrian workers employed in the capital rich oil-exporting countries, as well as in Lebanon and Jordan, which were estimated at almost a billion dollars annually at the end of the 1970s and the early 1980s.[18] As a result of these developments, the per capita GNP in Syria reached $1,670 by 1982, compared with only $350 in 1970, representing more than a five-fold increase in only 12 years (in current prices).[19]

Following the end of the "oil decade" in 1982 and the collapse of oil prices in 1986–87, the Syrian economy deteriorated to a state of severe recession, which continued until the end of the decade. Like the economic prosperity of the 1970s and the early 1980s, the economic recession of the latter half of the 1980s was mainly due to the changes in oil prices. First, the sharp decline in oil prices caused Syrian revenues from oil exports to substantially diminish. In addition, at the beginning of the 1980s, the capital inflow to Syria from the rich Arab oil-exporting countries started to decline sharply, mainly as a result of Syria's support for Iran in its war against Iraq.[20] Whereas the Arab transfers to Syria amounted to $1.8 billion in 1981, transfers fell to only $500 million during the years 1986–88.[21]

Furthermore, the scale of remittances of Syrian workers in the GCC countries, Libya and Jordan, was markedly reduced from 1983 onward due to the combination of the sharp decline in oil prices and the huge differences between the official rate of the LS and the real rate in the open markets.[22] These developments led to a chronic shortage of foreign exchange in Syria, which also severely affected the industrial sector. With the situation further exacerbated by two years of severe drought, the Syrian economy grew by less than one percent annually in real terms during the years 1982–85.[23] Moreover, the total GDP in 1985 fell below the 1981 level at constant prices.[24] The result was a sharp decline in the per capita GDP and income, since the annual population growth was much higher than the economic growth rates during that period.

Another negative consequence of the wide gap between the rates of population growth and economic growth was the increase in open and disguised unemployment rates during the second half of the 1980s. While during the late 1980s the official unemployment rate was 5.8 percent, according to unofficial sources the real figure was much higher, estimated at almost 10 percent.[25] The weekly publication *MEED* described the economic situation in Syria as it appeared to outside observers in November 1987:

> A chronic shortage of foreign exchange has left Syria unable to import much more than the barest essentials: industry has been starved of raw materials and spare parts, and the economy is running at a very depressed level. President Asad's policy of financing grand strategic designs from Arab aid has faltered. The aid is no longer flowing in sufficient quantities, and there are too few alternative sources of foreign exchange to fill the gap.[26]

The increase in the governmental budgetary deficits and the severe shortage of basic products, in parallel to the sharp devaluation of the LS, caused a price explosion during the years 1986–87. According to official Syrian figures, the consumer price index increased by 36 percent in 1986, and by 60 percent one year later, in 1987. However, according to unofficial estimates, the real inflation rate in each of these two years was more than 100 percent.[27] An IMF report published in February 1988 painted a gloomy picture of the economic situation in Syria during the mid-1980s, especially with regard to a sharp drop in foreign exchange reserves.[28] Two years later, in April 1990, the *New York Times* reported on the situation in the Syrian industrial sector:

> State-owned factories run at 40 percent of capacity because there is no foreign currency to buy spare parts. Two years ago, a plant manufacturing television sets simply closed because it could not afford imported components.[29]

The severe economic recession adversely affected the level of private consumption, with a continuous drop in the population's welfare. According to official figures, during the years 1981–89, the per capita GDP fell by approximately 20 percent in real terms. However, unofficial estimates indicate a much sharper decline in the real per capita GDP.[30] In 1989, the per capita GNP in Syria fell to only $890, compared with $1,670 (in current prices) seven years earlier, in 1982.[31] These developments soon found political expression in various displays of dissatisfaction with the economic deterioration, mainly the shortage of basic commodities such as sugar and coffee, and the rise in activity on the "black market," which led to escalating prices of basic consumer goods and foodstuff. In addition, as a result of shortages in electric power, five-hour power cuts were scheduled every day in the major cities, and the water supply was shut off at night.[32]

During the 1970s and the early 1980s, the Syrian government was able to allocate immense resources for military and security purposes and at the same time to achieve real economic growth and substantial improvement in the standard of living of the population. In the late 1980s, however, due to the steady shrinking of governmental revenues and foreign grants and loans, the negative effects of the high natural increase rates of the population came to the surface, and had an impact on both economic growth and the welfare level of the population. Thus, the economic crisis of the late 1980s was the combined result of the decline in oil prices after the end of the "oil decade" in the short run, and the negative consequences of the rapid population growth in the long run, in parallel to the huge costs of implementing the strategic balance policy.

Yet, in spite of the decrease in governmental revenues and the beginning of economic recession in 1983–84, the Syrian authorities continued to allocate sizable resources for military purposes and did not withdraw from the strategic balance policy. It seems that one of the major reasons for this decision was the Israeli invasion of Lebanon on June 6, 1982 and the direct confrontation between the Syrian and Israeli armies in Lebanon a few days later, which caused severe damage to the Syrian army, including the loss of 145 tanks and 100 aircraft.[33]

Finally, by the late 1980s, the Syrian authorities were obliged to recognize that they could not continue with the strategic balance policy because of its heavy socioeconomic and political costs. As a result, in June and October of 1987, the People's Assembly forced the resignation of four ministers. In November of that year, there were extensive cabinet changes, including the appointment of Mahmud al-Zu'bi to the office of Prime Minister. The first and most important mission of the new government was to reconstruct and revive the economy.[34] The newly appointed government began to enact revised social and economic policies. The first change was to limit the expenditures for military purposes in real terms, a process that has continued into the 1990s. While in 1985 the Syrian military expenditure was $5.432 billion, it declined to $3.563 billion (in current prices) ten years later, in 1995. In constant prices of 1995, the decline was from $7.445 billion to $3.563 billion, representing a reduction of more than 52 percent. Thus, the percentage of the Syrian GNP devoted to military expenditures declined from 21.8 percent to 7.2 percent during those years (see table 6.2). In terms of per capita, the military expenditure declined during that period from $709 to $236 (in constant prices of 1995). In 1996, according to the International Institute for Strategic Studies, Syrian military expenditure was $1.8 billion, representing approximately 11 percent of the GDP.[35]

The meaning of this policy change was clear: a delay, at least for the short term, in the implementation of the strategic balance policy. From the point of view of international politics, the Syrian withdrawal from the strategic balance policy reflected the realization of the Syrian leadership that the Soviet Union was not prepared to support and finance such a policy, despite the 1980 Soviet-Syrian Treaty of Friendship and Cooperation that guaranteed Soviet military support in case of direct

Table 6.2 Syrian military expenditures, 1985–96 ($US million)

Year	Military expenditures ($US million)		Arms imports ($US million)as		Military expenditures expenditures percentage of GNP	Per capita military ($US Constant 1995)
	Current	Constant 1995	Current	Constant 1996		
1985	5,432	7,445	1,500	..	21.8	709
1986	4,402	5,878	1,100	1,495	18.0	540
1987	2,880	3,727	2,000	2,635	11.7	330
1988	na	na	1,300	1,652	na	na
1989	3,748	4,491	1,100	1,342	14.3	370
1990	na	na	950	1,111	14.6	400
1991	na	na	800	900	na	na
1992	na	na	390	427	na	na
1993	na	na	270	288	na	na
1994	na	na	50	52	na	na
1995	3,563	3,563	110	112	7.2	236
1996	na	na	90	90	na	na

na = no data available

Source: United States Arms Control and Disarmament Agency (ACDA), *World Military Expenditures and Arms Transfers, 1996* (Washington, D.C., 1997), pp. 93, 144, tables, I and II; *1997*, p. 53, table II.

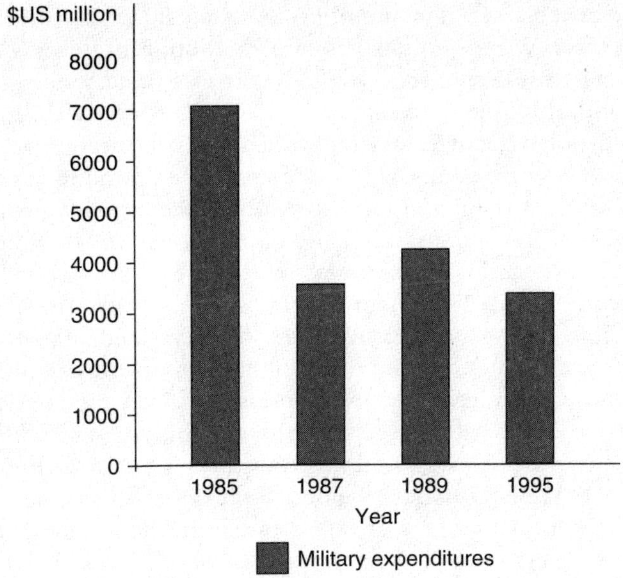

Figure 6.3 Syrian military expenditures, 1985–95
($US million – constant prices of 1995)

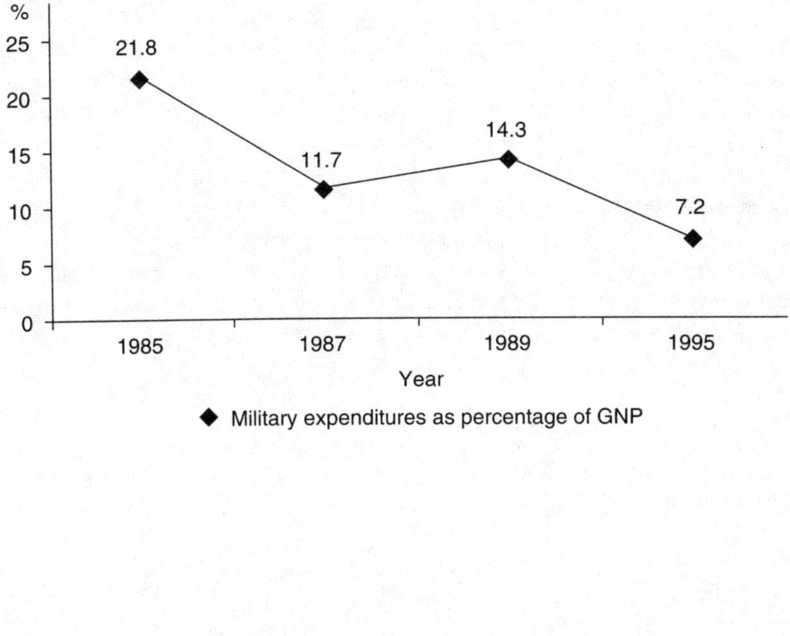

aggression against Syria.[36] Furthermore, the gradual withdrawal of the Soviet Union from world politics brought the Syrian authorities to the unavoidable conclusion that they would have to contend with the West, particularly with the United States.[37]

The second policy change was the decision of the Syrian leadership to adopt more direct measures in the field of family planning in order to achieve a substantial reduction in fertility levels. After a long period of time during which the Syrian authorities operated pro-natalist measures in order to achieve rapid population growth – among other things, to supply the heavy demands of manpower of the Syrian army and the various security units – they cancelled the financial and other benefits given to large families in 1987. At the same time, the Ministry of Health appealed to young families through the mass media to use family planning methods, and the range of activities of the Syrian Family Planning Association was widened. In addition, from the early 1990s, the Syrian authorities started to use official religious figures in order to convince the Muslim population that there were no Islamic restrictions against the use of contraceptives, a step that they had hesitated to take until then, mainly for internal political reasons.[38]

The shift of priorities in the allocation of resources from military purposes to socioeconomic development was accompanied by reforms in the economic policy, primarily through opening more fields to private sector activities; conducting trade reforms and adjusting the exchange rate of the LS; and reducing subsidies for basic commodities. It seems that the discussions and decisions of the Eighth Regional Congress of the Syrian Ba‘th party, held in January 1985, constituted the first step in changing Syrian economic policy. The final communique of the congress concluded with a sharp criticism of economic performance in the public sector and a call for increasing incentives for private sector investments in the Syrian economy.[39] Specifically, the first steps in the new economic reform consisted of Decision No. 186 (1985) to encourage private sector investment in tourism, and Law No. 10 (1986) to encourage the establishment of joint-venture agricultural companies.[40]

In addition to the economic crisis, the collapse of Communism in the late 1980s also influenced the decision-makers in Syria to increase the role of the private sector in overall economic activities. As Raymond Hinnebusch noted:

> The collapse of the communism has not only accelerated the ideological crisis, but, in threatening to deprive the public sector of East European aid, technology and export markets, further undermines the viability of statism.[41]

It seems that the decision of Asad to join the anti-Iraqi coalition during the 1990–91 Gulf crisis was also part of this new approach in policy. The crisis gave Syria the opportunity to support the West at a time when the US needed an alliance of Arab countries against Iraq. Syria was the first Arab country to condemn the Iraqi invasion of Kuwait. From the outbreak of the crisis, the Syrian regime supported the relevant UN Resolutions, including Resolution 678, which authorized the use of force against Iraq.[42] In exchange for sending about 20,000 troops to Saudi Arabia, Syria won significant economic benefits and, at the same time, considerable political advantage, both in the international arena and in the Arab world.

The large sum of cash that it received from the Gulf oil-exporting countries enabled Syria to re-equip its armed forces with modern aircraft, tanks and long-range missiles; to build power stations in order to overcome the chronic electricity shortage; to establish a working telephone network; and to improve water and waste-water facilities.[43] The total sum of cash that Syria received from the Gulf oil-exporting countries during the years 1977–94 amounted to almost $18 billion, of which more than $3 billion was received during the years 1991–94.[44] The $1.15 billion surplus in the Syrian balance of payments in 1991 was the outcome of the aid which Syria received from Saudi Arabia and its allies in the Gulf as payment for joining the anti-Iraqi coalition in the 1990–91 Gulf crisis.[45]

In addition to the aid which Syria received from the Gulf oil-exporting countries during the early 1990s, the Syrian economy also benefited from a sharp rise in oil revenues, caused by the increase in production to 600,000 b/d (barrel per day) in early 1996, from less than 200,000 b/d at the beginning of the 1980s. This level of production, it must be noted, is higher than that of Qatar and almost equal to that of Oman. As a result of such high production levels, governmental financial resources skyrocketed during the early 1990s,[46] when oil exports of 320,000 b/d gave Syria more than 60 percent of its export earnings.[47]

Moreover, in comparison to Jordan and, to a lesser extent Yemen – which were at the same time both labor-exporting and labor-importing countries – Syria adopted a wise labor migration policy during the 1970s and 1980s. The Syrian authorities conducted a selective migration policy, while temporary migration for employment purposes was allowed for unskilled and semi-skilled workers, in whom the government did not invest large sums of money for education and professional training. However, at the same time, heavy restrictions were placed on the migration of the most professional and skilled workers, in whose education and professional training the government did invest a considerable amount. Thus, their skills were put to work in the Syrian labor market for the implementation of national socioeconomic development plans.[48] Overall, during the 1970s and 1980s, the percentage of migrants from the total Syrian labor force amounted to only a few percent, as compared with tens of percent in Jordan and Yemen.[49] Consequently, throughout the first half of the 1990s, while Jordan and Yemen were occupied with the reconstruction of their economies and absorption of hundreds of thousands of returning workers and their accompanying family members, Syria did not have to deal with this overwhelming problem and was free to concentrate on the development of its economy and infrastructure facilities.

The increasing revenues from oil exports, accompanied by the financial support of the Gulf countries, in parallel to a wise migration policy during the 1970s and 1980s, brought about a renewal of economic growth in Syria during the first half of the 1990s. During the years 1990–94, GDP growth rates were extremely high – almost 7 percent annually on average.[50] By 1995, the GDP had increased by another 6 percent.[51] In that year, the per capita income was estimated at just under $1,000.[52] One year later, in 1996, the per capita GDP (at current prices) was estimated at almost $1,300. In comparison with the per capita GDP of $618 in 1988, this represents an increase of more than 100 percent during a period of only eight years (see table 6.3).[53] No less important than the renewal of economic growth, in terms of liberalization of the economy, was a rise in the rate of investments. By 1996, the GFCF in Syria was $5.6 billion, compared with less than one billion in 1988.[54] Also notable in this regard was the growth of the relative share of the private sector in total investments in the Syrian economy. In 1990, for the first time after the March 1963 Ba'th revolution, private sector capital investments were higher than those of the public sector.[55]

Investment Law No. 10 of May 1991 was intended to encourage investment by both the domestic and foreign private sector, especially with capital held by Syrians abroad. The law offers various bonuses to private investors, the most important being a tax exemption for 5–9 years, and exemptions from other taxes related to projects which have been approved within the framework of the law. Project applications must follow the overall development plans and incorporate a large local component and work force. Furthermore, the applications have to be export-oriented or promote import-substituting industrialization. The law also allows the formation of private joint stock companies for the first time in Syria since the "Socialist Rules" of July 1961. In addition, investors under Law No. 10 are exempted from the foreign exchange regulations initiated by Law No. 24 (1986). Accordingly, investors can open foreign exchange accounts and can also retain 75 percent of their export earnings for their own import or reinvestment requirements. The

Table 6.3 Syria: per capita Gross Domestic Product, 1988–97 (current prices, $US)

Year	Per capita GDP ($US)
1988	617.9
1989	645.0
1990	775.7
1991	845.8
1992	951.5
1993	1,020.2
1994	1,177.4
1995	1,229.4
1996*	1,289.5
1997*	1,370.5

Notes: * According to ESCWA estimates

Source: ESCWA, *National Accounts Studies of the ESCWA Region*, Bulletin No. 17 (New York, 1997), p. 9.

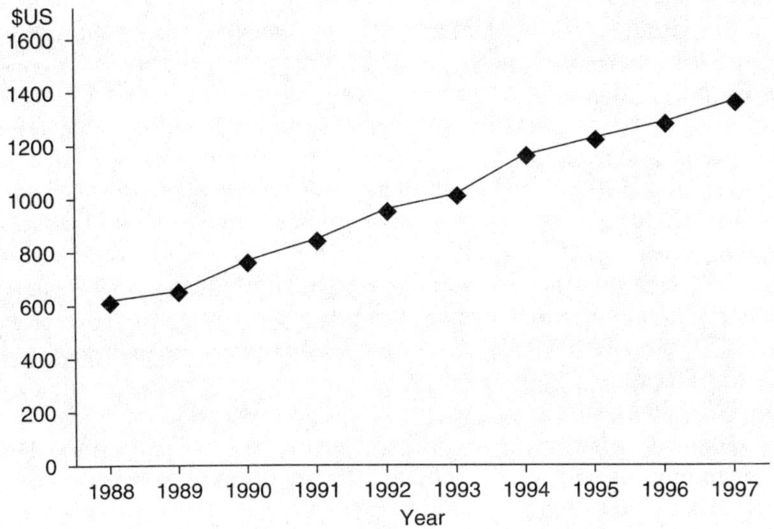

Figure 6.5 Syria: per capita gross domestic product, 1988–97 (current prices, $US)

remaining 25 percent must be turned over to the Commercial Bank of Syria at the rate of "neighboring countries."[56]

By September 1995, a total number of 1,251 projects had been approved at a planned investment of $5.5 billion. These projects would provide almost 90,000 new jobs.[57] At the end of November 1996, the number of projects approved by the Higher Council of Investment reached 1,457 with a planned investment of $8.65 billion.[58] Almost half of these projects were in the production and processing of chemicals, and another 30 percent were in the storing, packing, and processing of agricultural and other food products.[59] Despite these incentives, the United States Embassy Investment Climate Statement noted at the beginning of 1996 that only a small percentage of approved projects had even begun construction, much less operation.[60]

In addition, the banking sector, which was nationalized during the early 1960s along with many other private companies within the framework of the Ba'th socialist approach,[61] is still a state monopoly and is likely to remain so, at least in the foreseeable future. A reopening of the private banking system would enable the smaller and medium-sized local entrepreneurs to gain financing in Syria, which is currently almost impossible.[62]

Despite the difficulties, the scale of imports to Syria increased sharply as a result of the May 1991 Investment Law, reaching more than $5 billion for the first time, in 1995. However, even with the rapid increase in imports, Syria's account balance did not reflect concurrent high deficits. This was due to the parallel rise in the scale of exports, based primarily in three areas. The first was the oil export of about 400,000 b/d.[63] The second was the steady increase in receipts from the tourism industry, growing on average of 7 percent annually during the years 1985–95. By 1995, the total Syrian receipts from tourism had reached $1 billion,[64] as compared with only $204 million in 1987.[65] The third component consisted of the remittances of Syrians working abroad, many of them in neighboring Lebanon and, in smaller numbers, in Jordan and the GCC countries. These provided the additional funds required to meet local businesses' foreign exchange needs.[66]

It must be emphasized that despite of the liberalization measures, the Syrian economy still remains by and large state-controlled. The Syrian business community is now pressing for the abolition of Syria's multiple exchange rate system, under which many import items are priced at LS 11.2 to one $US, while the real rate in the open market is more than four times this amount.[67] In addition, they are pushing the government to establish a private banking system and to create a local stock exchange.[68] However, the Syrian government is insisting on the initial establishment of more shareholder-owned companies prior to initiating a stock exchange.[69]

Similar to other countries in the region, Syria has a substantial external debt, which amounted to approximately $16 billion at the end of 1994.[70] The largest component of the debt, more than 80 percent, is owed to the former Soviet Union. While this is unlikely to ever be paid in full, efforts are being made to reach an agreement on part of the debt.[71] In 1994, the Russian government offered to write off $9 billion of this debt if Syria repaid $3 billion. However, the Syrian government rejected the Russian proposal. It seems that the Syrian government was waiting for an offer of a complete write-off, either through the Middle East peace process or through the advent of time.[72] One Syrian analyst noted in early 1995: "Why should Egypt and Jordan have their debts written off and Syria be expected to pay theirs? It will be part and package of the deal."[73] David Lesch suggested that the debt issue between Russia and Syria was settled in the fall of 1998 when a Russian Defense Ministry delegation visited Syria. It seems that Syria will repay at least part of the debt in return for a rekindling of the arms relationship with Russia.[74]

However, more contentious is the $1.5 billion in arrears on Syria's debts to its main trading partners, namely, Japan, Germany, France, and other EU (European Union) countries. The Syrian government has held discussions with its creditors regarding this problem, but no solution has been reached.[75] The largest single creditor among these is Germany, which is owed approximately $900 million. Germany has taken over $500 million in principal from former East Germany. However, the Syrian government contests Germany's claim on it.[76] The failure of the Syrian government to fulfill its debt obligations means that its ability to secure future credit from sources other than the Gulf countries was limited. However, Syria's debt repayment deal with France in late 1996 was sure to boost its credibility, and relations with the World Bank and the IMF were set to improve after Syria began to pay off its $562 million World Bank debt in September 1997.[77] A lump of $270 million has already been paid, and the rest of the debt is to be paid in small monthly instalments.[78]

During the early 1990s, this set of developments engendered several economic and social outcomes in Syria. First and foremost, the level of private income and expenditure on consumption commodities began to increase. Imports of durable consumer goods increased by tens of percent. Moreover, an improvement in public services became clearly discernible. The population of Syria come to expect that the amelioration in its standard of living would continue.[79] However, the realization of such expectations demands a broader and more comprehensive application of the government's liberalization policy – in other words, opening the door to large investments by both domestic and foreign private sectors.[80]

It seems that one of the greatest dilemmas facing the Syrian leadership since the mid-1980s has been how to continue to uphold economic growth and privatization measures, while simultaneously adhering to the fundamentals of the political regime, which has hardly undergone any reforms since Asad came to power and thus continues to sustain its autocratic characteristics. Are economic liberalization and democratization simply two sides of the same coin? Is it possible to manage economic liberalization and privatization, including a private banking system and establishment of a stock exchange, in parallel to opening the country to millions of tourists every year, and at the same time to sustain the autocratic characteristics of the regime, without any changes in or participation by the private sector?

Volker Perthes has noted that: "Economic liberalization and private sector growth will not necessarily bring about democratization."[81] This is true, but to a limited extent. It is possible to increase the role, as well as the share, of the private sector in the economy without introducing fundamental changes in the basic autocratic characteristics of the regime, as evidenced in the Syrian case since the late 1980s. However, beyond a certain point (which changes according to the given socioeconomic conditions and political characteristics of each country), economic liberalization also requires taking some steps toward democratization, as proven by the experience of other Arab countries, such as Egypt. This is seemingly one, if not the major reason for Syria's slow steps toward economic reforms. The authorities fear that rapid economic reforms and fundamental structural changes could lead to social consequences that might threaten the continued stability of the current regime. Peter Kiernan noted in this regard that:

> Unlike some other Arab states, the country [Syria] is unlikely to undergo a rapid transformation toward a market oriented economy, for fears of risking political and social instability, which the regime of Hafiz al-Asad wants to avoid at all cost.[82]

The peace process between Syria and Israel touches on most of the economic and social variables mentioned above. It was, on the one hand, an outcome of the dismantling of the strategic balance policy, as well as a consequence of public pressure to bring about an improvement in the standard of living. On the other hand, it was one of the major levers for returning the Syrian economy to steady and rapid growth during the first half of the 1990s, which affected both the shape and the pace of

Syrian–Israeli peace negotiations. Egypt, the Palestinians, and Jordan all entered into peace negotiations with Israel when their economies were in such a severe situation that the economic recession clearly constituted a real danger to the continuation of the existing regimes. Heba Handoussa and Nemat Shafik claimed that: "Economic motives played an important part in Egypt's decision to sign a peace treaty – the country was facing a severe balance-of-payments crisis. Attempts to encourage private investment were floundering, and appeals for more aid were unrequited."[83] Boutros Boutros-Ghali, who served as the Egyptian Minister of State for Foreign Affairs, wrote that at the first meeting with his Israeli counterparts (Yigal Yadin and Ezer Weizman) in November 1977, "I described the effect of the population explosion on economic and social conditions in Egypt. Egypt, I said, needed peace so that it could confront its urgent economic and social issues. I wanted to convince the two Israeli ministers of the sincerity of the Egyptian quest for peace."[84] Thus, in order to achieve Egypt's economic goals, Sadat was willing to sign a separate peace treaty with Israel, which carried a heavy price, including the suspension of Egypt from the Arab League.

In the case of Jordan, the authorities had to face a variety of obstacles in addition to the severe economic recession of the late 1980s: the return of approximately 350,000 Jordanian citizens from the Gulf countries (the vast majority of them from Kuwait) and the loss of their remittances; the economic sanctions against Iraq (which, until the invasion of Kuwait, had constituted a lucrative market for Jordanian commodities); the elimination of aid from the Gulf oil-exporting countries; the huge external debt; and the increasing difficulties in obtaining loans in the international financial markets, due to Jordan's support of Iraq during the Gulf crisis. As a result, by the end of 1991, the official unemployment rate in Jordan skyrocketed to 23 percent, compared with less than 10 percent prior to the Gulf crisis.[85] As a result, the per capita GNP fell by more than 50 percent to $1,060 in 1991, compared with $2,250 only four years earlier, in 1987.[86] Clearly, the peace agreement with Israel in October 1994 not only improved the position of Jordan in international politics, particularly with the US, but also enabled Jordan to reschedule a substantial part of its foreign debt and to gain financial aid in order to revive its economy.[87]

The Palestinians faced a similar situation in the early 1990s due to Yasir 'Arafat's support of Iraq during the 1990/91 Gulf crisis. Not only were the vast majority of the Palestinians who were living in Kuwait prior to the Iraqi invasion expelled, but the generous financial aid previously provided by the Gulf countries was severely curtailed, making it extremely difficult for the PLO to fulfill its many financial obligations. This heavy financial burden, in parallel to the sharp deterioration in relations with both the international political system and the Arab world, forced the Palestinians to conclude an agreement with Israel within a short period of time, as well as to withdraw from some of their very basic demands.

In contrast, Syria, due to its improved economic situation in the first half of the 1990s, was able to manage slow negotiations with Israel and to insist on all of its basic demands, in the absence of economic pressure to conclude an agreement within a short period of time.[88] Moreover, in the previous peace negotiations between Israel and other Arab countries, the former was in a better position, due mainly to its superior economic situation which provided for increased leverage. In contrast, within the framework of the peace negotiations between Israel and Syria, the former is under greater pressure to conclude a final agreement within a relatively short period of time. This is primarily a result of the war in south Lebanon, which demands a very high price in loss of life, paralleled to the wide recognition in Israel that the Lebanese problem cannot be solved without Syria, which acts as the real authority in Lebanon.

However, over the period 1997/98, the rate of economic growth in Syria has slowed down. The main reason for this is the sharp decline in oil prices due to the drop in demand for oil by Asian countries, which is pushing the prices down. Since oil is the largest source of foreign currency in Syria, the decline in oil prices is adversely affecting the Syrian balance of trade in a period when the economy has already been slowing down, partly as a result of diminishing prospects for an Israeli-Syrian peace agreement in the foreseeable future. In addition, the decline in oil prices has led to cutbacks in the aid which Syria was used to receiving from the Gulf oil-exporting countries in the past. Thus, while the GDP growth was 6.7 percent in 1995, it fell to only 2 percent in 1996–97 on annually average, meaning decrease in terms of per capita.[89]

During the last decade, it seems that one of the major socioeconomic challenges of the Syrian authorities is how to produce large numbers of work opportunities in the productive sectors for the young generation. In the late 1990s, the number of new jobs needed for the graduates of secondary schools and higher education institutions in Syria was estimated at 140,000–200,000 annually. It seems now that economic growth rates will not meet the need and that if these rates continue at current levels, then the likelihood of rising unemployment rates in the future increases accordingly.[90]

However, in spite of the reduction in the economic growth rates during the past two years and the continuing of rapid population growth, it seems that Syria has good chances to overcome its socioeconomic problems, considering the demographic-economic factors and the scale of available natural resources, namely, agricultural land, water and oil. The core of

Syria's problems in this arena lies in its misguided allocation of resources and the wide base of its age pyramid, which has led to low rates of labor force participation and, thus, low per capita income. However, due to the steady reduction of fertility levels since the late 1980s, the wide base of the age pyramid is gradually narrowing, while the percentage of the population in the working age groups is steadily increasing. This process, which seems likely to continue in the coming years as well, combined with the steady improvement in women's educational level, will eventually bring about an increase in the overall rates of Syrian labor force participation, along with an increase in per capita income. At the same time, economic reforms must be continued in order to increase private investments, and in so doing, to multiply the number of work opportunities in the productive sectors to the point that high rates of both open and disguised unemployment can be avoided in the future. Without taking these measures, there is a growing danger that Syria will drop into the "population trap."

Today, it seems that there is no longer any doubt that during the last decade the Syrian economy has succeeded in implementing substantial structural economic changes, albeit limited in comparison to those that took place in Egypt during the latter part of the 1970s and throughout the 1980s. There is almost complete unanimity that the potential of the Syrian economy is enormous, especially in the fields of agriculture, light industry, oil, transport, and, in particular, tourism. It remains to be seen whether the Syrian regime will be able to utilize the country's high economic potential in the coming years, and how the economic situation in Syria will affect both the shape and the pace of Syrian–Israeli peace negotiations.

Notes

This chapter is based on the author's book: *Demographic Developments and Population Policies in Ba'thist Syria* (Brighton and Portland, 1999).

1 Rizkallah Hilan, "The Effects on Economic Development in Syria of a Just and Long-Lasting Peace," in Stanley Fischer, Dani Rodrik, and Elias Tuma (eds), *The Economics of Middle East Peace* (Cambridge and London, 1993), p. 61 [hereafter: Hilan, "The Effects on Economic Development in Syria;" and Fischer et al. (eds), *The Economics of Middle East Peace*]; see also: Moshe Ma'oz, *Syria and Israel: From War to Peace Making* (Or Yehuda, 1996), pp. 162–66 (in Hebrew) [hereafter: Ma'oz, *Syria and Israel*].

2 Gad G. Gilbar, *The Economic Development of the Middle East in Modern Times* (Tel Aviv, 1990), pp. 204–5 (in Hebrew) [hereafter: Gilbar, *The Economic Development of the Middle East*]; see also: Hilan, "The Effects on Economic Development in Syria," p. 60, table 3.1.

3 United States Arms Control and Disarmament Agency (ACDA), *World Military Expenditures and Arms Transfers, 1972–1982* (Washington, D.C., April 1984), p. 88, table II.

4 "Syria's Budget: Where the Cash Flows in '87," *The Middle East* (May 1987), p. 33; see also: Alan George, "Syria – An Economic Saved by Circumstances," *The Middle East* (December 1988), p. 27 [hereafter: *The Middle East* (December 1988)]; *Financial Times* (London), January 4, 1989, p. 3; *MEED*, May 28, 1982, p. 44.

5 *Financial Times*, June 2, 1986, p. 5.

6 *Financial Times*, December 8, 1986, p. 4.

7 The International Institute for Strategic Studies, *The Military Balance, 1988–1989* (London, 1989), pp. 334–25, table 4.

8 Gilbar, *The Economic Development of the Middle East*, p. 204; Moshe Ma'oz, *Asad – The Sphinx of Damascus: A Political Biography* (Tel Aviv, 1988), p. 193 (in Hebrew).

9 *Financial Times*, December 8, 1986, p. 4.

10 See, e. g., Syria, *Statistical Abstract-1990,* p. 51, table 1/2.

11 ESCWA, *Population Situation in the ESCWA Region, 1990* (Amman? 1992), p. 190, table 11.8.

12 ILO (International Labour Office), *Yearbook of Labour Statistics-1994* (Geneva, 1995), pp. 22–23, table 1.

13 Syria, *Statistical Abstract-1966*, p. 283, table 142; *1995*, p. 104, table 6/4.

14 Syria, *Statistical Abstract-1994*, p. 63, table 11/2.

15 Nabil Sukkar, "The Crisis of 1986 and Syria's Plan for Reform," in Eberhard Kienle (ed.), *Contemporary Syria: Liberalization between Cold War and Cold Peace* (London and New York, 1994), p. 27 [hereafter: Sukkar, "The Crisis of 1986 and Syria's Plan for Reform;" and Kienle (ed.), *Contemporary Syria*]; idem, "Economic Liberalization in Syria," in Hans Hopfinger (ed.), *Economic Liberalization and Privatization in Socialist Arab Countries: Algeria, Egypt, Syria and Yemen as Examples* (Gotha, 1996), p. 147 [hereafter: Sukkar, "Economic Liberalization in Syria"].

16 Regarding the resolutions of the November 1978 Baghdad Arab Summit, see: Avraham Sela, *Unity within Conflict in the Inter-Arab System: The Arab Summit Conferences, 1964–1982* (Jerusalem, 1983), pp. 159–80 (in Hebrew).

17 Alasdair Drysdale, "The Asad Regime and its Troubles," *Merip Reports*, Vol. 12, No. 9 (November/December 1982), p. 5; *MEED*, May 22, 1981, p. 38.

18 See, e.g., World Bank, *World Tables*, 1995 edition, pp. 650–51. Regarding the effects of the October 1973 "oil boom" on the Syrian economy, see, e.g., Eliyahu Kanovsky, "Middle East Economies and Arab-Israeli Peace Agreements," *Israel Affairs*, Vol. 1, No. 4 (Summer 1995), p. 28 [hereafter: Kanovsky, "Middle East Economies and Arab-Israeli Peace Agreements"].

19 World Bank, *World Tables*, 1989–90 edition, pp. 544–45.

20 *The Economist* (London), May 3, 1986, p. 51.

21 Raymond A. Hinnebusch, "Syria," in Tim Niblock and Emma Murphy (eds), *Economic and Political Liberalization in the Middle East* (London and New York, 1993), p. 188 [hereafter: Hinnebusch, "Syria"].

22 See: *MEED*, May 1, 1985, p. 34; April 11, 1987, p. 36. A discussion on the Syrian official and unofficial exchange rates appears in: Onn Winckler, *Demographic Developments and Population Policies in Ba'thist Syria* (Brighton and Portland 1999), pp. 105–8 [hereafter: Winckler, *Demographic*

Developments].
23 Sukkar, "The Crisis of 1986 and Syria's Plan for Reform," p. 27.
24 *MEED*, April 11, 1987, p. 36; November 14, 1987, p. 49.
25 *Al-Hayat* (London), January 26, 1992.
26 *MEED*, November 14, 1987, p. 49.
27 Sukkar, "The Crisis of 1986 and Syria's Plan for Reform," p. 28; see also: *Financial Times*, December 8, 1986, p. 4.
28 *Financial Times*, May 6, 1988, p. 3; Sukkar, "The Crisis of 1986 and Syria's Plan for Reform," p. 28; Volker Perthes, "The Private Sector, Economic Liberalization, and the Prospects of Democratization: The Case of Syria and some Other Arab Countries," in Ghassan Salamé (ed.), *Democracy Without Democrats? The Renewal of Politics in the Muslim World* (London and New York, 1994), p. 245 [hereafter: Perthes, "The Private Sector, Economic Liberalization, and the Prospects of Democratization"].
29 *The New York Times Magazine*, April 1, 1990, p. 33; see also: *Financial Times*, January 4, 1989, p. 3.
30 Kanovsky, "Middle East Economies and Arab-Israeli Peace Agreements," p. 29.
31 World Bank, *World Tables*, 1995 edition, p. 649.
32 See: *Financial Times*, December 8, 1986, p. 4.
33 Ma'oz, *Syria and Israel*, p. 157; see also: Ze'ev Shif and Ehud Ya'ari, *Milhemet Sholal* [The Misleading War] (Tel Aviv, 1984), pp. 203–4 (in Hebrew).
34 *The Middle East* (December 1988), p. 27.
35 EIU, *Country Profile-Syria, 1997–98*, p. 8.
36 Regarding to the October 1980 Soviet-Syrian Treaty of Friendship and Cooperation, see: Galia Golan, *Soviet Policies in the Middle East from World War Two to Gorbachev* (Cambridge and New York, 1991), pp. 153–55; Robert O. Freedman, *Moscow and the Middle East: Soviet Policy since the Invasion of Afghanistan* (Cambridge and New York, 1991), pp. 92–93.
37 See: Volker Perthes, "Incremental Change in Syria," *Current History*, Vol. 92 (1993), p. 24 [hereafter: Perthes, "Incremental Change in Syria"].
38 See the discussion on the Syrian natalist policies in: Winckler, *Demographic Developments*, pp. 109–18.
39 Yahya M. Sadowski, "Cadres, Guns, and Money: The Eight Regional Congress of the Syrian Ba'th," *Merip Reports* (July/August 1985), p. 6.
40 Alan George, "No Going Back," *The Middle East* (November 1996), p. 20. [hereafter: *The Middle East* (November 1996)]; on Law No. 10 of 1986, see, e.g., Sylvia Pölling, "Investment Law No. 10: Which Future for the Private Sector?" in Kienle (ed.), *Contemporary Syria*, pp. 15–19 [hereafter: Pölling, "Investment Law No. 10"].
41 Hinnebusch, "Syria," pp. 188–89.
42 Eberhard Kienle, "Syria, the Kuwait War, and the New World Order," in Tarek Y. Ismael and Jacqueline S. Ismael (eds), *The Gulf War and the New World Order* (Gainesville, 1994), p. 385.
43 *MEED*, September 29, 1995, p. 10.
44 *MEED*, November 18, 1994, p. 10.
45 *The Jerusalem Post*, January 21, 1992.
46 *MEED*, September 29, 1995, p. 12; February 9, 1996, p. 2; *Ha'aretz* (Tel Aviv), September 9, 1992.

47 *Jordan Times* (Amman), April 11–12, 1996.
48 On the Syrian labor migration policy, see: Onn Winckler, "Syrian Migration to the Arab Oil-producing Countries," *Middle Eastern Studies*, Vol. 33, No. 1 (1997), pp. 113–17.
49 See, e.g., Ismail Serageldin, James A. Socknat, Stace Birks, Boy Li, and Clive A. Sinclair, *Manpower and International Labor Migration in the Middle East and North Africa* (Oxford and New York, 1983), p. 72, table 8.2. On the phenomenon of replacement migration in the Middle East, see: Ian J. Seccombe, "Immigrant Workers in an Emigrant Economy: An Examination of Replacement Migration in the Middle East," *International Migration*, Vol. XXIV, No. 2 (June 1986), pp. 377–403; Onn Winckler, *Population Growth and Migration in Jordan, 1950–1994* (Brighton, 1997), pp. 64–68.
50 *MEED*, May 24, 1996, p. 7.
51 ESCWA, *Survey of Economic and Social Developments in the ESCWA Region-1995* (New York, 1996), p. 27.
52 *MEED*, February 9, 1996, p. 2.
53 See also: *Jordan Times*, June 13–14, 1996.
54 ESCWA, *National Accounts Studies of the ESCWA Region*, Bulletin No. 17 (New York, 1997), p. 15.
55 Perthes, "The Private Sector, Economic Liberalization, and the Prospects of Democratization," p. 249.
56 Pölling, "Investment Law No. 10," p. 20; Sukkar, "Economic Liberalization in Syria," p. 148; *The Wall Street Journal* (New York), January 4, 1994; *Financial Times*, July 28, 1995, p. 16.
57 *MEED*, September 29, 1995, p. 14; see also: "Syria: Secretive Power Play," *The Middle East* (January 1994), p. 32; Mariam Shahin, "Syria-Secret to the Economic Future," *The Middle East* (February 1995), pp. 27–28 [hereafter: *The Middle East* (February 1995)].
58 *Yedi'ot Aharonot* (Tel Aviv), November 27, 1996.
59 *MEED*, September 29, 1995, p. 14. See also: Lesch's and Efrat's chapters in this volume.
60 *The Middle East* (November 1996), p. 20. See also: Glenn E. Robinson, "Elite Cohesion, Regime Succession and Political Instability in Syria," *Middle East Policy*, Vol. 5, No. 4 (January 1998), p. 162.
61 See, e.g., Ziad Keilany, "Socialism and Economic Change in Syria," *Middle Eastern Studies*, Vol. 9 (1973), pp. 61–72.
62 *The Middle East* (February 1995), p. 28.
63 *MEED*, May 24, 1996, p. 8.
64 *Jordan Times*, May 7, 1996.
65 World Tourism Organization, *Yearbook of Tourism Statistics-1990*, 43rd edition (Madrid, 1991), p. 113.
66 *MEED*, May 24, 1996, p. 8; see also: November 18, 1994, p. 8.
67 *The Middle East* (November 1996), p. 20.
68 *MEED*, February 9, 1996, p. 2.
69 *The Wall Street Journal*, November 7, 1996.
70 *MEED*, September 29, 1995, p. 10.
71 *MEED*, May 24, 1996, p. 8.
72 EIU, *Country Profile–Syria, 1997–98*, p. 32; see also: *MEED*, November 18, 1994, p. 10.
73 *The Middle East* (February 1995), pp. 28–29.

74 See Lesch's chapter in this volume, p. 75, note 12.
75 *MEED*, September 29, 1995, p. 11.
76 EIU, *Country Profile–Syria, 1998–99*, p. 29.
77 EIU, *Country Profile–Syria, 1997–98*, p. 32; *MEED*, September 29, 1995, pp. 10–11; November 18, 1994, p. 10.
78 EIU, *Country Profile–Syria, 1998–99*, p. 30.
79 See, e.g., *MEED*, October 8, 1993, p. 3.
80 On the distribution among the private and the public sectors in the Syrian various economic activities by mid-1996, see: *Jordan Times*, June 13–14, 1996.
81 Perthes, "The Private Sector, Economic Liberalization, and the Prospects of Democratization," p. 268.
82 Peter Kiernan, "Syria's Economic Dilemma," *The Middle East* (March 1999), p. 35.
83 Heba Handoussa and Nemat Shafik, "The Economics of Peace: The Egyptian Case," in Fischer et al. (eds), *The Economics of Middle East Peace*, p. 19. See also: Gilbar, *The Economic Development of the Middle East*, pp. 197–202.
84 Boutros Boutros-Ghali, *Egypt's Road to Jerusalem: A Diplomat's Story of the Struggle for Peace in the Middle East* (New York, 1997), p. 23.
85 *Jordan Times*, October 14, 1991.
86 World Bank, *World Tables*, 1995 edition, p. 385.
87 Onn Winckler, "The Economic Factor of the Middle East Peace Process: The Jordanian Case," in Joseph Ginat and Onn Winckler (eds), *The Jordanian-Palestinian-Israeli Triangle: Smoothing the Path to Peace* (Brighton and Portland, 1998), pp. 156–77.
88 On the Syrian–Israeli peace negotiations during the years 1992–96, see: Itamar Rabinovich, *The Brink of Peace: Israel & Syria, 1992–1996* (Tel Aviv, 1998, in Hebrew).
89 EIU, *Country Profile – Syria, 1998–99*, pp. 13, 33, reference table 3.
90 A report of Reuters from Damascus dated July 19, 1998.

Part III

Socio-Demographic Aspects

7

The Question of Citizenship of the Algerian Immigrants in Syria, 1847–1900

Ş. Tufan Buzpınar

Algeria was under Ottoman rule from the first quarter of the sixteenth century until the 1830s. In July 1830, French forces occupied Algiers and the areas nearby without encountering significant resistance, though unexpected resistance led by Amir 'Abd al-Qader al-Jazairi (1807–83) began in November 1832. It ended in December 1847 when Amir 'Abd al-Qader surrendered, with his 15 years of struggle against the French over, leaving the French in complete control of the country.[1] Thereafter, many Algerians refused to live under French rule and began leaving Algeria. The overwhelming majority of the immigrants who left Algeria between 1847 and 1900 settled in towns and villages in Syria. In this chapter, the question of citizenship of the Algerian immigrants in the Ottoman Syrian province will be examined, based primarily on Ottoman documents.

The first group of Algerians to apply in 1847 to the French authorities in Algeria for permission to leave the country was one headed by Ahmad b. Salim, 'Abd al-Qader's *Khalifa* in Hamza, east of Algiers.[2] His first application received no response, but Ahmad b. Salim insisted that he and his followers were determined to leave Algeria. In the end, French Marshal Bugeaud officially informed the group that they were free to choose to live either in Algeria or in the East.[3]

By the term "East," both sides apparently meant Syria. In fact, Syria suited both the French and the Algerians. For the French, having Algerians in Syria could mean being able to increase their influence, and for the Algerians, Syria was the only fertile Arab land available for settlement.

Thus, late in 1847, 560 Algerian immigrants arrived in Syria under the leadership of Ahmad b. Salim. In principle, the authorities in Syria were ready to accept the immigrants, seeing them as Ottoman subjects "moving from one Ottoman province to another." However, one thing needed to be clarified before deciding the future of the immigrants: the question of their citizenship. First of all, the military and civil authorities in the province wanted to know whether the immigrants possessed French citizenship or any other official link that might be used by the French as a pretext to intervene in the internal affairs of the province. Hence, they obtained the authorization documents of the immigrants translated from Arabic into Ottoman Turkish. Upon closer examination, there was nothing found to indicate any links to the French. Although this was a point in the immigrants' favor, it was apparently not enough to satisfy the Ottoman authorities in Syria. In order to prevent any future links with the French, the authorities requested that the immigrants present a written promise to the effect that they and their descendants would retain Ottoman citizenship and not apply for foreign protection under any circumstances, as well as carry out all their obligations as Ottoman citizens.

At the first meeting of the Provincial Council, attended by the military authorities and some of the 'ulama and *shaykhs*, including *Shaykh* Ahmad b. Salim who was representing the immigrants, the representatives of the immigrants were asked to present their case. They were then informed of the above-mentioned conditions, which were accepted without hesitation. At a second meeting, held at the military headquarters in Damascus, all of the adult male immigrants signed a written promise and gave it to the Council.[4] Since all of the requirements put forth by the authorities had been met, the Council decided on January 12, 1848 that the state should provide the expenses for about thirty 'ulama and shaykhs, as well as for some poor people, and that the rest of the immigrants should be settled in the *sanjak* (sub-district) of 'Ajlun as farmers. For those who were unable to obtain the basics for farming, allowances of 120,000 Ottoman kuruş were proposed.[5] 'Ajlun was chosen for two reasons: first, because it was remote from the Mediterranean coast and thus was relatively safe from foreign infiltration and second, because there was vast arable state land available. By offering 'Ajlun, the Ottoman authorities were able to utilize state land and, more importantly, bring it under Ottoman civil administration.[6]

In a separate letter, the Wali and the commander of the Eyalet-i Şam, Safveti Pasha, and the commanders of the Anatolian Army, Mehmet Rashid, and the Arabian Army, Mehmed Namık, asked the Porte to complete the procedure in Istanbul in the shortest possible time given the desperate condition of the immigrants and the arrival of the agricultural season. Moreover, they informed the Porte that due to the urgency of the case, and as a temporary measure, they had already begun to implement the decisions of the Provincial Council. The other reason for prompt implementation of the decisions was that they had received news that a sizable number of poor immigrants from Algeria were on their way to Syria.[7]

On March 5, 1848, the Supreme Council of Judicial Ordinance (the Meclis-i Vâlâ-yı Ahkâm-ı Adliyye) met to discuss the suggestions made by the Provincial Council in Syria. The Supreme Council members were also presented with a report sent by the British consul in Damascus to the British ambassador in Istanbul, in which the consul drew attention to the possibility that in the future either the French authorities could claim that the Algerian immigrants in Syria were French subjects or the immigrants themselves could claim French protection in order to avoid their official obligations.[8] Also attending the Supreme Council's meeting was the Anatolian Army Commander, Mehmet Rashid, who had made a special trip to Istanbul. In the meeting, Mehmet Rashid explained the situation in Syria and supported the suggestions made by the Provincial Council. However, the Supreme Council members, seemingly much affected by the British consul's warning, were not convinced by the arguments of the provincial authorities or by the written promises of the immigrants. Consequently, it was decided that the immigrants would be settled in Anatolia in Teke and Alaiye (the present-day Antalya and Alanya on the Mediterranean coast). As for the other issues, the Supreme Council unanimously agreed upon giving Ahmad b. Salim 500 Ottoman kuruş, the ʻulama and the shaykhs 30,000 Ottoman kuruş, and the farmers the allowance of 120,000 Ottoman kurus, as suggested by the provincial authorities.[9]

While presenting the Supreme Council's decision to the Sultan, Grand Vezir Mustafa Rashid Pasha expressed disagreement with the place chosen for the settlement of the Algerian immigrants. He claimed that although the climate and physical conditions of Teke and Alaiye were suitable, the area was not safe from foreign influence, and furthermore, the immigrants were too weak to go there. ʻAjlun, on the other hand, was out of the way of foreigners and offered vast arable state land. Therefore, he supported the Provincial Council's suggestion that the immigrants be settled in ʻAjlun.[10] The Sultan accepted the Grand Vezir's view and added that after the immigrants were settled in ʻAjlun, their attitudes and activities should be monitored by both the provincial and central authorities.[11]

From 1847 onward, the sporadic arrival of Algerian immigrants in Syria continued until the decade after 1910. In 1855, the resistance leader

Amir 'Abd al-Qader al-Jazairi along with his family and servants, arrived in Damascus after a period of captivity by the French from 1848 until 1852 and then a three-year stay in Bursa in Western Anatolia. In 1857, about 90 Algerians, including the Amir's brothers and close relatives, came to Damascus.[12] Following 1847, the immigrants were settled in small groups in Akka, Aleppo, Beirut, Damascus, Haifa, Ladhiqiya, Sayda, Tarablus, and Jaffa. Since they arrived in Syria by both official and unofficial means, it is impossible to know the exact number of the immigrants. The French consular reports from Damascus state that in Damascus alone, the number of Algerians in 1883 was about 4,000, while there were about 3,700 Algerian farmers in Safed and Tiberias in 1870.[13]

Despite the considerable number of immigrants, until 1882 no serious problems arose between the Ottoman and the French or, indeed, between the Ottoman authorities in Syria and the Algerian immigrants. It seems that some of the immigrants accepted Ottoman citizenship while others did not, and that this did not cause any noticeable crisis. In fact, Amir 'Abd al-Qader received allowances from both the French and the Ottoman governments. The Amir's brothers in Damascus also received allowances from the Ottoman government.[14] One of the reasons for the absence of any serious problems could be that during his stay in Damascus, Amir 'Abd al-Qader particularly avoided associating himself with any political faction and concentrated mainly on the mundane activities of the immigrants, on his religious duties as a *shaykh* of the Qaderi Sufi order, and on learning.[15] The other reason might be that the Ottoman authorities tried to solve the problems created by the immigrants on their own without allowing any interference from the French. This meant that the problems of the Algerian immigrants were contained and their illegal behaviors tolerated.[16]

Be that as it may, from 1882 onward, a considerable change in the attitudes of the Ottoman authorities toward the Algerian immigrants emerged, particularly toward Amir 'Abd al-Qader's relatives and followers. The reason for this shift was that in the view of the Wali of Syria of 1880–85, Hamdi Pasha, Amir 'Abd al-Qader had begun protecting certain Algerians following his arrival in Damascus. According to Hamdi Pasha, some of Amir 'Abd al-Qader's followers who had committed crimes were seeking refuge in his house and were growing accustomed to defying governmental authority. Moreover, some of these criminals were claiming French protection of citizenship in order to escape punishment. Hamdi Pasha argued that such defiance would seriously endanger tranquillity and public order and would harm the authority of the government in Syria. He added that until that time, the provincial governors had tolerated the crimes committed by the Amir's followers, but that they were now facing a situation of a government within a government. Needless to say, this was the cause of innumerable political troubles.[17]

Also disturbing the Ottoman authorities was the French attitude toward the Algerian immigrants. The French had a long history stretching back to the Crusades in Syria. In the nineteenth century, as a result of competition between England and France to increase overseas possessions, France began to emphasize its traditional links with the Christians of Syria and with Syria generally. The French expedition to Syria in 1860 marked the high point of this effort, but the French defeat in the Franco-Prussian war of 1870–71 led to a temporary halt to French activities in Syria. With the heavy defeat of the Ottomans in the Ottoman–Russian war of 1877–78 and with the British occupation of Cyprus in 1878, followed by the visit to Syria of the British Ambassador in Istanbul, H. Layard, in the autumn of 1879, the French began to reassert their position in Syria. The first serious initiative was begun in 1880 with the dispatch of Louis de-Torcy, the French Military Attaché in Istanbul, to Syria, where he stayed for two months.[18]

Besides intensifying their activities among the Christians, the French sought out the Algerian immigrants, a number of whom already possessed some sort of link to them. Their goal was to increase the number of Algerians who had French citizenship or at least French protectorship. Obviously, the key to achieving their objective was to win the support of the leading figure among the Algerians, Amir ʻAbd al-Qader.[19] Well aware of the threat posed by the French initiatives in Syria, especially after the French occupied Tunis in 1881, and of ʻAbd al-Qader's influence over the Algerians, Hamdi Pasha suggested to the Sultan that Amir ʻAbd al-Qader be persuaded to encourage the Algerian immigrants to obey the Ottoman government rather than the French and that the Amir and his close associates be made more aware of the authority of the Ottoman government.[20] Amir ʻAbd al-Qader, on his part, responded by filing complaints to the Porte and to the Palace in Istanbul, as well as to the French diplomats in Damascus. The Porte sent a soothing letter to ʻAbd al-Qader, but also let Hamdi Pasha know that the central government had complete confidence in him. In essence, without compromising his policies, Hamdi Pasha created an opportunity for reconciliation with ʻAbd al-Qader and restored his pride.[21]

Meanwhile, the government decided that those immigrants who had settled permanently in Ottoman territories would be treated as Ottoman citizens, while those who were staying temporarily, that is, less than two years, would be able to claim French protection. In addition, those claiming French protection would have to leave the country at the end of two years. This policy produced the desired effect, and in 1882 alone, 1,500 of the Algerian immigrants who had settled in Galilee in 1862 registered as Ottoman citizens and gained ownership of the land which they had been using.[22]

In the wake of Amir 'Abd al-Qader's death in May 1883, Hamdi Pasha intensified his efforts to separate the Algerian immigrants from their traditional links to the French consulate in Damascus. The Wali especially tried to gain the support of the two eldest sons of the Amir, Muhammad and Muhyi al-Din, since they had already accepted Ottoman citizenship and had received the rank of *Mirmiranlik*. In the end, Hamdi Pasha's efforts proved successful. The two sons refused a French offer to the effect that if they were to accept French citizenship, their father's allowance of 300,000 francs (equivalent to 60,000 Ottoman kuruş) would be paid to them. However, they did so with the expectation that they would receive a satisfactory salary from the Ottoman government. In fact, over the following three months they received nothing. At that point, the Pashas, Muhammad and Muhyi al-Din, politely warned Hamdi Pasha that if the Ottoman government was not prepared to support them financially in order to care for one hundred or so dependants, then they would have to accept the French offer. Hamdi Pasha immediately wrote a letter to the Palace in which he drew the Sultan's attention to the French efforts aimed at gaining the support of 'Abd al-Qader's sons and to the influence of this family on Arabs in Syria, Tunisia, and Algeria. He claimed that Muhammad had promised him that if they were paid a salary, then all of the Algerian immigrants in Syria would accept Ottoman citizenship. Hamdi Pasha added that if this promise were kept, not only would the French influence in Syria be seriously damaged, but the Ottomans would gain the means to disturb the French in Tunisia and Algeria. Therefore, he strongly urged Sultan Abdulhamid II (r. 1876–1909) to order the payment of a monthly salary of 25,000 Ottoman kuruş for the two Pashas.[23] Also, Muhammad Pasha himself, in a telegram dated September 16, 1883, informed the Sultan that he needed government support in order to look after his family and dependants. Hamdi Pasha, upon receiving no response for a month after his first letter, felt the need to reiterate his views and re-emphasize the urgency of the matter.[24] Finally, on September 24, 1883, the Sultan's decree accepting the Wali's proposals was issued. The Wali was secretly informed of the decision and was asked first to solve the question of citizenship of the immigrants before implementing it.[25]

Now it was left to Hamdi Pasha to achieve his aims concerning the Ottomanization of the Algerian immigrants in Syria. Not surprisingly, he consistently tried to win over the Algerians to his side without making any serious compromises. Although his consistency did finally convince the Algerians to turn to the Ottomans for citizenship, they did request some favors: exemption from conscription, the establishment of two military companies, and some arable land in Houran. Upon Hamdi Pasha's acceptance of these requests, Muhyi al-Din declared that the "extraordinary efforts of the French were made futile and all of the immigrants of their own volition registered as Ottoman subjects and received their certificates."[26] It appears, however, that only a majority, rather than all, of the immigrants accepted Ottoman nationality and that before Hamdi Pasha died in 1885, only one company of Algerian immigrants had been established. Meanwhile, the French had succeeded in obtaining pledges of loyalty from Hashem, the fifth son of the Amir, and his followers. In return, Hashim received 80,000 francs a month from the French.[27]

Hamdi Pasha's successor, Rashid Nashid Pasha (1885–88), did not follow his predecessor's policies and adopted a less flexible attitude toward the Algerian immigrants. For instance, he did not allow them to establish the second company and required some of them to serve in the Ottoman army. This strained relations between the new Wali and the immigrants and increased the number of Hashim's followers.[28] Two incidents occurred in January and February 1888 that strained relations even further. In both instances, a number of Algerian criminals took refuge in the French Consulate in Damascus in order to escape from the Ottoman police. When the police attempted to arrest them in the Consulate, minor fighting between the two sides took place.[29] The French protested and requested the dismissal of the Wali. They also threatened to send two corvettes stationed in Rhodes to the Syrian coast. The Ottomans in return asked for the dismissal of the French consul in Damascus.

In March 1888, both the Wali and the French consul were dismissed, but the Ottoman and French negotiations over the question of citizenship of the Algerian immigrants continued. Both sides sent separate investigators to the area. At the end of the mission, the Ottoman investigator, Hüseyın Rıza, prepared a report dated April 19, 1888, in which he warned the Porte that unless the citizenship question of the Algerian immigrants was solved, incidents like the ones that had occurred in January and February of that year were likely to take place again. As a solution, he suggested that the Porte stick to its previous policy of treating the immigrants who were staying permanently as nationals, while allowing those staying only temporarily to claim French protection.[30]

The French investigator, Imbert, also prepared a report dated May 1, 1888, in which he summarized developments up to that point and suggested that France insist on the Algerian immigrants becoming French citizens in order to extend her influence in Syria. He also proposed that some Algerians, especially the late Amir's close relatives, be employed by the French.[31] Meanwhile, the Porte sent Muhyi al-Din Pasha to Syria in order to encourage the Algerians to accept Ottoman citizenship. While in Syria, Muhyi al-Din, along with his brother Muhammad, worked hard to accomplish this mission. The French were very disturbed by Muhyi al-Din's activities and, after repeated requests, Montebello, the French ambassador in Istanbul, got him recalled.[32]

The official responses to the suggestions made by Hüseyın Rıza were not clear, but relations between the Ottoman government and the Algerian immigrants were steadily improving. In October 1887, another of 'Abd al-Qader's sons, 'Ali, was granted a salary of 3,500 Ottoman kuruş.[33] In early 1888, Muhyi al-Din became a member of the Council of State, and Muhammad was granted *Mecidi* of the second class in September 1888.[34] A month later, Amir 'Abd al-Qader's wife, Shafiqa, was granted some arable lands in Syria.[35] At about the same time, the late Amir's three nephews, Muhammad Abu Taleb, Muhyi al-Din b. Mustafa, and 'Abd al-Qader Efendi, applied to the Ottoman government stating that at Muhammad Pasha's urging, they were prepared to become Ottoman subjects and stop taking salaries from the French government as long as they were granted similar financial support. In the end, Muhammad Abu Talib and Muhyi al-Din b. Mustafa were granted salaries of 800 Ottoman kuruş a month, while 'Abd al-Qader Efendi was granted a salary of 500 Ottoman kuruş a month.[36] Finally, in 1892, the late Amir's other son, 'Abd al-Malek, accepted Ottoman citizenship and was granted a salary of 3,000 Ottoman kuruş a month. The following year, 'Abd al-Malek was given the rank of captain and joined the army.[37] From among the sons of the late Amir, only Hashim maintained official ties with the French, and in 1892 he left for Algeria.[38]

Despite the improved relations of the Algerian immigrants with the Ottoman government, the question of their citizenship remained unresolved. In July 1888, Abdulhamid II asked Montebello to present a memorandum containing his government's views on this question. In reply, Montebello submitted a memorandum dated July 22, 1888, in which he complained about the local officials' unfriendly attitude to the pro-French Algerians in Syria. He suggested that the French accept the voluntary claims of French citizenship by the Algerians, that the Algerians be free to choose either Ottoman or French citizenship, and that finally, in order to prevent any future conflict, the Algerians not be allowed to change their nationality without the prior consent of either side.[39] Three days after Montebello's memorandum was written, Muhyi al-Din Pasha, probably again at the Sultan's request, presented the Sultan with his views on the same subject. Muhyi al-Din Pasha pointed out that the overwhelming majority of the Algerian immigrants would accept Ottoman citizenship if the second company was allowed to be established, if some arable lands in Houran were allocated to the immigrants, and if some official positions and honors were bestowed on the leading Algerian figures and their salaries paid regularly.[40]

On August 2, 1888, the Special Council of Ministers (*Encümen-i Hususi-i Vükelâ)*, consisting of the Ministers of Education, Judicial and Foreign Affairs as well as the President of the Council of State and the Grand Vezir, met to discuss the aforementioned memorandums. After lengthy discussions, the Special Council agreed that the fundamental reason for the Algerians' reluctance to become Ottoman subjects was conscription. Therefore, they decided that the Algerians be exempted from conscription for twenty years and that some arable land be allocated so that they would be encouraged to choose a settled life. As for Montebello's proposals, the Special Council members unanimously agreed that the status of the Algerians who accepted French citizenship prior to their arrival in Syria would not be changed, that the Ottoman government would be free to expel those who subsequently claimed French protection, and that those Algerians in Kudüs would be subject to the same rules. The Sultan approved the Council's decisions on August 11, 1888.[41]

While the discussions between the French and the Ottomans were continuing in Istanbul, the Ottomans were making gains on the ground in Syria. The local authorities were consistently making the Algerian immigrants Ottoman subjects. Realizing that developments were unfavorable in Syria, Montebello had a certain Kazım Bey take a threatening message to the Palace in late May 1889. His message stated that he had been asked by his government to return to Paris to explain the ill-treatment of the Algerian immigrants in Syria who held French citizenship. He added that not stopping such ill-treatment might result in the cutting of diplomatic ties and a tough French response.[42] The Sultan, Abdulhamid II, was disturbed by this message, for he interpreted it as meaning that the French were contemplating using the disagreements over the citizenship of the Algerian immigrants as a pretext to attack Syria. The Sultan immediately sought the advice of Kamil Pasha, the Grand Vezir, whose reply was quite telling and calmed the Sultan. He stated that the French ambassador had been telling his close associates for a month that he planned to go to Paris for two weeks to pick up his wife, and he added that it was impossible for the French to send a military expedition to Syria. Thus, he was only using threatening messages in an attempt to achieve the objectives of the French in Syria. In fact, their main objective was to have 5,000–10,000 male Muslim citizens there that they could use for their own purposes when needed.[43] He concluded that the Ottoman view be reiterated: that the Algerian immigrants in Syria were Ottoman subjects because they had been so prior to the French occupation of Algeria and because they had accepted the conditions of the Ottoman government in order to settle in Syria. In addition, if they wished to reject Ottoman citizenship, then the Ottoman government had the right to expel them from Ottoman territories. As for particular individual claims of French citizenship, these cases needed to be checked by local officials with consular registers and then settled.[44]

Apparently, the French ambassador's view was that Kamil Pasha had hardened the Ottoman position and that it was easier to reach an agreement with the Sultan than with the Porte; hence his insistence thereafter that the Sultan find a solution to the problem. Finally, in early November 1889, Abdulhamid II decided that since both sides had failed to find a permanent solution, the best course would be a continuation of the status quo and a warning to the respective officials in Syria to avoid creating problems.[45] At least in this way, a deterioration of the present good relations between the two countries could be prevented until a permanent solution was achieved. The French ambassador seemed satisfied with the Sultan's response and decided to leave for Paris. Before leaving Istanbul, Montebello paid Kamil Pasha a visit, perhaps in order to bid him farewell, at which time he disclosed the Sultan's decision. Kamil Pasha was quite upset and immediately expressed his disappointment to the Sultan about not being informed of this decision beforehand. He also reminded the Sultan that the issue had already been discussed at the Porte and that certain principles had been agreed upon.[46] Kamil Pasha's hard stance led the Sultan to reverse his decision and ask Montebello to delay his journey for a week. The following day, the Sultan informed Kamil Pasha that the ambassador had agreed to the delay so that a solution could be reached.[47] Kamil Pasha was not satisfied with the Sultan's response and asked for the exact wording given to the French ambassador and whether the message had been given verbally. Furthermore, he requested that the intermediaries, Artin Pasha, Under-Secretary of the Foreign Ministry, as well as Emin Bey and Dyresse Pasha, both working for the Palace, put in writing the message that they had conveyed to the ambassador and send the text to him the next day.[48]

While these communications were going on between the Porte and the Palace, news that more Algerian immigrants had arrived in Beirut reached the Palace. At this time, for unknown reasons, the Sultan changed his mind and decided to stick to his earlier decision, that is, the continuation of the status quo. The Sultan then informed Kamil Pasha that a permanent decision regarding the Algerians in Syria would be made at the proper time in the future and that for the moment, the main consideration was the treatment of the Algerian immigrants who had already migrated, as well as those who would migrate in the future, as Ottoman subjects.[49]

Kamil Pasha immediately convened a Special Council for this purpose and on November 18, 1889 presented the Sultan with the following draft agreement:

> a. Those Algerians who have migrated to and settled in Syria as part of a group are Ottoman subjects. Of those in this category, anyone who wishes to be a French subject has to leave the Ottoman territories within a certain time.
> b. Those Algerians who arrived as individuals and possessed French passports before their arrival, and who are registered as French citizens in the French consular registers, are to be retreated as French subjects. Those who have worked as Ottoman officials, served in the army, or settled on and been using state land are considered to be Ottoman subjects. If they wish to be French subjects, they have to leave the Ottoman territories within a certain time.
> c. Those Algerians holding French citizenship are not allowed to marry Ottoman nationals, and anyone disobeying this rule will be expelled.
> d. From among the French nationals in Syria, anyone identified as one who disturbs the peace will be expelled from the Ottoman territories.
> e. The consular registers containing records of French nationals of Algerian origin will be given to the Porte, and a joint commission will identify the French and Ottoman nationals.
> f. During the implementation of these rules, if a conflict occurs between the provincial authorities and the French consulate, the case will be referred to the Porte and the French Embassy in Istanbul.
> g. The Porte has also been informed of some Jews claiming to be French subjects, and these cases should also be sorted out.
> h. Those Algerians who have settled in Kudüs and in other parts of the Ottoman territories will also be subject to these rules.
> i. From now on, all newcomers will be treated as Ottoman subjects, and those newcomers who already hold French passports will have to leave the Ottoman territories within two years.

The Sultan gave his consent to the Council's draft agreement and added that it should be sent to the provincial authorities along with solemn warnings to the effect that serious attention be paid to avoiding any conflict with the French consulate over these matters and that the French ambassador be informed of the solemn orders sent to the provincial government in order to prevent any possible objections from him.[50]

Initially, Montebello did have serious reservations about the Ottoman proposals and especially objected to the two-year time limit placed on the

French nationals of Algerian origin and to the treatment of newcomers as Ottoman subjects. However, he agreed to send the document to his government. The Sultan also sent Artin Pasha to Montebello so as to persuade him to take a positive view of the proposals. In the end, the Ambassador seemed to agree to the proposals on the condition that the provincial government put an end to its Ottomanization policies toward the Algerian immigrants.[51]

It appears that the Sultan deliberately opted for a continuation of the status quo because after the death of Amir 'Abd al-Qader, a majority of the Algerian immigrants agreed to become Ottoman subjects and those who were still not subjects tended to follow the behavior of the majority. Moreover, the Sultan consciously avoided making a formal agreement with the French, believing that it could be interpreted as Ottoman recognition of the French occupation of Algeria. Be that as it may, the Ottomans achieved most of their objectives. All of the late Amir 'Abd al-Qader's sons, with the exception of Hashim, became Ottoman subjects. With the departure of Hashim from Syria in 1892, the leadership of the French nationals of Algerian origin passed to his son 'Omar, who apparently was much weaker than his father. In 1896, Amir 'Abd al-Qader's son 'Ali was given the rank of Pasha and was appointed as the *Kaymakam* of Quneitra. Meanwhile, the immigration of Algerians to Syria continued. In 1893, for instance, a group of Algerians arrived in Beirut and, despite the initial refusal by the Sultan, were settled on arable state land in Tiberias. Without exception, all of the newcomers accepted Ottoman citizenship.[52]

In conclusion, it can safely be stated that the Ottomans, right from the beginning, identified the most important problem that the Algerian immigrants might cause: the possibility that they would seek out French protection, using their links to the French. Other problems such as those arising from settling them or from any difficulties that they themselves might have in integrating into Syrian society or in earning their livelihood did not prevent the Ottomans from viewing the issue correctly. The question of their citizenship was clearly assessed. In fact, the citizenship question did not arise with all of the Algerian immigrants to Syria, but only with Amir 'Abd al-Qader and his relatives and followers. The Amir's death in May 1883 meant that the pro-French faction of the Algerians lost their leader. His death also prompted the Ottomans into intensifying their efforts to Ottomanize the Algerians. From 1884 onward, the dominant tendency among the late Amir's dependants was to become Ottoman subjects, and by the end of the century, the overwhelming majority of the Algerians in Syria had become Ottoman subjects. The French also made attempts to win the Algerians to their side, but these failed due partly to the consistency of the Ottoman policies toward the Algerian immigrants and partly to the tendency of the Damascene notables to view themselves as Ottomans.

Acknowledgment

I want to thank my colleagues Butrus Abu-Manneh and Joseph Nevo of the University of Haifa; İdris Bostan, İsmail Kara and Ali Akyıldız of Maramara University; Ahmet Kavas and Karen Wolfe of the Center for Islamic Studies who at various stages in the preparation of this article have all made invaluable contributions. Similarly, appreciation goes to the TDV Center for Islamic Studies for their financial support of the research carried out for this article.

Notes

1 For details of Amir 'Abd al-Qader's resistance to the French occupation of Algeria, see: Raphael Danziger, *'Abd al-Qadir and the Algerians* (New York, 1977), passim.
2 For the Amir's relations with Ahmad b. Salim who surrendered to the French in February 1847, see: *ibid.*, pp. 159, 167, 186, 235.
3 For the Ottoman Turkish translation of the authorization document given to Ahmad b. Salim, see: Başbakanlık Osmanlı Arşivi (BOA), İrade-Mesail-i Mühimme (I. Mes. Müh.), 2079, undated.
4 For the original Arabic document signed by the 204 adult males and its Ottoman Turkish translation, see: BOA, İ. Mes. Müh., 2079, Gurre-i Safer 1264/8 January 1848.
5 BOA, I. Mes. Müh., 2079, 5 Safer 1264/12 January 1848. Also in the same file are Ahmad b. Salim's two letters containing the same demands and two lists of Algerians immigrants: the first, included those who could do agricultural work, and the second, those who could not.
6 For more information about the Ottoman efforts to bring 'Ajlun and its environs under civil administration and the significance of the Algerians' role in it, see: Eugene Lawrence Rogan, *Incorporating the Periphery: The Ottoman Extension of Direct Rule Over Southeastern Syria (Transjordan), 1867–1914* (unpublished Ph.D. thesis, Harvard University, 1991), pp. 64–94.
7 BOA, İ. Mes. Müh., 2079, 5 Safer 1264/12 January 1848.
8 For the Turkish translation of the Consul's report dated 5 January 1848, see: BOA, İ. Mes. Müh., 2079.
9 BOA, İ. Mes. Müh., 2079, 29 Rebîülevvel 1264/5 March 1848.
10 For the Grand Vezir's views on this question, see: BOA, İ. Mes. Müh., 2079, 5 Rebiyulahir 1264/11 March 1848.
11 For the Sultan's decree on all of the issues presented to him in connection with the Algerian immigrants, see: BOA, İ. Mes. Müh., 2079, 16 Rebîülevvel 1264/22 March 1848.
12 Pierre Bardin, *Algériens et Tunisiens dans L'empire Ottoman de 1848 a 1914* (Paris, 1979), pp. 7, 128 [hereafter Bardin, *Algériens et Tunisiens*]; Nadiya Tarshun, "al-Hijrat al-Jazairiyya ila Bilad al-Sham fi Matla' al-Qarn al-'Ishrin (1909–1911), *Dirasaat Tarihiyya*, Nos. 27–28 (1987), pp. 161–89.

13 Bardin, *Algériens et Tunisiens,* pp. 8, 15–16.
14 For a brief analysis of the Amir's life in Syria and his family's relations with the French, see: Linda Schatkowski Schilcher, *Families in Politics: Damascene Factions and Estates of the 18th and 19th Centuries* (Wiesbaden–Stuttgart, 1985), pp. 215–18. For the allowances paid to the Amir and his relatives by the Ottoman government, see: BOA, İrade-Meclis-i Vâlâ, 25247, Rebîülahir 1277/October 1860 ve 10 Cemaziyelevvel 1283/20 September 1866; İrade-Meclis-i Vâlâ, 25484, 13 Şevval 1283/18 February 1867; İrade-Dahiliye, 37653, 37298, 37376; İrade-Hariciye, 5915 ve 6040.
15 Linda Schatkowski Schilcher, *Families in Politics* (Stuttgart, 1985), p. 215; John King, "Abd el-Kader and Arab Nationalism" in John Spagnolo (ed.), *Problems of the Modern Middle East in Historical Perspective:* Essays in Honour of Albert Hourani (Reading, 1992), pp. 145–48.
16 BOA, İ. Mes. Müh.. 2079, Damascus Provincial Council to the Porte, 12 January 1848.
17 BOA, YEE 18/417/3/40, Hamdi Pasha to the Porte, 11 Temmuz 1298/23 July 1882, document No. 67. Similar views were expressed by Hamdi Pasha in documents Nos. 69 and 71 dated 12 Temmuz 1298/24 July 1882, and 13 Temmuz 1298/25 July 1882 respectively.
18 John Spagnolo, "French Influence in Syria Prior to World War One," *Middle East Journal*, Vol. 23 (1969), p. 45ff.
19 BOA, YEE 18/417/3/40, Hamdi Pasha to the chief secretary of the Mabeyn, document No. 43, 5 Eylül 1298/17 September 1882.
20 *Ibid.*
21 BOA, YEE 18/417/3/40, Muhyi al-Din b. 'Abd al-Qader to the Palace, the Porte, Interior Ministry, Foreign Affairs, Judicial Affairs, and Darussaade Agasi, document No. 28, 8 Temmuz 1298/20 July 1882. See also: Engin Deniz Akarli, "Abdulhamid II's Attempt to Integrate Arabs into the Ottoman System," in David Kushner (ed.), *Palestine in the Late Ottoman Period* (Jerusalem and Leiden, 1986), pp. 81–82.
22 Bardin, *Algériens et Tunisiens*, pp. 40–41.
23 BOA, İrade-Dahiliye, 71127, Hamdi Pasha to the Palace, 11 Şevval 1300/ 15 August 1883.
24 BOA, İrade-Dahiliye, 71127, Muhammad's telegram, 4 Eylül 1299/16 September 1883 and Hamdi Pasha's letter, 5 Eylül 1299/ 17 September 1883.
25 BOA, İrade-Dahiliye, 71127, 22 Zilkade 1300/24 September 1883.
26 BOA YEE 14/ . . . . 126/11 Muhyi al-Din b. 'Abd al-Qader to the Palace, 3 Temmuz 1304/25 July 1888.
27 Bardin, *Algériens et Tunisiens,* pp. 46–47.
28 BOA YEE 14/ . . . . 126/11 Muhyi al-Din b. 'Abd al-Qader to the Palace, 3 Temmuz 1304/25 July 1888.
29 Public Record Office, Foreign Office (FO), 195/1613 Dickson to White, No. 5, Damascus, 3 February 1888; Bardin, *Algériens et Tunisiens,* pp. 55–56.
30 BOA YEE 14/244/126/7 Hüsayın Rıza to the Porte, 8 Şaban 1305/19 April 1888.
31 FO 195/1613 Dickson to White, No. 10, Damascus, 24 February 1888; Bardin, *Algériens et Tunisiens,* pp. 60–63.
32 BOA, Yıldız-Sadaret Hususi Maruzat Evrakı (Y. A. Hus.) 226/1, 4 Şevval 1306/3 June 1889; Bardin, *Algériens et Tunisiens,* p. 59.

33 BOA, İrade-Meclis-i Mahsus (İ.M.M.), 3935, 13 Muharram 1305/1 October 1887; MV, defter. 24, evrak. 59. In August 1888 the Amir's son 'Abdallah asked the government to raise his salary from 2,500 kuruş to the level of his brother 'Ali's salary, but his request was refused. M.V., defter. 34, evrak. 47, 23 Zilkade 1305/1 August 1888.

34 BOA, Yıldız Mütenevvi Maruzat Evrakı (Y. MTV.), 31/34, 27 Şubat 1303/10 March 1888; MV., defter. 30, evrak. 57, 21 Receb 1305/3 April 1888; İrade-Dahiliye 86171, 15 Ağustos 1304/28 August 1888 and 5 Eylül 1304/18 September 1888; İrade-Dahiliye 86143, 15 Eylül 1304/28 September 1888.

35 BOA, İrade-Dahiliye, 86399, 7 Safer 1306/14 October 1888.

36 BOA, I. Mec. Mah., 4340, their petitions are dated 12 Eylül 1304/25 September 1888. The Wali's views on their petitions are dated 24 Muharram 1306/1 October 1888; and the date of the Sultan's irade is 2 Rebîülahir 1306/6 December 1888. I. Mah., 87018, 2 Rebîülahir 1306; MV, defter. 37, evrak. 57, 22 Rebîülahir 1306; MV, defter. 41, evrak. 42, 23, Receb 1306.

37 BOA, Y. A. Hus. 263/92, 25 Muharram 1310/19 August 1892; Y. MTV. 72/117, 9 Şaban 1310/26 February 1893.

38 Before his departure from Syria Hashim's relations with the local authorities as well as with the locally influential families steadily deteriorated. See: BOA, MV, defter. 29, evrak. 46, 17 Cemaziyelahir 1305/1 March 1888; BOA, MV, defter. 43, evrak. 38, 20 Ramazan 1306/20 May 1889; Yıldız Sadaret Hususi Maruzat Evrakı (Y.A.Hus.), 225/54, 24 Ramazan 1306/24 May 1889; İ. Dah. 88806, 24 Ramazan 1306/24 May 1889; MV, defter. 43, evrak. 38, 20 Ramazan 1306/20 May 1889; BOA, Y.A. Hus. 277/118, 26 Zilhicce 1310/10 Temmuz 1893 and Bardin, *Algériens et Tunisiens,* p. 134.

39 BOA, YEE, 14/... b/126/11, 22 July 1888. For the second copy of the memorandum, see: I. Mec. Mah., 4221.

40 BOA, YEE, 14/ . . . b/126/11, Muhyi al-Din to the Mabeyn, 13 Temmuz 1304/25 July 1888.

41 BOA, İ. Mec. Mah., 4221, 24 Zilkade 1305/2 August 1888, and 3 Zilhicce 1305/11 August 1888.

42 BOA Yıldız Sadaret Hususi Maruzat Evrakı, 226/1, 4 Şevval 1306/3 June 1889.

43 *Ibid.*

44 *Ibid.*

45 BOA İ. D., 90747, 17 Rebîülevvel 1307/11 November 1889.

46 *Ibid.*

47 BOA, İ. D., 90748, 18 Rebîülevvel 1307/12 November 1889.

48 BOA, İ. D., 90746, 21 Rebîülevvel 1307/15 November 1889.

49 BOA, İ. D., 90728, 22 Rebîülevvel 1307/16 November 1889.

50 BOA İrade Meclis-i Mahsus, 4625 and Yıldız Sadaret Resmi Maruzat Evrakı, 49/39 Rebîülevvel 1307/20 November 1889.

51 Bardin, *Algériens et Tunisiens,* pp. 76–77.

52 BOA, M.V., defter. 46, evrak. 39; M.V., defter. 61, evrak. 42, 30 Cemaziyelevvel 1308/11 January 1891; BOA İrade-Dahiliye, 1311 M-47, 13 Muharram 1311/27 July 1893; Irade-Dahiliye, 1311 R-40, 26 Rebîülahir 1311/6 November 1893.

8

European Foreigners in Damascus and Aleppo During the Late Ottoman Period

Yoram Shalit

Accounts by travelers of the time show that the Muslim population of Damascus, in contrast to that of Aleppo, was renowned for its intolerant and fanatical attitude toward foreigners. This view is also held by Orientalists[1] and thus arouses intellectual curiosity as to whether this was actually the case, and if so what were the reasons?

Damascus and Aleppo are two Syrian Muslim cities in close geographical proximity to one another. Both were situated within the boundaries of the Ottoman Empire; both were *Wilaya* capitals, with a Wali (governor) in residence; both contained a relatively large non-Muslim population. Damascus, with several of Islam's "forefathers" buried in its precincts, was considered to be a "holy city" and from the beginning of Muslim rule served as a gathering point for starting out on the *Hajj* caravan. It also served as a center for peripheral trade in close affinity with the *Hajj*. Aleppo, in contrast, was a cosmopolitan city involved in the internal trade system as well as in the transit trade between Europe and the Orient.

The available data regarding foreigners in Aleppo and Damascus during the eighteenth and nineteenth centuries (see tables 8.1 and 8.2) lead to the following conclusions: First, in Aleppo, the number of French and English traders combined never exceeded 150 during the period under discussion. Second, during the course of the eighteenth century, up to 1791, the number of French and English traders in Aleppo declined drastically from their seventeenth century level. Third, in contrast to Aleppo, no European traders at all were to be found during the eighteenth century in Damascus, though European professionals and missionaries

Table 8.1 French presence in Aleppo and Damascus, 1630–1820

Year	Damascus	Aleppo Consul	Secretary	Trading Houses	Traders	Profressionals	Missionaries	Total
1630	1	1			40			
1653	–	1			15			
1660	–	few						
1670	–	1			60		8	
1681	–	1						28
1693	–	1			6			
1698	–	1	1		19	7	13	
1717	–	few						
1731	–	1		11			about 15	
1740–3	–	1						
1759	–	1		7				
1764	–	1			12			
1765	–	1	9					42
1772	–	1	6					
1781	–	1	9					
1783–5	–	1	7					
1789	–	1	9–10					
1791								
1794	1						few	
1800								
1810				3				
1816		1						
1817	1			–				
1820				2				

Source: Shalit, p. 199.

Table 8.2 English presence in Aleppo and Damascus, 1662–1841

Year	Damascus	Aleppo Consul	Secretary	Trading Houses	Traders	Profressionals	Missionaries	Total
1662–70	–	1		50	60			
1680	–			30–40	60			60
1699	–	1	1+1			1		40
1725	–				30			
1734	–			15	15			
1737–8	–				10–12			
1740	–			7–8				
1741	–	1	1		10	2	14	
1743	–			10				
1748	–			7				
1750	–			5–6				
1753	–	1		8				
1772	–	1		4				
1781	–			3				
1783	–			2				
1783–5	–	–		2				
1791	–	–			few		few	
1799	–							
1800	–							
1803	–	1						
1806	–	1						
1812	1							
1824	–	1						
1825				–				
1833	1							
1833–41		1						

Source: Shalit, p. 201.

did settle there. Fourth, French and English traders returned to Aleppo and set foot in Damascus at the beginning of the nineteenth century. Fifth, although the data points to a decrease in the number of foreign traders in Aleppo, this does not indicate a decline in the general population of foreigners, which, paradoxically, increased due to the accretion in the number of clergy.

These data raise some questions: First, what accounts for the foreign presence (trading stations, consuls and European traders) in eighteenth-century Aleppo and its absence in Damascus? Second, what caused the decline in the number of French and English traders in Aleppo, and are the reasons identical for both nationalities? Third, why did the French and English traders reappear at the beginning of the nineteenth century in both Aleppo and Damascus? Fourth, how could so few foreigners exercise such a powerful impact, out of all proportion to their number? Finally, what significance can be ascribed to the presence in Damascus of European professionals and missionaries?

The Legal Status of the Foreigners in Damascus and Aleppo

A distinction must be drawn between the status of non-Muslims and that of foreigners in the Ottoman Empire since the former were subjects of the Sultan, whereas the latter were not. In its perception of foreigners, the Ottoman law relied on Islamic law, the *Shari'a*, which regards the foreigner as a *Must'amin*, that is, as a person receiving an *Aman*, which is the guarantee of life and property from the Muslim ruler.[2] This *Aman* was granted for a limited period of time, generally one year, in contrast to the permanent *Aman* conferred on the non-Muslim, the *Dhimmi*. The *Shari'a* requires a foreigner wishing to reside for an extended period in a Muslim country to convert to the status of *Dhimma*, with all that this implies.[3]

In order to adapt Ottoman law to European commercial interests, a step dictated by the might of the European powers, and to enable foreigners to remain in the Empire without changing their status and becoming subjects of the Sultan, the Sultans conferred on foreigners special rights, based on contracts extrinsic to the *Shari'a*. These contracts were drawn up directly between the Ottomans and the monarchs of the European powers. Called *Imtiyazat* in Turkish, they are generally known as "Capitulations."[4] The contract concluded by the Sublime Porte and France, in February 1535, served as the basis for subsequent arrangements whereby other Western nations obtained corresponding privileges.[5] The contracts were renewed and ratified by successive Sultans.[6]

The February 1535 French–Ottoman agreement established the legal status of foreigners in the Ottoman Empire.[7] Hamilton Gibb and Harold Bowen stated that the foreigners remained subject to the authority of the "civil" and "criminal" law of their countries of origin, whose representatives and agents were the Consuls in the Ottoman territory.[8] A precise juridical analysis of the agreement shows it not only defining the Consuls' powers, but also conferring extraterritorial status and immunity on foreigners by excluding them from the Ottoman judicial and tax systems. The agreement also granted foreigners privileges which do not derive from the Islamic law.

The French Community in Aleppo

The first French trading station in Aleppo was set up in 1562 and became firmly established in 1612.[9] The legal basis for the station's activity was provided, as indicated, by the French–Ottoman Capitulation agreement. The community's organization and administrative structure were formed during the course of the seventeenth century and the first half of the eighteenth century.[10] The dominant figure in this regard was Colbert, Louis XIV's Finance Minister. The trading stations (Echelles) were subordinated to the Chamber of Commerce in Marseille. The French community in Aleppo was made up of the following elements: The consuls and the traders operating the trading station; professionals; clergy; and wards (both foreign and non-Muslim). Of these, the consuls and traders were the most dominant in the community.[11]

The English Community in Aleppo

In 1583, Richard Forster was appointed as England's first Consul to Tripoli, Aleppo, Damascus, Jerusalem, Amman, and all other port cities in Syria and Palestine, with Tripoli chosen as his official abode. In that same year John Barret was already operating in Aleppo as acting English Consul.[12] In 1589, Aleppo supplanted Tripoli as the center of English business operations in Syria.[13] The activity of the consuls and traders at that time was founded on the Capitulation from 1580 and on the Royal Charter, issued on September 11, 1581, for a monopoly which led to the establishment of the Levant Company.[14] The English trading station operated in Aleppo until 1791. Thereafter, only a few traders remained in the city without any consul. Only in 1803 did an English Consul return to the city (see table 8.2). The English community in Aleppo was similar in make-up to that of the French.

Transient travelers and guests were not an organic part of the station, though at times they took part in its activity. As in the French community, the English consuls and traders formed the most dominant group, but unlike the French station, the organization, structure, and procedures were determined almost at the outset in the English station. For this reason, of the two stations, the English one was earlier in establishing itself,[15] a fact which was also reflected in the development of the community and its leisure culture.

For the English living in Aleppo in the eighteenth century, the daily routine alternated between periods of intense activity and periods of almost total inactivity. This routine was an outcome of the work at the station, which revolved around two main events: The gathering of the silk cocoons and the arrival of the ships bringing in and taking out goods.[16] Thus it is probable that the period toward springtime, as well as other intervals during the year, were dead seasons in terms of the station's activities.

The English at the trading station in Aleppo conducted their own internal community life. In contrast to the French, who held a yearly carnival, the English were much more active all year round, working to break the monotony of life and to ease their exile by extending hospitality to others, making merry and exhibiting a gay and sportive spirit. They brought with them to Aleppo the social life and the forms of entertainment and recreation they had known in their homeland. In the winter and spring they went on rabbit and wild goose hunts twice a week, while in the searing summer heat they went horse-back riding at sunset. To this end, the traders kept their own horses and hunting dogs. They also played cricket, went on nature trips and held picnics at which they ate, drank wine and played games.[17] So strong and entrenched among the English is the tradition of spending time outside the city that even the members of the small community remaining in Aleppo at the beginning of the nineteenth century went on hunting parties, as in the days of John Barker, the English Consul, who would invite travelers and guests to join him in the chase.[18] During the seventeenth century, and for as long as the English community maintained its numerical strength in the eighteenth century, it presented a more unified and cohesive front than its competitors, at least as far as the community's social life was concerned. In other words, there was a direct correlation between the size of the community and the nature of its social life.[19]

The lifestyle portrayed above points to healthy relations, despite commercial competition, and to a sense of security, especially during Constantine Volney and Richard Pococke's time. The fact that the station was composed of young unattached males unquestionably contributed to this lifestyle. They set up the so-called "Order of the Knights of the Salt Valley," and the community held festive ceremonies to crown the "Knight of the Salt Valley," as well as ceremonies in which visiting Englishmen were awarded a title. Henry Teonge's description refers to the 1670s, but is indicative of the community's lifestyle so long as it maintained its numerical strength.[20] The English community was able to adapt itself to the local lifestyle, albeit that the climate differed greatly from that with which its members were familiar. One of the institutions of relaxation and rejuvenation in Aleppo, as indeed in every Muslim city, was the *Hammam*. The English in Aleppo adopted this tradition; parties were held separately at the *Hammam* for men and women.

All the foregoing raises the question of why the English were more enterprising than the French and other Europeans in giving variety to their lives and breaking the monotony, and what enabled them to present a more united and cohesive front. The answer is not a difference in social background, since it appears that the English and the French serving at the stations came from similar backgrounds (well-established trading families in London and Marseille, with close ties to high society); rather, the difference between the two communities stemmed from the following factors:

1 The English preceded the French in setting selective criteria for the traders of the Levant Company. Moreover, the criteria set by the English were more strict and rigid than those set by the French, and the English applied these criteria more rigorously than the French.
2 The rules and regulations laid down by the French with respect to membership in and conduct of the "Assemblee" (assembly) were different than those of the English and aroused internal disagreements, particularly in light of the necessity of financing bankruptcies and repaying debts from the station's funds.
3 The French traders maintained an inner hierarchy: The first were the "les Regisseurs" and "les negociants" (the most prominent merchants and agents), who were the station's aristocracy. They alone formed the "Assemblee" and were entitled to elect and to be elected. The second were "les Commis" and "les Fateurs," who were almost equal in number to the first category, but were not members of the "Assemblee."

These different categories created tensions among the French community in Aleppo, to the extent that it was said that it would be difficult to find an organization whose members so liked to foster differences of opinion and disputes with such fervor as the French traders did among themselves and between themselves and the Consul.[21] Although the French were more numerous than the English in eighteenth-century Aleppo, the English projected a more homogeneous and united image due to the superior quality of the English manpower. To this one must add the difference in social traditions which each community brought with it from its homeland.

In England, the club and the coffeehouse were the center of social activity, where the art of conversation was formed and ideas evolved, albeit with less finesse and taste than in France. The Londoner's amusements were wine, women and dice, including card games in the clubs. Entertainment in England of that time was of a popular nature and included sports, such as cockfighting and pitting bulldogs against bears. Other forms of entertainment were horse racing, raising thoroughbred horses, fox hunting, cricket, and boxing. In France, the people followed what went on in Paris, where activity centered around the "Salons," in which opinions were formed and fashions created, and around the gatherings of *Nouvellistes*, who would congregate in the different Paris gardens to interpret and analyze foreign policy, literature, and language. The cultural predilection in France was clearly urban, including theater, opera, etc., with the city enthusiastically imitating the Royal Court.[22]

The Relationship between Locals and Foreigners: The Fanaticism of the Damascus Inhabitants

Whereas in eighteenth-century Aleppo there were trading stations and foreign communities, in Damascus these were totally nonexistent. Neither do we find European Consuls residing in Damascus, and only a very few even passing through or visiting there. Only in the early nineteenth century is a change evident, with consuls residing in Damascus as well. The explanation which has gained the widest currency is that only in Aleppo were the Europeans benefiting from a sufficient degree of liberalism and respect on the part of the local population, which was more courteous, jovial, pleasant and easygoing than in other places in the Ottoman Empire in its attitude toward Europeans.[23] The Damascus population, in contrast, was renowned for its intolerance and fanaticism toward foreigners.[24]

Thus, we are now at a point where the questions posed at the beginning of this chapter can be answered: namely, why were the Damascus inhabitants regarded as intolerant and fanatical toward foreigners, and was this the reason for the absence of foreigners in Damascus in the eighteenth century? And was the European impression of Aleppo inhabitants correct, and was this the reason for the presence of foreigners in Aleppo?

Damascene intolerance, religious bigotry, and fanaticism originate in the holy nature of the city. Although not on the same level of sanctity as Mecca, Medina and Jerusalem, it certainly ranks after them as one of the starting points of the *Hajj* caravan – hence its designation as *Bab al-Janub* (the Gate of the South) – and as the abode of the *Khalifas* and the site of the Umayya Mosque. In Damascus there developed a local elite based on the 'ulama, landholders who exerted influence over the al-'Azm Walis and the *Mufti* (both local appointees), as well as the Janissaries. These circumstances bred a strong religious atmosphere that undoubtedly led to the attitude that foreigners were impure. This atmosphere characterized Damascus not only in the eighteenth century, but in the nineteenth century as well.[25] But if this was the real reason for the absence of foreigners in Damascus in the eighteenth century, why did it not prevent the appearance of foreigners in the city in the nineteenth century? Is, then this depiction of the attitude of the city's population to foreigners correct?

Indeed, the general atmosphere in Aleppo was more comfortable for foreigners, as their greater numerical presence would seem to indicate, and the city's economic dependence on the European trade taught the parties to live symbiotically, side by side. The local Muslim population became accustomed over time to cooperating with the foreigners and even fostered excellent relations with them around economic interests, a fact which allowed the Europeans to lead a quiet and secure life in their own closed community.[26] But the question still to be answered is whether the Aleppo population was less fanatical and intolerant than the Damascus population?

Day-to-day life for foreigners in Aleppo was not without its difficulties. In the eighteenth century foreign residents continued to live in *khans*. (A *khan* is an inn for travellers, built around a central courtyard.)When the number of English declined and space was vacated in the *khan* douane, it was taken over as warehouse space by local traders. Despite the general instability of the Ottoman Empire, which was at the time undergoing a process of decline, paradoxically, foreigners in Aleppo felt relatively secure, for reasons indicated above. However, consuls still had need of the Janissaries' escort. In day-to-day life, although the Capitulations conferred protection against formal antagonisms, the Europeans were exposed to insults and beatings, mostly from the lower stratums. They therefore had to camouflage themselves in Oriental garb, so as not to draw attention to themselves.[27] It should be noted, however, that decent shopkeepers and Muslims intervened on the foreigners' behalf in cases of outright antagonism.[28] Thus, in Aleppo, as in Damascus, and contrary to the accepted notion, Europeans were also in danger from religious fanaticism.

European Consuls hosted Muslim guests from among governmental officials, city notables, etc. The French Consul even had a special room furnished in Oriental style, so that the guests would feel at ease on their visits.[29] However, very few Europeans visited Muslim homes.[30] Likewise, Muslim locals appeared only rarely in the European residential quarter.[31] Thus, European ties with the local population were generally limited to official ceremonies, commerce, and appearances in court. Regarding the entry of foreigners to Muslim homes, this apparently refers to the homes of dignitaries from the governing circle, the Janissaries, and the *A'yan* (the higher echelons of society in Aleppo). Paton referred to these dignitaries on his visit to Aleppo in the 1840s, stating that they showed more courtesy to foreigners who wore European garb than to foreigners attired as Orientals.[32]

The vested economic and commercial interests of these dignitary groups in Aleppo dictated their ties with foreigners – in contrast to Damascus, where in the eighteenth century it was the 'ulama who comprised the higher stratum of society. In Damascus, economic interests were connected more with the purchase of real estate, which provided the basis for economic strength; such interests did not necessitate ties with foreigners. In any case, the lower classes did not form part of the equation in either Damascus or Aleppo. They did not have the potential to trade with foreigners and were therefore also not accustomed to their presence.

The *Hammam* was an institution in every Muslim city. There were *Hammam*s for Muslims, Christians, and even Jews. The Consuls of Aleppo and their guests learned to adopt the lifestyle of the city, and this included visits to the *Hammam*. But which *Hammam*s did the foreigners visit – the Muslim or the Christian ones? It appears that both options were available to them and that they had no inhibitions about frequenting the Muslim *Hammam* and were even received there with honor. For example, John Lewis Burckhardt reports that his principal enjoyment was going to a Turkish *Hammam* in Aleppo, where the visit was almost ceremonial in nature. Here it was pleasant to have the body massaged by experienced adult servants, to soap and rub one's body in warm water, and afterwards to relax, drink coffee and smoke.[33] In contrast to the English attitude toward the *Hammam*, we have no record of the French attitude, and it is not clear whether they also frequented the *Hammam* or found other ways of refreshing themselves.

Thus far we have examined the relations between locals and foreigners during periods of calm. But what was their character during events connected with struggles between the different parties? Is there a difference between the struggle in the eighteenth century and that of the early nineteenth century in the standing of, and attitude toward, European foreigners?

In 1770, a struggle took place in Aleppo between the different power cliques. This struggle took the form of a rebellion in which the *Ashraf* attacked the *Sarai*. The Europeans sequestered themselves in their *khan*s and were subjected to stoning whenever they went out. During these riots, all the *Bazar* shops were closed, including those of the foreigners.[34]

During the period 1804–6, a power struggle again took place in Aleppo. By the end of this struggle, the Wali and the *Ashraf* had almost succeeded in subduing the Janissaries. The Europeans in Aleppo, who up until that time had been mere observers of the Wali's repressive tyranny over his subjects, began to feel concern for their own lives and property, particularly against the background of events in Ladhiqiya. In light of 'Ali Agha's treatment of the Europeans there, those in Aleppo feared that the city's inhabitants would interpret this as a permit to mistreat them. The Europeans learned how to protect themselves and developed a particular means of communication and assembling, whereby they passed from roof to roof in times of riots. Sharpshooting from the minarets stopped while any European was traversing the roofs, and when a European was caught in a clash between the Janissaries and the *Ashraf*, firing ceased by general consent. Whereas the Janissaries refrained from harming foreigners, the *Ashraf* incited such activities and themselves acted against foreigners.[35] This aggression was not so much due to the fact that the leaders of the *Ashraf* had no vested economic interests with the foreigners, but rather that religious fanaticism was the natural ally of the lower and poorer classes, which was the *Ashraf* power base. Although most of the Janissaries were also from the lower social classes, this group was characterized sociologically by its non-identification with the urban population.[36] The Janissaries, who realized the seriousness of the situation, did not hesitate to approach the foreign consuls and request them to intervene on their behalf and mediate between them and the Wali. The consuls, having vested interests of their own, were willing to do so, and the terms of compromise with the *Ashraf* were brokered by the consuls.

When the Janissaries foresaw defeat in their struggle against the Wali, they did not hesitate to conceal their property (precious stones) by depositing it with foreign traders, who were the consuls of the Jews (*al-Tujjar al-Ajanib Qanasil al-Yahud*). At least in one instance, in 1813, the proprietors of a European trading house, with whom such property had been deposited, refused to comply with the Wali's demand to hand over the property of the Janissaries. However, lest it be thought that this refusal arose from a sense of loyalty to the depositors, it must be pointed out that on the return of the Janissaries to Aleppo several years later, the holders of the deposit refused to return it to them as well.[37]

Thus as we can see from the foregoing, foreigners played a role in the struggles between the different power cliques in the city. Their role as intermediaries derived from the fact that the different groups recognized their standing with the Wali, which rose in parallel to the increase in the volume of trade and the importance of their contribution to the city's economic development, as well as to the Wali's private pocket. Muhammad al-Tabbakh is thus correct in regarding the consuls and the foreign communities as a group having vested economic interests in mediating and restoring calm so as to enable the continuation of the trade which was their *raison d'être*.[38]

Thus, non-Muslims and foreigners were respected by the Janissaries, but not by the *Ashraf*, who, when pressed, incited the masses against foreigners and non-Muslims in order to obtain their support.[39] In other words, there was actually no difference between the intolerance and fanaticism of the inhabitants of Aleppo and those of Damascus; however, demonstrations of this attitude were moderated in Aleppo due to economic considerations. This being so, it follows that it is not religious fanaticism or intolerance that accounts for the absence of foreigners in Damascus in the eighteenth century, but rather economic interests connected with trade products.

During this period, while Damascus was a potential market for consumer goods from Europe, it had no attractive product like silk to offer the Europeans in return.[40] Significant proportions of the Damascene trade were connected with the *Hajj* caravan. However, due to religious reasons, only Muslims could engage in this trade.[41] Lacking an economic interest, there was no reason for European traders to locate a trading station in Damascus. It was preferable to distribute consumer goods through local traders from Aleppo or from some other existing trading station.

Nevertheless, there were foreigners in Damascus during this period however; data shows that in the 1630s, there were present in Damascus a French Consul and Venetian traders whom de Fermanel regarded as living in excessive freedom, and in the course of the eighteenth century and the early nineteenth century, there resided in the city Capucin some Jesuit and Terra Santa missionaries, as well as a few isolated European physicians who stayed in Damascus over extended periods.[42] The physician Chaboceau, for example, who, among other things, was the Wali's personal physician, was a preferred guest in the most exclusive palaces and was able to move about after dark without fear for his life.[43]

Another noteworthy fact is that the sources do not ascribe to the missionaries in Damascus the same degree of proselytization as to the missionaries in Aleppo. Could this be due to the fact that Damascus had no European trading stations and that the local inhabitants did not identify the missionary activity with that of the trading stations? When a decree was issued by the Sublime Porte in 1724 prohibiting contact between subjects of the Ottoman Empire and the French missionaries, this was at the request of the Greek Orthodox Patriarchs in Istanbul, Jerusalem, and Antakya. This decree was reissued in 1746, threatening those praying in the missionaries' churches with imprisonment and fines.[44] In exchange for a bribe paid to the governor, permission was given to pray at the churches in the European monasteries (*dayr al-Ifranj*). The fact that repeated decrees were necessary shows that the Christian inhabitants of Damascus supported the Catholic missionaries – both physically and economically.[45] The diligence of the Catholic missionaries coincided with the struggle for Arabism against an alien Greek priesthood, and had great influence on the appointment of Cyrillus in Damascus and Athanasius in Aleppo.[46]

The situation of the missionaries frequently depended on the arbitrariness of the Wali. For example, in 1759 the Damascus Wali, 'Abdallah al-Shatiji, blackmailed them for having built a monastery.[47] The missionaries were thus caught between the Christian communities in their struggle among themselves and with the Wali, who, in many cases, was exploiting this state of affairs to augment his income. In 1818, for instance, following the riots between Roman Catholics and the Greek Orthodox, Catholic missionaries were forbidden by the Wali to preach on religious themes.[48]

Relations between the missionaries and the Muslim population were initially passive, since the missionaries did not operate among the Muslim inhabitants and the local population actually gave their tacit consent to the missionaries' activities among the Christian population. However, a significant change occurred in 1807, when the Muslim inhabitants of Damascus were influenced by the pervasion of the *Wahabiyya*'s ideology. The inhabitants of Bab Tuma then began mocking the European missionaries, and it seemed to them a worthy deed to kill the monks and destroy the monastery. The monks suspected this impending occurrence and paid the *Qadi* and the Aghas of the Janissaries for protection. The *Qadi*, for his part, threatened the Muslims, who complained to the Wali, but the latter replied that he would not intervene.[49]

Although the same fanatical atmosphere prevailed during the nineteenth century as in the eighteenth century,[50] foreigners were present in Damascus at that time. In 1812, the English Consul Barker took up residence in the city, maintaining influential ties and contacts with the Wali. During that same decade, a physician and French consular agent also resided there. If the population of Damascus had been exceptionally fanatical, as described by European sources, one would have assumed that such fanaticism would have forced them to leave the city – for the very reason that they were individual and isolated Europeans without the support and backing of an established and influential trading colony – but this was not the case.[51]

Foreigners began to operate in Damascus not because of the sudden appearance of local goods that interested them, but because of compelling political factors, such as the rule of Muhammad ʻAli in Syria. Muhammad ʻAli was interested in increasing his income from customs duties and expanding the silk trade, as well as in securing himself against European opposition to his expansionist policy. In order to achieve this aim, he was in need of foreign traders to accelerate trade and increase profits from customs. To this end he brought about a change in the status of the non-Muslims in Syria. The timing was perfect because European countries were in the midst of the Industrial Revolution, with a search for new markets for their consumer goods as well as their raw materials. This was the point at which Damascus opened up to foreign traders, who now had a special economic interest in marketing textile products.[52]

ʻAbd al-Karim Rafeq argues that French traders did not settle in Damascus because the rebellions and power struggles in the city and the Bedouin forays convinced the eighteenth-century French authorities that it would be dangerous to send traders or to maintain a consul there.[53] However, this argument is questionable, since Aleppo at that time suffered from restiveness even more than Damascus, and trade caravans to Aleppo were also subject to Bedouin raids.

The Decreasing Number of Foreigners in Aleppo

The economic decline of Aleppo during the course of the eighteenth century occurred simultaneously with the decrease in the number of French and English traders as compared to past centuries. This raises the question of a connection between these two developments.

Some historians believe that there is a link between these two developments and that it was the economic eclipse of Aleppo that caused the number of foreign traders to diminish.[54] But the answer to this question is more complex. As shown in tables 8.1 and 8.2, one can see that at the beginning of the eighteenth century, the English community in Aleppo numbered approximately the same as that of the French, while the English had a more substantial share of the trade. Only in the course of the eighteenth century did a change occur, as the figures reflect a decline in the size of both communities. Regarding the English, there is indeed a connection between the drop in the number of English traders and the economic decline of Aleppo, with the English even contributing to and accelerating this process by diverting English trade to the Persian Gulf and Izmir.[55] Despite this connection, however, there were other reasons for the decrease in English traders in Aleppo. One major reason was that in the late 1730s many English traders in the city departed back to London and transferred the management of the trading houses to veteran and well-established firms in Aleppo. Among other things, this was the outcome of internal processes at the Levant Company in London, which itself experienced a drastic drop in the number of members between 1670 and 1753. Another reason was that several Levant traders and trading houses went bankrupt, or their owners began to deal in other business due to the reduced attractiveness of the trade.[56]

In contrast, the French continued to maintain all their Syrian stations and eventually came to dominate the trade in the Syrian region. However, there was also a decline in the number of French traders in Aleppo. This was the outcome of administrative decisions adopted in France, including restricting the number of trading stations in 1743 and fixing set periods of time for remaining at the stations in 1731. These regulations were economically motivated by the desire to increase the selling price of French goods and to reduce the spot purchase prices by limiting competition between the French trading houses. In addition, the regulations were intended to prevent the creation of a monopoly by the existing trading houses, thus allowing new traders a share in the Levant trade.[57]

Proof that there was no link between the decrease in the number of French traders and Aleppo's economic decline can be found in the fact that despite the number of trading houses being restricted to nine or ten, and despite the French traders' diminished numbers as compared to the seventeenth century and the early eighteenth century, the scope of French trade in Aleppo increased from a pre-1715 level of million livres (old French currency), to 1.4 million Livres in 1760.[58] It would appear that during this period the French took the place of the departing English traders in Aleppo and even gained from their departure.

However, starting in 1789, the French no longer maintained any trading houses in Syria, renewing their presence only in 1820 when they reopened two.[59] The reasons for the closing of the French stations were political, including the French Revolution and the French army's expedition to Egypt, which caused a cooling off in relations between France and the Ottoman Empire.[60] Accordingly, there is no apparent connection between the decrease in the number of French trading houses and the economic decline of Aleppo, though the same cannot be said with respect to the English.

Summary

One major conclusion arising from this research is that the Damascus Muslim inhabitants were not more intolerant and fanatic towards foreigners than were those of Aleppo. It was their economic interests that caused the Europeans to settle in Aleppo and not in Damascus, where the trade, to a large extent, was connected with the *Hajj* caravan and was limited to participation by Muslims due to religious reasons. Moreover, while Damascus was a potential market for consumer goods from Europe, it had no attractive product to offer the European traders in return. Thus, the European traders preferred to distribute their consumer goods in Damascus through local traders or through some other existing trading station in the Syrian region. Both in Damascus and Aleppo, if the European foreigners were exposed to danger during the seventeenth and eighteenth centuries, it was only from the lower stratums of society. It was clearly economically advantageous for the upper classes to maintain a connection with the foreigners, at least in Aleppo. During the nineteenth century, however, when economic development in the Syrian region was substantially accelerated, particularly under the rule of Muhammad 'Ali, European traders operated and settled in Damascus as well. Here again, mutual economic interests took precedence over any feelings of intolerance.

Notes

This chapter is based on the author's Ph.D. dissertation *Nicht Muslime und Fremde in Aleppo und Damaskus im 18 und in der Ersten Halfte des 19 Jahrhunderts* [Non-Muslim and Foreigners in Aleppo and Damascus during the 18th and the First Half of the 19th Centuries], Friedrich-Alexander Universität, Erlangen-Nürnberg, 1995. The dissertation was written under the supervision of Professor Thomas Philipp from Friedrich-Alexander Universität. It is published under the same title by Klaus Schwarz Verlag, Berlin, 1996.

1 M. C. F. Volney, *Voyage en Egypte et en Syrie 1783, 1784, 1875* (Paris, 1959), pp. 51, 54, 152 [hereafter: Volney]; G. A. Olivier, *Voyage dans*

L'Empire Ottoman l'Égypte et la Perse (Paris, 1807), Vol. II, p. 313 [hereafter: Olivier]; H. A. R Gibb and H. Bowen, *Islamic Society and the West* (London, New York, and Toronto, 1962), Part I, pp. 309–10 [hereafter: Gibb and Bowen]; L. D'Arvieux, *Memoire du Chevalier D'Arvieux, Envoyé Extraordinaire du Roi à la Porte, Consul du Alep 1653–1685* (Paris, 1735), Vol. III, pp. 534–35, Vol. VI, p. 414 [hereafter: D'Arvieux]; J. Sauvaget, *Alep: Essai sur le Développement d'une Grande Ville Syrienne: des Origines au Milie du XIXe Siècle* (Paris, 1941), p. 204 [hereafter: Sauvaget]; Muhammad Raghib al-Tabbakh, *I'lam al-Nubala' bi-Ta'rikh Halab al-Shahba'* (Aleppo, 1923–26), Vol. III, p. 238 [hereafter: al-Tabbakh]; P. Masson, *Histoire du Commerce Français dans le Levant aux 17–18 Siècles* (Paris, 1911), XVIIIeme siècle, p. 286 [hereafter: Masson]; Robert Paris, *Histoire de la Chambre du Commerce de Marseille de 1660 à 1789* (Paris, 1957), Vol. V, p. 413 [hereafter: Paris]; W.G. Browne, *Travels in Africa, Egypt and Syria from the Years 1792–1798*, 2nd edn (London, 1806), pp. 442, 459, 460 [hereafter: Browne]; K. Niebuhr, *Travels through Arabia and other Countries in the East,* 1761–1767 (Edinburgh, 1792), Vol. II, p. 241 [hereafter: Niebuhr].

2 This conception is based on *Qur'an*, Sura 9, Verse 6; Willi Heffening, *Das Islamische Fremdenrecht* (Hannover, 1925), pp. 15–37.

3 A. Fattal, *Le Statut Légal de Non-Musulmans en Pays d'Islam* (Beirut, 1958), p. 73.

4 Gibb and Bowen, Part II, p. 213.

5 A. C. Wood, *History of the Levant Company* (London, 1964), p. 8 [hereafter: Wood]; J. C. Hurewitz, *Diplomacy in the Near and Middle East: A Documentary Record 1535–1914* (Princeton, 1956), Vol. I, p. 1 [hereafter: Hurewitz].

6 Hurewitz, pp. 5–6, 7–9, 25–35; Wood, pp. 6, 8; Richard Hakyluyt, *Voyage* (London, 1962), Vol. III, pp. 57–60 [hereafter: Hakyluyt].

7 For the texts, see: Hurewitz, Vol. I, p. 502.

8 Gibb and Bowen, Part II, p. 213.

9 AE (Affaire Etrangeres) BI (serie), 81 cc Alep 1729–1732, tome 6, p. 81, Memoire; Sauvaget, p. 201; Masson, XVIIeme siècle, p. 78–79. According to Masson, the first French Consul arrived from Tripoli in 1612.

10 On the establishment of the French station (Echelle) in Aleppo during the sixteenth and seventeenth centuries, see: Masson, XVIIeme siècle, Chapter 5; Sauvaget, pp. 200–2.

11 AE BI, 76 Alep 1696–1707, État de la Ville d'Alep 1698, pp. 358–59, la Nation de France Alep; AE BI, 94 cc Alep tome 19, 1777–79, Memoire 16, April 1777, p. 29; AE BI, 96 cc Alep. 1784–86, tome 21, État des Francais Alep 1783, Paris, pp. 232, 235–38, 290; AE BIII, 290 and ACCM. J 904 a letter from Peleran; A. Russell, *The Natural History of Aleppo*, 2nd edn (London, 1794), Vol. II, pp. 5–7 [hereafter: Russell].

12 Hakyluyt, Vol. III, pp. 115–17, September 5, 1583; Wood, p. 15.

13 Masson, XVIIeme siècle, p. 379; John Sanderson, *Travels of 1584–1602 Hakyluyt Society* (London, 1931), p. 130 [hereafter: Sanderson]; Wood, p. 24.

14 See: Yoram Shalit, *Nicht Muslime und Fremde in Aleppo und Damaskus im 18 und in der Ersten Halfte des 19 Jahrhunderts* [Non-Muslim and Foreigners in Aleppo and Damascus during the 18th and the First Half of the

19th Centuries], (Berlin, 1996), pp. 16–20 [hereafter: Shalit]; Wood, p. 11; Hurewitz, pp. 9–15 (the charter).

15 Sanderson, p. 167; Public Record Office State Papers (SP) 105.118, p. 27; SP 105.148, June 8, 1623; SP 105.151, October 30, 1649; A. de la Montraye, *Travels through Europe, Asia and into Parts of Africa, 1696* (London, 1732), Vol. I, p. 153.

16 Ralf Davis, *Aleppo and Devonshire Square* (London, 1967), pp. 76–78 [hereafter: Davis]; Leonard Charles Ibby, *The Travels in Egypt and Nubia, Syria and Asia Minor During the Years 1817–1818* (London, 1985), p. 235 [hereafter: Ibby].

17 Russell, Vol. II, pp. 9, 15–18; Henry Maundrell, *A Journey from Aleppo to Jerusalem in 1697* (Beirut, 1963), pp. vi, 198 [hereafter: Maundrell]; Volney, p. 152; Revd Henry Teonge, *Dairy 1675–1679* (London, 1825, 1928), pp.146, 159 [hereafter: Teonge]; Richard Pococke, *Description of the East (*London, 1743–45), Vol. II, Part 1, p. 152 [hereafter: Pococke]; Wood, p. 242; Davis, pp. 46, 49, 87. The French merchants also kept horses, see: Robin L. Fedden, *Syria an Historical Appreciation* (London, 1947), pp. 215–16 [hereafter: Fedden]. See also: Shalit, pp. 199–297.

18 Ibby, pp. 233–34.

19 Henry Maundrell, *A Journey from Aleppo to Jerusalem in 1697* (Beirut, 1963), p. xxiii; Pococke, Vol. II, Part 1, p. 152 ; Wood, pp. 237, 240; Davis, pp. 22, 79–80.

20 Teonge, pp. 153–55, 167–68.

21 Sir John Chardin, *Travels into Persia, 1671* (London, 1686), pp. 7–8; Wood, p. 237.

22 Russell, Vol. II, p. 18; Andre Maurois, *Histoire d'Angleterre* (Tel Aviv, 1960), pp. 270, 278–90 (translated to Hebrew); Idem, *Histoire de la France* (Tel Aviv, 1960), pp. 175–77, 199–201, 206 (translated to Hebrew).

23 Volney, pp. 51, 54, 152; Olivier, Vol. II, p. 313; Gibb and Bowen, Part I, pp. 309–10; D'Arvieux, Vol. III, pp. 534–35, Vol. VI, p. 414; Sauvaget, p. 204; al-Tabbakh, Vol. III, p. 238; Masson, XVIIIeme siècle, p. 286; Paris, Vol. V, p. 413; Browne, p. 442.

24 Volney, p. 152; Gibb and Bowen, Part I, p. 310; Browne, pp. 459, 460; Niebuhr, Vol. II, p. 241; Fedden, pp. 34, 35, 37; Mikha'il al-Dimashqi, *Ta'rikh Hawadith al-Sham wal-Lubnan min Sana 1197 ila Sana 1357 Hijriyyan* (Beirut, 1912), p. 22 [hereafter: al-Dimashqi].

25 'Ali Bey, *Travels of 'Ali Bey in Syria and Turkey between the Years 1806 and 1807* (London, 1816), p. 272 [hereafter: 'Ali Bey]; Alphonse de Lamartine, *Impressions, Pensées et Paysages Pendant un Voyage en Orient 1832–1833* (Stuttgart, 1839), pp. 65–67 [hereafter: Lamartine]; J. P. Durbin, *Observation in the East, Chiefly in Egypt, Palestine, Syria and Asia Minor* (New York, 1845), p. 68 [hereafter: Durbin]; A. W. Kinglake, *Eothen* (Lincoln, 1985), p. 344 [hereafter: Kinglake].

26 AE BI 76 cc Alep. September 30, 1682; D'Arvieux, Vol. III, pp. 534–45, Vol. XVI, pp. 249, 414; Volney, pp. 274–75, 385; Henry Maundrell, *A Journey from Aleppo to Jerusalem in 1679* (Beirut, 1963), p. 148; Russell, Vol. I, pp. 226–27, Vol. II, pp. 2, 11; Fedden, p. 51; 'Ali Bey, p. 296; Sauvaget, p. 204.

27 Russell, Vol. I, p. 184, Vol. II, p. 24; Davis, p. 5; J. L. Burckhardt, *Travels in Nubia, Memoire* (London, 1822), p. xxxviii [Hereafter: Burckhardt].

28 Russell, Vol. II, p. 24.

29 Masson, XVIIeme siècle, p. 464.
30 Niebuhr, Vol. II, p. 221; Teonge, pp. 150–52.
31 See: Shalit, pp 272–85; Davis, p. 80; Russell, Vol. II, p. 11.
32 A. B. Paton, *The Modern Syrians* (London, 1844), p. 225.
33 Katherine Sim, *Desert Traveller: The Life of J.L. Burckhardt* (London, 1969), p. 83 [hereafter: Sim]. See also: Lamartine, pp. 183–86.
34 See, e.g., Masson, XVIIIeme siècle, p. 286; Paris, Vol. V, p. 414; Fr. Charles Roux, *Les Echelles de Syrie et de Palestine aux 18 Siècle* (Paris, 1928), p. 214; About the conflicts, see: al-Tabbakh, Vol. III, p. 281.
35 Ibby, p. 238; Fedden, p. 215; Sim, pp. 80–81; Burckhardt, p. XXVII, Memoire, Letter from May 22, 1809, describes the high position of the Consul among the Janissaries.
36 See: Shalit, pp. 63–74
37 E. Barker, *Syria and Egypt under the Last Five Sultans of Turkey* (London, 1826), Vol. I, p. 140; Kamil ibn-Husayn ibn-Muhammad ibn-Mustafa al-Halabi al-Ghazzi, *Nahr al-Dhahab fi Ta'rikh Halab* (Aleppo, 1342–5/1923–6), Vol. III, p. 318.
38 Al-Tabbakh, Vol. III, pp. 319–20.
39 Ferdinand Taoutel, *Watha'iq Ta'rikhiyah 'an-Halab* (Beirut, 1940), Vol. I, p. 123; AE BIII 243, Bobin 2, *Rapport sur l'État Commercial et Politique de Syrie 1848.*
40 Davis, p. 123.
41 K. K. Barbir, *Ottoman Rule in Damascus 1708–1758* (Princeton, 1980), pp. 108, 161–67; Y. Hofman, *Muhammad 'Ali in Syria*, (Ph.D. thesis, the Hebrew University of Jerusalem, 1963), pp. 259–60 (in Hebrew) [hereafter: Hofman]; 'Abd al-Karim Rafeq, *The Province of Damascus 1723–1783* (Beirut, 1966), p. 73 [hereafter: Rafeq].
42 Masson, XVII siècle, pp. 386, 388, 458; Masson quotes M. de Fermanel, *Le Voyage d'Italie et du Levant de M. Fermanel en 1630–32* (Rouen, 1687), pp. 312–21; and D'Arvieux, Vol. I, pp. 339–46, Vol. II, pp. 462–67; J. Thevenot, *Relation d'un Voyage Fait au Levant (Roune, 1665)* Vol. II, pp. 25–40; Ibby, pp. 282–83.
43 Jean Haslip, *Lady Hester Stanhop* (London, 1934), pp. 139, 143; Ibby, p. 283.
44 Mikha'il Buraik, *Ta'rikh al-Sham 1720–1781* (Harisa, 1935), p. 19 [hereafter: Buraik]; A. Rabbath, *Documents Inédits pour Servir à L'Histoire de Christianism en Orient* (New York, 1973), Vol. I, p. 565.
45 Buraik, pp. 13, 19–20; 'Ali Bey, p. 272; Lamartine, Vol. III, pp. 96–97.
46 Rabbath, Vol. I, p. 592.
47 *Ibid*, p. 65.
48 Al-Dimashqi, p. 42.
49 *Ibid*, p. 22.
50 Fedden, pp. 34–37; Lamartine, Vol. III, pp. 65–67.
51 Ibby, p. 240.
52 T. S. Ashton, *The Industrial Revolution* (Tel Aviv, 1981), pp. 53–78 (in Hebrew); Hofman, pp. 253, 267; Wood, p. 192; Lamartine Vol. III, pp. 65, 92–93; Kinglake, pp. 326–27; 'Ali Bey, p. 272; Durbin, p. 68.
53 Rafeq, pp. 138, 178.
54 H. L. Bodman, *Political Fractions in Aleppo* (Chapel Hill, 1963), p. 128; Masson, XVIIIeme siècle, p. 521.

55 Masson, XVIIIeme siècle, p. 520; Davis, pp. 27, 36.
56 Davis, pp. 62–63, 89, 240, 242.
57 Masson, XVIIIeme siècle, pp. 25–28, 157. Masson relies on the ordonnance from 1731 and 1743.
58 Masson, XVIIIeme siècle, p. 522.
59 Davis, pp. 28–29; Masson, XVIIIeme siècle, p. 523; AE BIII 243, Bobine 2, Renseignement sur le commerce du Levant, Division par les Échelles, et tableau des établissements, May 13, 1825.
60 Sauvaget, pp. 180–92; A. Luzki, "The Francus in Aleppo and the Influence of the Capitulations on its Jewish Inhabitants," *Zion*, Vol. 6 (1940), p. 63.

9

Betwixt and Between: The Arab Al-'Aramshah Tribe of Southern Lebanon

Joseph Ginat

Arab al-'Aramshah is a Bedouin tribe located on both sides of the Lebanese-Israeli border. There are two different assumptions as to the origin of the tribe. Some of the tribe's elders claim that the tribe originated in Iraq, while others think that it originated in the Syrian desert. Those who claim Iraqi origins use as proof the fact that the tribe's vernacular has some similarities to Iraqi dialect. They use some words of Iraqi origin, whereas other tribes in the region do not. They indicate that the tribe stayed in the Syrian desert for several generations after it left Iraq.

The name of the tribe is derived from the given name "'Armoosh" or "'Armooshi," who the tribe members believe is the founder of the lineage. Some of the elders, as well as the scholar Moshe Gabay from Kibbutz Eilon, think that the tribe arrived at its contemporary location around 200–220 years ago. The author of this article thinks that the al-'Aramshah people arrived in the area about 160 years ago, based on the genealogical data collected from the late Jaber 'Ali, as well as from the elders of Megheis *Khams* (co-liable groups) [Marx, 1967]. Jaber's widow, who is still alive at approximately 106 years of age, verified the information that the late Jaber had given me, namely, that his grandfather was born in the present location of the tribe, while his great-grandfather 'Abdallah was born in the Syrian desert. In the Encyclopedia of 'Umar Ridha Kahala (1949, 1994) the entry "al-'Aramshah" identifies a sub-tribe (far'a) of al-Judr of the al-Jabur al-Waie in Iraq. 'Aramshah (al-Bo) is a *fakhed* (another term for sub-tribe) of al-Badri in Iraq. 'Umar Ridha stated that al-Bo Badri *fakhed* were famous for breeding Arabian horses and camels (new edition, 1994, Volume V: 34, 36).[1]

In 1875, the French traveler, Guerin, mentioned that he arrived in the region on September 16 and took notes of his observations (Guerin, [1877] 1880, Vol. VII: 84). His description specified the area of Khirbet 'Irribin, where he found ruins of homes, the remains of a church and subterranean storage. He stated that he saw several Bedouin grazing their herds, but he did not indicate their tribal identity. Guerin mentioned another ancient site on the same plateau. Khirbet Idmit is on the opposite edge of the plateau. He found two cisterns and two ancient buildings there, in addition to two houses where *fallahin* (peasants), not Bedouin, lived.[2]

The contemporary al-'Aramshah Bedouin in the communities of Zahirah in Lebanon and Jurdie and Nawaquir in Israel claim that Guerin was mistaken in calling the inhabitants *fallahin*.[3] Instead, the al-'Aramshah believe that these people were probably the original tribe members who came from the Syrian desert. In his book, Guerin includes a map that depicts the area, but the tribe is not mentioned on the map whatsoever. Another map from approximately the same time period, published by the Palestine Exploration Fund (PEF) in 1880, shows the name "al-'Aramshah" on the site of their present location.[4]

At the end of World War I, England and France held detailed negotiations about the division between their Mandates. The negotiations took a relatively long time despite the fact of the agreement between Sykes and Picot in 1916 regarding the distribution of the area, which had formerly been part of the Ottoman Empire. The goal of the French was to include as many minority groups as possible under their jurisdiction, which, indeed, was the final outcome (Hof, 1985: 3–17; Aharoni, 1999: 2). Both the French and the British insisted on having tight border restrictions in order to prevent the smuggling of goods and the transfer of disease or epidemics. However, the new border divided the *dirah* (tribal territory) of the al-'Aramshah tribe. Political and military decisions do not usually take into consideration social, economic and other cultural structures.

In 1926, arrangements were made by the British and French authorities to enable the al-'Aramshah tribe members on either side of the border to cross for pasturing or watering their herds. The Bedouin were asked for the first time in history to brand their herds and flocks with two different kinds of marks – instead of one mark per tribe – in order to know which were from Lebanon and which were from Palestine. Usually each tribe had its own distinct mark or *wasam*.[5] The British and the French also asked the al-'Aramshah people to carry an identification card, something they had never previously done.

The names of the locations of the al-'Aramshah in Palestine and Lebanon, according to Murad al-Dabagh, are Khirbet Nawqir and Khirbet

Jurdie; whereas, in Lebanon the name of the location is Zahirah. In Zahirah, he mentions another tribe by the name of Qulitat. He states that according to the statistics of 1931, there were 199 people in the entire al-'Aramshah area, of whom 109 were males ([1964] 1988, Vol. VII: 341). Ashkenazi (1938: 253) gives similar details to those of al-Dabagh. The names of the places mentioned by al-Dabagh were used by the British and French authorities. As to the number of tribal members, Walid Khalidi claims that in 1945, there were 360 Bedouin of the al-'Aramshah tribe in the area (1992: 17–18).

From the establishment of the state of Israel in 1948 until the Sinai campaign of 1956, the Bedouin of the al-'Aramshah tribe were allowed to cross the border. The Israeli part of the tribe used to shop in the towns north of Zahirah. The cemetery for both parts of the tribe was located on the Lebanese side. After the 1956 war, however, the Lebanese army prohibited the Israeli al-'Aramshah Bedouin from crossing the border into Lebanon. Neither could the Lebanese al-'Aramshah come into Israel any longer. Despite the border closure, the two parts of the tribe kept in contact.

Jaber told me that he had learned from his father and that it was also the oral tradition among the tribe members that they had been driven out from the Syrian desert by the Rwala because of a drought. He said that the Rwala were the strongest tribe in its federation of tribes, though he did not remember the name of the federation, which is, in fact, "'Aneze." Musil, who studied the Rwala Bedouin beginning in 1908, wrote that "Rwala belonged to the 'Aneze group (Musil, 1928: xiii). William and Fidelity Lancaster, who started studying the Rwala in 1972, stated that: "The Rwala are the largest tribe of the 'Aneze confederation (W. Lancaster, 1981: 8).[6] In drought years, the stronger tribes raid the weaker tribes. First, they graze on the *dirah* of the weaker tribes. In the second stage, they raid the villages on the fringe of the desert and the sown. Schumacher reports that in 1912, the Rwala raided the Circassians on the Golan, who fired on them and chased the Rwala back into the desert. Schumacher witnessed the encounter between the Rwala Bedouin and the Circassians. He saw thousands of camels with young Bedouin running fast into the desert as a result of the Circassian shots. One armed Circassian told Schumacher that the Rwala Bedouin left and would never come back (Schumacher, 1888: 146–47).[7] The case of the defeat of the Rwala in the raid on the Circassian field was known all over south Lebanon and the Galilee. The al-'Aramshah gloated at the Rwala's misfortune, feeling that God was punishing the Rwala because they had raided the al-'Aramshah and driven them out of the Syrian desert, which caused them to become semi-sedentarized.

The Bedouin usually prefer nomadism to sedentarization. The Lancasters emphasized the preferred option of the Bedouin: "We have never heard anyone claim that nomadism was forced on them as the only option available; on the contrary, all the nomads we have come across regard nomadism as their preferred choice" (William and Fidelity Lancaster, 1998: 25). Salzman states that sedentarization is "preferred upon nomadic people by external forces (1980: vii).[8] Within the external forces, we should include those such as drought years (Khazanov, 1994). In recent publications, Khazanov indicates that "when drought strikes, many animals perished from lack of fodder" (1998: 25). Epidemics cause nomads to move to other places and, in many cases, to sedentarize (Beck, 1986: 129ff.; Black-Michaud, 1986: 83–84; Irons, 1975; Tapper, 1979). W. Lancaster mentions in his book on the Rwala (1981) that there were periods of long-lasting drought years. In the Syrian desert, he reports on six consecutive years of drought between 1956 and 1962. (Lancaster, 1981: 18, 112, 145, 148). In the Saudi desert, " . . . the drought lasted from 1956 to 1972, but the Rwala, of course, could exploit rainfall in Syria and Iraq" (*ibid.*: 100).

In her study on the raids, Louise Sweet (1970) distinguishes between reciprocal raids conducted by equal nomad tribes and unilateral raids perpetrated by stronger tribes on weaker tribes or on settled Bedouin and *fallahin*. The strong Bedouin tribes on the East Bank of the Jordan River, such as Bani Sakhir (Alfayez, 1995), would raid the fields of the Jewish settlements in the Beit She'an and Yizrael Valleys. The historian Malamat, in his discussion on the Midianites and his analysis of their penetration and retreat in Gideon's period, notes the raid of the Bedouin from the Eastern Bank of the Jordan River to the West Bank in the year 1947, which was a year of drought (Malamat, 1964: 110–23). The al-'Aramshah case belongs to the unilateral type of raid in which they were driven out of the Syrian desert because of drought. The Rwala needed more space for their pasture. For the Rwala at that time, it appears not to have been an exceptionally difficult drought. In contrast, when they raided the Circassians on the Golan Heights, it was most likely a far heavier drought.

The al-'Aramshah Bedouin moved from the Syrian desert close to the Golan and then west to the area which became Lebanon after World War I. When they reached the present location in their encampment, they suffered epidemics from which many of their animals died. According to the elders of the tribe, until 1948 they suffered three times from epidemics and twice from heavy drought. Jaber, as well as other elders of the tribe, told me that one of these drought periods was in the time of World War I, especially during the years 1916–17. Jaber graphically described the hardships endured: "We would take the barley grains out of the camels' manure, wash it, and make bread out of it. The Turkish soldiers would trade a rifle for half a pita bread." The al-'Aramshah used to graze their animals in the nearby valleys by day and encroach the *fallahin's* fields at night. Until 1948, the al-'Aramshah tribe belonged to the category of semi-nomadic Bedouin, pitching their tents in different locations of their *dirah*.

After the 1948 establishment of the state of Israel, most of the al-'Aramshah Bedouin continued to live in tents. In the late 1950s and early 1960s, they became sedentarized and moved into lean-tos and then buildings in both Lebanon and Israel. As mentioned earlier, the members of the two parts of the tribe were keeping in close contact. After June 1982, when Israel invaded Lebanon, the Israeli al-'Aramshah resumed burying their dead in the cemetery of the tribe on the Lebanese side. In order to maintain cohesiveness between the two parts of the tribe, they conduct marriage unions between the Israeli and Lebanese parts of the tribe. Some of these unions are between members of the same *khams*, and between relatives (in-group marriages), while others are from different descent groups.[9] Of course, the Lebanese as well as the Israeli al-'Aramshah continue to marry from other tribes and even from other villages.

Marriage unions, serve to establish political alliances, termed by Peters as "weaving ties" (1965). It was important to the al-'Aramshah elders to direct marriage unions with their new neighbors after arriving in their present location. By conducting unions with other tribes in the region, the resulting political alliances prevented raids from newly established relations. Moreover, such alliances by marriage even helped to protect against raids by a third party. Such marriage unions were established between the al-'Aramshah and the Qulitat Bedouin in Lebanon and between the al-'Aramshah and the al-Haib in the northern Galilee. This latter marriage alliance misled al-Dabagh to claim that the al-'Aramshah originated from the al-Haib federation of tribes ([1964] 1988, Vol. 7: 413). Granqvist focused on marriage patterns in her study on Irtas (1931, 1935), a Palestinian village located south of Bethlehem on the fringe of the desert. From her we learn that in all cases of unions between the Irtas people and the Bedouin, the female came from Irtas. The villagers built these alliances by giving their daughters to the Bedouin in order to gain their protection.[10] While the Judean Desert Bedouin took the women of Irtas, they never gave any of their women to the villagers.

In the marriage union between the al-'Aramshah Bedouin of Lebanon and that part of the tribe in Israel between the years 1974 and 1982, the Israeli al-'Aramshah girls married into the Lebanese al-'Aramshah. However, since 1982 none of the Israeli al-'Aramshah girls have married into Lebanon, while eight al-'Aramshah girls from Lebanon have been married to Israeli al-'Aramshah. The Israeli al-'Aramshah do not know what will happen in southern Lebanon after the Israelis withdraw, worrying that the Lebanese will prevent any contact of the al-'Aramshah tribe on both sides of the border. Since 1982, the political situation is unclear for the inhabitants who live in the security zone controlled by the Israeli Defense Forces (IDF) and the South Lebanese Army (SLA). Any time there is a statement or suggestion by an Israeli politician to withdraw from Lebanon, it increases the tension among the dwellers of this security zone, including the al-'Aramshah tribe on both sides of the border. The Israeli al-'Aramshah think that in case Israel withdraws from south Lebanon, they might be cut off from their relatives on the other side of the border, thus losing contact with their daughters who married Lebanese al-'Aramshah men. On the other hand, the al-'Aramshah tribe members in Lebanon want to strengthen the ties with their relatives and with others from different *khams* of the tribe living in Israel. For those in Lebanon, the uncertainty of who will rule their area and what the political situation will be after the Israeli withdrawal drives them to seek more support from their relatives in Israel.[11] By creating stronger bonds through marriage, that is, by giving their daughters to Israeli al-'Aramshah, the receiving families will be more obliged to help in times of future need.

It should be noted, however, that the status of women in the al-'Aramshah tribe is much higher than in other Bedouin tribes in the region and elsewhere, and even higher than among the *fallahin*.[12] The al-'Aramshah girls and women do not cover their faces with a veil and are not excluded from the company of men in public. They can go freely within the tribe or the tribal territory and talk to men when they meet them outdoors. In wedding ceremonies, they dance together with men, which is a unique cultural phenomenon in Arab societies. Women play an important role in their own mate selection as well as that of their offspring. Unlike other Bedouin societies and the *fallahin* in the region, the bride and groom can meet freely beforehand without a chaperone. However, when it comes to political alliances or sometimes even economic ties, the elders of the tribe make the decisions. In the case where a political alliance has determined the match, the bride or groom can reject the assigned partner. Then the families will try to find a different partner from within the *khams*.

In marked contrast, even Palestinian women who were empowered by their participation in the *Intifada* in Gaza Strip and the West Bank still did not achieve much personal freedom in relations between the sexes. Suha Sabbagh, in her book *Palestinian Women of Gaza and the West Bank*, pointedly notes: "and despite women's growing political activism, their status in society is not greatly changed" (1998: 11).[13] As indicated above, the women of the al-'Aramshah do have a higher status in the family and the community. However, in times of uncertainty, the political calculation overrules free mate selection. Here we see the dichotomy between the two parts of the tribe. While the Lebanese want to strengthen the ties, the Israelis are reluctant to gives their daughters to the Lebanese in case the border closes in the future.

In this uncertain atmosphere, the al-'Aramshah elders in Lebanon look for other avenues by which to increase the interactions with their fellow tribe members in Israel. They try to be involved in the mediation of conflicts that occur within different co-liable groups among the Israeli al-'Aramshah and between the al-'Aramshah and other tribes in the region. They have also increased their involvement in mediation among different groups in south Lebanon. Mediation in Arab society is known by the term *wasita*, or *wasta* in colloquial Arabic. The mediator serves as a go-between in solving conflicts and is usually a person with some authority (Barth, 1968: 96–97; Black-Michaud, 1975; Farsoun, 1970: 269–70; Gellner, 1969: 12; Ginat, 1997: 55–99; Gulliver, 1979: 209, 214, 218, 227; Marx, 1981). An important quality of a successful mediator is his reputation (Ginat, 1997: 55). As William Lancaster says: "Reputation is based on how closely a person demonstrates virtues, honor, bravery, generosity, political acumen and mediation abilities" (1981:43). George Simmel, in his analysis of the "stranger" with respect to the mediator, stresses that he is objective and that both sides trust him (1971: 146).

The Lebanese al-'Aramshah elders understand that the role of mediation is important and that by accumulating cases which contribute to their reputation, they will be needed whatever the political future brings. Whenever there are rumors that the Israelis are discussing the possibility of withdrawal from the security zone, the elders and the other members of the tribe usually meet in one of the *diwan* (guest room) or "regular private gathering of friends and associates for conversation or discussion" (Eickelman, 1997: 332, 375).[14]

The al-'Aramshah Bedouin in Lebanon are betwixt and between the Israelis, who control the security zone in south Lebanon, and the SLA, on the one hand, and between the Lebanese army and the Hizballah Shi'a, on the other hand. The Israeli government decided on January 14, 1984 to redeploy troops from territories in Lebanon and to establish a secure buffer zone in south Lebanon (Ma'oz, 1995). In March of 1985, the SLA encompassed 1,890 soldiers, whereas it numbered 2,500 by August of 1986. This was the same number of SLA soldiers at the end of 1997 (Erlich, 1997:15). The establishment of the security zone controlled by the IDF and the encounters with the new enemy, the Hizballah, founded by Iran and encouraged by Syria, started a new era for the

150,000 inhabitants of the secured buffer zone. The presence of the IDF was not demarcated by any specific time period. The Madrid conference in October 1991 and the discussions between Israel and the Syrians in the US, which started in the fall of 1991 and continued in July 1992,[15] indicated the beginning of uncertainty for the residents of the security zone.

This was even more the case for the al-'Aramshah tribe. General Yossie Peled, who was responsible for the north of the country plus the security zone, indicated that between 1989 and 1995, the IDF transferred seven fortified military installations to the SLA. Israel turned over increasing responsibility to the SLA, while the number of Israeli soldiers in Lebanon steadily decreased (Peled, 1997: 3). Such actions and, moreover, their announcement caused more tension among the al-'Aramshah tribe members. Another incident giving cause for concern was: "In August 1996, soon after assuming office, Prime Minister Benjamin Netanyahu proposed a 'Lebanon first' plan, whereby Israeli troops would withdraw entirely from Lebanon in exchange for Syrian guarantees to disarm Hizballah, facilitate the deployment of the Lebanese army southward to the border with Israel and protect Israel's SLA allies" (Zittrain Eisenberg, 1997: 7). The Syrian President, Hafiz al-Asad, rejected Netanyahu's proposal.

In the past several years, one can hear politicians from both major Israeli political parties expressing their support for the idea of a unilateral withdrawal from Lebanon. One of them, the Knesset (the Israeli Parliament) Member Yossi Beilin, who was Deputy Minister of Foreign Affairs and later a minister in Shimon Peres' government, has stated that the best solution would be a withdrawal in agreement with the Syrian government. However, if this cannot be achieved, then he would prefer a unilateral withdrawal rather than prolonging the current problems (Beilin, 1997). Retired General Shlomo Gazit, who was the head of the IDF Intelligence Unit, stated in a lecture given to the Peace and Security Association (September 29, 1997) that the entire population of south Lebanon smells the end of the IDF presence. Gazit suggested that Israel come to an agreement with the Lebanese government via a mediator, preferably President Mubarak of Egypt. According to Gazit, President Mubarak knows that any step forward in the peace process would contribute to stability in Egypt. Gazit emphasized that the withdrawal should take place as soon as possible. Another supporter of policy change is Michael Eitan, a Deputy Ministry in the Prime Minister's Office and previously the Minister of Science in Netanyahu's government, who declared that Israel has to make a brave decision to reassess its presence in Lebanon (*Ha'aretz*, November 19, 1998).

In October 1998, Asad delivered a secret message to President Clinton indicating that if Israel agreed to a full pullback from the Golan Heights, he would make sure that there would be no further Hizballah attacks in south Lebanon (*Ha'aretz*, November 30, 1998). On November 26, 1998, Prime Minister Netanyahu said that Israel was ready to revise security arrangements to pave the way for an IDF withdrawal from Lebanon (*Jerusalem Post*, November 27, 1998). Yet, at the same time, the Hizballah attacked the IDF and SLA, which provoked an Israeli retaliation. As the *New York Times* reported: "Israeli forces bombarded suspected Hizballah guerilla targets in southern Lebanon overnight in retaliation for deadly attacks on its soldiers . . . The Israeli army warned Lebanese civilians that it was preparing to bombard a string of areas close to the occupied border area" (November 29, 1998). Moreover, Hizballah has recently intensified its recruitment of people from the security zone, mainly from the Shi'a community. *Shaykh* 'Abbas Muhsayn 'Ali Fadlallah, from the village of Kila, was arrested on October 29, 1998 by the SLA. He was charged with planning to kidnap an Israeli soldier and to smuggle him to the Hizballah headquarters (*Ha'aretz*, November 25, 1998). Danny Rabinovich, an Israeli anthropologist, in his analysis of the situation of the security zone, has indicated that the civilian population of south Lebanon is suffering the most. He predicts that more and more of the Shi'a population will collaborate with Hizballah and that the high command of the SLA will have to evacuate from south Lebanon to Israel or Europe (*Ha'aretz*, November 30, 1998). In reference to relations with Hizballah, Laura Zittrain Eisenberg suggests that: "The SLA and Lebanese Christian nationalists sympathetic to Israel vigorously oppose a unilateral withdrawal for fear of a wholesale massacre of SLA members and their families by Hizballah" (Zittrain Eisenberg, 1997: 7). On the Israeli side, however, the most recent public poll conducted by Ephraim Yaar and Tamar Harman found that there is a significant increase in the number of people who support a unilateral withdrawal from south Lebanon (Yaar and Harman, *Ha'aretz*, December 2, 1998).

The atmosphere among the al-'Aramshah in Lebanon is even worse than among the other people of south Lebanon. They are Sunni-Muslim, rather than Shi'a like the majority of the region's population.[16] They reside next to the Israeli border and, as indicated earlier, half of the tribe lives on the other side of the border. There have been some incidents of Hizballah shelling in which Katyusha missiles meant for Jewish settlements fell on buildings of the al-'Aramshah people on both sides of the border. In one case, when a Lebanese Bedouin was killed, the Israeli members of the tribe crossed the border and paid their respects to their relatives.[17] When an IDF soldier who was a member of the al-'Aramshah tribe was killed by a Hizballah attack,[18] the Lebanese tribe members came to his family's *diwan* to be with their relatives in time of grief. Some of the al-'Aramshah even serve in the SLA and fight alongside the IDF against the Hizballah.

In an interview with elders of the Israeli part of the tribe (June 1998), I learned that it has only been in the past few years that some of the Lebanese young men of the tribe went to Beirut and were drafted by the Lebanese National Army (LNA). I was told that two of them even achieved the rank of officer. I then met with two men of the Lebanese al-'Aramshah tribe and several people from villages neighboring Zahirah. From the information I gathered, I verified the fact that some of the tribe members have served in the LNA. It is interesting to note that those of the neighboring villages were less reluctant to talk about the al-'Aramshah youth serving in the LNA than were the tribe members themselves. As one of the al-'Aramshah tribe members stated: "We are Lebanese and there is one official government in Lebanon, and we should be loyal to our government." Another older tribe member said, "*Al-hayya madraseh*" (Life is school), emphasizing that even though he was illiterate, the school of life had taught him many wise things. He went on to say: "You Israelis were in the Sinai and Gaza Strip two times. Every time you left, those who were suspected of collaborating with your people were brutally murdered." He continued giving examples of people who were murdered in Syria and in Lebanon and concluded, "Not only Hizballah is trigger-happy, but it is also an old Lebanese trait." A Christian from a neighboring village was more open and said: "Israel would always act according to its interest. When the UN decided in 1978 in favor of a total Israeli withdrawal from all Lebanese territory, Israel did not take that resolution seriously."[19] On the other hand, he added:

> When there is an increase in the Israeli public opinion to withdraw from south Lebanon, we have no doubt that the IDF will withdraw even though the Minister of Defense and the other high command of the IDF are against unilateral withdrawal. If you come to the various *diwan* of the al-'Aramshah and other villages in the region, the only discussions you hear are focused on this subject. We believe that the withdrawal will be soon, but we do not know what the fate will be of those who live in the region.

In such a period of uncertainty and fear of the unknown, one can understand the strategy of the al-'Aramshah youth joining the LNA. To a certain extent, it is a psychological relief. However, this situation causes some difficulties in the daily lives of their families. Those who serve in the LNA are cut off from their families and the community as a whole. They cannot cross the security line of the buffer zone and cannot stay in contact with their families. Theoretically, it might be a situation where, in the course of encounters between the SLA and the IDF with Hizballah, the Lebanese government may or may not decide to send troops to that area. It could happen that brothers or cousins serving in the LNA would have to shoot at their relatives who serve in the SLA and vice versa.

The underlying reason for al-'Aramshah youth serving in the LNA is to avoid unknown problems or consequences that might arise after the Israeli withdrawal. When a member of the al-'Aramshah tribe proclaims his loyalty to the central government, it is the "emic," whereas the "etic" has to be analyzed in terms of their seeking a secured solution.[20] They want to prove to the Lebanese government that they are not supporting Israel even though they live on the border and that it is not by choice that the tribe is divided between Israel and Lebanon. Above all, it is not by choice that they are part of the security zone. Their greatest concern is that Hizballah might take over the area after the Israeli withdrawal. There is no way that they can establish any alliances with Hizballah. Thus, the best solution for them is to live in the dichotomy of serving in the SLA and the LNA simultaneously.

The situation in south Lebanon is, of course, not an easy one for the 150,000 people who live there. But the al-'Aramshah case is much more complicated than for any other ethnic group. The members of the tribe who live in Zahirah on the Lebanese-Israeli border are encapsulated betwixt and between Israel, the SLA, Hizballah, and the Lebanese authorities. They are aware of the fact that they will face many difficulties when Israel finally withdraws. At the present time, they are trying to find any kind of safety valve in order to protect themselves from known as well as unknown dangers.

Appendix

Resolution 425 (1978)

Adopted by the UN Security Council at its 2074th meeting on 19 March 1978,
The Security Council,

Taking note of the letters from the Permanent Representative of Lebanon and from the permanent Representative of Israel,

Having heard the statement of the Permanent Representatives of Lebanon and Israel,

Gravely concerned at the deterioration of the situation in the Middle East and its consequences to the maintenance of international peace,

Convinced that the present situation impedes the achievement of a just peace in the Middle East,

1 Calls for strict respect for the territorial integrity, sovereignty and political independence of Lebanon within its internationally recognized boundaries;
2 Calls upon Israel immediately to cease its military action against Lebanese territorial integrity and withdraw forthwith its forces from all Lebanese territory;
3 Decides, in the light of the request of the Government of Lebanon, to establish immediately under its authority a United Nations interim force for southern Lebanon for the purpose of confirming the withdrawal of Israeli forces, restoring international peace and security and assisting the government of Lebanon in ensuring the return of its effective authority in the area, the Force to be composed of personnel drawn from member States;
4 Requests the Secretary General to report to the Council within twenty-four hours on the implementation of the present resolution.

Resolution 426 (1978)

Adopted by the Security Council at its 2075th meeting on 19 March 1978,
The Security Council,

Approves the report of the Secretary-General on the implementation of Security Council resolution 425 (1978), contained in document S/12611 of 19 March 1978,

1 Decides that the United Nations Interim Force in Lebanon shall be established in accordance with the above-mentioned report for an initial period of six months, and that it shall continue in operation thereafter if required, provided the Security Council so decides.

Acknowledgment

I would like to express my thanks to Professor Norman Stillman, University of Oklahoma, for his valued comments and to Reuben Aharoni of Haifa University who studied the history of the al 'Aramshah tribe and was kind enough to exchange information and ideas for this chapter.

Notes

1 'Umar Ridha Kahalah, 1949, new publication, 1994. Vol. V, pp. 34, 36, based on al-Ghazawi, *'Ashayir al Iraq* .256/4, 89/3.

2 Reuben Aharoni who also interviewed residents of al-'Aramshah was given the same information. A family of *fallahin* origin inhabited the buildings in Khirbet Idmit up to 1956. That family had property in Lebanon. Several families of the al-'Aramshah cultivated the *fallah's* land close to Khirbet Idmit and received half of the crops. The name of the family was Mamluk. There is a local legend that the founder of the family was the only *Mamluk* who, with his horse, succeeded in escaping from the fortress in Cairo when Muhammad 'Ali had a "party" for the *Mamluks* where he killed them (1811).

3 Victor Guerin, 1977, translated into Hebrew by Haim Ben-'Amram (according to the original French publication, 1880), Vol. VII, The Galilee (II), p. 84.

4 G. Falah, *The Process and Patterns of Sedentarization of the Galilee Bedouin, 1880–1982* (Unpublished Ph.D. thesis, University of Durham, 1982), p. 2. The map that he uses in his work is PEF The Map of Western Palestine 1880, sheet II–VI, *Memoirs 1881–83*; Vol. II, pp. 73–74; see also: Falah (1983).

5 Each tribe has its own mark called *wasam* in Arabic. This is done in order to identify lost livestock. The al-'Aramshah tribe had the same *wasam* for both parts of the tribe in Lebanon and Palestine. A new arrangement was demanded for each half of the tribe to have a different brand in order to cross from Lebanon to Palestine and vice verse. Lane, in his Arabic-English lexicon, referring to the *wasam* (sima), says "a brand or mark of a figure made with a hot iron upon an animal." Vol. VIII (1863–1893), p. 3053. See also the same interpretation by Ayalon and Shenar, 1962 (1947), p. 415. Muhammad Murtadha al-Zabidi, 1888/89–1892/93 (1310 *Hijrah*) *Taj al-'Arus* 9, pp. 92–93 refers to the same explanation of the term. Musil, who studied the Rwala Bedouin, in his description of searching for lost sheep, says "They found a piece of the skin of the first sheep, which by the marks on his heads, the owner recognized as belonging to his flock. Before sunset, they found the second and the third sheep, which had the same mark (1828: 460). Other researchers refer to the *wasam* in their studies; see: Ashkenazi, 1938; Burkhardt, 1831, Vol. I, pp. 198–99; 'Aref al-'Aref, 1933, 1934; Oppenheim, 1939; Bar Zvi, 1991; Levi, 1987; Kay, 1978; al-Hashash, 1991; al-Qusus, 1972.

6 For further analysis on the concept of federation of tribes, see: Sharon Bastug's description of the segmentary lineage system (1998). See also: Barth (1992).

7 For the description of the Golan (Jaulan) and its inhabitants prior to World War I, see: Schumacher, 1888; Schumacher, Oliphant, and Le Strange, 1889.

8 External forces could be governments that plan oil drilling or other programs as well. Jamil, 1956; Hiatt, 1984; Fazel, 1970; Katakura, 1977; Cole, 1981; Fabietti, 1982; W. Lancaster, 1981; Scholz, 1981; Medzini, 1998; Kliot and Medzini, 1985; Janzen, 1986; Behnke, 1980; Salzman, 1980. Anatoly Kazanov has an excellent analysis on the subject in his book: *Nomads and the*

Outside World (second edition, 1994), as well as in his paper: "Pastoralists in the Contemporary World: The Problem of Survival," 1998. For the different reasons for sedentarization due to external forces, see: N. N. Lewis, 1987.

9 The Bedouin of north Israel as well as south Lebanon adopted the *fallahin* term *hamula* either for the lineage or for the descent group. For further discussion on the *hamula* either as lineage or clan, see: Cohen, 1965: 3; Antoun, 1972: 44–45; Ginat, 1982: 22, footnote 8; Peters, 1990: 84–111; Tapper, 1983: 10.

10 The author of this chapter conducted a field study in Egypt on the ordeal by fire – the *bish'a* (Ginat, 1998). Some of the members of the *Mubasha's* (the person who conduct the *bish'a*) *khams* married women of peasant origin. The Mubasha' stated that: "We take their women, but we do not give our women to the *fallahin.*" The same statements were given by Bedouins in Israel whose relative married a woman from a rural community. See: Marx, 1967. Musil specified the restrictions to marry the daughters of blacksmiths, or other mechanics who camp with the Rwala (1928: 136–37). W. Lancaster emphasizes that no one among the Rwala "wished to lower his or her reputation so marriage tends to take place between individuals and groups with roughly similar reputation (1981: 46).

11 For changes in marriage patterns in times of uncertainty in Arab villages, see: Ginat, 1982: 88–149. The marriage has been analyzed according to sub-periods. For an example of sub-period division of the al-'Aramshah Bedouin, see: *Ibid*: 242.

12 For comparison on women's status, see: Abu-Lughod, 1986; C. Eikelman, 1984; Ginat, 1982: 151–217; Goodwin, 1994; Peters, 1990: 243–77; Wikan, 1991 (1982). For the status of married women in Lebanon, see: Lamia Rustum Shehadeh, 1998. In her paper, which was focused on legal status, Shehadeh indicates that: "Further, according to the Sunni and Ja'fari [Shi'a] sects, the husband has the right to admonish and discipline, as well as inflict physical punishment, when the wife is recalcitrant" (1998: 506). For further sources of Islamic Law, classical Muslim Family Law and modern Muslim Family Law reforms in some Arab countries, see: Esposito, 1982. This does not, of course, apply to al-'Aramshah women, who have higher status.

13 Suha Sabbagh took upon herself a very important task of editing the book. The book deals with women's activities at the time of the *Intifada*. However, it would be important to have materials on women's status post-*Intifada*. As we know, after the *Intifada*, women's status regressed. When we refer to the al-'Aramshah women, there are no fluctuations in the status and role in both, the family and community.

14 In some Arab countries, the *diwan* is called *diwaniyyah* (Eikelman, 1997: 332, 375). Another term being used is *madhafa*. This derives from *dhaif*, which means guest. In Iraq, the *madhafa* is known as *mudhif* (Ibid., p. 377). Before the members of the al-'Aramshah tribe became sedentarized, they used the Bedouin term, "shiq," the part of the tent for the guest.

15 For the description and analysis of the peace talks between the Israelis and the Syrians, see: Rabinovitz, *The Brink of Peace, Israel and Syria, 1992–1996* (1998). For the relations between Israel and Syria at that period including the situation in Lebanon, see: Ma'oz, 1995. Rabinovich in his book claims "the best and most comprehensive book on Israel's conflict and relations with Syria

in those years is Moshe Ma'oz , *From War to Peace Making* (1998: 266).

16 The Shi'a community in Lebanon is estimated at 35 percent of the Lebanese total population, where the Sunnis are estimated at approximately 24 percent of the total population. The Christians are estimated at about 35 percent, and the Druze about 6 percent. See: W. W. Harris, 1998: 476.

17 This event took place in July of 1993. Ma'oz refers to the event by saying: "During the first two weeks of July 1993, the Syrian-directed Hizballah and the Syrian-controlled Jibril group ('Popular Front for Liberation of Palestine – General Command') launched several attacks, including Katyusha rockets, against Israeli targets in southern Lebanon and northern Israel, killing five soldiers and wounding eight. Israel responded with a large-scale artillery and air bombardment against terrorist/guerrilla positions and villages in southern Lebanon. In this operation (named in Hebrew *Din ve Heshbon* or 'Accountability'), which lasted seven days, some 50 to 70 'terrorists' and 113 civilians were reportedly killed, 400 to 500 wounded, and several hundred thousand Lebanese villagers fled their homes" (Ma'oz, 1995: 235).

18 This case took place in April 1996, during the operation "Grapes of Wrath." For more details on the operation, see: Savir, 1998: 288–91; W. W. Harris, 1998: 477–83.

19 The man referred to Resolution 425, dated March 17, 1978. See the text of Resolution 425 and 426 in the attached Appendix 1.

20 For explanation of "emic" and "etic," see: M. Harris, 1970.

References

Western Languages

Abu Lughod, Laila. *Veiled Sentiments: Honor and Poetry in a Bedouin society.* Berkeley, 1986.

Antoun, R. T. *Arab Village: A Social Structural Study of a Transjordanian Peasant Community*. Bloomington, 1972.

Ashkenazi, T. *Tribus Semi-Nomades de la Palestine du Nord.* Paris, 1938.

Barth, F. *Political Leadership among the Swat Pathans.* London and New York [1951], 1968.

——. "Comment" in *Man*, Vol. 27, No. 1 (1992), pp. 175–77.

Bastug, S. "The Segmentary Lineage System: A Reappraisal." In: *Changing Nomads in a Changing World.* edited by J. Ginat and A. M. Khazanov. Brighton, 1998, pp. 94–123.

Beck, L. *The Qashga'i of Iran.* New Haven, 1986.

Behnke, R. L., Jr. *The Herders of Cyrenaica: Ecology and Kinship Among the Bedouin of Eastern Libya.* Urbana, Illinois Studies in Anthropology, 1980.

Black-Michaud, J. *Cohesive Force: Feud in the Mediterranean and the Middle East.* Oxford, 1975.

——. *Sheep and Land: the Economies of Power in a Tribal Society.* London and Paris, 1986.

Burkhardt, J. L. *Notes on the Bedouin and Wahabys.* 2 Vols. London, 1831.

Cohen, A. *Arab Border Villages in Israel: a Study of Community and Change in a Social Organization.* Manchester, 1965.

Cole, D. P. "Bedouin and social Change in Saudi Arabia." *Journal of Asian and*

African Studies, Vol. 16, Nos. 1–2 (1981), pp. 128–49.
Eickelman, C. *Women and Community in Oman*. New York, 1984.
Eickelman, D. F. *The Middle East and Central Asia: An Anthropological Approach*, third edition. Upper Saddle River, 1997.
Esposito, J. L. *Women in Muslim Family Law*. Syracuse, 1982.
Fabietti, U. "Sedentarization as a Means of Detribalization: Some Policies of the Saudi Arabian Government Towards the Nomads." In: *State, Society and Economy in Saudi Arabia*. Edited by T. Niblock. London, 1982.
Falah, G. *The Process and Pattern of Sedentarization of the Galilee Bedouin, 1880–1982*. Unpublished Ph. D. thesis, University of Durham, 1982.
——. "Patterns of Spontaneous Bedouin Settlement in Galilee." *Occasional Publication* (New Series), No. 18. Durham: University of Durham, Department of Geography, 1983.
Farsoun, S. K. "Family Structure and Society in Modern Lebanon." In: *Peoples and Cultures of the Middle East*, Vol. 2, *Life in the Cities, Towns and Countryside*. Edited by L. E. Sweet. Garden City, 1970.
Fazel, G. R. "The Encapsulation of Nomadic Societies in Iran." In: *The Desert and the Sown: Nomads in the Wider Society*. Edited by C. Nelson. Research Series 21, Institute of International Studies, Berkeley, 1970.
Gellner, E. *Saints of the Atlas*. Chicago, 1969.
Ginat, J. *Women in Muslim Rural Society: Status and Role in Family and Community*. New Brunswick, 1982.
——. *Blood Revenge: Family Honor, Mediation and Outcasting*. Brighton, 1997.
——. "Preservation and Change in Bedouin Societies in Israel." In: *Changing Nomads in A Changing World*. Edited by J. Ginat and A. M. Khazanov, Brighton, 1998, pp. 171–201.
Goodwin, J. *Price of Honor, Muslim Women Life: The Veil of Silence on the Islamic World*. Boston, 1994.
Granqvist, H. *Marriage Conditions in a Palestinian Village*. Societas Scientiarum Fennica, Commentationes Humanarum Litterarum, Vol. 3, No. 8 and Vol. 6, No. 8. Helsinki: Akademische Buchhandlung, 1931–1935.
Gulliver, P. *Dispute and Negotiations: A Cross-Cultural Perspective*. New York, 1979.
Harris, M. *The Rise of Anthropological Theory: A History of Theory of Culture*. New York, 1970.
Harris, W. W. "Lebanon." *MECS* (Middle East Contemporary Survey), Vol. XX (1996). Edited by M. M. Weitzman. Boulder, 1998 (Tel Aviv University, Dayan Center, 1998), pp. 472–501.
Hiatt, J. M. "State Formation and the Encapsulation of Nomads: Local Change and Continuity among Recent Sedentarized Bedouin in Jordan." *Nomadic People*, Vol. 15 (1984), pp. 1–11.
Hof, F. C. *Galilee Divided: The Israel–Lebanon Frontier, 1916–1984*. Boulder, 1985.
Irons, W. *The Yomut Turkman: A Study of Social Organization among Central Asia Turkish-Speaking Population*, Vol. 48. Museum of Anthropology, Anthropological papers. Ann Arbor: University of Michigan, 1975.
Janzen, J. *Nomads in the Sultanate of Oman: Tradition and Development in Dhofar*. Boulder, 1986.
Katukura, M. *Bedouin Village: a Study of a Saudi Arabian People in Transition*. Tokyo, 1977.

Kay, S. *The Bedouin*. New York, 1978.
Khalidi, W. (ed.). *All That Remains: The Palestinian Villages Occupied and Depopulated by Israel in 1948*. Washington, D.C., Institute for Palestinian Studies, 1992.
Khazanov, A. M. *Nomads and the Outside World*, second edition. Madison, 1994.
——. "Pastoral Nomads in the Past, Present and Future: A Comparative View." In: *The Struggle for the Land: Indigenous Insight and Industrial Empire in the Semiarid World*. Edited by P. A. Olson. Lincoln and London, 1990, pp. 81–99.
——. "The Problem of Survival." In: *Changing Nomads in a Changing World*. Edited by J. Ginat and A. M. Khazanov, 1998, pp. 7–23.
Kliot, N. and Medzini, A. "Bedouin Settlement Policy in Israel 1964–82: Another Perspective." *Geoforum*, Vol. 16, No. 4 (1985).
Lancaster, W. O. *The Rwala Bedouin Today*. Cambridge, 1981.
—— and Lancaster, F. "Who are These Nomads? What do They Do? Continuous Change or Changing Continuities?" In: *Changing Nomads in a Changing World*. Edited by J. Ginat, and A. Khazanov. Brighton, 1998, pp. 24–37.
Lane, E. W. *An Arabic-English Lexicon*. London, 1863–93.
Lewis, N. N. *Nomads and Settlers in Syria and Jordan, 1800–1980*. Cambridge, 1987.
Ma'oz, M. *Syria and Israel: From War to Peacemaking*. Oxford, 1995.
Marx, E. *Bedouin of the Negev*. Manchester, 1967.
——. "The Anthropologist as Mediator." In: *The Future of Pastoral People: Proceedings of a Conference held in Nairobi, Kenya, August 4–8, 1980*. Edited by J. G. Galaty, D. Aronson, and P.C. Salzman. Ottawa: International Development Research Center, 1981.
Medzini, A., "Bedouin Settlement Policy in Israel, 1964–1996." In: *Changing Nomads in a Changing World*. Edited by J. Ginat, and A. Khazanov. Brighton, 1998, pp. 58–67.
Musil, A. *The Manners and Customs of the Rwala Bedouins*. New York: American Geographical Society, Oriental Explorations and Studies, No. 6, 1928.
Oppenheim, M. Von. *Die Beduinen*, 4 Vols. Leipzig and Wiesbaden: Otto Harrassowitz, 1939–68 (Vol. 1, 1939).
Peters, E. L., "Aspects of the Family among the Bedouin of Cyrenaica." In: *Comparative Family Systems*. Edited by M. F. Nimkoff. Boston, 1965; pp. 191–96.
——. *The Bedouin of Cyrenaica: Studies in Personal and Corporate Power*. Edited by Jack Goody and Emanuel Marx. Cambridge, 1990, pp. 84–111.
Rabinovich, I. *The Brink of Peace: The Israeli Syrian Negotiations, 1992–1996*. Princeton, 1998.
Sabbagh, S. "Introduction." In: *Palestinian Women of Gaza and the West Bank*. Edited by S. Sabbagh. Bloomington, 1998, pp. 1–38.
Salzman, P. C., "Preface." In: *When Nomads Settle: Process of Sedentarization as Adaptation and Response*. New York, 1980, pp. vii–viii.
Savir, U. *The Process: 1,100 Days that Changed the Middle East*. New York, 1998.
Scholz, F. (ed.). *Beduinen im Zeichen des Erdöls: Studien zur Entwicklung im Beduinischen Lebensraum sudost-Arabien*. Wiesbaden, 1981.
Schumacher, G. *The Jaulan*. London, 1888.

——, Oliphant, L., and LeStrange, G. *Across the Jordan: Being an Exploration and Survey of Part of Hauran and Jaulan*. London, 1889.
Shehadeh, Rustum, L. "The Legal Status of Married Women in Lebanon." *IJMES*, Vol. 30, No. 4 (1998), pp. 501–19.
Simmel, G. "On Individuality and Social Forms." In: *Selected Writings*. Edited and with introduction by D. N. Living. Chicago, 1971.
—— and Sweet, Louise E. "Camel Raiding of North Arabia Bedouin." In: *Peoples and Cultures of the Middle East*, Vol. 1: Depth and Diversity. Edited by Louise E. Sweet, New York, 1970, pp. 265–89.
Tapper, R. *Pasture and Politics: Economic Conflict and Ritual among Shahsevan Nomads of Northwestern Iran*. London, 1979.
——. "Introduction." In: *The Conflict of Tribe and State in Iran and Afghanistan*. Edited by R. Tapper. New York, 1983.
UN. "The Rhodes Agreement: Armistice Agreement Between Israel and the Hashemite Kingdom of Jordan." In: Security Council, Official Records: Fourth Year, Special Supplement, No. 1, 1949. New York, 1949.
UN Resolutions, 425, 426, (1978). UN Security Council at its 2074th and 2075th meetings on 19 March 1978.
Wikan, U. *Behind the Veil in Arabia: Women in Oman*. Chicago, 1991 (1982).
Zittrain Eisenberg, L. "Israel's Lebanon Policy." In: *Meria Journal*, Issue No. 3, September 1997. [This article draws on the author's "Israel South Lebanon Imbroglio," *Middle East Quarterly*, Vol. 4, No. 2 (June 1997), pp. 60–69.

Hebrew

Aharoni, R., *'Arab al-'Aramshah* (forthcoming 1999).
Ayalon, D. and Shenar, P. *Arabic-Hebrew Dictionary*. Jerusalem, 1962 (1947).
Bar-Zvi, S. *The Jurisdiction among the Negev Bedouin*. Tel Aviv, 1991.
Beilin, Y. "Unilateral Withdrawal from Lebanon." In: *The Security Zone in Lebanon: A Reconsideration*. Edited by Y. Bar-Siman-Tov. Jerusalem: Leonard Davis Institute for International Relations, the Hebrew University of Jerusalem, 1997, pp. 47–52.
Erlich, R. "Perception on the Secured Zone and Subjecting it to the Test of Reality." In: *The Security Zone in Lebanon: A Reconsideration*. Edited by Y. Bar-Siman-Tov. Jerusalem: Leonard Davis Institute for International Relations, the Hebrew University of Jerusalem, 1997, pp. 9–28.
Gazit, S. "Lebanon and Israel." Lecture at the "Peace and Security," meeting, September 29, 1997.
Guerin, V. *Geographical, Historical and Archaeological Description of Eretz Israel (Palestine)*. Jerusalem, 1977 (Translated into Hebrew by Haim Ben-'Amram, according to the Paris Publication 1880), Vol. 7, *The Galilee*, No. 2.
Levi, S. *The Bedouin in the Sinai Desert: A Pattern of Desert Society*. Tel Aviv, 1987.
Malamat, A., "The War of Gideon and Midian." In: *The Military History of the Land of Israel in Biblical Times*. Edited by J. Liver. Tel Aviv, 1964, pp. 110–23.
Peled, Y. "The Background for the IDF Presence." In: *The Security Zone in Lebanon: A Reconsideration*. Edited by Y. Bar-Siman-Tov. Jerusalem: Leonard Davis Institute for International Relations, the Hebrew University of Jerusalem, 1997, pp. 29–34.

Yaar, E. and Harman, T. Article based on results of November 1998 poll regarding the peace process. *Ha'aretz*, December 19, 1998.

Arabic

Abu Khusah, M. *Encyclopedia of the Main Tribes and Confederations of Be'er-Sheva* (Bir al-Sab'a). Amman, 1994.
Alfayez, M. *Bani Sakhir Tribe*. Amman: Aljamiah al Urduniyyah Markaz al-Lughat, 1995.
'Aref, A. al. *Bedouin Justice*. Jerusalem, 1933.
——. *History of Be'er-Sheva (Bir al-Sab'a) and its Tribes*. Jerusalem, 1934.
Al-Dabagh, M. M. *Palestine Our Country*. Kafar Qar'a, 1988 (Beirut, 1964), 10 Vols. (New edition) Vol. 7, No. 2.
Al-Hashash, A. *Customary Jurisprudence*. Amman, 1991.
Al-Jamil, M. *The Nomadic Bedouin Tribes in Iraq*. Baghdad, 1956.
Al-Qusus, A. *Bedouin Justice*. Amman, 1972.
Kahalah, U. R. *Encyclopedia of the Ancient and Contemporary Bedouin (al-Arab) Tribes*. (Damascus, 1949, and Beirut, new edition, 1994), Vol. 5.
Al-Zabidi, M. *Taj al-'Arus Min Jawahir al-Qamus*. Cairo, 1306–1310 A.H. (1888/89 - 1892–93).

Daily Newspapers

Hebrew

Ha'aretz (Tel Aviv).

English

Jerusalem Post.
The New York Times.

Part IV

Regional Relations

10

The Franco-Syrian Treaty Negotiations and the Question of Lebanon, 1936–1939

Meir Zamir

In a treaty signed in Paris on September 9, 1936, France, the mandatory power, undertook to grant Syria independence after a three-year probation period and to incorporate in it Jabal Druze and the ʻAlawi region. Two months later in Beirut, France signed a treaty with Lebanon guaranteeing its territorial integrity and its existence as an independent state. During the negotiations on both treaties, the Syrian Arab nationalist movement, led by the National Bloc,[1] waged a vigorous campaign for Syria's independence and unity and demanded that either Lebanon be linked politically and economically to Syria, or that its borders be revised. The National Bloc's campaign among the Muslims in Beirut, Tripoli, Sidon, Tyre and Baʻalbak, urging unity with Syria and opposing Lebanon's alliance with France, sparked confrontations between Syria and Lebanon and between Christians and Muslims within Lebanon. The negotiations and the signing of the Lebanese treaty in November were subsequently accompanied by violent demonstrations by the Muslims in the coastal cities.

Syria's formal stand regarding Lebanon's borders during the treaty negotiations was defined in a letter sent by Hashim al-Atasi, head of the Syrian delegation, to Damien de Martel, the French High Commissioner for Syria and Lebanon, on July 6, 1936. (For the letter and the French response, see Appendices.) The events leading up to the letter had begun on June 11, when the Syrian representatives officially requested the return of the "Syrian" regions annexed to Lebanon in 1920. The reports of Syria's territorial claims infuriated the Lebanese Christians, especially the Maronites, and prompted Pierre Viénot, the Under-Secretary for Foreign

Affairs, to dispatch a letter to Lebanese President Emile Eddé, officially reiterating France's commitment to maintaining Lebanon's independence and territorial integrity.[2]

Since Lebanon's establishment in 1920, the Syrian nationalist leaders had been demanding its reunion with Syria, in particular the Biqa' valley and Tripoli. The Biqa' valley, which separated the mountains of Lebanon and the anti-Lebanon and comprised the districts of the Biqa', Ba'albak, Rashaya and Hasbaya, was part of the *Wilayets* of Damascus and Beirut. After 1918, it was administered by Faysal's Arab government in Damascus before it was annexed to Lebanon. The Syrians were determined to restore this strategically and economically important region to their state. For the same reason, the French military command in the Levant was resolute that the Biqa' valley remain under its direct administration. Throughout the 1920s, the Syrians strove to regain control over what they referred to as "the four casas," making great efforts to undermine the Lebanese administration and French influence there. In 1926, they appeared to have succeeded to some extent when Henry de Jouvenel, the French High Commissioner, recommended annexing to Syria part of the Biqa' valley, including Ba'albak. This plan was never implemented, however, as his successor, Henri Ponsot, met with strong opposition from French military circles and his own staff, as well as from the Maronite Church.[3]

In the 1920s and 1930s, the Syrians repeatedly raised their territorial claims on Tripoli. Moderate leaders, such as Prime Ministers Ahmad Nami and Taj al-Din al-Hasani and the head of the Parliament, Subhi Barakat, and such nationalists as Hashim al-Atasi, Jamil Mardam, Sa'adallah al-Jabiri, Fakhri al-Barudi and Shukri al-Quwatli, reiterated these claims on numerous occasions. They argued that Syria was becoming increasingly dependent on Beirut for imports and exports, and that the construction of a port in Tripoli, its natural outlet to the sea, was essential for their country's economic viability and prosperity. They also stressed that Lebanon already had its own port and that most of Tripoli's inhabitants were Muslims, who sought union with Syria. The decision to build a terminal in Tripoli for the Iraqi Petroleum Company's pipeline from Mosul increased its strategic and economic importance and further strengthened Syria's determination to gain control there. The claims on Tripoli were motivated, however, not only by economic considerations, but also by the Syrian nationalists' vision of their future state – a modern, liberal, independent Arab state which, while being an integral part of the Arab Muslim world, would also maintain close ties with Europe.

Both Robert de Caix, Secretary General of the High Commission in 1923, and Henri de Jouvenel in 1926, had agreed to return Tripoli to

Syria. But as was the case with the Biqaʿ valley, such a step was opposed by the Maronite Church, by military circles, by officials in the High Commission and the Quai d'Orsay, and by French companies with economic interests in Beirut. They all warned that it would severely weaken Beirut, where France had important economic and strategic interests, and argued that Syrian control of Tripoli would separate Lebanon from the autonomous ʿAlawi region. After the completion of the oil pipeline in 1935, which provided part of France's oil supply, and the decision to build a large refinery in Tripoli, few French officials in either Beirut or Paris were willing to seriously consider acquiescing in Syria's demands.[4]

Following Syria's failure in November 1933 to negotiate with France an agreement similar to the 1930 Anglo-Iraqi treaty, and the subsequent suspension of the constitution and adjourning of the parliament by the French High Commissioner, the National Bloc reconsidered its tactics in Lebanon. Some of its members argued that demands for the revision of Lebanon's borders were undermining Syrian efforts toward independence. In the face of Syrian threats to the very existence and territorial integrity of their state, the Maronites, they claimed, would seek continued French protection despite their misgivings regarding the Mandate. The French, they pointed out, were exploiting Lebanese Christian fears of the Muslims to justify retention of the Mandate not only in Lebanon but in Syria as well. National Bloc leaders such as Riad al-Sulh, and later Fakhri al-Barudi and Jamil Mardam, proposed that Syria shelve its political and territorial claims in Lebanon and strive to win the Maronites' trust in order to undermine France's position there. They anticipated that when the Mandate ended and the two states achieved their independence, Syria would be able to take advantage of its superiority so as to gain control of Lebanon, both politically and economically. Riad al-Sulh argued against detaching regions with large Muslim populations, such as Tripoli and Baʿalbak, from Lebanon, claiming that this would increase the Christian majority and thereby strengthen Lebanon's separatist tendencies. Thus, throughout 1934 and 1935, the National Bloc successfully exploited the disillusion and resentment toward the Mandate of Christian political and economic groups in Lebanon in order to rally opposition to France. It targeted in particular the Maronite Church, headed by Patriarch Pierre Antoine Arida, and the Constitutional Bloc, led by Beshara al-Khuri. These tactics were especially effective during the tobacco monopoly crisis of 1935.[5]

In early 1935, the National Bloc had ample opportunity to pursue its new tactics in Lebanon. Opposition to the French Mandate and to de Martel's policy had been growing in Beirut among the influential

Christian merchant and financial class, whose interests were being adversely affected by a recession. They criticized de Martel's economic policy and resented the privileged position accorded to French and foreign concessionary companies. Furthermore, Christian politicians, especially Beshara al-Khuri, who was competing with Emile Eddé for the presidency, were angered by the High Commission's support for Eddé. Arida, the powerful Maronite patriarch, who considered himself to be the spokesman of Lebanon's interests, publicly criticized de Martel's economic policy. The High Commissioner's decision in January to restore the tobacco monopoly provoked popular protest in Lebanon and provided the National Bloc leaders with the opportunity to incite the Lebanese Christians against France. They were more than willing to allow Arida, whom they depicted as the "Patriarch of the Arabs," to head a national protest against the Mandate as long as it served their interests.

In February and March, they went to Bkerki, the seat of the Maronite Patriarch, to thank Arida for adopting a patriotic stand and to ask him to lead the united Syro-Lebanese struggle against the tobacco monopoly. Muslim politicians in Lebanon were urged to back Arida's stand against de Martel. In Damascus and other Syrian cities, Muslim religious leaders publicly acclaimed Arida, and students and pupils demonstrated in the streets in his support. Syrian newspapers praised the new-found Muslim–Christian solidarity against the French Mandate. However, behind closed doors, Syrian leaders continued to express their lack of trust in the Lebanese Christians.[6]

The National Bloc's success in coercing prominent Lebanese figures into cooperating with Syria against the French Mandate caused much concern in the High Commission and the Quai d'Orsay. French officials repeatedly warned Arida and his Bishops, as well as Christian politicians, of the National Bloc's true intentions. They claimed that collaboration with the Syrians and the Muslims in Lebanon was not only undermining French interests in the Levant, but was endangering Lebanon's very existence. In February, the Sûreté Générale ordered Fakhri al-Barudi to leave Beirut immediately, and two months later banished Riad al-Sulh to Qamishli in the Jazira area. While the tobacco monopoly crisis convinced de Martel and the Quai d'Orsay to adopt a more conciliatory policy toward the Lebanese Christians' political and economic demands, it served to deepen French hostility toward the Syrian National Bloc.

In February 1936, however, after boycotting the Syrian nationalists for two years and refusing to negotiate on their demands for a treaty and Syrian unity, de Martel had to change his policy following seven weeks of general strikes and violent demonstrations instigated by the National Bloc. On March 1, he reached an agreement with the Syrian representatives led by Hashim al-Atasi, head of the National Bloc, whereby France would undertake to grant Syria a treaty similar to the 1930 Anglo-Iraqi agreement; a Syrian delegation would leave immediately for Paris to negotiate its terms; and all detainees arrested during the riots would be released. In mid-March, a Syrian delegation left for Paris to negotiate what was believed in Damascus and Beirut to be a treaty granting Syria independence and unity.

In Paris, the National Bloc negotiators, led by Atasi and Mardam, faced the old dilemma regarding their stand on Lebanon: Should they continue to seek rapprochement with the Christians in Lebanon, or should they renew Syria's claims over Tripoli and the Biqa' valley? There was a clear advantage in pursuing the former option, as in early March, following Syria's example, seven members of the Constitutional Bloc had presented a memorandum to de Martel requesting the replacement of the Mandate with a treaty "like that of our Syrian brethren." Moreover, renewing demands for the revision of Lebanon's borders at such a sensitive stage in the negotiations would have antagonized the Maronites and their influential supporters in France, and thus would have jeopardized Syrian goals of ending the Mandate and restoring Jabal Druze and the 'Alawi region to Syria. Nevertheless, some National Bloc leaders, in particular Atasi and Quwatli, argued that Syria could not forgo its standing claims in Lebanon, especially in Tripoli, in negotiations that were to determine its borders. They warned that the Maronites could not be trusted, and that France, after ending its Mandate in Syria, would turn Lebanon into its major strategic base in the Middle East, thereby posing a permanent threat to Syria's independence and unity. The National Bloc, they asserted, could not morally ignore the appeals of the Muslims in Lebanon for union with Syria. Thus, from March to May 1936, nationalists in both Damascus and Paris sent conflicting messages to the Christians and the Muslims in Lebanon. While Syrian leaders assured Arida that the National Bloc had no intention of demanding the revision of Lebanon's borders so long as the country strove to end the Mandate and attain national sovereignty, others incited the Muslims in Lebanon, particularly in Tripoli, to call for union with Syria.[7]

The Syrian delegation's decision to formally present their country's territorial demands on June 11 resulted directly from the victory of Léon Blum's Popular Front – a coalition of Socialists, radical Socialists, and Communists – in the French general elections. Both the Socialist and Communist parties had criticized France's traditional policy of favoring the Maronites and other Syrian minorities (particularly the Druze and the 'Alawis), which, they claimed, was antagonizing the Muslim majority and the influential Syrian Arab nationalist movement. Socialist and

Communist deputies, as well as newspapers allied with the two parties, backed the National Bloc's calls to end the Mandate and grant Syria independence and unity. Indeed, during informal discussions in April and May with the Syrian negotiators, French leftist politicians had endorsed Tripoli's return to Syria and revision of the borders between the two states in the Biqa' valley. The Syrian representatives were therefore confident that the new French government would be more supportive of Syria's interests in Lebanon. Although the publication of Viénot's letter to President Eddé on June 20 somewhat shook their confidence, some still believed that it was merely a tactical move intended to placate the French right and the Maronites (see Appendix A). Relations within the Bloc also played a part in their decision. Under pressure from the more militant members of the National Bloc in Damascus, the delegation aimed to demonstrate an uncompromising stand toward the French.[8]

At the end of June, members of the Syrian delegation in Paris and nationalists in Damascus began urging pro-Syrian Muslim leaders in Tripoli, Beirut and Sidon, as well as Shi'ite notables in Tyre, Jabal Amil and the Biqa' valley, to send petitions to the French authorities and the Permanent Mandates Commission in Geneva and to organize demonstrations in support of union with Syria. On July 5, delegates from Tripoli, Beirut, Nabatiya, Marj Ayoun, Tyre and Bint Jubeil met in Sidon and passed a resolution upholding Syrian unity. They also called for a plebiscite to be held in the regions annexed to Mount Lebanon and authorized the Syrian delegation in Paris to present their national aspirations. Their resolution was forwarded to the French government, the National Assembly and the Permanent Mandates Commission, as well as to the Syrian delegation in Paris and the National Bloc leaders in Damascus. In the following days, general strikes and large-scale demonstrations were held in Sidon, Tripoli and Beirut, as well as in Syria. Syrian newspapers accused the Maronites of pursuing an isolationist policy that was undermining Syria's national interests, while Lebanese newspapers harshly criticized Syria and its supporters in Lebanon for attempting to jeopardize Lebanon's territorial integrity and its very existence as an independent state. In Paris, Ignatius Mubarak, the Maronite Bishop of Beirut, traded insults in the press with the Syrian representatives, while Prime Minister Léon Blum and Foreign Minister Yvon Delbos were inundated with protests from Lebanon, including from Patriarch Arida and President Eddé. The President demanded that his country be allowed to dispatch its own delegation to Paris in order to defend its national interests against the Syrian ambitions.[9]

Despite repeated French warnings that Syria's territorial demands and campaign of incitement in Lebanon were jeopardizing the treaty negotiations, the Syrian delegation restated its political, territorial and economic claims on Lebanon throughout July and August. Reports from Beirut that 'Alawi notables were petitioning the High Commission, the Quai d'Orsay and the Lebanese government to unite their region with Christian Lebanon fueled Syrian hostility toward the Lebanese state. French opposition to Tripoli's annexation to Syria and rumors that Britain was considering the partition of Palestine and the establishment of a Jewish state prompted the Syrian representatives to propose turning Sidon into a Syrian port. This, they hoped, would link the Shi'ites in south Lebanon to Damascus and, at the same time, would insert a wedge between Christian Lebanon and the proposed Jewish state in Palestine.[10]

After its demands were refused, the Syrian delegation changed its tactics and proposed that the issues of Syria's borders with Lebanon and future economic relations between the two states be negotiated directly by their respective governments. It also proposed that a Syro-Lebanese organization replace that of the Common Interests (a body which was controlled by the High Commissioner and administered customs duties in the mandated territories) in order to regulate economic ties between them. This organization would comprise representatives of the two countries according to the size of their populations and would enjoy considerable power in economic and political affairs. This initiative aimed in actual fact to create a Syro-Lebanese confederation under the guise of common economic interests. Well aware of the Syrians' intentions to exploit their superior position in bilateral negotiations so as to force Lebanon to acquiesce in their demands, the Quai d'Orsay rejected these proposals and made it clear that France would neither grant Syria and Lebanon independence nor sponsor their admission to the League of Nations until those issues were settled.[11]

In the Franco-Syrian treaty, finally signed in September 1936, France agreed to end its Mandate, grant Syria independence, and restore to it Jabal Druze and the 'Alawi region. In return for these two areas, the Syrian delegation was obliged to renounce its territorial demands in Lebanon. Officials in the Quai d'Orsay proudly pointed to their success in excluding Lebanon from the negotiations and in persuading Syria to recognize its separate existence within its 1920 borders. However, their satisfaction was premature – already during the signing ceremony, Atasi reiterated Syria's desire to form a federation with Lebanon. During negotiations on the Franco-Lebanese treaty in the next two months, it became apparent that despite French efforts, Syria was unwilling to recognize Lebanon's independence and territorial integrity.[12]

The National Bloc's most immediate concern was to prevent France from using the Lebanese treaty as a military alliance and from turning

Lebanon into a permanent base for its military, economic and cultural influence in the Levant. Its members were well aware of the pressure put on the Quai d'Orsay by the army, navy and airforce high commands to ensure France's complete freedom of action in Lebanon, considered vital for its strategic needs in the eastern Mediterranean. They also knew that certain Lebanese politicians, especially President Eddé, viewed the treaty as a means to defend Lebanon against Syria. They subsequently intensified their efforts to persuade Beshara al-Khuri and other Constitutional Bloc members who opposed Eddé to insist on a treaty identical to that of Syria and to demand "complete national sovereignty" from France. At the same time, they encouraged pro-Syrian Muslim leaders on the coast to participate in the Lebanese delegation to the treaty negotiations.[13]

Aware of Syrian nationalist intentions, the French aimed to conclude a treaty with Lebanon before the end of November, when the Syrians would still be engaged in the parliamentary elections provided for by their own treaty. Moreover, as long as France had not yet published the decrees regarding the annexation of Jabal Druze and the 'Alawi region to Syria, the nationalist leaders, they reckoned, would have to proceed carefully in Lebanon. The High Commission also exploited the outbreak of violent clashes in early October between Muslims and Christians in Aleppo as a way to caution the National Bloc against any provocation of inter-sectarian tension in Lebanon. In order to finalize the negotiations without delay, the French pressed the Christian leaders, especially Eddé and Khuri, to shelve their personal and factional rivalries and to collaborate in the negotiations against the Syrian threat. They also urged Patriarch Arida, President Eddé and Christian politicians to accord the Muslims in Lebanon more equality, including allowing the nomination of a Sunni as prime minister, so as to undermine Syrian efforts to persuade them to support union with Syria. Viénot also instructed the High Commission to consider granting Tripoli greater autonomy within the Lebanese state. In October and early November, de Martel frustrated the National Bloc's efforts to intervene in the negotiations with Lebanon and convinced Eddé and Khuri to cooperate. Accordingly, Muslims were informed that by retaining its influence, France would be better able to protect their rights in an independent Lebanon. Shi'ite notables were reminded of the inferior status of their brethren in Iraq and were assured that their community would be better off in Lebanon than in a Sunni Arab Syrian state controlled by Damascus. Although the High Commission refused to give Tripoli autonomy, it separated the city from the district of North Lebanon and granted it the status of an independent municipality with its own Muslim governor.[14]

De Martel's success in persuading Eddé and Khuri to form a joint delegation to the treaty negotiations caught the National Bloc by surprise. Some moderates, including Jamil Mardam, advocated caution at that stage, but the majority called for increasing pressure on the High Commission and the Lebanese Christians in order to prevent them from turning the treaty into a military alliance. On October 16, one day after the Lebanese Parliament's approval of the composition of the Lebanese delegation to the negotiations, al-Jabiri, Afif al-Sulh and Riad al-Sulh met in Sofar in Lebanon with 'Abd al-Hamid Karameh and 'Abd al-Latif Bisar from Tripoli, and Salim 'Ali-Salam and Omar Bayhum from Beirut for the purpose of deciding on steps to be taken by the Muslims in Lebanon in order to undermine the negotiations. In the following weeks, Muslims in Beirut and Tripoli held strikes and demonstrations against the Lebanese state and in support of union with Syria. The demonstrations soon escalated into riots and violent confrontations with the French army, resulting in scores being killed, hundreds wounded and many others detained. On October 23, a conference to protest the treaty was held in Beirut, attended by hundreds of Muslim delegates. The resolution adopted by the participants and sent to de Martel, the Quai d'Orsay and the Permanent Mandates Commission called for either Lebanon to be linked in a confederation with Syria or a decentralized system to be implemented in Lebanon, whereby Muslims in the annexed regions would enjoy an autonomous status similar to that of the 'Alawis, Druze and Turks in Syria.[15]

At the same time, the Syrian press stepped up its attacks on the Lebanese Christians, particularly the Maronites. It accused them of "harming the Syrians and the supporters of Syrian unity" and described Emile Eddé as "a Maronite president known for his hatred of the Arab race and culture." Newspapers called for the Maronites to take note of the events in Palestine and stressed that neither France nor any other European power could prevent the Arab people from being united. They warned that Lebanon would become isolated economically, as an independent Syria would lower its customs barriers with Iraq, Palestine and Trans-Jordan and would direct its trade with Europe through Haifa instead of Beirut. An editorial in the Damascan newspaper *Fata al-Arab* stressed that Syria would play a greater role in the Arab world in the future and that Lebanon would therefore not continue to threaten it for long. It warned ominously that Lebanon could not "close its gates, because it has many breaches and the Arab people have ways of penetrating those breaches."[16]

Faced with organized opposition from the Muslims in Lebanon and attacks from Syria, de Martel conducted the negotiations in complete secrecy. He pressured the Lebanese representatives to hasten their conclusion, and consequently the entire negotiations lasted for only three weeks. In the evening of November 12, the High Commission unexpectedly declared that an agreement had been reached, and the following morning the treaty was signed by de Martel and Eddé amidst elaborate security measures taken by the French army. Although the High Commission had made sure that the Lebanese treaty would appear identical to that of Syria in order to limit Syrian criticism and Muslim opposition in Lebanon, France had attained its goal. In contrast to the Syrian treaty, the military protocol in the Lebanese treaty granted the French army, navy and airforce complete freedom of action in Lebanon for the entire 25–year duration of the treaty.[17]

The news of the signing of the treaty provoked a hostile reaction from Damascus. Likewise, thousands of Muslims in Beirut turned out to demonstrate against the treaty and the Lebanese state, following inflammatory speeches by Riad al-Sulh and other Muslim leaders. They marched to the city center where they set fire to cars and trams, looted shops, stormed government offices and French concessionary companies, and threatened to lay siege to the seat of the Lebanese government. Youth movements in the Christian quarters, headed by the *Phalanges*, prepared to defend Christian lives and property, while Maronites from the villages in the Mountain threatened to descend to the city to protect their brethren. Fearing escalation into inter-sectarian clashes, the High Commission rushed French forces to the center of Beirut, where they battled throughout the day with the demonstrators. Hundreds were wounded before they were able to restore law and order. In the following days, violent riots and demonstrations also took place in Tripoli during which scores were wounded.[18]

In telephone conversations and later at meetings in Damascus, French officials accused the National Bloc of instigating the riots in Beirut and Tripoli. They warned that the events in Lebanon were sowing doubt within the French government, the National Assembly and the public regarding Syria's ability to uphold its obligations as stipulated in its own treaty, including protection of its minorities. Under such circumstances, France, they cautioned, could not continue to fulfill its obligation to annex Jabal Druze, the 'Alawi region and Alexandretta to Syria. A similar warning was sent by Viénot in a telegram to Hashim al-Atasi. The Syrian nationalists denied any involvement in the crisis in Lebanon, and Shukri al-Quwatli even went so far as to claim that Emile Eddé, and not Riad al-Sulh, was responsible for the riots in Beirut. Nevertheless, fearing that France would not implement the Syrian treaty, the National Bloc immediately dispatched Mardam and al-Jabiri to Beirut to calm the situation. The two prominent Syrian leaders urged the Muslim notables there to prevent further demonstrations against the Lebanese treaty lest they jeopardize Syria's own agreement with France. From Beirut they proceeded to Tripoli, where they conveyed a similar message to the city leaders, some of whom, including Karameh and Bisar, had been imprisoned by the French authorities.[19]

The Muslims in Lebanon were extremely disappointed with the Syrian nationalists' conduct during the crises in Beirut and Tripoli in November and December. After urging them to demonstrate against the Lebanese treaty and to support union with Syria, the National Bloc had abandoned them, fearing that its own treaty with France was in danger. Muslim politicians argued that with Lebanon soon to gain independence, their community should secure its own rights in the country rather than aspire to a confederation with Syria. De Martel and Eddé encouraged them by nominating Khair al-Din al-Ahdab of Tripoli as the first Sunni Prime Minister in January 1937. Ahdab had supported Syrian unity during the late 1920s and early 1930s, but later became an outspoken opponent of Syrian ambitions in Lebanon during his tenure as Prime Minister.[20]

Having miscalculated in the treaty negotiations in Lebanon, the Syrian government, now controlled by the National Bloc, had good reason to proceed cautiously. With its own Christian communities voicing fear for their future, and with the French Right using the issue of Syria's inability to protect its minorities to delay the treaty's ratification, Syria could not afford to appear responsible for inter-sectarian strife in Lebanon. Yet, in 1937 and again in 1938, the Syrian government renewed its territorial, political, and economic claims in Lebanon and encouraged pro-Syrian Muslim leaders on the coast to oppose the Lebanese state. The Syrian stand resulted from a combination of the crisis in Alexandretta; Eddé's attempt to unilaterally ratify the Franco-Lebanese treaty; and Lebanon's resistance to Syria's demands regarding future economic ties between the two states.

During the negotiations in Paris, whenever the Syrian delegation demanded Tripoli as Syria's port, French officials countered that Syria already had a port in Alexandretta. After the conclusion of the Franco-Syrian treaty, Turkey opposed the annexation to Syria of the *Sanjak* (province) of Alexandretta, which had a large Turkish population and had enjoyed a certain degree of autonomy since 1921.[21] With the increasing threat of war in Europe, Turkey exploited France's desire to ensure its neutrality as a way to gradually alter the *Sanjak's* status and to finally annex it in July 1939. Faced with the Turkish ambitions in Alexandretta, the Syrian government requested Tripoli as compensation. Thus, in early 1937, the National Bloc renewed its activities in Tripoli, encouraging its supporters there to petition the French and the Permanent Mandates

Commission for the city's annexation to Syria. It also initiated the visit of a delegation from Tripoli to Paris in the summer of 1937 to present similar demands. At the same time, the Syrian press repeated accusations that the Lebanese government was seeking economic dominance over Syria through its control of Beirut and Tripoli.[22]

Syria's campaign to detach Tripoli caused great concern in Beirut. President Eddé protested to the Quai d'Orsay, while Premier Ahdab visited the city, undertook to increase government investment there, and called for its leaders to counter Syrian ambitions. In Paris, the Ministers of War, Navy and Airforce sent letters to the Prime Minister opposing any change in the city's status. Despite warnings from Foreign Minister Delbos and his Under-Secretary Viénot, during a visit to Paris in June 1937, Syrian Prime Minister Mardam reiterated his country's claims on Tripoli, provoking an open confrontation with Eddé who was also in Paris at the time. Syrian anger and disappointment with the French position intensified after the High Commission acquiesced in the Lebanese government's demands and revised the border near Tripoli by annexing villages to Lebanon that were part of the 'Alawi region. The French decision sparked protests from the Syrian President and government, but to no avail.[23]

The issue of the ratification of both treaties by France became another source of contention between Syria and Lebanon. French rightist deputies and senators, as well as colonialist circles who had opposed the Syrian treaty from the start, prevented its ratification in 1937 and 1938. The growing threat of war in Europe reinforced opposition from the French army, which argued that the treaty would limit its freedom of action in Syria. Even Mardam's consent to revise it in December 1937, and again in November 1938, could not convince the National Assembly to ratify it. Unwilling to wait for the Syrian treaty to be ratified, Eddé, who regarded Lebanon's treaty with France as a military alliance protecting the Christians against Syria, sought to ensure its unilateral ratification. He was supported by General Huntziger, commander of the French army in the Levant, and by many in the National Assembly, but the Syrian government strongly objected, fearing that such a move would jeopardize its efforts to ratify its own treaty. Relations between Syria and Lebanon deteriorated further during Eddé's visit to Paris in June 1937, when he sought separate ratification of the Lebanese treaty. His declarations to French politicians and the press regarding the Christians' loyalty to France and the freedom of action enjoyed by the French army in Lebanon, in contrast to Syria, provoked a hostile reaction in Damascus. Mardam and Sa'adallah Jabiri, who were then in Paris, refused to make a courtesy call on Eddé, who, in return, reacted by instructing his ministers to boycott the two Syrian statesmen upon their return to Damascus via Beirut.[24]

Economic issues became another source of tension between the two governments. As provided for in their treaties with France, they were to reach agreement on administration of the Common Interests and division of the revenue from customs duties. The negotiations involved issues crucial to the economies of both states, such as their continuation after independence as one economic bloc with a common currency and no customs barriers. Disagreement had emerged even before the official negotiations began in April 1937, when the Lebanese government, despite Syrian opposition, renewed the Banque Syrie-Liban's concession for another 25 years. Both governments were running budgetary deficits and were anxious to secure a larger portion of the Common Interests budget. Syria demanded 70 percent of the revenue, based on the size of its population, while Lebanon insisted on parity, arguing that the Lebanese, with their higher standard of living, consumed the greater part of the imported goods. The negotiations were also overshadowed by political considerations. While the Syrian government sought close economic ties between the two states, Maronite leaders in Lebanon, particularly Eddé and Arida, advocated separation in order to ensure their country's independence. In March 1938, the negotiations broke down, with each side blaming the other.[25]

France's refusal to ratify the treaties left open the issue of Syro-Lebanese relations. In November 1943, the decision made by the Lebanese Christians, headed by President Beshara al-Khuri, to sever their traditional ties with France and to struggle for complete independence, in parallel to Lebanon becoming one of the founding members of the Arab League, left the Syrian government no choice but to agree to the Lebanese state's separate existence within its 1920 borders. Referring to Syria's stand on Lebanon, Jamil Mardam wrote in September 1939: "In the littoral we have recognized a separate but not a foreign state. Lebanon will always be part of us, despite itself and despite ourselves."[26] This statement was to accurately reflect relations between Syria and Lebanon after independence. Syria's ambitions in Lebanon, which had eluded the National Bloc between the two world wars, were finally realized by President Hafiz al-Asad in the May 1991 Treaty of Brotherhood, Cooperation, and Coordination which effectively subjugated Lebanon to Syria.

Appendix A

Delegation of the Syrian Republic Paris, July 6, 1936
His Excellency
M. de Martel
Ambassador of France
High Commissioner of the Republic in Syria*
President of the French Delegation
Paris

Mr. Ambassador,
In your letter of June 27 last, Your Excellency informed me that the French government had no intention of calling into question the Syro-Lebanese borders as decided upon on August 31, 1920. At the same time, you sent me a copy of a message from Mr. Viénot to the Lebanese President, in which the Under-Secretary-of-State for Foreign Affairs defined his government's stand regarding Lebanon's current territorial status.

It is my duty to inform Your Excellency that the Syrian delegation was painfully surprised by this decision and, on the basis of assurances which reached me following the publication of Mr. Viénot's message, I allow myself to draw the attention of the government to the fact that the attitude expressed in the said message may give rise in Lebanon to a hotbed of irredentism, which would make it difficult to maintain cordial relations, which the Syrian people – of whose sympathies for the Lebanese Your Excellency is aware – is striving to establish between the two brotherly and neighboring states.

I must make it clear here that at no time did the Syrian delegation intend to dispute the issue of the borders without the knowledge of the Lebanese people or without the participation of their qualified representatives in negotiations necessary for the settlement of the issue. In acting otherwise, it would have run counter to the frequently expressed wishes of the Syrian National Bloc to shape its attitude out of concern not to endanger Syro-Lebanese friendship.

Besides, the question of territorial status is one of justice and rights, and it is difficult for us to admit that Lebanon would refuse to agree to its negotiation in the same spirit of agreement and collaboration.

Your Excellency knows, for the same reason as his predecessors, that the decree of August 31, 1920 was a unilateral act by which the French representative, exercising his almost sovereign powers, disposed of 400,000 Syrians, fundamentally attached to Syria, with no regard to their wishes, despite the fact that this decree was made when the principle of the right of peoples for self-determination was in full blossom.

This decree was an administrative act before being raised to the level of an international instrument. But in neither of its forms did it succeed in severing the spiritual ties of the inhabitants of the territories, which it disposed of, with Syria, or in transforming the character of these territories which were, and remain, Syria's outlet to the sea and its natural ports.

It is therefore in the spirit of the message from Mr. Viénot to Mr. Eddé, as well as of the letter of Your Excellency, that the intangibility of Lebanon's territorial status is a function of the international character of the guarantee that affirms this status at the initiative of and concern of the French government.

I must, at this point, remind Your Excellency that this international character has not always secured the intangibility of Lebanon's territorial status, nor that of Syria.

Your Excellency knows, in fact, that following his predecessors' decisions, and after the decree of August 31, 1920 was registered in Geneva [League of Nations], Lebanon was obliged to give up to England, on two separate occasions, strips of its most richest land. As for Syria, the international guarantee seemed never to have played to its advantage, as its heritage served, on numerous occasions – and without intervention from Geneva – to satisfy the appetites of irascible neighbors, and of others who appeared to have special claims to the sympathies of the French representatives. Thus Lebanon saw torn from it the fertile region of El Houlé, and Syria was dispossessed of large areas in the north, with no objection being raised or concern shown – so rapidly demonstrated today – for respecting the international character of guarantees regarding the territories of these two states.

Whatever the case, the Syrian delegation could only formally object to the questioning of Syria's right to natural access to the sea. It believed it useful to recall on this occasion that the late Mr. de Jouvenel in 1926, and Ponsot in 1927, had admitted this principle; Mr. Eddé, President of Lebanon, had declared himself on each occasion to be a convinced advocate [of that policy]. At the same time the delegation asks, on the eve of what it hopes will be a new era, for the French government, through a wise dispensation of justice between the two neighboring states and an acceptable application of the principles of the League of Nations, to help to establish friendly relations and a close understanding between the two states.

It does not ask for an arbitrary act for Syria, as it cannot ignore the fact that whoever benefits from such an act will one day expose himself to the arbitrariness of others. It only requests that the territories torn away from it be allowed to express their wishes in a free plebiscite.

The Lebanese government, full of the satisfaction that Mr. Viénot's message appears to have given to Lebanon's elected representatives, will not, we are sure, consider as unfriendly the proposition of a plebiscite which could confirm, perhaps, its point of view, and would finally put an end to the situation in whose settlement the two nations have an equal interest.

While asking that a question of such great importance raised originally by a simple administrative decision be settled by a free plebiscite, the Syrian delegation believes it has given, as much to France as to Lebanon, the best proof of the good intentions of the nation which it has the honor to represent.

With deep respect,

Hashim al-Atasi

* De Martel's official title was "High Commissioner of the [French] Republic in Syria and Lebanon"
Source: Archives du Ministère des Affaires Etrangères, Paris, Syrie et Liban, Vol. 493, pp. 75–78

Appendix B

His Excellency Hashim al-Atasi — Paris, July 7, 1936
President of the Syrian Delegation
Hotel "Continental"
Paris

Mr. President,

The High Commissioner of the French Republic has sent me the letter of the 6th of the month in which Your Excellency thought it necessary to raise again the issue of the Syro-Lebanese borders as defined on August 31, 1920 and confirmed by the Mandate granted to France on July 24, 1922.

I have the honor of informing Your Excellency that the High Commissioner's letter of June 27 to which you refer was given to me before it was sent to you, and that I approved all its terms. I can only confine myself to the conclusions that the document intended to inform the delegation. The Syrian delegation, by insisting on introducing an issue foreign to the program established in the joint agreement of March 1, would raise problems, whose evocation, by their very nature, would risk compromising the satisfactory and rapid conclusion of the current negotiations – a conclusion which Your Excellency knows how much I anticipate.

With deep respect,
Pierre Viénot

Source: MAE, Nantes, Syrie et Liban, Carton 478.

Notes

1 The National Bloc was the most important political organization during the Mandate period, comprising prominent Syrian nationalists from Damascus, Aleppo, Homs and Hama.

2 Archives du Ministère des Affaires Etrangères (hereafter: MAE), Paris, Syrie et Liban, Vol. 478, "Délégation de la République Syrienne: Etudes Critiques des Projets Français," Paris, June 11, 1936; MAE, Nantes, Syrie et Liban, Carton 478, Viénot's letter to Eddé, Paris, June 20, 1936.

3 Meir Zamir, *The Formation of Modern Lebanon, 1918–1926* (London, 1985), pp. 176–89 [hereafter: Zamir, *The Formation of Modern Lebanon*];

idem, "Faisal and the Lebanese Question, 1918–1920," *Middle Eastern Studies*, Vol. 27, No. 3 (July 1991), pp. 404–26.

4 MAE, Nantes, Syrie et Liban, Carton 926, Information No. 3625, Beirut, October 29, 1934; Carton 457, "Note au Sujet de Tripoli," Tripoli, October 6, 1936; Zamir, *The Formation of Modern Lebanon*, pp. 116–18, 186–89, 196–97.

5 MAE, Nantes, Syrie et Liban, Carton 411, Information No. 208, Beirut, March 30, 1933; Carton 926, Information, Beirut, February 4, 1934; Information No. 319, Beirut, January 31, 1935; Carton 943, Information No. 181, Beirut, September 29, 1934; Meir Zamir, *Lebanon's Quest: The Road to Statehood, 1926–1939* (London, 1997), pp. 111–12, 154–55 [hereafter: Zamir, *Lebanon's Quest*].

6 MAE, Nantes, Syrie et Liban, Carton 1542, Information, Beirut, February 4, 1935; Zamir, *Lebanon's Quest*, pp. 167–71.

7 MAE, Nantes, Syrie et Liban, Carton 478, "Pourparlers avec la Délégation Syrienne au Sujet du Corps du Traité – Réunion du 27 Avril 1936"; Zamir, *Lebanon's Quest*, pp. 191–93.

8 MAE, Paris, Syrie et Liban, Vol. 492, Paris, May 30, 1936, Atasi to de Martel; Vol. 493, "Note: Négociations Franco-Syriennes," Paris, June 20, 1936; MAE, Nantes, Syrie et Liban, Carton 364, "Note sur les Négociations Franco-Syriennes," Paris, June 13, 1936.

9 MAE, Nantes, Syrie et Liban, Carton 457, Nos. 487–88, Beirut, June 8, 1936, High Commission to the Quai d'Orsay; "Note: Visite à Mgr. Arida à Dimène," Beirut, July 29, 1936.

10 MAE, Paris, Syrie et Liban, Vol. 494, No. 909, Beirut, September 11, 1936; Vol. 501, No. 823, Beirut, August 2, 1936; Meyrier to the Quai d'Orsay. See also: Laura Z. Eisenberg, *My Enemy's Enemy: Lebanon in the Early Zionist Imagination, 1900–1948* (Detroit, 1994), pp. 98–102.

11 MAE, Nantes, Syrie et Liban, Carton 478, "Réunion Tenue le 15 Juillet 1936 par le Sous-Commission Chargée de la Question de la Conférence des Intérêts Communs."

12 MAE, Nantes, Syrie et Liban, Carton 2990, Nos. 607–9, Paris, September 19, 1936, Quai d'Orsay to the High Commission. For the Franco-Syrian treaty, see: Albert H. Hourani, *Syria and Lebanon* (London, 1946), pp. 314–23 [hereafter: Hourani, *Syria and Lebanon*].

13 MAE, Nantes, Syrie et Liban, Carton 459, Information No. 552, Damascus, October 2, 1936; Information No. 3595, Beirut, October 3, 1936; Carton 460, Riad al-Sulh's speech at the Conference of the Coast, published in the newspaper, *Beirut*, October 25, 1936.

14 MAE, Nantes, Syrie et Liban, Carton 2990, Nos. 615–18, Paris, September 24, 1936; Quai d'Orsay to the High Commission; Nos. 798–800, Beirut, October 9, 1936; and No. 1,104, Beirut, November 6, 1936, de Martel to the Quai d'Orsay; Carton 457, Nos. 918–21, Beirut, October 29, 1936, de Martel to the Quai d'Orsay.

15 MAE, Nantes, Syrie et Liban, Carton 2,990, Nos. 821–27, Beirut, October 13, 1936; de Martel to the Quai d'Orsay; Carton 460, Information No. 3,840, Beirut, October 16, 1936; Information No. 4,037, Beirut, October 24, 1936. See also: Riad al-Sulh's speech at the Conference of the Coast.

16 MAE, Nantes, Syrie et Liban, Carton 459, Information *Fata al-Arab*, October 30, 1936.

17 MAE, Nantes, Syrie et Liban, Carton 2990, No. 1,147, Beirut, November 20, 1936, de Martel to the Quai d'Orsay. For the Franco-Lebanese treaty, see: Hourani, *Syria and Lebanon*, pp. 333–37.

18 MAE, Nantes, Syrie et Liban, Carton 459, "Rapport Spécial," Beirut, November 15, 1936; "Rapport sur les Événements du Novembre 15, 1936 Beyrouth," Beirut, November 24, 1936, Director of the Sûreté Générale to de Martel; Carton 460, No. 275, Tripoli, November 20, 1936, administrative adviser of north Lebanon to the French delegate in Lebanon.

19 MAE, Nantes, Syrie et Liban, Carton 459, No. 1,646, Damascus, November 16, 1936, the French delegate in Syria to de Martel; Information No. 633, Damascus, November 17, 1936; a telephone conversation between the French delegate in Syria and Faris al-Khuri on November 19, 1936.

20 MAE, Nantes, Syrie et Liban, Carton 2990, No. 1,179, Beirut, November 27; and No. 1,233, Beirut, December 11, 1936, de Martel to the Quai d'Orsay; Carton 460, Nos. 675–76, Beirut, June 11, 1937, Ahdab to the Quai d'Orsay.

21 On this regard, see also: Kushner's chapter in this volume.

22 MAE, Nantes, Syrie et Liban, Carton 460, Information No. 56, Damascus, February 12, 1937; "Revendications Syriennes sur Tripoli," Paris, March 6, 1937, Viénot to de Martel; Nos. 680–82, Beirut, June 12, 1937, Meyrier to the Quai d'Orsay; MAE, Paris, Syrie et Liban, Vol. 502, No. 358, Beirut, April 2, 1937, de Martel to the Quai d'Orsay.

23 MAE, Paris, Syrie et Liban, Vol. 502, Beirut, February 10, 1937, Letter from Eddé and Ahdab to Léon Blum; No. 199, Paris, February 17, 1937, Léger to de Martel; MAE, Nantes, Syrie et Liban, Carton 460, No. 442, Paris, February 24, 1937, Minister of Air to Minister of Foreign Affairs and the latter's reply; No. 137, Paris, March 6, 1937, Viénot to de Martel.

24 MAE, Paris, Syrie et Liban, Vol. 503, No. 685, Paris, June 18, 1937, Eddé to Ahdab; MAE, Nantes, Syrie et Liban, Carton 496, No. 670, Beirut, July 4, 1937, de Martel to the Quai d'Orsay. See also: George Hakim, "Fiscal System," in Sa'id B. Himadeh (ed.), *Economic Organization of Syria* (Beirut, 1936), pp. 337, 383.

25 MAE, Nantes, Syrie et Liban, Carton 944, Proceedings of the Lebanese Parliament on June 2, 1937; Information: "Clergé maronite", Beirut, November 15, 1937; MAE, Paris, Syrie et Liban, Vol. 495, No. 383, Beirut, April 10, 1937, de Martel to the Quai d'Orsay.

26 Jamil Mardam Bey, "The Legacy of Equivocation," in Salma Mardam Bey, *Syria's Quest for Independence* (Reading, 1994), pp. xv–xvi.

11

Syrian–Iraqi Relations: Iraq as a Factor in the Syrian Foreign Policy

Michael Eppel

Through most of the years of their existence, since World War I, relations between Syria and Iraq were characterized by asymmetry and an unequal balance of power. For many years, while Syria was under the French Mandate (1920–46) and thereafter as an independent state, Iraq intervened in Syrian domestic politics, posed a threat to its sovereignty and independence, and at times assisted it or forces within it against threats posed by its other neighbors. In the bilateral relations between Iraq and Syria, the former was more active, possessed more resources and more military power, and demonstrated expansionist trends aimed at domination of the latter in the name of Arab unity. Iraq was more involved and more influential in Syrian domestic politics and foreign policy; however, the developments within Syria, the changes in its regional and international orientation, and Iraq's failures to implement union with it or to achieve dominance over it had an effect on the regime in Baghdad. From the standpoint of the regime and the central politicians in Iraq during the Hashemite monarchy (1921–1958), the establishment of a federation or union with Syria was the way for Iraq to achieve a sound regional and international status while strengthening its own legitimacy and political status in the internal Iraqi arena.

The pattern of relations and mutual influence between the two states was a direct result of their weakness, the instability of their regimes, the socio-political conflicts inherent in Arab societies, and the "permeability" of the borders between them ("Permeability," in this context, refers to the ability of Syria's Arab neighbors, and especially Iraq, to interfere in its internal affairs, and the legitimacy with which Syrian politicians could request and receive financial and political assistance from Iraq, Egypt, Saudi Arabia and Jordan in the name of Arab unity). The weight of pan-

Arab orientation in the radical nationalist trends, which arose in the Arab world, including Syria, during the 1930s granted legitimization to the involvement of outside entities in internal politics in the name of pan-Arabism. This approach considered the borders between Arab states as no more than a Western colonialist dictate, opposed to the interests and goals of the Arab nation, as compared with the weakness of consciousness of territorial national identity.

The complex attraction–repulsion relationship between Syria and Iraq embodied – and still embodies to this day – the tension and ambivalence in the modern collective identification trends in the Arab world, between Arab national consciousness and the vision of Arab unity, on the one hand, and, on the other, consciousness of territorial identity within the framework of the presently existing borders, and the interests of forces within both Syria and Iraq in preserving and fostering the existing state entities and building their separate states.

The situation wherein Syria was the weaker, more passive and more divided, as against Iraq, which was the stronger in general and more active in the inter-Arab arena, began to change with the ascendancy of the Ba‘th regimes in both countries and the crystallization of the territorial state under those regimes.[1]

The weakening of the Iraqi threat to the Syrian regime was a direct consequence of the latter's coalescence as a territorial state, the stabilization of its regime, the growing feeling of Syrian Arab collective identity among its population, and the changes in the conditions prevailing in the inter-Arab arena. It was precisely (and paradoxically) the rise and strengthening of the Ba‘th regimes, in whose ideological message and political legitimization the principle of Arab unity played a central role, which led to reinforcing the justification for the separate existence of Syria and Iraq as separate and legitimate frameworks, whose individual integral territorial identity was more clear-cut than and took precedence over general Arab identity. Since the Iraqi invasion of Kuwait, against the background of the boycott and the internal sanctions, the balance of power between Syria and Iraq has shifted, for the first time, in favor of Syria. Iraq's policy, international status and internal developments are relevant to Syria's status and policy. Syrian interests in Iraq and Iraqi interests in Syria are related to the processes of their coalescence as states, the stabilization of their regimes, and the development of consciousness of collective identity among their populations. These processes in both countries are still going on. Yet, while Syria under Asad enjoys stability and conditions favorable to these processes, the situation in Saddam Husayn's Iraq is different. Admittedly, the state has grown stronger; yet, at the same time, trends toward internal dissension and disintegration continue to rise.

Syrian–Iraqi Relations before the Rise of the Radical Regimes

The Hashemite rulers of Iraq,[2] and many of its central policy-makers during the monarchical years, aimed to establish a federation or union with Syria and to achieve Iraqi domination of the Fertile Crescent. This aim in Iraq's regional policy resulted from its regional status, its internal conditions, and the nature of its leadership, taking into account the following factors:

1 The tenuous existence of the Iraqi state, which was established by the British, the lack of any cohesive common factor among its heterogeneous population, and the domination of the conservative élite belonging to the Sunni Arab minority.
2 The external threat represented by its stronger and more cohesive neighbors – Turkey and Iran – which enjoyed influence over parts of the Iraqi population and posed a threat against its vital interests, with Iran against the Shatt al-'Arab and Turkey against the petroleum-rich areas of Mosul and Kirkuk.
3 The rising dominance of pan-Arab ideology in the Iraqi political climate and its status as a means of enlisting support and legitimacy in Iraq's political arena, starting in the 1930s.
4 The socio-political conflict affecting the conservative Sunni Arab élite and politicians, in view of the rising new socio-political forces needing far-ranging reforms and changes in the social, economic and political status quo, whose preservation was an existential interest of that élite. The élite politicians needed the Westernized middle strata, which demonstrated political consciousness and was vital to the existence and function of state institutions and systems. They could not, however, provide a response to its needs, including accelerated modernization, changes in the electoral system, industrialization and agrarian reform. These were liable to undermine the status quo from which the ruling élite drew its strength.
5 Iraqi interests in Syria and Palestine as an outlet to the Mediterranean for Iraq and a direct link with Europe and the West.
6 The dynastic ambitions of the heads of the Hashemite royal house, which resulted from their world view, their evaluation of Iraq's chances to survive, and the need for legitimization of their status in Iraq.[3]

The National Bloc (*al-Kutla al-Wataniyya*), which was the central nationalist force in Syria during the Mandate, basically subscribed to a trend which, while it admittedly favored inter-Arab cooperation, in practice aimed for Syrian independence and unity. Most members of the National Bloc sought to maintain a republican regime in sovereign Syria and opposed the trends which supported the Hashemite monarchy and union with Iraq. However, during the 1930s, a change occurred in the National Bloc's attitude toward pan-Arabism, in the wake of the difficulties and stagnation in negotiations with France, and against a background of the conservative élite of notables' need to enlist the support of the modern middle strata, which was constantly expanding and whose younger members were becoming increasingly radicalized.[4] The desire to enlist the support of Iraq and Britain in their struggle against France, as well as the changes in the ideological climate in Syria, impelled the politicians to transfer the emphasis from Syrian territorialism to pan-Arab nationalism.

At the same time, throughout the entire period, there were also politicians in Syria who had connections with Iraq, and who viewed the strengthening of these connections, and even actual federation with Iraq, as the solution to Syria's problems. Some of these manipulatively exploited their connections with Iraq and the aid received from the latter country to promote power struggles within Syria, while others hoped that, should the federation come into being, they would be granted a special status in the framework of that federation. The Syrian trend toward seeking support from Iraq and the power of those supporting union between the two states increased during the times of crisis in Syria's relations with France: in 1933 and again in 1939–40.[5]

With the departure of the French from Syria and the granting of its independence in 1946, Iraq increased its pressure to transform Syria into an area of Iraqi influence and to establish a federation with it. The relative impotence of the Syrian state, the weakness of Syrian national-territorial identity as compared with the strength of regional, ethnic and tribal identities and loyalties within it, the tenuous legitimacy of its regime and the atomization of its social forces, made it easy for Iraq to meddle in Syrian internal affairs. Such central Syrian politicians as Hashim al-Atasi (President of Syria, 1943, 1949, 1954–1955), Fares al-Khuri (Prime Minister of Syria, 1944–45, 1954–55), and People's Party (*Hizb al-Sha'b*) heads Nazim al-Qudsi (Prime Minister, 1950–51) and Rushdi al-Kihya, as well as Sabri al-'Asli of the National Party[6] (Prime Minister, 1954, 1955, 1956–58) and others, sought to strengthen their ties with Iraq and were willing to establish a federative relationship with it. When these politicians were made to suffer distress by their rivals in the Syrian political arena, or when they feared possible cooperation between Syria's neighbors, Jordan, Turkey and Israel, they showed an increasing tendency toward *rapprochement* with Iraq and seeking assistance from it; at such times, they expressed their willingness to establish an alliance or a federation, or even to agree to Syria's incorporation into the Hashemite kingdom of Iraq. The pro-Iraqi Syrian politicians hoped that, within the framework of a federation or union with Iraq, their own position (relative to that of their rivals in Syria) would improve.

In 1946–47, as part of his efforts to bring about the signature of a pact between Iraq and Turkey, the Iraqi politician Nuri al-Sa'id attempted to gain recognition as the representative of Syrian interests before the Turks. In this way, Nuri aimed to depict Iraq as Syria's protector and strategic backer, and thereby to foster his own ambitions to Iraqi control or dominance of Syria.[7]

In the course of the 1948 War on Palestine, Syria felt increasingly threatened by what it perceived as cooperation between Israel, King 'Abdallah of Jordan, Turkey and Britain, with a view to bringing Syria under Hashemite rule and ripping away its northern territories in favor of Turkey. The feelings of weakness and anxiety in Syria constituted the background for the rising pro-Iraqi trend during the 1948 War.[8] The People's Party, whose power base was in the northern city of Aleppo, had a distinctly pro-Iraqi image; its platform included the establishment of a federation with Iraq, and its heads enjoyed connections with Iraq and received its support. However, even among its ruling rival, the National Party, whose President Shukri al-Quwatli led Syria to strengthen its relations with Saudi Arabia and Egypt, such central politicians as Sabri al-'Asli and Michail Ilian favored the reinforcement of connections with Iraq and even the establishment of a federation, forged new links with Iraq and enjoyed its support.

On March 29, 1949, Syrian Chief of Staff Husni al-Za'im launched a *coup d'état* and ousted President al-Quwatli. In the first days after the revolution, al-Za'im proposed to Iraq the signature of a military alliance between the two states.[9] His intimates hinted to Iraqi emissaries that Syria would be prepared for union with Iraq. This move by al-Za'im was a manipulation intended to gain support for his regime in view of his fear of a negative reaction by Egypt and Syria, and given the pressure exerted by King 'Abdallah and the possibility that he might exploit Syria's instability and attempt to take it over. Al-Za'im's maneuver was meant to neutralize the Egyptian-Saudi threat and simultaneously to drive a wedge between the Hashemite states which aimed to win Syria. However, a few days later, when al-Za'im realized that Egypt and Saudi Arabia were prepared to accept the ouster of their ally al-Quwatli and to maintain relations with the new regime in Damascus, provided that it did not adopt a pro-Hashemite stance, he turned his back on Iraq and returned to Syria's former policy of seeking support from Egypt and Saudi Arabia.

The pro-Iraqi trend in Syria reached its height under Sami al-Hinnawi, who launched a *coup d'état* ousting al-Za'im in August 1949. Following that coup, the status of pro-Iraqi forces rose in Syria, the People's Party became the ruling party, and Hashim al-Atasi was elected President. Syria was overcome by a pro-Iraqi euphoria; it appeared that a federation or union with Iraq had become not only a real possibility, but an imminent certainty. Yet, Iraq itself, at the time, was showing obvious hesitation and mixed approaches. While the Regent 'Abd al-Ilah and his supporters worked to seize this opportunity to realize their ambitions in Syria, Nuri al-Sa'id – the prominent Iraqi politician identified with Iraq's aim for control of Syria and dominance in the Fertile Crescent – kept his action cautious and avoided any hasty moves. While Nuri admittedly continued to aim for the traditional Iraqi objectives, he sought to establish the union on terms which would favor Iraqi dominance and prevent the Syrian instability from polluting Iraq and endangering its regime.

Hashim al-Atasi, leaders of the People's Party and other pro-Iraqi politicians viewed the rapid establishment of a federation or union with Syria as a move intended to reinforce their rule in Syria, frustrate their rivals, and neutralize the threat of an additional intervention by the Syrian Army. The increasing trends toward union with Iraq aroused objection on the part of Egypt, Saudi Arabia and France, and serious fears on the part of National Party politicians and Army officers. These fears were a central motive for the subsequent of another *coup d'état* led by Adib al-Shishakli in December 1949.

In 1952–54, during Shishakli's direct rule, Iraq was actively, though not effectively, engaged in attempts to oust him from power.[10] Once again, Iraqi policy was characterized by conflicting trends. The Regent 'Abd al-Ilah and Fadhil al-Jamali (Prime Minister of Iraq, September 1953–March 1954) sought to remove al-Shishakli from office. Nuri al-Sa'id, on the other hand, examined the possibility of negotiating with him, based on his assessment that al-Shishakli's stable pro-Western regime served the Iraqi interests of preventing penetration by Egypt or the rise of radical forces in Syria which could endanger the regime in Iraq.[11] All in all, the role of Iraq's activity in al-Shishakli's ouster in February 1954 was minimal, and the collapse of the regime in Syria resulted mainly from internal Syrian processes.

Following al-Shishakli's fall from power, the conditions prevailing in Syria appeared *prima facie* to be convenient for Iraq and its supporters. Pro-Iraqi politicians held most of the central posts in the Syrian regime. The Presidency was restored to Hashim al-Atasi. Serving as Prime Minister was Sabri al-'Asli of the National Party, who had maintained connections with Iraq since 1948. The posts of Foreign Minister and Minister of the Interior were held by al-Atasi and 'Ali Buzo, both heads of the People's Party, whose platform included the establishment of a federation with Iraq as one of its goals; both al-Atasi and Buzo were receiving financial support from Iraq. However, this situation, convenient as it may have been for Iraq, did not give rise to a close and stable relationship between the two states, nor did it enable Iraq to achieve dominance of Syria. Despite their status in the political arena, the pro-Iraqi politicians were unable to halt the rising leftist-radical ideological trends and political forces, based on the modern middle strata and especially on educated and semi-educated young men and young Army officers. The pro-Iraqi politicians from the conservative élites had no response to the leftist-nationalist-radical ideological messages of the Ba'th or to revolutionary Egypt, which increased its activity in Syria in 1954 and provided a source of inspiration to radical young men and officers, whose strength and power began to grow.

Between 1954 and 1958, Syria became a battlefield between pro-Western Iraq, a country controlled by the conservative élite, which the young nationalist radicals perceived as a symbol of reaction and surrender to the West, and revolutionary Egypt, with its neutralist orientation and its ties to the Soviet Union. The fall of the pro-Western, Iraq-friendly Fares al-Khuri government in February 1955, against a background of the struggle over the Baghdad Pact, was a turning point in which the pro-Iraqi conservative forces in Syria lost their political positions. Sabri al-'Asli, who became Prime Minister in February 1955, shifted his own and his regime's orientation from pro-Iraqi to pro-Egyptian (at least on a public level), in order to gain popularity with the radical anti-Iraqi, pro-Egyptian forces which were drastically on the rise in Syria. Hashim al-Atasi and senior pro-Iraqi politicians from the People's Party desired to bring about an Iraqi military intervention in Syria, in order to block the rising power of the radical officers – the Ba'th and the Communists – but did not dare to express their desires publicly.[12]

During 1955–57, Iraq encouraged and assisted the unsuccessful attempts to organize a conspiracy which would overturn the regime in Damascus, with a view to preventing the rise and growth of leftist radical forces, especially among Army officers and members of the Ba'th. These attempts at toppling the regime, with the assistance of Iraq and the West, only increased the instability and general confusion prevailing in Syria. This prepared the ground for the radical Army officers' approach to Gamal 'Abd al-Nasser in January 1958 with a proposal which led to the establishment of UAR in February 1, 1958. The union between Syria and Egypt was a defeat for Iraq and the Hashemite regime. This defeat and the wave of pro-Egyptian fervor which swept the Arab world in 1958 represented an important catalyst for the *coup d'état* led by Army officers under 'Abd al-Karim Qassem, which put an end to the monarchical regime and the ruling élite of Iraq in July 1958.

When an acute conflict broke out, in the autumn of 1958, between the radical-revolutionary forces – the UAR under 'Abd al-Nasser and Iraq under Qassem – Syria, then the northern district of the UAR, became a target for Iraqi activity intended to harm 'Abd al-Nasser. By contrast to the Hashemite regime, Qassem favored Iraqi territorialism. Accordingly, Iraqi activity *vis-à-vis* Syria was intended primarily to strike at 'Abd al-Nasser and impel Syria to separate from Egypt, in order to remove the threat beyond Iraq's borders, rather than as an attempt to take over Syria itself.[13] Iraq itself had now become a proponent of Syrian independence. Following Syria's secession from the UAR in September 1961, the politicians of the restored old conservative élite, who were pressured by the radical forces supported by Nasserist Egypt, cooperated with the revolutionary Iraqi regime under Qassem. Syria's secessionist conservative President, Nazim al-Qudsi, and the radical ruler of Iraq, 'Abd al-Karim Qassem, held a conference on March 14–16, 1962 in Abu-Kemal, near the Syrian–Iraqi border, in order to create an alliance against Nasserist Egypt. The Syrian conservatives were compelled in the face of the Nasserist and the radical challenge to collaborate with Iraq in spite of its radical regime.

The Vision of Arab Unity and the Reinforcement of Territorialist Trends in Syrian–Iraqi Relations Under the Ba'th

The rise to power of the Ba'th party in both Iraq and Syria in 1963; the internal struggles in the Syrian Ba'th between 1962 and 1970 and the Iraqi Ba'th in 1963; and the rift between the two parties, gave the relations between the two states an ideological dimension which affected the legitimization of their regimes.[14] The ideological partnership and the centrality of the idea of Arab unity in the ideology and legitimization of the Ba'th Party regimes created conditions whereby, during that period of internal political instability, the regimes were exposed and sensitive to mutual subversion in the name of Arab unity.

The rivalry between the two Ba'th parties and each one's claim to be the sole true Ba'th transformed the existence of each regime into an existential threat for the other. The power struggles and disputes which resulted from the two states' national interests were expressed and amplified in the ideological dispute which affected the legitimacy of both regimes. In the course of the struggles which took place in the Syrian Ba'th between 1962 and 1966, the struggling factions sought assistance from factions within the Iraqi Ba'th. Thus, for example, the leftist-radical faction of the Syrian Ba'th, led by Hamud al-Shufi, was assisted by the 'Ali Salih Sa'di faction of the Iraqi Ba'th.[15] The fall of the Iraqi Ba'th regime in November 1963 and that of Sa'di's leftist faction had an effect on the Syrian Ba'th and its internal struggles.

Following the intra-Ba'th coup of February 1966, which brought Salah Jadid's leftist faction to power in Syria and led to the expulsion from Syria of Michel 'Aflaq and Salah al-Din al-Bitar – the founders and historic leaders of the Ba'th – came a new stage in the relations between the two Ba'th parties. As long as both Ba'th regimes had remained weak and insufficiently cohesive, the question of mutual legitimization and delegitimization had played a central role in the relations between them. Asad's takeover of Syria in 1970 and the restoration of the Ba'th to power in Iraq following the coups of July 17 and July 30, 1968, created a complex situation whereby a rift between the Ba'th parties became a rift between the states themselves. The asylum found by Ba'th founder and ideologue Michel 'Aflaq in Iraq reinforced the Iraqi Ba'th's claim to legitimacy and supremacy.[16] The stabilization and reinforcement of the Ba'th regimes during the 1970s intensified the struggle between them for regional dominance and contributed to the relative decline in the importance of the struggle between them for legitimacy and recognition.

In 1977 came a lull in the tension prevailing between Iraq and Syria. The two states underwent a rapprochement as a consequence of the separate peace between Egypt and Israel. Following Egyptian President Anwar al-Sadat's peace initiative in November 1977, Asad launched an initiative for the improvement of relations between Syria and Iraq. However, Iraq's attempt to take on the leadership of the Arab world, its objection to UN Resolutions 242 and 338 (which were accepted by Syria), and its demands for drastic action against Egypt impeded the rapprochement between Syria and Iraq. In the autumn of 1978, an initiative for reconciliation between Iraq and Syria was launched, following Egypt's persistence in the course of a separate peace with Israel. Syria sought to strengthen its status *vis-à-vis* Israel and Egypt, whereas Iraq softened its rigid position and brought about an inter-Arab common denominator against Egypt.[17]

In October 1978, Asad visited Baghdad and discussed a Syrian–Iraqi union with Iraqi leaders. This initiative and the moves to intensify relations between the two states came to a halt in July 1979, following Saddam Husayn's decisive takeover of Iraq and its Ba'th party. According to several sources, the idea of a union with Syria was raised against the background of struggle between Saddam and his rivals, as an attempt by President Hassan al-Bakr and his supporters to block Saddam. Indeed, immediately following Saddam's rise to power, the Iraqi administration announced the discovery of a conspiracy to overturn the Iraqi regime with Syrian assistance.[18] This led to the breaking off of relations between Syria and Iraq and the renewal of the rift, accompanied by mutual attacks. In April 1982, Syria closed its border with Iraq, shut down the pipeline from the Kirkuk oil fields to the Syrian port of Banias, and severed diplomatic relations. The Iranian military success in May 1982 and the deterioration in relations with Syria pushed Iraq to promote closer ties with Egypt.

The relations between Iraq and Syria reached a nadir when Syria allied itself with Iran in its war against Iraq between 1980 and 1988. The struggle for regional dominance and the atmosphere of mutual suspicion led Syria to support Iran, the non-Arab, radical-Islamic enemy of Ba'thist Arab Iraq. Syria's support of Iran, when most Arab states supported Iraq as an expression of the historical struggle between the Arabs and the Persians, its rejection of Islamic radicalism that was endangering the existing Arab regimes, as well as its insistence on a hard line concerning Egyptian isolation following its separate peace agreement with Israel (March 1979), led to Syria's own isolation in the inter-Arab arena throughout most of the 1980s.

It was precisely under the Ba'th regimes, in whose ideology and legitimization the principle of Arab unity constituted a central component, that the concept of the territorial state was reinforced in both Syria and Iraq and the consciousness of a separate territorial identity took root among their populations. (This statement, of course, must be qualified with a reservation regarding Iraq, in which Saddam Husayn's policy of cruelty against the Kurds and Shi'is, starting in the late 1980s, and the loss of state control over Kurdish and Shi'i areas, due to the Iraqi invasion of Kuwait, led to the strengthening of trends which favored ethnic and tribal identification.)

Each of the Ba'th parties is a reflection of the unique conditions characterizing its country. The expansion of Ba'thist ideas from Syria to Iraq resulted from a complex combination of circumstances: a certain similarity in the conditions which characterized the growth of the modern middle strata (some of whose members were attracted by Ba'thist ideas), the unique circumstances affecting Iraq in the 1950s, and the political conditions and intellectual-ideological climate of the Arab world during the same period. The ideological similarity and the shared messages were but one stratum – constituting, in fact, a rather thin conceptual and terminological cover – in the ways and circumstances governing the historical development of the two states and their respective parties. The power and validity of the pan-Arab ideological component resulted from the lack of internal cohesion in both states, as well as from the weakness of their respective national identity and the weakness and tenuous legitimacy of their regimes, against the background of the social structures and broad range of identity trends among their populace.

The changes in the political and social conditions prevailing in the Arab states since the 1970s, the reduced attractiveness of the vision of Arab unity and radical pan-Arab ideology, and the changes occurring in the conditions of the inter-Arab arena reduced the capacity of the two regimes for mutual de-legitimization. The ability of the Iraqi Ba'th regime to effectively subvert its Syrian rival lasted only as long as the Syrian Ba'th was plagued with struggles and the Syrian regime remained fragile.

Syrian–Iraqi Relations Following the Iraqi Invasion of Kuwait

Following the Iraqi invasion of Kuwait in August 1990, Syria joined the Arab-Western coalition led by the United States against Iraq. This Syrian move, which was vital to the formation of the anti-Iraqi coalition, resulted from the strategic shift in Syrian policy which had begun in 1987–88. In visits by Asad to the Soviet Union in 1985 and 1987, his hosts explained to him that they intended to put an end to the global Cold War and achieve peaceful solutions of regional conflicts. In view of the change in Soviet policy under Gorbachev and against the background of Syrian economic recession,[19] Syria began to change its policy in an attempt to improve its relations with Western European countries and the United States.

At the same time, a gradual thaw began in relations with Egypt. Syria, which had broken off relations with Egypt due to the latter's separate peace agreement with Israel, and which had maintained the most rigid position with regard to the boycott of Egypt, began to slowly change its attitude in late 1987. Full normalization between Syria and Egypt was achieved in 1991, when Syria joined the Arab-Israeli peace process. The change in Syrian strategy resulted not only from the change in the status and policy of the Soviet Union and the severe economic recession within Syria, but possibly also from Syrian fear of Saddam Husayn's aggressive tactics. The growth and expansion of the Iraqi army during the war against Iran changed the balance of power to Syria's detriment. Syria now found itself facing a neighbor with vast military power – an army of a million soldiers led by a threatening, ambitious tyrant. In 1989, Syria became concerned about Iraqi assistance to the anti-Syrian government of General Michel 'Awn in Lebanon. Since the beginning of the Civil War in 1975, Iraq has supported the anti-Syrian forces rebelling against the status-quo in the Lebanese backyard of Syria.

Syria's decision to join the anti-Iraqi coalition created an internal problem for the Ba'th regime in Damascus. Starting in the earliest days of the Ba'th regime, Syria's propaganda, communication and educational systems had portrayed the American government as a hostile, imperialistic force, dangerous to the Arab nation and to Syria.[20] Now the heads of the regime had to explain the change in the approach, whereby Syria had become the ally of the United States against an Arab state which flew the anti-American flag and used pan-Arab nationalist slogans as emblems of the Arab nation's struggle against imperialism. In view of the confusion among the Syrian public and its expression of identification with Iraq, the senior Ba'th speakers had to work hard to explain their country's policy to party activists, army officers, students and the general public of Syria.[21] Saddam Husayn was accused by Syria of breaching the sovereignty of an Arab state, destroying the partnership between Arab states, serving the interests of Zionism by distracting attention from the Arab struggle against Israel, and creating a situation in which the Arab states were forced to consent to American intervention.

The Gulf War in the winter of 1991 and the sanctions imposed on Iraq, which severely damaged its military power and economic strength, changed the balance of power between Iraq and Syria in favor of the latter. The Iraqi threat against Syria dwindled and effectively disappeared, at least in the short term. At the same time, however, Syrian suspicion and criticism of Saddam Husayn did not waver. The Syrian interests regarding Iraq are presently as follows:

1. Weakening and toppling Saddam Husayn's regime, or at least neutralizing its capacity for threatening stability of the region in general and of Syria in particular.
2. Maintaining the territorial integrity of Iraq.
3. Obtaining Iraq's long-term cooperation and support in Syrian relations *vis-à-vis* Israel and Turkey, following the decline and fall of Saddam Husayn's regime.

Since the 1980s, various organizations opposed to Saddam Husayn's regime have been active in Damascus. In addition to the anti-Saddam branch of the Iraqi Ba'th, a Communist group, and Kurdish factions, Damascus also hosts the Shi'i organization *Da'wa*, which sought to avoid falling under Iranian protection. The activity of the Iraqi opposition organizations in Damascus is much more intensive than that of its counterparts in Baghdad. At the same time, it must be stated that the total effectiveness of all the organizations opposed to Saddam – those operating from Syria, Iran, Britain or other places – is very limited, and that they do not constitute a real threat to his regime, due to the dissension and struggles between them, as well as to the nature of the Iraqi regime.

Notwithstanding the hostility directed against Saddam Husayn, the preservation of Iraq's territorial integrity is an important national interest for Syria. The crumbling of Iraq is liable to constitute a dangerous precedent by undermining the existing borders in the Middle East and encouraging separatist movements, which endanger the stability of the Arab states in general and of Syria in particular. The possibility of Iraq falling apart, leaving its northern areas to become a Kurdish state or to fall under Turkish control or influence, while the southern and central areas would be dominated by the Shi'is and protected by Iran, constitutes a threat to Syria and contradicts the basic world outlook of Asad's Arab nationalism and that of the Syrian leaders.

The commonality of interest between Syria and Iran against Iraq would come to an end were Iraq to fall apart, giving Syria cause to fear Iran's increased influence over Iraq. Therefore, it is in Syria's interest to preserve Iraqi territorial integrity and independence, while ensuring that Iraq remain free of ambitions for regional dominance. This Syrian approach is reflected both in its leaders' official declarations and in the pressure exerted by the Syrian authorities on Iraqi opposition organizations, especially the Kurds, to refrain from harming the integrity and unity of Iraq. In June and July 1997, the Syrian Foreign Minister, Faruq al-Shar', emphasized the common interest of Syria, Egypt and Saudi Arabia in preserving Iraq's unity, and expressed fear of Turkish intervention in northern Iraq.[22]

Since the spring of 1997, there has been an improvement in the relations between the two countries. Syria has begun to show a thaw in its relations with Iraq, set against the background of its disappointment in the stagnation of the peace process with Israel. This is in view of the United States' failure to pressure Israel into withdrawing from the Golan Heights and in view of the reinforced military cooperation between Israel and Turkey, which Syria perceives as a grave strategic threat. In March 1997, at a meeting of delegates from Socialist parties to the European Parliament, Iraqi Deputy Prime Minister, Tariq 'Aziz, expressed his satisfaction with the positive development of relations with Syria.[23]

In May 1997, a delegation of the Syrian Chambers of Commerce and Industry visited Baghdad.[24] Two months later, in July, Syria stopped the broadcasts of the Damascus radio station operated by organizations in opposition to Saddam Husayn's regime. Likewise, Iraq closed down the Voice of Arab Syria radio station, which had broadcast anti-Asad propaganda from Baghdad.[25] In August, a delegation of Iraqi merchants and industrialists, headed by the Chair of the Iraqi Industrial Federation, visited Syria and met with Syrian Minister of Economy, Muhammad al-Imadi.[26] Syria was awarded a contract for export to Iraq in the amount of $13 million, and crossing points for merchandise and travelers were opened along the Syrian–Iraqi border. On August 7, Iraqi Minister of Petroleum, Amir Muhammad Rashid, told a press conference in Baghdad that Iraq was prepared to resume running petroleum through a pipeline that passes through Syria.[27] A similar announcement was made by Syrian sources.[28] 'Adnan al-Qudsi, head of the Iraqi Industrial Federation, stated: "There is an Iraqi political approach which favors giving priority to the offers made by Syrians regarding the export of Syrian products to Iraq according to the UN Resolution 986" (food for oil).[29] The 44th Damascus International Fair, held at the end of August, was attended by an Iraqi economic delegation headed by the Iraqi Minister of Commerce, Dr. Muhammad Mahdi Salih, whose ministry signed economic agreements with the Syrians.[30]

In political statements regarding the resumption of trade relations, significant differences may be observed between Iraqi and Syrian speakers. Iraqi Foreign Minister, Muhammad al-Sahaf, sent a message to Syria expressing his hope that the economic relations would lead to a resumption of diplomatic relations and a reconciliation between the two countries. Iraqi UN Ambassador, Nizar Hamdun, noted that steps were being taken toward improving relations with Syria.[31] The Iraqis emphasized the political importance of the economic ties with Syria as a way to break through the walls of Iraq's economic isolation and to take a step toward normalization in Syrian–Iraqi relations. The Iraqi periodical *Babil* called for normalization of relations with Syria in order to establish a front against imperialism and Zionism.[32]

Syrian statements, on the other hand, have emphasized that the new relations are economic ties only and have no political significance. Syrian Foreign Minister, Faruq al-Shar', referred to the rumors of an impending coalition between Syria, Iraq and Iran as a dangerous illusion which must not be allowed to mislead.[33] Other Syrian entities, however, have unofficially told the press that the thaw in relations with Iraq represents Syria's anger at the stagnation of the peace process with Israel and the rapprochement between Israel and Turkey.

Regarding the crisis which burst out in November 1997 between Iraq and the UN concerning the inspection by UN inspectors of the royal palaces and sites suspected as being used for manufacture of biological weapons, Syria adopted a position opposed to the use of force against Iraq. Much ado was made of Iraqi Deputy Prime Minister, Tarik 'Aziz's, arrival for talks in Damascus, after no senior Iraqi personage of state had set foot in Syria for 17 years.[34] Syria's position expressed rage and suspicion, in view of the cooperation between Israel and Turkey and the stagnation of the peace process.[35] However, up to the end of 1998, the limited thaw in Syria's relations with Iraq has taken the form of demonstration and pressure on the United States, rather than any overall expression of strategic change in Syrian policy.

During the crisis, which broke out anew starting on January 13, 1998, when the United States prepared to strike a military blow against Iraq,[36] Syria took a definitive stand against the use of force. Asad even held talks with Iraqi Foreign Minister, al-Sahaf, in order to emphasize Syrian objection to the military move planned by the United States. Following the arrangement negotiated by UN Secretary-General, Kofi Annan, the Foreign Ministers of Iraq and Syria held a long discussion at the initiative of the Iraqi Foreign Minister. According to a Jordanian source, al-Sahaf took this opportunity to praise the Syrian position adopted during the crisis. The same source added that the Syrians expressed their satisfaction with al-Sahaf's declarations regarding Syria's positive role in Lebanon.[37] (It should be remembered that, in times of tension between Iraq and Syria, Iraqi spokesmen had attacked Syrian policy in Lebanon, and Iraq had even attempted to render assistance to anti-Syrian forces in Lebanon.)

In July 1998, Iraq's Oil Minister, Amir Muhammad Rashid, announced that Syria and Iraq had agreed to reopen the pipeline from the Kirkuk oil fields in Iraq to the Syrian port of Banias.[38] The reopening of the pipeline, which had been closed since 1982, and the agreement to build an additional new pipeline was an important breakthrough toward strengthening economic cooperation between the two states. In September of that year, Syria's trade center was reopened in Baghdad. Concurrently, officials of the two states hinted about the possibility of resuming diplomatic relations.[39] Notwithstanding the growing tendency to strengthen economic cooperation during 1998, it seems that Asad and the Syrian leadership remain suspicious regarding Saddam's Iraq.

Conclusion

The positions and opinions of Asad and Saddam Husayn are of especial importance in shaping the relations between the two states, considering the nature of their respective regimes and the status of their heads of state, despite the great differences between the two regimes and between the two men. Syrian statements regarding Saddam Husayn are notable for their contempt, rejection and apprehension, justified in national and political terms. The personal mistrust and hostility between the two leaders reduces the chances for rapprochement and long-standing alliance between their countries, but does not negate tactical cooperation.

Continued stagnation of the peace process, combined with the rapprochement between Israel and Turkey, and the continuation of the Turkish threat to the Euphrates waters – all considered strategic threats against Syria – constitute grounds for a thaw in Syrian relations with Iraq in order to demonstrate Syria's dissatisfaction and to exert pressure on the West. If any severe deterioration in Israeli-Syrian relations occurs, along with a simultaneous deterioration in the water dispute with Turkey, then the chances for moves toward reconciliation with Iraq will improve.

The development of relations between Syria and Iraq depends on the nature of the relationship between their domestic politics and their regional foreign policy, and the degree to which the regimes will try to reinforce their domestic legitimacy and power by adopting a policy aimed at regional domination.

As long as either Syria and/or Iraq continues to suffer from internal weakness and instability and aims for dominance in the Fertile Crescent, mutual suspicion and tension will prevail. The socio-political processes in Syria and the development of the Syrian state will lead, in the long run, to conditions favorable to stable relations with Iraq. This is only if post-Saddam Iraq (whenever his regime eventually comes to an end) maintains its unity and stability, and does not get involved in a protracted inter-ethnic struggle, dragging in such external forces as Iran, Turkey, Saudi Arabia, Syria, and so forth. Then and only then will there be any real chances (from the Syrian point of view) for long-lasting and stable cooperation between two states which do not pose a mutual threat to each other's regimes. This can only come to pass when the weight of the drive for regional dominance and power as a component of domestic stability declines and is replaced by development, modernization and industrialization as the main components of the two regimes and their respective political systems.

The reinforcement of Syria as a nation-state and the change in the meaning and functions of nationalism in Arab societies, in the ideological climate in Arab states and in the inter-Arab arena, have decreased the ability of Iraq to influence Syrian politics. However in the visible future, the fate of Iraq and its foreign policy still have considerable importance for the regional posture and strategic interests of Syria.

Notes

1 The Iraqi Ba'th regime first rose to power in 1963 and returned in 1968.
2 King Faisal I, 1921–33; King Ghazi, 1933–1939; Regent 'Abd al-Ilah,

1939–53; King Faisal II, 1953–58.
3 Reeva Simon, "The Hashemite 'Conspiracy': Hashemite Unity Attempts 1921–1958," *IJMES*, Vol. 5 (1974), pp. 314–27.
4 Philip S. Khoury, *Syria and the French Mandate* (Princeton, 1987), pp. 310–11, 359.
5 *Ibid.*, p. 585.
6 Sabri al-'Asli adopted a pro-Iraqi orientation in the National party starting in 1948, in contrast to the pro-Egyptian and pro-Saudi attitude of its traditional leadership. In 1955, under pressure by the officers and radical forces, al-'Asli changed his policy and, as Prime Minister of Syria, distanced himself from Iraq. During his term in office, Syria underwent a rapprochement with Egypt under 'Abd al-Nasser and opposed the Baghdad Pact. While he was Prime Minister in 1956–58, Syria turned its back on Iraq and formed a union with Egypt in February 1958.
7 Michael Eppel, "Iraqi Politics and Regional Politics 1945–1949," *Middle Eastern Studies*, Vol. 28 (1992), pp. 108–19.
8 Michael Eppel, "Syrian–Iraqi Relations during the 1948 Palestine War," *Middle Eastern Studies*, Vol. 32 (1996), pp. 74–91.
9 Patrick Seale, *The Struggle for Syria: A Study in Post-War Arab Politics* (London and Oxford, 1965); Michael Eppel, *Iraqi-Syrian Relations 1945–1958* (unpublished Ph.D. thesis, Tel Aviv University, 1990), Vol. 1, pp. 101–83 (in Hebrew).
10 *Mahkamat al-sha'b* (People's Trials), protocols of the trials of members of the monarchical regime in Iraq, drawn up by the authorities of Qassem's revolution in 1958, Vol. 1 (Baghdad, 1959), p. 131; *ibid.*, Vol. 2, pp. 453, 471, 531. Testimony in the trials of Iraqi intelligence figures involved in activity intended to topple the al-Shishakli regime in Syria; *ibid.*, Vol. 3, p. 1099, the trial of Fadhil al-Jamali.
11 Michael Eppel, "The Fadhil al-Jamali Government in Iraq, 1953–1954: The Last Attempt at Changes and Reforms in the Conservative Regime Before the Revolution," *Journal of Contemporary History*, Vol. 34 (1999), pp. 417–42; Mohammed Fadhel Jamali, "Iraq under General Nuri," *Middle East Forum*, Vol. XL (1964), p. 13; *Mahkamat al-sha'b*, Vol. 4, p. 444, the trial of 'Abd al-Jalil al-Rawi, former Iraqi Ambassador to Syria.
12 *Ibid.*, p. 1070; Michael Wright (British Ambassador to Iraq) to FO, no. 455, April 13, 1955, PRO/FO/371/115506/Y/1073. *Ibid.*, No. 176, April 15, 1955
13 Uriel Dann, *Iraq under Qassem* (Jerusalem, 1969), p. 263.
14 In Iraq, the Ba'th seized power in February 1963, but was ousted by 'Abd al-Salam 'Arif in November of that year. The Ba'th returned to power in Iraq in 1968, following a coup in two stages on July 17 and July 30.
15 Itamar Rabinovich, *Syria Under the Ba'th, 1963–1966: The Army-Party Symbiosis* (Jerusalem, 1972), pp. 79, 99, 107.
16 Eberhard Kienle, *Ba'th vs. Ba'th: The Conflict Between Syria and Iraq, 1968–1989* (London and New York, 1990), pp. 48–57.
17 Amatzia Baram, "Ideology and Power Politics in Syrian–Iraqi Relations, 1968–1989," in Moshe Ma'oz and Avner Yaniv (eds.), *Syria Under Assad: Domestic Constraints and Regional Risks* (London, 1986), pp. 133–37.
18 *Ibid.*, p. 135.
19 Regarding the economic recession in Syria during the latter part of the 1980s, see: Lesch's, Efrat's and Winckler's chapters in this volume.

20 Michael Eppel, "Syria: Iraq's Radical Nemesis," in Amatzia Baram and Barry Rubin (eds), *Iraq's Road to War* (New York and Haifa, 1993), pp. 177–90.
21 *Ibid*., p. 185.
22 *Al-Ahram* (Cairo), July 14, 1997; BBC SWB, June 12, 1997, according to Syrian Arab Republic Radio.
23 *Al-Hayat (*London), March 20, 1997.
24 *Gulf States Newsletter* (West Sussex), Vol. 22, No. 563, June 16, 1997.
25 EIU, *Country Report – Iraq*, No. 4 (1997).
26 BBC SWB, August 18, 1997.
27 *Ibid*., August 12, 1997.
28 Peter Feuilherade, "Mending Fences," *Middle East International* (MEI), June 13, 1997.
29 *Al-Hayat,* August 18, 1997.
30 BBC SWB, August 28, 1997, according to INA (Iraqi News Agency), August 26, 1997.
31 *MEI*, June 13, 1997.
32 *Babil* (Baghdad), August 20, 1997.
33 *MEI*, June 13, 1997.
34 *Al-Hayat*, November 22, 1997.
35 BBC SWB, November 24, 1997.
36 Due to Saddam Husayn's refuse to allow the UN inspectors free and unlimited access to all sites in Iraq suspected of manufacturing biological and chemical weapons of mass destruction.
37 BBC SWB, March 4, 1998, according to the Jordanian weekly *al-Majd*.
38 Reuters, August 8, 1998.
39 Reuters, September 4, 1998.

12

Turkish–Syrian Relations: An Update

David Kushner

In a discussion of the present state of Turkish–Syrian relations, it might be useful to briefly summarize the findings of an article published ten years ago in which I tried to describe and analyze Turkish–Syrian relations as they appeared then, mostly from the Turkish viewpoint.[1] In reviewing the course of relations between the two countries since Syria acquired its full independence after World War II, it was possible to distinguish between two main phases of development. In the first phase, lasting until after the collapse of the UAR in September 1961, relations moved from a rather chilly beginning toward a state of confrontation. They were affected by memories of past relations between Turks and Arabs, especially of the World War I period, when Arab nationalists rose up to throw off the Ottoman rule which had lasted four centuries. While Arabs saw their revolt as a legitimate step toward acquiring national independence, the Turks regarded it as nothing but a "stab in the back" that undermined their wartime effort against the entente powers. Relations were later further affected by the secularist and Westernist course adopted by the Turkish Republic, seen by many Arabs as a betrayal of traditional Islamic principles. Last but not least, and with a particular impact on the Syrians, was the fact that the borders between Syria and Turkey, as delineated in agreements between Turkey and the Powers, left in Turkish hands extensive lands considered by Arabs as their own. The most thorny border question was that of the province of Alexandretta (Iskenderun), handed over to Turkey by France in 1939 to be incorporated in Turkey as the province of Hatay.

This combination of memories, differences, and conflicts accounted for the chilly beginning of relations. Later on, in the 1950s, it was Turkey's role as the bastion of Western interests in the Middle East, along with its developing relations with Israel, on the one hand, and Syria's movement into the radical revolutionary and pro-Soviet camp in the Arab world, on the other, which caused the two countries to view each other with intense suspicion and hostility. There were two interruptions in this process. One was created by the regime of Husni al-Zaim, the pro-Western officer who held power in Syria for several months in 1949 and who viewed friendship with Turkey as one of the pillars supporting both the independence of Syria and the stability of his rule. The second was brought about by the ascendancy of the People's Party in Syria in 1954–55 and its readiness to enter into a pro-Western alliance with both Iraq and Turkey. However, both periods were of relatively short duration and conflicted with the general trend of politics in Syria, which was definitely one of radicalization and growing anti-Westernism. From the mid-1950s onward, Syria adopted an increasingly nationalist and pro-Soviet orientation, closely cooperating with Nasserist Egypt. With turbulence engulfing Jordan, Lebanon and Iraq in 1957 and 1958, and the new levels of tension emerging between the pro-Western and pro-Soviet camps in the Middle East, relations with Turkey further deteriorated, and it appeared on more than one occasion that both countries might even drift into war. The formation of the UAR by Syria and Egypt in early 1958 could only contribute to further suspicion and tension.

However, there was a turn toward accommodation in relations between Turkey and Syria after the dissolution of the UAR in September 1961. In Syria, the intense pan-Arab nationalism of former years, never abandoned, gave way to a certain "withdrawal," which was aimed at reconstruction and guarding the country's newly-established independence. The rise in late 1970 of the regime of Hafiz al-Asad, taking over from the strongly pro-Soviet and socialist Salah Jadid, contributed to the adoption of realistic and pragmatic policies. Overall, tensions between the major "camps" in the Middle East began to dissipate, reflecting broader changes in relations between the Eastern and Western world blocs. Much of Syria's attention during the 1960s and 1970s was focused, in fact, on its relations with Israel and the situation in Lebanon. By then, Turkey, too, had adopted a more flexible approach toward the two major world blocks, moving away from its close identification with Western interests and making a sustained effort to build bridges with the Soviet block and the non-aligned countries. In the mid-1960s, Turkey began to actively seek the friendship of the Arab countries in the Middle East, taking care not to intervene in the affairs of the Arab world and not to side with one camp or another. It cooled its relations with Israel and adopted an increasingly pro-Arab position on the Arab–Israeli conflict.

Taken together, all these changes were bound to have their effect upon Turkish–Syrian relations. Although still having their ups and downs, they had lost their threatening confrontational nature and were marked by a growing willingness to put aside their sentiments, solve outstanding problems between the two countries, and establish good neighborly relations. Trade expanded, several agreements of cooperation were signed, and mutual contacts assumed a higher level than had been previously customary.

Still, it was clear that with all the cooperation achieved during this second phase in relations between Turkey and Syria, their full potential was never reached. The confrontational era in the Middle East in general, and in the relationship between the two countries in particular might have passed, but important "irritants" continued to cast a shadow over the nature of relations. Among them were the problem of Turkish properties nationalized by Syria and the problem of security along the border. Two major issues, in particular, were of a highly disruptive nature. The first was the deep disagreement between the two countries over the proper apportionment of river waters; and the second was the alleged direct or indirect support given by Syria to various terrorist organizations, which were responsible for the growing restlessness in Turkey. All diplomatic efforts toward resolution proved fruitless, and these issues, vital to the security and welfare of both countries, only served to deepen suspicions and hostilities and to exercise their negative impact on their bilateral relations.

The period of some ten years which have elapsed since the above-mentioned review of Turkish–Syrian relations was written has witnessed important changes on the Middle East scene. The weakening and eventual collapse of the Soviet Union brought an end to the Cold War, along with the serious challenge that the Soviet Union had previously posed to Western positions and influence in the Middle East. States such as Syria, which had for decades been supported politically, militarily and economically by the Soviet Union, found themselves operating in the new world order where the West, and more specifically the United States, had the final word. Deprived of its former Soviet backing, the inevitable result was a growing interest on the part of Syria in accommodating itself to the new realities and mending its relations with the West, particularly with the United States. Turkey, for its part, could also sense a new feeling of "loneliness." Having for years been viewed as a most valuable strategic asset for the West in its attempt to block Soviet expansionism southward, and having thus been assured of substantial Western support, it now experienced a nagging sense of lost worth and began searching for new challenges and roles in order to strengthen its position as an important regional power. These changes of outlook on both sides of the Turkish–Syrian border were bound to eliminate some of the traditional "sting" in the relations between the two countries.

Moreover, and in an unprecedented way, a common interest of significant importance presented itself to both countries as the Gulf crisis erupted in August 1990, namely, the Iraqi invasion of Kuwait. This, more than ever before, demonstrated to all concerned the threat that Saddam Husayn's regime posed to regional stability. In the months ahead and throughout the Gulf War in early 1991, both Turkey and Syria found themselves on the same side of the fence, joining hands with the United States and the West in an anti-Iraqi coalition. The danger emanating from Iraq to the security of Syria was as big as the one which faced Turkey. Nor was the elimination of the threat by Saddam Husayn the only common denominator in the interests of Turkey and Syria. As the ensuing years were to show, both countries, while obviously hostile to Saddam Husayn's regime and striving for his downfall, nevertheless agreed on the need to preserve the unity of Iraq as a country. Turkey, following its traditional policy, was wary of the possibility of Iraq's disintegration and the emergence of a Kurdish state close to its own borders. Suspicions, voiced early during the crisis, that Turkey might be planning to take advantage of the situation by attempting to "restore" Mosul to Turkish hands, were dissipated as it became clear that Turkey's first priority was the full preservation of Iraq's integrity and sovereignty. Syria, if perhaps less concerned with the impact of such a Kurdish entity on its own relatively small Kurdish minority (approximately 8–9 percent of the total Syrian population), could not part, ideologically or politically, from its strong adherence to Arab nationalism and its support for the territorial integrity of Arab lands.

If the talk heard sometimes during the Gulf crisis of a real "spring" in Turkish–Syrian relations proved to be perhaps too premature, these developments had the effect of reinforcing, not weakening, the trend toward accommodation and cooperation already apparent between them. This becomes clear when one examines both the content and the form of relations between the two countries over the last decade. First, beginning with the visit of Vahit Halefoğlu to Damascus in 1989, there has been, after an interval of six years, a frequent exchange of visits and meetings between the Foreign Ministers of both countries. Moreover, recent years have witnessed the first reciprocal visits by Turkish and Syrian Prime Ministers since the visit of Turkey's Prime Minister Adnan Menderes to Damascus in 1955 failed to induce the Syrians to join the proposed pro-Western regional alliance (the Baghdad Pact). In March 1986, the Syrian Prime Minister, 'Abd al-Rauf al-Qassem, came to

Ankara, and in July 1987, Turgut Özal of Turkey paid an official visit to Damascus. In January 1993, Turkish Prime Minister Süleyman Demirel visited Syria within the framework of his tour of several Arab countries on what was described as a "goodwill mission." These high-level contacts did not in themselves indicate a warming up of relations, but in sharp contrast to the situation during the previous "confrontational" period, they at least underscored the importance given by the two countries to their neighborly relations and their interest in maintaining these relations on a normal basis. The level of contacts represented a definite departure from past practices and was therefore significant in itself.

In addition, trade, including lively border trade, played an important role in the developing relations between the two countries and demonstrated the ability of Turkey and Syria to separate between their political differences and their economic interests. In the period between 1987 and 1993, for example, Turkey increased its volume of exports to Syria from $60.6 million to $238.8 million, while Syria raised its exports to Turkey from a mere $55.2 million to $68.5 million.[2] There has also been growing cooperation between the two countries in a number of fields. During his visit to Damascus in 1987, Özal signed a protocol for economic cooperation that included trade, banking, transportation, telecommunication, the transfer of electrical power, and exploration of oil and natural gas. Several agreements have also been made to facilitate the crossing of Turkish pilgrims heading toward the Holy Cities in Saudi Arabia. In June 1993, an agreement was reached for interconnecting the electricity grid of Turkey, Syria and several other Arab countries. Agriculture has been yet another area of cooperation, and both sides have worked together on such matters as animal health and irrigation.

However, in contrast to these positive developments, there have been several incidents during the period under survey which did not contribute at all toward a better atmosphere between the two countries. In 1985, a Syrian diplomat in Ankara was involved in a murderous assault on the Jordanian embassy and succeeded in escaping from the country. There have also been several cases of shooting across the border, and in October 1989, a Turkish civilian aircraft was shot down by a Syrian fighter over Hatay. As always, Syrian maps showing Hatay as part of Syria, or at least marked as a "controversial" area, have, from time to time, drawn the attention of the Turkish public to the fact that Syria has never really given up its old claims to pieces of Turkish territory. Beyond the bilateral level, Syrian policy toward the question of Cyprus has never been to Turkey's liking. To this was added the cool position adopted by Syria toward the question of the Bulgarian Turks, which greatly preoccupied Turkey and Turkish public opinion in the late 1980s.

More than any other matter, however, the dividing issues of water distribution and Syria's apparent support of terrorism in Turkey have continued to produce the most negative effects upon the relationship between Turkey and Syria. These two issues have dominated the agenda between the two countries throughout the period, and in fact, they have tended to become even more serious and consequential as time went on.

The question of water has assumed greater proportions as the need for this precious commodity has grown in both countries due to rapid population growth and the increasing irrigation areas. The issue has gained additional momentum with Turkey's steady progress in its vast development project for southeast Anatolia – the GAP (Güney Doğu Anadolu Projesi), involving plans for the construction of a whole system of dams and reservoirs for the expansion of irrigation and the production of electric power. According to the commitments made by Özal during his visit to Damascus in 1987, Turkey was to allow at least 500 cm. (cubic meters) per second to flow down from the Euphrates River into Syria. This was accepted by the Syrians as a temporary arrangement, but not as a permanent solution to the problem. The Syrians have argued continuously that the water allowed to flow across the border is both insufficient in quantity and polluted. They have contended, more importantly, that since the Euphrates River is shared by three countries – Turkey, Syria and Iraq – the amount of water allocated to each state should not be determined by one country alone, dependent on its goodwill. Rather, the apportionment of the river waters should be undertaken within the framework of a multiparty agreement between the "partners" and determined according to each country's actual needs, both present and future.

In contrast, Turkey's position has been that the Euphrates River waters (since they cross international borders and do not form them) are basically Turkish, and while Turkey would always be willing to provide Syria and Iraq with all of their water needs, there is no question of recognizing the river as international. Turkey has also argued that Syria and Iraq are getting more than sufficient quantities of water and that, in fact, the GAP is a blessing to Syria, as well, because it assures it a permanent supply of water even when the river flow is low. According to the Turkish viewpoint, there has been a considerable waste of water on the part of Syria and Iraq, creating the need for technical studies to determine the precise needs of each of the countries, with particular consideration given to the most efficient and rational methods of irrigation. It has also been Turkey's position that a comprehensive scheme to include other rivers flowing through both countries (like the Asi and the Tigris) was needed.

Turkey has countered Syrian accusations by pointing out that Syria was not considering Turkey's needs with regard to the Asi River, which flows from Syria into Turkish territory. All along it has also blamed the Syrians for doing their best to obstruct the progress of the GAP project by exerting pressure on financial institutions around the world not to provide any assistance to Turkey as long as it refuses to reach a proper agreement with Syria. The failure of the Peace Water project, first raised by Turkey in 1986, to get off the ground, has also been partly attributed to Syrian insistence on an independent consortium to carry out and operate the project.

It was inevitable that with the completion by Turkey of more and more dams as part of the GAP project, and with Turkey's temporary reduction of water flow into Syria in order to start filling the reservoirs, Syria's apprehension and anger would grow. Such was the case in January–February 1990, for example, when Turkey began holding back water for the large Ataturk dam. Turkey had earlier allowed larger quantities of water to flow down the river in order to compensate Syria and Iraq for the temporary loss, but Syria insisted that the no-flow period be much shorter than planned by Turkey, which eventually turned out to be about one month. Once again, Syria presented its demand that matters related to the flow of the river water not be left to the discretion of Turkey alone, but instead be regulated by all the countries concerned. As it would do on other similar occasions, Syria turned for support to other Arab countries and to the Arab League, a move that irritated the Turks and exacerbated the controversy. With the inauguration of the Ataturk Dam in July 1992, the issue was once again brought to the fore. While Arab ministers were invited to take part in the ceremony, and Turkey repeated its commitment to keep the water flowing, Prime Minister Demirel found it opportune to reiterate the Turkish position that the water was Turkey's just like oil belonged to the Arabs and that it had the right to do with it what it wished.[3] The statement, though predictable, had a most chilling effect on Turkish–Syrian relations, and Syria again brought the matter before the Arab League. Demirel's visit in January of 1993 did not quite allay Syrian fears and did not resolve the issue, although it was agreed between the countries that a solution must finally be found within the same year.

While Syria's position in wanting to sign an international agreement and in confining itself to the Euphrates River alone can well be understood as one which would best assure its interests, the same might be said of the Turkish stance on the issue. With Turkey having actual control of the Euphrates, it is clear that there is no strong motivation on the Turkish side to reach a quick solution, let alone one which would come in the form of an international agreement, as demanded by the Syrians. Turkey seems, in fact, to be quite content to leave matters as they are, as it would be against its interests to commit itself to a specific quantity or portion of water, given the significant fluctuations in precipitation and water flow from one year to another and given the uncertainty of water requirements in the future. The Turks' insistence on including other rivers in an agreement is also understandable insofar as it would reduce the share of the Euphrates to be allocated to Syria and Iraq. Apart from these considerations, the water issue likewise serves Turkey well as a means of applying pressure on Syria to cease its support of militants and insurgents in Turkey. Although the water issue is an explosive one and has the potential of disrupting the relationship between the two countries, it is also more likely to act as a deterrent against any Syrian aggression against Turkey. Confident that Syria will continue to depend on Turkish waters, Turkey has had no real reason to rush into a hastily concluded agreement.

Syrian support for terrorism and rebellion in Turkey continued indeed to feature as the other major issue afflicting the Turkish–Syrian relationship. Turkey maintains that Syria has for years been providing all kinds of assistance to terrorist organizations whose purpose was to bring lawlessness and instability to Turkish life. The identity of the terrorists might have changed over the years, but the basic features of Syrian support have remained the same. During the 1970s many of the terrorists, who were then mostly Turks, were said to have been trained and armed in camps in Syria or Lebanon, sometimes in close collaboration with Palestinian organizations.The same was said to be the case with Armenian terrorists, mostly associated with ASALA (The Armenian Secret Army for the Liberation of Armenia), who, in the late 1970s and early 1980s, engaged in frequent assaults on Turkish diplomats and officials abroad. In more recent years, particularly since 1984, when the Kurdish underground organization, the PKK (Partiya Kerkeran-i Kurdistan) began its all-out uprising against Turkish authorities in Anatolia, it has largely been the Kurdish separatists who, according to the Turks, have received open or tacit Syrian support. Once again, Kurdish terrorists (some of them Syrian nationals) are said to have been trained in Syria or in Syrian-controlled Lebanon and then allowed to infiltrate into Turkish territory. In addition, the Turks claim, there has been considerable smuggling of arms and money into Turkey for the use of the PKK.

To top everything else, Syria has served at times also as the very headquarters of the PKK. Some of the congresses of the PKK are said to have been held in Syria, and the founder and long-time leader of the movement, Abdullah Öcalan, is said to have maintained his residence in the country.

As with the water issue, there have been endless contacts between Turkey and Syria with the purpose of resolving the matter, with the issue acquiring particular urgency as the Kurdish insurgence intensified and as more evidence was found by Turkish authorities proving a Syrian connection. Turkish officials have been in the habit of passing the evidence on to the Syrian authorities, demanding quick action against the terrorists and issuing harsh warnings to Syria to desist from its support. At times there have been actual threats: In his tour of South Eastern Anatolia in August 1989, Özal, for example, warned Syria and other neighbors of Turkish action to destroy PKK bases.[4] Reports – perhaps leaks – would often appear in the press that Turkey was actively considering reprisals and cross-border operations against Syria. The Syrians have invariably reacted to Turkish accusations by denying any sort of help accorded to Turkish or Kurdish terrorists. They have maintained that it was not Syria's policy or intention to harm the stability of Turkey, with which Syria wished to have good neighborly relations, and that Syria would never allow its territory to become a base for attack or intrigue against Turkey's security. Syrians have often claimed a lack of knowledge of any subversive activities against Turkey conducted from their territory. At other times they have argued that they are not always able to control operations carried out in places like Lebanon or along the long border between Syria and Turkey. With regard to Öcalan, Syria has constantly disavowed any knowledge of his whereabouts and denied that PKK congresses and meetings have ever taken place in Syrian-controlled areas.

On occasion, agreements were signed between Turkey and Syria committing both countries to observing the security of their common border and to preventing any action aimed against the territory of the other. Such was, for example, the protocol of security signed during Özal's visit to Damascus in 1987. It did lead for a while to more determined action on the part of the Syrians, by taking care not to support the terrorists actively and by closing bases on Syrian soil proper. However, bases in Lebanon that were claimed not to be under full Syrian control apparently remained active, and it was not long before they once again became the subject of Turkish complaints and warnings. Turkey argued that Syria, contrary to its claims, was, in effect, in control of Lebanon, and that it was not doing all it could to prevent the activities of terrorists and their infiltration through Syrian territory into Turkey. In 1992, matters deteriorated enough to bring the Turkish Minister of the Interior to Damascus, where he signed another security agreement in which both countries accepted that the PKK was an outlawed organization and promised to cooperate in ending its presence in the Biqa‘ valley in Lebanon. They also agreed to actively cooperate against terrorism and to establish a supervision mechanism. Once again, as on many previous occasions, the agreement brought some temporary relief and, due partly to American pressure on Syria, PKK terrorists were, in effect, removed from the Biqa‘. Shortly afterwards, however, matters reverted back to where they had been before.

In the eyes of the Turks, Syrian denials of its support for destructive actions against Turkey were not made in good faith. The same goes for its commitments to help in eradicating the terrorists' bases. The Turks believed that Syria's policy was partly based on its long-term interest in weakening Turkey in a way which might lead to its break-up and the redrawing of its borders, and partly on its wish to retain its own valuable trump card against Turkey on the water issue. There was little doubt, of course, that a game of cards was, in fact, being played between the two countries. Syria, given the sensitivity of the "terrorism" issue, never admitted, and indeed could never admit, that it was virtually encouraging terrorism in a neighboring country. Its actions, however, spoke for themselves, and it was not accidental, for example, that after Syria's failure to get a satisfactory response from Turkey on the water issue early in 1993, there was a resurgence of activity through the Turkish–Syrian border later that year. The Turks, on their part, could also not easily admit to using the vital matter of water as a trump card, but at times, and especially when terrorism in their country was on the rise, did use language which thinly veiled their readiness to punish Syria for its doings. Thus, for example, in a speech in 1989 in Şanliurfa, Özal warned Syria that Turkey would continue to supply Syria with the promised quantities of water as long as it had enough and as long as Syria stuck to the conditions set down in the 1987 agreement.[5] Turkey did not, in fact, shy away from making its point even clearer by, at least on one occasion, closing the flow of water without prior warning to Syria.[6]

In the mid-1990s, there was a noticeable deterioration in the state of Turkish–Syrian relations, derived primarily from the prolongation and occasional intensification of the major issues dividing the two countries. The steady progress of Turkish irrigation projects, to include even the Tigris river, with no settlement of the distribution issue, increasingly worried and annoyed the Syrians, who once again turned to the support of other Arab countries. Turkey voiced a complaint of its own regarding the reduction of the allocation made by Syria in the Asi River, leading to only 10 percent of its water being allowed for use by Turkey. Cases of infiltration from Syria into Turkey also increased and, to make things worse, there was a particular increase of activity along the borders of the province of Hatay. During the first months of 1996, Turkey's reaction became unprecedentally harsh, with Prime Minister Mesut Yılmaz warning Syria that "this neighbor will have to either give up taking hostile actions against us or sooner or later end up paying the price for its enmity toward us." Associating Syria's activity with its designs on Hatay, he reminded the Syrians that Turkey had no territory to give away and no one should doubt "that Hatay is one of the provinces to which we attach great importance and give priority."[7] Turkish spokesmen were by this time ready, as never before, to directly refer to Syria's support of terrorism. For instance, pertaining to the seizure of arms and ammunition destined for the PKK on the border, the Turkish Minister of Interior reminded his listeners that Syria was still listed by various Western countries as a country which supports terrorism and that it was nothing new for Syria "to use the terrorist organizations in the region as a means of threatening the internal security of various countries."[8]

Into this old–new state of tension in Turkish–Syrian relations was now added yet another factor: growing Turkish–Israeli cooperation. Turkey's recognition of Israel in 1949 and its ongoing relations with it had always been resented and suspected by Syria. When Turkey began, in the mid-1960s, to cool its relations with Israel and to court the Arab world, the issue lost much of its earlier importance. However, starting in the late 1980s, a gradual rapprochement between Turkey and Israel took place, based as it was, among other things, on the common struggle against terrorism in the area. More recently, the process has been greatly accelerated and has found expression in two military agreements which were concluded in the course of 1996 between Turkey and Israel: one for cooperation in air force training and the other for the upgrading of Turkish F-4 fighter bombers by the Israeli Aircraft Industries. The agreements were never described by either Israel or Turkey as forming a military pact in any way, although the new military cooperation between the countries was significant in itself. It may have indeed been partly induced, on Turkey's part, by the newly conceived threat coming from Syria – its growing support for the Kurds, its accelerated armament, and the close relations formed between Syria and Iran, on the one hand, and Syria and Greece, on the other.

In any event, the new accords signed between Turkey and Israel were enough to arouse considerable suspicion in Syria and the Arab world at large. They invoked memories of the now well-known "periphery pact" secretly concluded between Turkey, Israel and other countries in the late 1950s, and whatever the truth behind their meaning, were viewed by Syria as being aimed against it. They aroused Syria's old fears that Turkey and Israel would be in a position to simultaneously pressure Syria on both its northern and southern borders were the need to arise. Continuous reports about actual joint military exercises, courtesy visits by war vessels, and frequent mutual exchanges by Turkish and Israeli military commanders only served to heighten Syrian apprehensions.

Syria was therefore the prime mover behind the loud and nervous reaction to these agreements within the Arab world in the summer of 1996. On the ground, there was evidence of a Syrian build-up along the border with Turkey, only to be countered by the apparent dispatch of Turkish reinforcements. Turkish naval exercises were said to have been deliberately conducted close to the Syrian waters and were widely interpreted as a warning to Syria. The whole situation was reminiscent, if on a smaller scale, of the sabre-rattling which erupted on more than one occasion during the tense years of confrontation in 1957 and 1958.

It is against this background that in July 1996 a new government came to power in Turkey, headed for the first time by an Islamist party, the Welfare Party. The party and its leader, Necmettin Erbakan, who became Prime Minister, have been on record for many years as ardent advocates of a more Islamic regime at home and of an active and wholehearted orientation toward the Islamic world as a basis of Turkey's foreign relations, involving the playing down or reduction of Turkey's relations with the West and with Israel. The initial steps taken by Erbakan and his friends in power did betray a preference for an Islamist foreign policy, and Erbakan's first foreign trips were conducted with the aim of fostering relations with Islamic countries in Asia and Africa. Although Erbakan's visits did not include Syria, the new government, in both word and deed, showed special regard toward Turkey's southern neighbor, and Turkish gestures were greatly welcomed by Syria as a deliberate attempt to set Turkish–Syrian relations on a new friendly course. The Syrian ambassador in Ankara was the first one to be received by the new prime minister, and, undeterred by American displeasure, government circles let it be known that Erbakan was seeking the cooperation of Syria, as well as Iraq and Iran, for the settlement of the Kurdish problem in northern Iraq and other areas. It was clearly the new prime minister's thesis that Islamic bonds could serve as a useful instrument for bringing about cooperation between Muslim countries, otherwise engulfed by mutual conflicts and squabbles.

Yet, if there was any lesson to be learned from the experience of Erbakan's government, it is that not even an Islamist prime minister with an Islamist orientation was able to bring about a meaningful change in the nature of Turkish–Syrian relations. Realities on the ground did not change and, while it is true that Erbakan's language toward Syria was milder in tone than that of his predecessors, no progress was made toward a solution of any of the outstanding problems between the two countries. Consequently, there was little change, if any, in what other Turkish statesmen and officials were saying on the subject. In an interview published in an Israeli newspaper at the end of September 1996, President Demirel had this to say on Turkish–Syrian relations:

> As most members of the international community know by now, Syria gives all kinds of support to the terrorist organizations which carry out subversive, separatist activities against Turkey. Although Turkey strives to maintain amicable relations and to promote cooperation with Syria, Damascus for its part seems to be seeking to undermine Turkey's stability and to weaken it. Its policy toward Turkey aims to foment economic, social and political mayhem . . . With this policy Syria is trying to enhance its bargaining chip in the matter of water, secure better terms in reciprocal trade and reiterate that it has never forfeited its territorial claim to the Hatay region.[9]

It was during the term of office of Erbakan's successor, Mesut Yılmaz, that a new low point in bilateral relations occurred, assuming the proportions of a serious crisis. In October 1998, also motivated perhaps by internal political considerations, the Turkish government decided to force Syria to desist once and for all from supporting the PKK by bringing matters to the brink of war. Warnings of military action, unless Syria were to take concrete steps against PKK activities, were phrased in unusually harsh and threatening terms and were accompanied by the movement of troops along the border. Public opinion was aroused, and government and military spokesmen were joined by opposition parties and the press in a display of a high level of national determination. The crisis was diffused only after Egypt and Iran stepped in to mediate, and Turkish and Syrian officials met in Adana to work out a new security agreement between the two countries. According to this agreement, replacing the earlier 1987 and 1992 accords, Syria declared that Öcalan was "no longer" in Syria and that PKK camps were "no longer" in operation on its soil and undertook to fully cooperate with Turkey against the PKK, which it recognized as a terrorist organization. Several measures to combat terrorism were agreed upon between the two countries, and Turkey declared that it would henceforth closely monitor the implementation of the agreement by the Syrians.

With the conclusion of the 1998 crisis, it seemed that Syria had this time come to understand the importance of the security issue to Turkey and was, at least in the short term, willing to translate its commitments into action. Abdullah Öcalan was forced out of Syria and seems to have gone to Russia, only to move on to other havens, and finally be captured in Kenya and brought to trial in Turkey. It remained to be seen, however, how long the new understanding between Turkey and Syria would last. Both countries have indeed manifested a preference for accommodation, knowing that the other alternative is confrontation and war, which would cost them both dearly. Yet, it is similarly clear that no real friendship and cooperation could be easily attained between the two countries. This stems partly from the fact that there is relatively little which binds them in the way, for example, that the Kurdish issue or oil trading have often brought Turkey and Iraq together. There is, on the contrary, plenty of resentment and suspicion between the two countries. Hatay is still a deep wound in the hearts of the Syrians, and the water apportionment issue is far from being settled to their satisfaction. Both of these issues give rise to fears among the Turks that Syria, interested as it is in changing the situation in its favor, cannot but harbor ill intentions toward them. Syrian support for the PKK in the past has demonstrated to the Turks the extent of their neighbor's willingness to disrupt stability and security in their country, and, in their eyes, there is no guarantee that the same will not recur in the future. The issues between Turkey and Syria are deeply divisive, and their explosive potential is real. As put by Philip Robins, "The best that can be hoped for in the foreseeable future is that the structural problems which divide the two sides can be managed in such a way as to promote compromise and defuse tension."[10]

Notes

1 David Kushner, "Conflict and Accommodation in Turkish–Syrian Relations," in Moshe Ma'oz and Avner Yaniv (eds), *Syria under Assad:Domestic Constraints and Regional Risks* (London and Sydney: Croom Helm, 1986), pp. 85–104. Other works which have treated the subject in recent years are H. Fahir Alacam, "Turkish–Syrian Relations," *Turkish Review of Middle East Studies*, Vol. 8 (1994–95), pp. 1–17; Muhammad Muslih, "Syria and Turkey: Uneasy Relations," in Henri J. Barkey (ed.), *Reluctant Neighbor: Turkey's Role in the Middle East* (Washington, D.C.: US Institute of Peace, 1996), pp. 113–30; Murhaf Jouejati, "Water Politics as High Politics: The Case of Turkey and Syria," in *ibid.*, pp. 131–46; Daniel Pipes, *Syria Beyond the Peace Process,* Policy Papers No. 40 (Washington, D.C.: The Washington Institute of Near East Policy, 1996), pp. 53–67; see also: Philip J. Robins, *Turkey and the Middle East* (New York: Council on Foreign Relations, 1993).

2 Ayşegül Kibaroğlu, "Prospects for Cooperation in the Euphrates Tigris River Basin," *Turkish Review of Middle East Studies*, Vol. 8 (1994–95), p. 149.

3 *Hürriyet* (Istanbul), July 25, 1992; *Cumhuriyet* (Istanbul), July 27, 1992.

4 *Cumhuriyet*, August 28, 1989.

5 *Cumhuriyet*, October 2, 1989.
6 *Hürriyet*, January 14, 1992.
7 Anatolia Radio, April 20, 1996, quoted by BBC, *Summary of World Broadcasts: Central Europe and Balkans,* April 22, 1996.
8 TRT TV, January 24, 1996; *ibid.*, January 27, 1996.
9 *Ha'aretz* (Tel Aviv), September 22, 1996, quoted in *ibid.*, September 24, 1992.
10 Robins, *Turkey and the Middle East*, p. 53.

Part V

Strategy toward Israel

13

Syria's Struggle over Water with Israel, 1959–1967

Moshe Shemesh

The conflict over the diversion of the Jordan River's water and its use by Israel was a key issue on the Arab world's political agenda from September 1959 until the June 1967 War. The Arab countries perceived this conflict as essentially a political problem and the core of the struggle against Israel. Arab discourse centered on the correct response to Israel's plan: Should they prevent implementation of the plan by diverting the Jordan River's tributaries, or should they take military action? Egypt and Syria held opposing views about solving the problem. Eventually 'Abd al-Nasser's position won out. The main aim of this chapter is to illustrate the dilemma that Syria faced while planning its strategy on this issue, as a result of the gap between its ideological extremism (represented by the Ba'th party) and its inability to carry out a policy based on it.

The first crisis between Israel and Syria over water diversion occurred in September 1953, when Israel commenced work on a project to rechannel the Jordan River in the central demilitarized zone near the B'not-Ya'acov Bridge. The plan called for digging a canal two and a half kilometers long that would extend from the B'not-Ya'acov Bridge south to Tabha on the northern shore of the Sea of Galilee, where the differences in elevation would be utilized to produce electricity. On September 7, 1953, Syria filed a complaint before the Israeli–Syrian Mixed Armistice Commission in reference to Israel's use of heavy earth-moving machinery in the central region of the demilitarized zone. Syria also demanded that the UN observers call for "an immediate cessation of the work."[1]

On September 23, 1953, Major-General Bennike, the Chief-of-Staff of the UN Truce Supervision, requested the Israeli government to stop the work so as "to ensure that the authority which started work in the demilitarized zone on September 2, 1953, is instructed to cease work in the zone as long as an agreement is not arranged."[2] Encouraged by Bennike's attitude, Syria filed a complaint before the UN Security Council on October 12, 1953, charging that Israel had violated the armistice agreement on three counts:

1 Violation of the rights of the inhabitants in the demilitarized zone.
2 Prevention of the Syrian population residing along the river from using its water for irrigation purposes.
3 Military seizure of land in the demilitarized zone.[3]

In light of the ensuing Security Council debate, Israel was forced to halt work (October 28, 1953), mainly due to American pressure (the threat of postponing economic assistance unless Israel ceased further earth-moving operations).[4] The US was involved at that time in trying to achieve a comprehensive Arab-Israeli settlement of the water problem in the region, though it was not successful in its mission. In 1958, Israel initiated an alternative plan, tapping water from the Sea of Galilee and channeling it to the Negev via the National Water Carrier.

The issue of the Jordan River's diversion was first discussed in the Arab League Council in September 1959, when it was decided to form a committee that would present a series of recommendations.[5] The subject was also reviewed by the UAR (United Arab Republic) government in November 1959, which decided to call a special meeting of the Arab League Council to discuss the Israeli water scheme.[6] Thereafter, it became a major Arab issue with two opposing positions: the Egyptian stand, which supported a technical solution, and the radical Syrian position, which advocated the use of military force.

By the end of 1959, Israel's water diversion scheme had become a hot political issue as the result of several factors. First, Eric Johnston, on his own initiative, reported to UAR[7] officials that Israel was about to implement its plan for the Jordan River diversion. The UAR attached great importance to this information because of Johnston's prior involvement with the issue and his proximity to American officials. Moreover, the Israeli Finance Minister, Levi Eshkol, and the Minister of Agriculture, Moshe Dayan, had publicly declared the strategic importance of Israel's Water Plan and outlined a timetable for completing its first stage.[8] These announcements incited fear in the Arab states that the plan would soon go into effect. They regarded the Water Plan as a means for Israel to increase its power by facilitating the absorption of masses of new immigrants who would, in turn, reinforce its army. This, they charged, would endanger the Arab states and hamper a solution to the Palestinian problem.[9]

Both the Syrian and the Egyptian leadership (during the period of unity) were convinced, based on their accumulated, yet erroneous, information, that Israel would soon embark on its diversion of the Jordan River. As a result, any work pursued in the central demilitarized zone heightened suspicions that Israel was indeed moving forward with its original plan. This fear was evident, for example, in the Syrians' response to the drainage work carried out by Israel south of the B'not-Ya'acov Bridge in 1960. They vehemently objected to the project, maintaining that it was connected to the Jordan River diversion scheme. Due to the importance of the issue, they let 'Abd al-Nasser deal with it, but insisted on military action, if necessary, to stop the work. 'Abd al-Nasser, however, preferred to deal with the issue through the Mixed Armistice Commission.[10]

From 1959 until the June 1967 War, the issue of Israel's water diversion antagonized Syria (the UAR's northern region) more than any other Arab country. The Syrian Ba'th characterized Israel's water plan within the context of the Arab struggle against Israel as "the most urgent pan-Arab national problem (*qawmiya*) being discussed today in the Arab League" (January 1961). The Ba'th position was consistently vigorous and uncompromising, according to which the Arabs "must forcibly resist Israel's diversion of the Jordan's waters in order to prevent the complete eradication of the Palestinian problem by Israel." Akram Hourani, one of the Ba'th leaders and member of the UAR government, demanded in November 1959 that military action be taken against Israel in the central demilitarized zone so as to bar any form of diversion work from taking place. However, Hourani's position was rejected and, in combination with other reasons, led to the Ba'th ministers' mass resignation from the UAR government on December 24, 1959.[11]

The militant Ba'th position stemmed from the following motives:

1 It reflected the Ba'th strategy for a solution to the Arab-Israeli conflict, whose ultimate goal was "the annihilation of Israel." Therefore, it was contended that "diverting the Jordan River created the greatest of dangers to the rights of the Arabs in *Filastin* since the Catastrophe (*al-Nakba*) in 1948."[12]
2 Israel's diversion of the Jordan River was viewed primarily as a Syrian problem, whether it referred to the original Israeli plan for diverting the Jordan in the demilitarized zone or whether it meant Israel's pumping water from the Sea of Galilee at a point close to the Syrian border.
3 The Ba'th position also stemmed from rivalry with Egypt for Arab public opinion regarding the way to solve the Arab–Israeli conflict. The Ba'th represented the antithesis of Egypt, viewing the struggle

> against diversion of the Jordan River as the spearhead of the Arab-Israeli conflict and as the most essential part of the crusade that would lead to the "destruction of Israel." In order to achieve this goal, the Ba'th favored using all measures available, including armed force, to halt Israel's diversion scheme.[13]

At the beginning of the water crisis, in late 1959, the Ba'th party, which was a senior partner in the UAR government, hastened to arrive at a firm decision, relying on Syria's experience on the water issue.[14] Syria voiced its position not only in official statements and public declarations by Ba'th ministers, but at high-level discussions within the UAR government, in contacts between the two regions (North and South) during the period of unity, and also in secret memos passed from the Ba'th leadership to the parties in Lebanon and Syria. The controversy between the Syrian Ba'th and 'Abd al-Nasser over the appropriate response to Israel's diversion plans added another level to the frustration of the Ba'th leadership and brought on the Ba'th ministers' aforementioned resignation from the UAR government in late 1959.

The official Syrian Ba'th position, finalized between the end of 1959 and early 1960, stated: "The appropriate and definitive Arab response to Israel's diversion of the Jordan River is to block her from carrying out this scheme. Any other Arab decision [on our part] will only be deceitful and misleading toward Arab public opinion. The Arab deterrent should be a firm policy statement declaring that Israel will not be allowed to perpetrate its brigandage [and will be prevented] by all means available, including armed force if necessary."[15]

Concerning the use of force, the Syria Ba'th leaders announced in October 1960 that "Arab artillery could easily prevent Israel from continuing diversion of the Jordan by knocking out its equipment, and this is precisely what Arab cannon fire has been doing since 1953."[16] At that time (1953), Syria had sent urgent complaints to the Security Council and succeeded in forcibly preventing Israel from continuing its diversion work upon the Security Council's recommendation. Most of the Arab League's discussions between 1960 and 1963 revolved around the Arabs' own plans for diverting the Jordan's tributaries and the establishment of a United Arab Command (UAC), which would prepare Arab armies for the "destruction of Israel's military power."[17] The assessment was that Israel would complete its water project by 1963. However, no concrete measures were taken toward either one of these goals until the end of 1963.

After the Ba'th party came to power in Syria on March 8, 1963, the leadership's dilemma regarding the water issue was evident in two contradictory political statements. In the first, on behalf of the Ba'th's Sixth National Congress, in October 1963, it stated: "The Congress considers the issue of the Jordan River diversion [by Israel], whether by pumping from the Sea of Galilee or diversion (in the demilitarized zone), as a major threat, primarily a military one, to the Arab homeland. The party calls on all Arab states, especially Egypt, to challenge the plan, even if [military] force is required."[18] On the other hand, at a meeting of Arab Chiefs-of-Staff on December 7, 1963, the Syrian Chief-of-Staff, Yusuf Shukour, declared, according to 'Abd al-Nasser, that "Syria will not be able to divert the Jordan River's water in its own territory, for should it attempt to do so, Israel would attack, the water sources would fall into enemy hands, and Syria would be helpless to do anything about it."[19]

At a convention of the Arab Chiefs-of-Staff, held on December 7–9, 1963, to discuss Arab reactions to the impending opening of Israel's National Water Carrier, two proposals were presented:

1 To establish an Arab Joint Command to deal with military aspects of the Arab response.
2 To set up a special apparatus to execute technical counter-projects, such as the Arabs' own scheme for diversion of the Jordan's tributaries.[20]

At the same time, during the meeting of the Arab Chiefs-of-Staff, the Syrians launched a strident propaganda campaign against the Egyptians' unwillingness to take part in a large-scale offensive and against their rejection of the Syrian proposal to discuss an Arab attack in the case that Israel were to begin operating the National Water Carrier. In addition, the Syrians accused 'Abd al-Nasser personally of blatant cowardice and lack of will to fight Israel while he boasted of Arab military superiority. Israel's National Water Carrier, Syria charged, was a vital concern not only for Syria, but for all the Arab countries "because the dangers inherent in it threaten all of us . . . We must decide upon a unified Arab military plan to undermine the diversion scheme, one which is basically a military plan . . . Egypt shirks a military confrontation with Israel over diversion of the Jordan, and for this reason is a traitor to Arab interests."[21] On December 15, 1963, following the Arab Chief-of-Staff's meeting, the Syrians raised six alleged strategic threats to the Arab states which would result from the opening of Israel's National Water Carrier:

1 The project would enable Israel's absorption of four million more Jews into *Filastin*, representing an influx of new citizens that would allow Israel to concentrate greater manpower for a decisive campaign in the future.

2 The project would forever separate the Arab East (*al-Mashriq al-'Arabi*) from the Arab West by means of a tightly crowded human wall in the Negev, and would thus destroy Arab plans for unity and encirclement of Israel.
3 The project would increase Israel's manpower and economic strength, thereby placing it at an advantage *vis-à-vis* the Arab forces.
4 The project would bolster Israel's military potential and would thus encourage the launching of a new aggressive campaign against Arab lands.
5 The Jordan River diversion project would be only one in a series of Zionist-imperialist expansionist acts against the Arab homeland.
6 The Jordan River project would prove to be another link in the chain of aggression inherent in Israel's irredentist policy, which claims that its borders stretch from the Nile to the Euphrates, and whose goal is to expel the Arabs from the entire region and settle in their place twenty million Jews.[22]

Following an appeal by 'Abd al-Nasser, the First Arab Summit convened in January 1964 in Cairo in order to deal with the Arab response to Israel's completion of its National Water Carrier and its impending opening in May. 'Abd al-Nasser imposed his strategy on the Summit, stating that "the immediate goal [of Arab strategy] is diversion of the Jordan's tributaries and the creation of an effective deterrent force by strengthening the Arab armies."[23] At this stage, the Arab states were still endeavoring to avoid a confrontation with Israel that would lead to all-out war.

The Second Arab Summit, held in September 1964 in Alexandria, resolved to carry out the Arab plan for diverting the Jordan's tributaries. According to Ali Amir, the head of the United Arab Command, "Israel will take military measures, either during one of the stages of the Arab plan's implementation or toward the end of the project. In either case, Israel will launch an all-out war for which the Arab states must be prepared."[24] However, things did not turn out according to Amir's predictions. Syria's part in the Arab diversion was to build a 73-kilometer canal for carrying water from the Banias Springs southward toward the Yarmuk. In addition, the canal was intended to absorb the Hasbani's excess water, which was being diverted in Lebanon. Diversion of the Banias would bring 90 million cubic meters of water to be used for irrigating land around the river. Eighteen months were allotted for carrying out this plan.[25]

Syria's official policy emphasized the political importance of diversion, but failed to publicly acknowledge the potential economic benefits deriving from the diversion of the Banias, namely, the irrigation of 60–100 thousand dunams (15–25 thousand acres). While criticizing the Arab Summit's resolutions on the water issue, Syria attached its signature to them with deep reservations, claiming that:

1 "The Summit decision is not coping seriously with the problem, unless immediate action is taken. Diversion of the tributaries is absolutely essential . . . The ideal solution should have been preventing Israel from starting diversion of the Jordan River's water. Rechanneling the tributaries is an empty recompense for the Arabs' helplessness."[26]
2 "Diversion has to be integrated into a comprehensive military plan for the liberation of *Filastin* . . . It cannot be considered a substitution for liberating *Filastin*, but part of a practical plan for liberating *Filastin* . . . The diversion is accepted as a minimum border, so long as Arab countries refuse to declare an all-out war of liberation at the present time, but this is not a satisfactory response."[27]
3 "Though diverting the tributaries has been delayed for four to five years, the urgent need to exploit our water for developing our resources can no longer be ignored. The continuation of the project is based on our need for survival, and defending the enterprise will be the task of our deterrent forces. This justification cannot be denied."[28]

Against the background of Syria's firm ideological stand and basic political attitudes, it is understandable that once the Second Arab Summit gave the green light to start the Arab diversion work, Syria was the first state to begin operations in her own territory (opposite Tel-Dan) in November 1964. Syria initiated this work, free of any external Arab pressure, in a sensitive area exposed to the Israeli border near the armistice line. Only Syria continued to clear away the path for water diversion even after damage caused by Israeli land attacks and air strikes against the work.

Israel's reaction to Syrian rechanneling was not slow in coming. On November 13, 1964, hostilities flared up in the Tel-Dan area (where Syrian diversion work had already begun), when Israeli bulldozers clearing away a patrol road were fired upon. The Dan River was the only one of the Jordan River's sources whose springs were inside Israel's borders, and in order to defend it, Israel had opened up a patrol road around it in 1962. Claiming that the road passed through their territory, the Syrians attacked with anti-tank and machine-gun fire from the Nuchila fire-base opposite Tel-Dan, and afterwards continued to pump recoilless gun shells into the Israeli positions. When the Israel Defense Force (IDF) returned the fire, the incident escalated with concentrated

Syrian shelling from other gun positions, as well as the engagement of tanks. Again, the IDF returned fire with all available weapons on the front, including heavy armor, and war planes were called in to silence the Syrian artillery. The Syrians linked the whole incident to the diversion work being carried out, claiming that "Israel's goal was to test the seriousness of the Arabs' decision to execute their own water diversion project . . . The Syrian Army is able to defend its plans and insure their completion."[29]

This incident did not prevent the Syrians from continuing their earth-moving work to the north and south of the Banias, encompassing four sections simultaneously and employing ten bulldozers. Four months later, on March 17, 1965, after an Israeli patrol was shot at, the IDF again struck at the Syrian digging operations in the Tel-Dan region. Israeli tanks blasted away at the sources of Syrian fire and zeroed in on the heavy earth-moving equipment at a range of 2000 meters. The Syrians, however, did not respond, apparently because their front-line officers had instructions not to respond unless they received direct orders from the High Command. Until this incident, the Syrians had managed to clear away a north–south path nearly 15 kilometers long, just west of the Banias, but as a result of the firefight, they stopped their work along this entire sector.

Diversion work was renewed on April 15, 1965 at a new point south of the B'not-Ya'acov Bridge, opposite the Israeli agricultural settlement of Mishmar ha-Yarden, five kilometers from the border. On May 13, 1965, an IDF patrol traveling south of Mishmar ha-Yarden opened fire on Syrian earth-moving equipment. IDF tanks struck at Syrian machinery at a range of five to six kilometers from the B'not-Ya'acov Bridge, putting three Syrian tractors out of action. Although the Syrians continued to avoid a military confrontation, the recurrence of Israeli belligerency highlighted the need for a reassessment by Syria and the Head of the UAC. The Israeli reaction, testing the Arab strategy regarding the Jordan River diversion, came as a surprise to the Arab leaders, especially the Head of the UAC. As already mentioned, his prediction (during the Second Summit meeting) had been that Israel would respond only toward the end of the project. Instead, Israel's reaction had come as soon as work commenced,[30] thus making it clear that Israel was determined to obstruct Syria's diversion operations at all costs.

The IDF's vigorous response presented Syria with a dilemma. On the one hand, work stoppage would harm Syria's integrity and prestige, both internally as well as in the rest of the Arab world. On the other hand, Syria consistently avoided any deterioration in the situation along the border that might have occurred due to Israel's attacks. Syria could not afford the risk of allowing the border to deteriorate until it was assured of

Egypt's political support and military assistance in the case of war. The Syrians correctly calculated that the diversion area's close proximity to the border would enable Israel to hinder earth-moving operations at will. Its persistence in doing so strengthened the Syrian assessment that Israel's objective went beyond preventing diversion work, and that its ultimate goal was to occupy the demilitarized zones by means of an extended military action.

Syria subsequently requested that UAC air units be stationed on its territory in order to challenge Israel's aerial supremacy. The Syrians made a proposal to the Egyptian government regarding severe retaliatory measures against Israeli settlements following the Israeli attack. In addition, Syria sought reinforcement in the form of a deterrent force together with the preparation of Arab armies capable of immediate deployment in the event of Israeli hostilities. Syria also demanded a comprehensive Arab mobilization for a worst-case scenario, which meant stationing Egyptian troops in the Sinai and the Gaza Strip and evacuating UN emergency forces along the border. In a nutshell, Syria was calling for "a clearly defined war strategy against Israel, not just a water diversion plan." However, Egypt, as well as the UAC, adamantly insisted that the incidents were only local skirmishes, a claim intended to point to Syria as the sole responsible Arab party.[31]

At the end of May 1965, after a reevaluation of the brewing tensions, and in accordance with the Egyptian strategy, ʻAli Amir suggested that diversion work continue further away from the Israeli border, until such time as the UAC had completed preparation of its defenses.[32] In a meeting with President Shihab of Lebanon in late May 1965, ʻAbd al-Nasser recommended that Lebanon postpone the implementation of the diversion plan in her territory, stating that: "If Israel destroys a tractor and I have to retaliate by attacking the next day, it means that Israel is the one who determines the time for war."[33] Nonetheless, the Syrians proceeded with their work, transferring it further south to Qubat Qarʻa, about 10 kilometers from the Israeli border. On August 12, 1965, the IDF responded with tank fire that destroyed Syrian earth-moving equipment. Again, the Syrians kept silent and continued their work at a slower rate.

At the Third Arab Summit, held in September 1965 in Casablanca, the assessment prevailed that: "Israel had succeeded in sabotaging the Arabs' plans to divert the Jordan's tributaries, thus bringing them to a halt." However, the Syrian Chief-of-Staff emphasized that Syria would not stop the diversion project even though he was "expecting a fourth, a fifth and a sixth attack." The Third Summit granted freedom of action to all countries working on diversion projects, as long as Arab military power, including its air forces, was not strong enough to defend the operations or capable of deterring Israeli attacks on them.[34] This decision actually signalled the formal withdrawal of the Arab Summit's support of the Syrian diversion project.

In spite of the Summit's resolution, Syria continued its rechanneling, moving it further south, and away from the border out of range of Israeli armor. An IDF military operation on August 12, 1965, caused a Syrian work stoppage for three days, after which the work on clearing a diversion path continued until the middle of October 1965. At that time, most of the equipment was brought further south to the Ein Hamoud sector, which was even more removed from the border. Until January 1966, the work in the Qubat Qar'a sector progressed slowly and employed minimal equipment in preparing a path six kilometers long. In mid-January 1966, the work proceeded only in the Ein Sufeira sector, 12 kilometers from the border, but advanced so slowly that by July 1966, only three and a half kilometers of the designated water course's top soil had been cleared away, while a mere one and a half kilometers of canal had actually been excavated.

The Israeli reaction to the Syrians' continued diversion work became a question of proper timing, and on July 14, 1966, the IDF launched an air strike against Syrian earth-moving machinery. Five bulldozers were destroyed at Ein Sufeira, and in the course of a dog fight between Israeli and Syrian jets, one Syrian MIG-21 was shot down. Again, the Syrians refrained from reacting.[35] This attack in effect capped the lid on Syria's diversion activity, although some minor "cosmetic" clearing away continued until the June 1967 War.

In conclusion, we can see that Syria was the only Arab state which attempted to carry out its share of the Arab diversion plan, even though the finished product was inconsequential. For all the effort made, the top soil along a 40-kilometer swath was cleared away, and a canal only three kilometers in length was excavated. Lebanon ceased all diversion work after the incident of May 13, 1965. Jordan, through its Yarmuk Plan, kept to the framework of the original Johnston Plan.

The Ba'th party, which took part in the UAR government and had been ruling Syria since early March 1963, was trapped by the water issue between its ideological commitments and its inability to implement them. The Ba'th party's problem, as defined by one of its leaders, constituted "accomplishments on the theoretical level, but failures on the performance level."[36] In this context, it may be concluded that one of the main reasons behind the stability of Asad's regime has been its success in narrowing the gap between ideology and praxis. Syria called for the use of force to thwart Israel's diversion of the Jordan River and to counteract her attacks against the Syrian diversion efforts. However, in practice,

Syria had to admit that it could not fight Israel alone. This was evident from the instructions given to front-line Syrian soldiers, directing them not to respond to any Israeli provocation unless they received specific orders from high-ranking officers. The objective was to prevent Israel from having any excuse for further attacks on Syria's diversion operations.

Syria's failure was also part of the overall shortcoming of Arab strategy in the water conflict. The need to compensate itself for this failure and bolster its shattered prestige led Syria to support the *Fatah* organization's guerrilla attacks against Israel. The question remains whether, and to what extent, Syria's failure and frustration contributed to the deterioration leading to the June 1967 war, which, as we know, started with a Syrian warning that Israel was deploying large forces on its borders.

Notes

1 See: Yemima Rosental (ed.), *Documents on the Foreign Policy of Israel*, Vol. 8, 1953 (Jerusalem, 1995), p. 645, note 5; see also: Aryeh Shalev, *The Israel-Syria Armistice Regime 1949–1955* (Tel Aviv, 1993), pp. 168–69 [hereafter: Shalev, *The Israel-Syria Armistice Regime*].

2 See: Major-General Van Bennike's letter to Moshe Sharett from September 23, 1953, in Rosental (ed.), *Documents on the Foreign Policy of Israel*, Vol. 8, 1953, document No. 381, pp. 673–76.

3 Shalev, *The Israel-Syria Armistice Regime*, p. 172.

4 Rosental (ed.), *Documents on the Foreign Policy of Israel*, Vol. 8, 1953, document No. 444 (editor's note), pp. 769–71; see also: document No. 473, p. 812 (editor's note).

5 *Middle East Record* (Shiloah Research Center – Tel Aviv University), Vol. 1 (1960), pp. 204–7; see also: *al-Hayat* (Beirut), September 2, 1959; December 27, 1959.

6 *Al-Ahram* (Cairo), December 2, 1959.

7 The UAR was the official name of the unification of Egypt and Syria during the period February 1958–September 1961.

8 See: Moshe Dayan, *Ha'aretz* (Tel Aviv), October 5, 18, 19, 1959; Levi Eshkol, *Ha'aretz*, November 19, 1959; see also: *Davar* (Tel Aviv), December 10, 1959; *al-Hayat* (Beirut), December 19, 1959.

9 See: *Filastin*, (East Jerusalem-Jordan), January 5, 1961; General Muhammad Ibrahim, *Egyptian Gazette* (Cairo), November 1, 1960; *al-Ahram*, December 5, 1959, January 5, 1960; *Cairo Radio*, commentaries, December 5, 6, 1959.

10 For details see: Moshe Shemesh, "Arab Struggle Over Water Against Israel 1959–1967," *Iyunim Bitkumat Israel* (The Ben-Gurion Research Center, Sede-Boker, Israel), Vol. 7 (1997).

11 See: Hasanayn Haykal, quoting from the protocol of the UAR's government debate of late November 1959, *al-Ahram*, May 18, 1962; on Akram Hourani's version on this debate (November 29, 1959) see his article published in: *al-Ayam* (Damascus), June 13, 1962.

12 See: *al-Sahafa* (the Ba'th organ in Lebanon), Beirut, February 16, 1960; see also: *al-Ba'th wa Qadiyat Filastin*, Vol. 4, 1959–64 (Beirut, May 1975), p. 30; *Nidal al-Ba'th, al-Qutr al-Lubnani 1951–61*, Vol. 8 (Beirut, March 1972),

pp. 67–68 [hereafter: Nidal al-Ba'th, Vol. 8].

13 See: *al-Sahafa*, February 16, 17, 1960; *al-Ba'th wa Qadiyat Filastin*, Vol. 4, pp. 29–34; *Nidal al-Ba'th*, Vol. 8, pp. 67–68.

14 Shalev, *The Israel-Syria Armistice Regime*, pp. 51–80, 165–92.

15 *Al-Sahafa*, February 16, 17, 1960; see also: *al-Ba'th wa Qadiyat Filastin*, Vol. 4, pp. 29–34.

16 *Al-Sahafa*, October 19, 1960; *al-Ba'th wa Qadiyat Filastin*, Vol. 4, pp. 57–59.

17 See: 'Abd al-Nasser, Cairo Radio, January 13, 1964; *al-Ahram*, April 27, 1961; Haytham al-Keilany, *al-Istiratijiyat al-'Askariya lil-Hurub al-'Arabiya al-Israiliya 1948–1988* (Beirut, 1991), p. 261–62 [hereafter: Keilany, *al-Istiratijiyat al-'Askariya*].

18 See: *Nidal Hizb al-Ba'th al-Arabi al-Ishtiraki, Abr Mu'tamaratihi al-Qawmiyya 1947–1964* (Beirut, 1971), p. 166.

19 See: 'Abd al-Nasser, *al-Jumhuriyya* (Cairo), November 19, 1965; *Cairo Radio*, December 23, 1963, February 22, 1964, May 1, 1964, July 1, 1964; *al-Ahram*, March 12, 13, 1965, November 20, 1965.

20 See: al-Keilany, *al-Istiratijiyat al-'Askariya*, p. 262.

21 See: *al-Thawra* (Damascus), December 5, 6, 7, 10, 1963; *Damascus Radio*, December 4, 1963.

22 *Damascus Radio*, commentary, December 15, 1963; see also, *al-Ba'th* (Damascus), December 11, 1963; *Damascus Radio*, December 18, 1963.

23 On the resolution of the first Arab Summit, see: *Keilany*, *al-Istirajiyat al-'Askariya*, pp. 260, 264, 284, 286.

24 See: Ahmad al-Shuqayri, *'Ala Tariq al-Hazima* (Beirut, June 15, 1972), pp. 268–69 [hereafter: al-Shuqayri, *'Ala Tariq al-Hazima*].

25 Details of the Arab diversion plan, see: *al-Jumhuriyya*, October 24, 1964.

26 See: *al-Ba'th*, January 16, 21, 1964; *al-Ba'th wa Qadiyat Filastin*, Vol. 4, pp. 143–47.

27 See: *al-Ba'th wa Qadiyat Filastin 1964–1969*, Vol. 5 (Beirut, May 1975), pp. 97–111, 120–21 [hereafter: *al-Ba'th wa Qadiyat Filastin*, Vol. 5]; Munif al-Razaz, *al-Ba'th*, September 22, 1965.

28 See: *al-Ba'th wa Qadiyat Filastin*, Vol. 5, pp. 97–111.

29 *Damascus Radio*, commentaries, November 14, 15, 1964; *al-Thawra*, November 14, 1964.

30 Shuqayri, *'Ala Tariq al-Hazima*, pp. 268–69.

31 See: Mahmud Riyad, *Mudhakirat*, Vol. 2 (Beirut, 1986), pp. 300–1; Munif al-Razaz, *al-Ahrar* (Beirut), June 7, 1965; *al-Ba'th wa Qadiyat Filastin*, Vol. 5, pp. 94–97.

32 Shuqayri, *'Ala Tariq al-Hazima*, pp. 39–40, 65; 'Abd al-Nasser, *Cairo Radio*, May 31, 1965; *al-Hayat* (Beirut), May 30, 1965.

33 See: Mahmud Riyad, *Mudhakirat*, Vol. 2, p. 300; 'Abd al-Nasser, *Cairo Radio*, May 31, 1965.

34 See: Mahmud Riyad, *Mudhakirat*, Vol. 2, pp. 303–9; Shuqayri, *'Ala Tariq al-Hazima*, pp. 85, 268–69; *Keilani*, *al-Istirajiyat al-'Askariya*, p. 263.

35 Details on this event, see: *Ha'aretz*, July 15, 1966; *Damascus Radio*, July 14, 1966 (announcement by military spokesman).

36 See: *Nidal Hizb al-Ba'th al-Arabi al-Ishtiraki, Abr Mu'tamaratihi al-Qawmiyya 1947–1964* (Beirut, 1971), introduction of the editor to the Report on the Ba'th's Seven National Congress held in February 1964, p. 254.

14

Changes in Syria's Regional Strategic Position vis-à-vis *Israel*

Moshe Ma'oz

Background

One of the main characteristics of the Syrian quest for pan-Arab and anti-Israeli leadership was the dichotomy between the grand design and the ability to carry it out. Ideologically, Syria has long considered itself as the "beating heart of Arabism," the center of Arab nationalism and the struggle against Zionism. These concepts derived from the emergence of modern Arab nationalism in Syria in the early twentieth century, the rise of the pan-Arab Ba'th party in the 1940s and the establishment of the Ba'th regime in Syria in early March 1963, and contributed to underlining Syrian ambitions to unify the Arab world and lead its conflict with Israel.

In practice, however, for a long period of time Syria was unable to realize these grand goals because of its ongoing domestic problems, notably the instability of the political system and the centrifugal tendencies of its compact minorities, as well as the tension between the ruling upper class and the new middle class. Syria also suffered from the absence of a strong national leader capable of unifying the nation and advancing Syrian ideological aims and strategic interests in the Arab world, as well as *vis-à-vis* Israel. Rather than extending its influence into neighboring Arab countries, Syria, until the Ba'th ascendancy, was the object of the unitary or expansionist designs (and of subversive activities) of its neighbors. These included the "Fertile Crescent" unity scheme of the Iraqi leaders King Faysal I in the 1930s and Nuri Sa'id in the early 1940s, as well as the "Greater Syria" unity plan of King Abdallah of Jordan in the mid-1940s. Even Syria's union with Egypt (UAR) between 1958 and

1961, largely motivated by Syrian–Arab ideological concepts and strategic security interests, turned out to be partly an Egyptian endeavor to control the political system and exploit the economic assets of its Syrian partner. This traumatic experience lingered during the first seven years of the Ba'th rule, placing Damascus in a defensive posture *vis-à-vis* Cairo. To this trauma we should also add the sharp ideological, political and economic conflicts between the two Ba'thist pan-Arab regimes in Damascus and Baghdad. Despite Syria's militant policies, it failed to defeat Israel in both pan-Arab wars of 1948 and 1967. In the latter war, which Syria largely initiated, it also lost the Golan Heights.

The Asad Era – General Observations[1]

With the ascendancy of Hafiz al-Asad in 1970 (in fact he had already become Syria's strong man in 1969), previous constraints and limitations on the country's regional leadership were likely to diminish, if not disappear completely. For the first time in its contemporary history, Syria had a powerful ruler with a unique combination of leadership qualities on both national and regional levels, as well as a strong ambition to achieve pan-Arab influence. Indeed, Asad has been able not only to establish, for the first time, a strong centralized regime, but also to achieve remarkable political stability and military might for Syria as well. Possibly aspiring to succeed Gamal 'Abd al-Nasser (who died in 1970) as a pan-Arab leader, Asad's grand ideological and strategic goals were, during the early 1970s, to achieve all-Arab solidarity, if not unity, primarily in order to carry out a coordinated struggle against Israel.

Given these aims, the Egyptian–Syrian war against Israel in 1973 initially appeared to be a unique act of pan-Arab solidarity and cooperation among several Arab countries. In fact, however, Asad not only played a secondary role in the war, but he realized after a few days that Sadat's strategic aims were essentially incompatible with his own. Following his military defeat by Israel, Asad was unable either to coordinate a joint diplomatic strategy or to prevent Sadat from concluding separate agreements with Israel. Subsequently, Asad himself tried to recover the Golan Heights by means of diplomatic efforts, directed mainly toward the United States, but to no avail.

Having failed to implement his aims, Asad, the realistic and pragmatic strategist, changed his course during the mid-1970s. He turned his efforts toward the achievement of a "Fertile Crescent" political–military union or cooperative arrangement with Iraq, as an alternative to Egypt. Yet, facing severe obstacles in realizing this alternative scheme, Asad simultaneously endeavored to forge a "Greater Syria" union with Jordan, Lebanon and the PLO, again as an alternative to the "Fertile Crescent" (and pan-Arab) scheme. Here again, Asad encountered great difficulties, largely owing to the Israeli and Iraqi challenges.

At this juncture, Asad opted for the first time and with growing Soviet military help, to single-handedly establish a strategic balance with his formidable enemy, American-backed Israel, as well as to extend his regional design beyond the inter-Arab context and to establish an alliance with a non-Arab power, Iran. This approach was initiated in order to strengthen his shaky regional position, to neutralize potential Israeli and Iraqi threats, and to improve his maneuvering capabilities among various Arab states.

Yet, despite his Soviet backing and links with Iran, Asad failed again to achieve regional hegemony and to match Israel's military superiority. His only strategic regional gain was the extension of Syria's dominance over (most parts of) Lebanon. The major causes for this failure were:

1 The acute economic crisis generated *inter alia* by the arms race with Israel.
2 Syria's growing inter-Arab isolation created by its support of Iran in the war against Iraq, with the end of the war in 1988, at Iraq's advantage, further aggravating Damascus' regional-strategic predicament.
3 The significant change in Soviet policy toward Syria and the subsequent disintegration of the Soviet Union, which seriously undermined Damascus' strategic military backing. Under these circumstances, Syria has been induced, since 1988, to adopt a new regional strategy *vis-à-vis* various Arab countries, the United States and particularly Israel.

Before examining Syria's new regional strategy and its future prospects, it would be worthwhile to dwell upon and explain its previous failures to acquire regional hegemony and to challenge Israel. Such an inquiry may also help to evaluate the constraints on Damascus' present and future regional strategy.

Asad, Israel and the Pan-Arab Dimension

Under the neo-Ba'th regime (1966–70), against the background of Syria's regional isolation and Israeli threat, Asad aspired to achieve the following interconnected goals:

1 To improve Syria's relations with most of the Arab countries, irre-

spective of their socio-political regime, and particularly to become the co-leader of a large Arab union alongside Egypt, the most powerful Arab country, while winning financial backing from Saudi Arabia, the most affluent Arab country.
2 To recover the Golan Heights, as well as other Arab lands occupied by Israel in the June 1967 war.

In order to implement those strategic goals, Asad employed ideological concepts and political and diplomatic initiatives, while simultaneously increasing the military build-up.

On the ideological level, Asad used the Ba'thist concepts of pan-Arabism and the historic struggle against Zionism and imperialism, notions that were still influential among the Arab peoples. In many public speeches and interviews, Asad and other Syrian leaders hailed the ideal of Arab unity as a major cure for the problems of the Arab nation and stressed the need to fight Israel, the major enemy of the Arabs.[2] However, being aware of inter-Arab rivalries, on the one hand, and Israel's military might on the other, Asad developed a more realistic policy toward Arab unity and the struggle against Israel, namely, aiming at inter-Arab co-operation in forming a strategic balance with Israel and employing both military and diplomatic means to recover the occupied territories.

Thus, in late 1970, Syria joined the federation of Arab Republics, along with Egypt and Libya, ostensibly as a step toward a comprehensive Arab union "from the Atlantic Ocean to the Arab Gulf." At the same time, Damascus endeavored to renew or imprint relations with the conservative Arab states of Saudi Arabia, Kuwait, Morocco, Lebanon and Jordan, in order to advance inter-Arab military, political and economic cooperation. Similarly, while systematically developing, with massive Soviet help, a strong military force to confront Israel, Asad declared for the first time, in March 1972, that Syria would no longer oppose the implementation of UN Security Council Resolution 242 (November 1967). That is, he would accept a political settlement, provided Israel withdrew from all Arab lands occupied in the June 1967 war and the Palestinians achieved their national rights.[3]

However, as Israel rejected Syrian (and Egyptian) demands to withdraw from the occupied territories, Damascus stepped up its military preparations for war against Israel. Yet, Asad realized that Syria was unable to confront Israel single-handedly on the battlefield and that it badly needed to join forces with either or both Arab regional military powers – Egypt and Iraq – in order to effectively fight Israel and consequently gain an important regional standing. Syria preferred the partnership with Egypt owing to the latter's stronger strategic position and military power, as well as its deep motivation to regain the occupied territory through a combination of military and political means.

The subsequent alliance between Syria and Egypt in the October 1973 War against Israel enabled Damascus, for the first time, to reach the position of a "shared" regional hegemony with Egypt, while several other Arab countries rendered military, diplomatic, and economic support to both Syria and Egypt in an impressive demonstration of pan-Arab solidarity. However, the Syrian–Egyptian partnership did not last long, as Sadat, partly with American encouragement, signed a series of separate agreements with Israel starting in late 1973 and culminating in the March 1979 Egyptian-Israeli peace treaty.

The Iraqi Connection

Although in the aftermath of the October 1973 war Syria's new regional position was strengthened, it was still unable to match Israel's military superiority without the full participation of Iraq, the second most powerful Arab country after Egypt. Such a partnership between the two pan-Arab Ba'thist regimes indeed had great potential as the core of a Fertile Crescent strategic configuration (together with Jordan, Lebanon and the Palestinians) and as a formidable military–political power in the Arab region. However, as things turned out, several attempts made by Damascus during the 1970s to conclude a union or alliance with Baghdad were a complete failure due to ideological, strategic (political and economic), and personal conflicts between the two Ba'thist regimes. To begin with, each government claimed to represent the authentic Ba'thist doctrine, while both of them were engaged in a strategic-political competition for hegemony in the Fertile Crescent region. Syria periodically blocked the Euphrates River waters flowing into Iraq and/or demanded high royalties for the passage of Iraqi oil through its territory. Furthermore, when Saddam Husayn came to power in the late 1970s, he and Hafiz al-Asad developed an intense personal enmity.

Yet notwithstanding their ideological rivalry, Damascus appealed to Iraq for military help during the 1973 war, whereupon Baghdad dispatched two armored divisions to help Syria fight Israel in the Golan Heights. Iraq recalled its forces immediately after Syria accepted UN Resolution 338, labeling Damascus as "defeatist" and accusing it of recognizing Israel. In 1974 and 1975, Asad proposed that Iraq establish a political–military union with Syria, but was repeatedly rejected because of his readiness to "make peace with the Zionist enemy."[4] Only following the Camp David accords between Egypt and Israel (1978) did the Iraqi president, Ahmad Hasan al-Bakr, offer to cooperate with Asad in foiling those accords. Consequently, in October 1978, the two leaders signed a charter for Joint National Action, providing for the "closest form of unity ties," including "complete military unity," as well as "economic, political and cultural unification . . . " being an "historical pan-Arab step . . . in confronting the present Zionist onslaught . . . against the Arab nation."[5]

However, this Syrian–Iraqi agreement did not last long, first because Asad probably became concerned about the ambition of the newly self-appointed (1979) Iraqi president, Saddam Husayn, to lead the new union as well as the unified Ba'th party; second, because of Asad's refusal of the Iraqi demand that he renounce Syria's acceptance of UN resolutions 242 and 338, which Baghdad considered as recognition of Israel; and finally, because of Asad's objection to a full merger with Iraq and to the deployment of Iraqi troops in Syria. With the eruption of the Iraq–Iran war in 1980, the renewed Syrian–Iraqi conflict reached its highest peak, as Damascus backed Teheran against Baghdad.

The Greater Syria Scheme[6]

Without the strategic partnership of either of the two powerful Arab countries, a more promising avenue for Asad's regional leadership and confrontation with Israel was the creation of a Greater Syria alliance, or union, ("federation" in Asad's words) with Jordan, Lebanon and the Palestinians. In addition to its common historical and geographical background, this region could provide important strategic, political and economic assets to a new Damascus-led union, with Syria being the most powerful party in such an alliance. Employing military power and political skill while taking advantage of his neighbors' predicaments, Asad indeed managed during the period 1975–77 to almost unify Greater Syria under his leadership. As Patrick Seale observed in 1977:

> Asad saw Syria's immediate neighbors, Lebanon and Jordan, as a natural extension of its territory . . . The three-nation grouping is already a fait accompli . . . Asad now rules by proxy in Lebanon, while progressive integration with Jordan is well advanced. If the Palestinians ever recover a West Bank homeland, they too will inevitably join this complex.

Like Seale, other Western commentators also defined Syria in 1977 as a "new regional power," "a new power center," and "a new dominant power in the Middle East," while Asad was depicted as "the star of the Arab homeland."[7] This "new regional power," however, was not sufficiently cohesive and solid, and thus disintegrated before it became a political reality. By late 1977, Jordan, the most important strategic component of this Syrian-led alliance, began to worry *inter alia* about Damascus' rejectionist policy toward the Egyptian-Israeli peace process. Seeking to regain his inter-Arab freedom of maneuverability, King Husayn gradually broke away from Asad's grip in favor of a new alliance with Iraq's strong man and Asad's rival, Saddam Husayn.

PLO leader, Yasir 'Arafat, developed somewhat similar relations with Asad during the 1970s and early 1980s. Following a Syrian-led anti-Israeli strategic cooperation, which culminated in a 1975 Syrian offer to establish a joint military and political command with the PLO, Asad and 'Arafat became sworn enemies in 1976. This occurred against the background of the Lebanese Civil War (of 1975–76) and Asad's support of the Christian Lebanese forces in their conflict with the Lebanese leftist–PLO alliance. Thus, for example, in June 1976 the PLO–Lebanese leftist alliance inflicted heavy losses on the invading Syrian army near Sidon; and in August 1976 Christian-Maronite forces, backed by Syrian troops, attacked and killed many Palestinians in the Tal al-Za'atar refugee camp near Beirut. Although Syria mended its fences with the PLO in 1977, it did not help the Palestinians in March 1978 during the Israeli offensive against the PLO bases in south Lebanon.

Following another period of Syrian–PLO rapprochement after the 1978 Camp David accords, Syria again did not "defend the Palestinian existence" during the 1982 Israeli invasion of Lebanon.[8] With the final rift between Asad and 'Arafat (who was deported from Damascus in 1983), Syria lost its remaining influence over the mainstream PLO, while also failing to gain any significant hold among Palestinians in the Israeli-occupied West Bank and Gaza Strip. The PLO peace agreement with Israel (the Declaration of Principles – the Oslo accord of 1993) further alienated Asad of 'Arafat.

Dominance in Lebanon

The only substantial achievement in Asad's Greater Syria strategic design has materialized in Lebanon, although not without great difficulties. Indeed, in 1978, Syria started to encounter growing opposition to its control of Lebanon from the Christian–Maronite Lebanese forces, which were receiving increasing military aid from the Likud-led Israeli government. Following the 1982 Israeli invasion, a pro-Israeli Lebanese government was established in Beirut, while Syrian forces were forced to withdraw from large parts of the country. This severe setback occurred only several months after the Asad regime encountered its worst domestic predicament ever: the militant Islamic rebellion, which was crushed in the 1982 Hama repression, claiming many thousands of civilian lives and causing the destruction of large parts of the city.

Amazingly, however, at the lowest ebb of Syria's regional and domestic crises, Asad managed to recover his protectorate over most of Lebanon, albeit after several years. Employing various Lebanese and Palestinian armed organizations, as well as his own personal skill, Asad had the 1983 Lebanese-Israeli strategic agreement abrogated and caused the withdrawal of Israeli forces from Lebanon in 1985 (except for a "security zone" along the border, manned by the Israeli-controlled SLA). Subsequently, Damascus established a pro-Syrian government in Beirut and turned Lebanon into its satellite state, by way of two bilateral agreements: the Ta'if agreement (October 1989) and the "Friendship and Cooperation" agreement (May 1991). In the end, Damascus' control of Lebanon, particularly of its defense and foreign policies, has constituted the major achievement of both Asad's regional strategy, notably his Greater Syria scheme, and his contest with Israel over Lebanon.

Yet, while succeeding in gaining a strategic advantage with regard to Lebanon, Syria totally failed to achieve an overall strategic balance with Israel or induce it to give up the occupied territories within the framework of a comprehensive Arab-Israeli political settlement.

Syria's Strategic Balance with Israel and Strategic Alliance with Iran

Following the October 1973 war, Asad made several serious attempts to prevent Sadat from signing separate agreements with Israel. Asad insisted on forming a unified Arab delegation in the negotiations with Israel, with the intent of dictating to Israel the terms of a pan-Arab–Israeli settlement. Endeavoring to gain American goodwill and backing (and to overcome his strategic predicament), Asad publicly offered in 1974, 1975, 1976 and again in 1977 to sign a "peace agreement" with Israel (in fact, a non-belligerency agreement with no diplomatic relations, etc.).

In return, Israel was to withdraw from all Arab territories occupied in 1967, and a Palestinian state was to be created in the West Bank, the Gaza Strip and East Jerusalem. Asad's suggestions were rejected not only by Israel, but also by the United States and by Egypt – all of whom preferred a step-by-step approach in the peace process, beginning with an Egyptian–Israeli peace treaty. Although the American President, Jimmy Carter, was inclined to seek a comprehensive settlement to the

Arab-Israeli conflict, however, the historic journey of Sadat to Israel in November 1977 influenced him to initiate the Egyptian–Israeli Camp David accords (August 1978) to the deep disappointment of Asad.

In the late 1970s, having failed to prevent Egypt from signing a separate peace agreement with Israel, on the one hand, and establish a Fertile Crescent or Greater Syria strategic alliance, on the other, Asad embarked on a new, ambitious strategic scheme. His doctrine of "strategic balance," seeking to build a powerful military force, as well as a cohesive society and stable economy, was to enable Syria to single-handedly achieve the following three goals: deter Israel from attacking Syria; allow an attack on Israel at the appropriate time; and negotiate a political settlement with Israel from a position of military strength.[9] This doctrine, which Syria tried to implement with massive Soviet military assistance, was also aimed at extending Syrian influence in Jordan, Lebanon and among the Palestinians, as well as at countering a potential military threat from the rival Iraqi regime. In 1979, alongside his doctrine of strategic parity, Asad initiated, also for the first time, a strategic alliance with the new Islamic revolutionary regime in Iran. The purpose was to complement and enhance Syria's new regional strategy, notably *vis-à-vis* Israel and Iraq. As Asad himself said:

> This (Islamic) revolution introduced important changes in the strategic balance . . . from a regional and global point of view [it] supports the Arabs, without hesitation, in actions for the sake of liberating our land . . . how will we be allowed to lose a country like Iran of the Islamic revolution . . . with all its human, military and economic potential?[10]

Asad and other Syrian leaders also blamed Saddam Husayn for starting a "wrong war" against Iran, a war that constituted a "waste of the Arab potential – human and material – which would have been directed to serve the struggle of our nation against the Zionist enemy." Damascus thus supported Iran with the expectation that the Iraqi regime – not Iraq as a state – would collapse: "An Iranian victory in the Gulf War will allow for the establishment of the three states – Iran, Iraq, Syria – as the principal front against the Zionist state of Israel."[11]

In such an "Eastern Front" alliance, Syria, as the major "confrontation state" against Israel, would enjoy the huge strategic depth of Iraq and Iran and thus play a leading role in the new regional confrontation. Simultaneously, or alternatively, Damascus expected that its alliance with Teheran would at least weaken the Baghdad regime and neutralize its threat to Syria. It would thrust Damascus into a position of mediator between Iran, on the one hand, and Saudi Arabia, Kuwait and even Iraq, on the other, and would consequently improve Syria's strategic, political and economic assets. However, it turned out that Asad's remarkable yet hazardous strategic design did not materialize and indeed aggravated Syria's regional position. In fact, Damascus' isolation in the Arab world increased as a result of the consistent Syrian support of Iran in its war with Iraq, while at the same time Arab (Gulf) financial aid was being drastically reduced. To Baghdad's advantage, those setbacks became even more critical with the end of the Iraq–Iran war (1988).

Parallel to this painful débâcle, by 1988 Damascus had also failed to achieve its strategic balance with Israel, while its huge expenditure on military reinforcements caused a severe economic recession in Syria.[12] If all those predicaments were not sufficient to cause a radical change in Asad's policies, the dramatic upheaval in Soviet policy toward the Middle East, following the advent of Gorbachev's administration in 1985, finally convinced Asad to reassess his regional strategy. Already in April 1987, on his visit to Moscow, Asad received the following blunt statement from Gorbachev: "The reliance [of Syria] on military force in settling the Arab-Israeli conflict has completely lost its credibility." The Soviet leader also pointed out that Moscow would no longer support Syria's doctrine of strategic parity with Israel and urged Asad to seek a "balance of interests" within a political settlement to the Middle East conflict.[13]

Developing a New Strategy

Consequently, even before the demise of the Soviet Union, Syria was already forced in late 1988 to develop a new two-track strategy. On the one hand, Damascus has continued to build a credible military power and sustain its alliance with Iran, in order to deter Israel (and possibly also Iraq) from attacking Syria; to negotiate a political settlement with Israel from a position of relative military strength; as well as to maintain its control in Lebanon and reassert its influence in Jordan and among the Palestinians.

On the other hand, and more emphatically, Syria has embarked on a course of rapprochement with Egypt and Saudi Arabia, as well as with the United States, in order to achieve the following goals: first, to integrate with a pragmatic inter-Arab alliance which would curb the Iraqi threat; second, to gain American diplomatic and financial support; and third, to join the Arab-Israeli peace process in coordination with Egypt and the United States. This strategy has as its aim the retrieval of the Golan Heights and resolution of the Arab-Israeli conflict in accordance with the Arab notion of a "just and comprehensive peace."

In December 1988, Asad publicly stated, for the first time since 1978, that he "acknowledged the importance of Egypt in the Arab arena" and that Syrian–Egyptian cooperation had always been compatible with the interests of the Arab world. A year later, full diplomatic relations were restored between Syria and Egypt. On that occasion, Asad announced in Cairo that: "We are ready to join the peace process . . . we accept UN Resolutions 242 and 338 and we still call for a just and comprehensive peace."[14]

Simultaneously, Syria improved its relations with the United States, and in November 1990 Asad met President Bush in Geneva – his first meeting with an American president in thirteen years. Subsequently, in an extraordinary and unprecedented move, Syria joined the American-led Western–Arab coalition against the Iraqi occupation of Kuwait, expecting to realize the above mentioned goals and to obtain tacit American and Arab approval of its indirect control in Lebanon. In addition, Damascus sought to have the United States erase its name from the list of countries supporting international terrorism, this being in line with Syria's endeavors since the late 1980s to attract foreign investment and improve its economy.

In order to settle its bitter conflict with Israel, Syria joined the American-engineered Middle East peace process in July 1991 and, significantly, adopted flexible positions for the first time. On the eve of the Madrid peace conference (October 1991) initiated by Washington,[15] Syria agreed to conduct direct negotiations with Israel even in the absence of previous Israeli commitments to withdraw from the occupied territories and agree to Palestinian statehood. It also accepted that the peace conference would be a "regional conference," rather than an international one, and that it would be convened under American and Soviet sponsorship rather than under the auspices of the UN Security Council.

The Madrid Peace Process and its Breakdown

At the Madrid conference, however, Syria still insisted on a total Israeli withdrawal from all occupied territories – the Golan, southern Lebanon, the Gaza Strip and the West Bank, including Arab (East) Jerusalem. In return, Syria was ready to offer "peace" to Israel, which in fact stopped short of full recognition, normalization, and diplomatic relations and could be interpreted as no more than a non-belligerency agreement.

Probably this rigid Syrian attitude at the Madrid conference and in the subsequent bilateral negotiations with Israel represented not only Damascus' unchanged ideological stance, but also a bargaining position *vis-à-vis* Israel. As it happened, the Israeli government under Prime Minister Yitzhak Shamir was still unwilling to give up the Golan Heights (let alone the West Bank), even for full peace with Syria.[16]

It was only a few months after his election as Israel's Prime Minister that Yitzhak Rabin stated for the first time, in August 1992, that Israel considered UN Resolution 242 to be also applicable to the Golan Heights. Subsequently, he declared that the extent of Israeli withdrawal from the Golan would depend on the extent of the Syrian peace agreement.

At this juncture, in September 1992, Asad was probably prepared to conclude a peace agreement with Israel, which would include diplomatic relations and security arrangements, but not full normalization. Syria also insisted on linking Israel's total withdrawal from the Golan Heights to its withdrawal from southern Lebanon; to the settlement of the Palestinian problem; and to the elimination of Israel's nuclear weapons.[17] No wonder, then, that the bilateral Syrian–Israeli negotiations continued at a slow pace for about four years and were characterized or accompanied by tough bargaining positions; periodic interruptions and military pressures in southern Lebanon; manipulation of the media; and diplomatic maneuvers directed largely at gaining American support.

Simultaneously, however, both parties also settled differences and made positive gestures toward each other while gradually preparing their publics: the Syrian people for a peace settlement and the Israeli public for relinquishing the Golan Heights.[18] For example, Israel acknowledged that the settlement of southern Lebanon was to be linked to that of the Golan Heights, while Syria, after the signing of the Oslo Israeli-Palestinian Accords, ceased in fact to insist on a Palestinian-Syrian linkage in the settlement with Israel.

Consequently, by late 1995 or early 1996, Syria and Israel became rather close to concluding a peace agreement, as they reached a mutual understanding concerning issues of withdrawal from and demilitarization of the Golan; the settlement of the southern Lebanon problem; diplomatic relations; and certain elements of economic cooperation, including water projects. By contrast, however, both parties could not agree on the final border between the countries: Israel was apparently prepared to withdraw to the international boundary, whereas Syria insisted on the June 4, 1967 line, which included strategically important areas on the Israeli side of the international border that Syria had seized in the 1948 war. Syria also rejected Israeli demands to thin out its massive military concentration beyond the Golan and to expand the arenas of normalization. In March 1996, Shimon Peres, Israel's new Prime Minister, decided to suspend the bilateral talks with Syria on the basis that Damascus did not denounce the bloody terrorist attacks by Hamas in Jerusalem and Tel Aviv.

In fact, this unilateral action by Peres was largely related to his decision to advance the Israeli national election to late May 1996 (instead of late October), aimed at concluding and signing a peace agreement with Syria after the election. As it happened, the slow, highly cautious and suspicious Asad did not rush to seal a peace treaty with Peres (who also enraged Asad by ordering Israel's massive military operation in Lebanon – "Grapes of Wrath" – in April 1996). Asad apparently preferred to wait until after the Israeli election and then make his decisions accordingly.

Whether or not Asad miscalculated his moves or missed a unique opportunity to regain the Golan Heights remain open questions, for following the election of Benjamin Netanyahu as Israel's Prime Minister on May 29, 1996, Israel reversed its attitude toward Syria. Similar to Shamir's position in Madrid, Netanyahu was also prepared to make peace with Syria, but not to relinquish the Golan Heights. He suggested starting the bilateral negotiations again, but without taking into consideration the points of understanding that had been reached with Syria by the previous government, notably an Israeli withdrawal from the Golan Heights. Netanyahu and other *Likud* leaders also resorted to verbal attacks on Syrian leaders, while stepping up Israel's military cooperation with Turkey, Syria's northern adversary.

In reaction, not only has Syria accelerated its war of attrition against Israel in southern Lebanon through its Hizballah proxy, it has also increased and modernized its military arsenal, notably including ballistic missiles carrying chemical warheads. Moreover, while fostering its strategic alliance with Iran and expanding its military relations with Russia, Damascus has endeavored to forge a pan-Arab anti-Israeli camp. Its aims have been to reimpose a united Arab economic boycott on Israel and to induce those Arab countries, which had established diplomatic and economic relations with Israel to abandon them.

Such anti-Israeli efforts and actions are likely to be expanded and encouraged by Syria if the peace talks are not resumed according to a formula accepted by Damascus. In a worst-case scenario – and under suitable circumstances – Syria might venture to capture part of the Golan Heights in a surprise military attack, in order to shatter the stalemate and renew the political negotiations with new Syrian leverage. Such actions on Syria's part would be likely to resemble Sadat's strategy and surprise attack in October 1973, and would probably provoke a massive counter onslaught by Israel and deteriorate into an all-out war in which Egypt may not remain idle. Some analysts have even assessed that Syria, facing a continued stalemate on the Golan Heights issue, is likely to launch a strategic surprise attack into Israel, using ballistic missiles carrying chemical warheads. Other observers see little prospect of war between Syria and Israel in the short run.[19]

Following the election of Ehud Barak as Israel's Prime Minister in May 1999, the prospects for Syrian–Israeli peacemaking have once again become promising.

Notes

1 This section, as well as other parts of the chapter, are derived from my book, *Asad – The Sphinx of Damascus: A Political Biography (*London and New York, 1988 and 1990); see also: Patrick Seale, *Asad of Syria: The Struggle for the Middle East* (London, 1988).

2 See, for example: Karim Shaybani, *Hafiz al-Asad* (Beirut, 1972), pp. 10, 13; *al-Nahar* (Beirut), March 17, 1971; Radio Damascus, June 9, 1974.

3 Ma'oz, *Asad,* pp. 85–86, citing various sources.

4 *Al-Nahar*, March 27, 1974; *al-Hawadith* (Beirut), June 26, 1975. Cf. Ma'oz, *Asad*, pp. 112–13.

5 Text in *Journal of Palestine Studies,* Vol. 8, No. 2 (1979), pp. 200–2.

6 For details, see Ma'oz, *Asad*, chapter 9. For a general historical account of the Greater Syrian concept, see: Daniel Pipes, *Greater Syria: The History of an Ambition* (New York, 1990).

7 Cited in Ma'oz, *Asad,* p. 134; see also: *al-Thawra* (Damascus), June 23, 1977.

8 Ma'oz, *Asad,* p. 167. For a Syrian version of the 1982 war in Lebanon, see: Mustafa Talas, *al-Ghazu al-Israili Li-Lubnan* (Damascus, 1984), pp. 389–90 (in Arabic).

9 For a detailed analysis of Syria's doctrine of strategic balance, see: Ma'oz, *Asad,* p. 177ff; see also: Asad's speeches, Damascus Radio, March 15, 1980; March 9, 1981; September 17, 1982.

10 Mustafa Talas (ed.), *Kadhalika Qal al-Asad* (Damascus, 1984), pp. 389–90 (in Arabic).

11 See, respectively, Associated Press, April 30, 1987; *al-Shira'a* (Beirut), March 17, 1986.

12 Regarding the economic recession in Syria during the latter half of the 1980s, see: Lesch's, Efrat's, and Winckler's chapters in this volume.

13 Cited in Moshe Ma'oz, "Syrian–Israeli Relations and the Middle East Peace Process," *The Jerusalem Journal of International Relations*, Vol. 14, No. 3 (1992), p. 9; cf. H. Cobban, *The Superpowers and the Syrian–Israeli Conflict* (Washington, D.C., 1991), pp. 57–58.

14 *New York Times,* July 17, 1990. For a detailed study on the Syrian approach to the peace process, see: A. Drysdale and R. A. Hinnebusch, *Syria and the Middle East Peace Process* (New York, 1991).

15 For details, see: Moshe Ma'oz, *Syria and Israel: From War to Peacemaking* (Oxford and New York, 1995), pp. 208–9.

16 For details, see *ibid.*, pp. 210–15.

17 See, e. g., *Tishrin* (Damascus), July 14, 1992; *al-Ba'th* (Damascus), October 8, 1992.

18 Details in Ma'oz, *Syria and Israel,* pp. 223ff. See also: I. Rabinovich, *The Brink of Peace: Israel & Syria, 1992–1996* (Tel Aviv, 1998), pp. 80ff (in Hebrew).

19 See: *The Prospects for the Israeli–Syrian Peace Negotiations*, Baker Institute Study, No. 8 (August 1998), p. 5.

15

Asad's Art of the Double Game

Daniel Pipes

> Whoever does not dissimulate is a fool, for no intelligent person goes naked in the market.
>
> – 'Alawi saying[1]

> [Jimmy Carter found that] the word of Syrian was in fact a thousand and one words, and that what they agreed to one day, they rejected the next, returning to it the day after.
>
> – Anwar al-Sadat[2]

> [The Syrians] don't respect their word. They scheme, they promise you one thing and do something else on the side. They promised in the past, but they never lived up to any agreement.
>
> – Michel 'Awn[3]

What's going on with Syria? Is Hafiz al-Asad making peace with Israel or not? Is he ending his totalitarian rule or not? What are his goals?

The controversy surrounding these questions points to what is perhaps the Asad regime's most characteristic feature: an unwillingness to take a stand. Instead, it prefers to juggle several policies at the same time – what I shall call the art of the double game. This involves taking two contrary steps or pursuing two contrary policies, usually at the same time, sometimes sequentially.

In the domestic arena, the double game explains the Syrian regime's restricting to a small number of mainly 'Alawi military officers but making elaborate efforts to convince the population otherwise; and its attempt to both maintain state capitalism and encourage entrepreneurship. Our concern here, however, is with foreign affairs, where the double game helps explains the elusiveness and successes of Syrian policy. We begin with a look at Syrian relations with several Middle Eastern actors, then focus on relations with Israel.

Friendship and Enmity

In many of his Middle Eastern diplomatic relationships, Asad simultaneously maintains good and bad relations with other governments. In the case of Iraq, he works both with the Iraqi opposition groups intent on deposing Saddam Husayn (Kurdish and Shi'i ones in particular) and also with the Arab Liberation Front, a Baghdad-sponsored Palestinian group. In the case of Iran, Asad cooperates with the *Mullahs* where it suits him (supporting Hizballah in Lebanon, the Palestinian rejectionist groups, Iraqi territorial integrity) and works against them where it does not (supporting Saudi and Egyptian leaders). In the case of Jordan, the two governments outwardly get along; but when King Husayn took steps inimical to Asad, the latter often made life unbearable (for example, he unleashed a campaign of terrorist incidents in 1985).

With Yasir 'Arafat, a politician who plays the double game almost as expertly as Asad himself, things get especially complex. 'Arafat and Asad are not profound enemies, for they are neither attached to contrary political philosophies nor bound to permanently opposed interests. Rather, they come from similar political origins and share many assumptions, personal qualities, enemies, and aspirations. As tacticians, they conflict one moment and cooperate another. To be sure, they dislike each other intensely and their rivalry has a murderous edge – but what else can one expect from men of their temperament and accomplishments? Asad has killed tens of thousands of his own people; why not PLO members too? They resemble two Mafia dons who murder each other's men but also drink together at festivals and cooperate against outsiders. When two masters of the double game play together, the results are quadrupled.

As for Lebanon, General Michel 'Awn characterizes the Syrians' role there like that of "a pyromaniac firefighter":[4] they instigate a problem – smuggling, drug trafficking, skirmishes between the sects, attacks on Israel – then rush in with a solution that serves their interests.

Perhaps the most evident example of this pattern concerns the actions of Hizballah. To begin with, the Syrian leaders create the illusion that they do not control this ostensibly independent Lebanese fundamentalist Muslim group, whereas in reality it depends on them for its very existence. Hizballah not only receives Syrian funding, equipment, logistics, and information, but Damascus must approve all Iranian aid. The illusion works, for governments around the world treat Hizballah as though it were an autonomous organization.

Asad has used Hizballah to play a series of double games with Israel:

1 When Hizballah launches rocket attacks against Israel, Asad typically begins by publicly supporting the attacks (boosting his anti-Zionist credentials among the Syrian population and shoring up his alliance with Tehran), then he quietly instructs Hizballah to stop them (thereby winning credit with the US and Israeli governments). The Israelis realize that the Syrians "control everything Hizballah does,"[5] but can do little to stop the charade.
2 Asad used Hizballah as his shill in December 1993, when he announced that a five-man American congressional delegation would be allowed to travel to Syria and Lebanon in search of seven Israeli servicemen missing in action. Very nice; but within two days, Hizballah denounced this operation and said it would not cooperate. As Hizballah holds the remains of at least two Israelis, this statement effectively undid Asad's offer.
3 Asad from time to time cracks down on Hizballah, raiding its storehouses for weapons, explosives, and drugs. He arrested several leaders of Hizballah in April 1994, ostensibly retaliating for their staging an anti-Syrian demonstration in southern Lebanon. Uri Lubrani, the coordinator of Israeli government activities, accurately described this raid as "mere cosmetics" designed to show Syrian action without actually doing anything.[6]
4 Through the 1980s, Asad engaged in a complex ploy of gaining freedom for hostages whose capture he had been party in the first place. Hizballah could not have seized Westerners in parts of Lebanon occupied by Syrian troops or under their influence, then held them hostage for months or years without Syrian approval. Circumstantial evidence suggests it then released the hostages when so instructed by the Syrian authorities. Not surprisingly, grateful diplomats failed to point out Syrian complicity as they stood with the newly released hostage at the Foreign Ministry in Damascus; quite the contrary, regardless of their private thoughts, they profusely praised President Asad. This pattern recurred again and again during the eight-year period, 1983–91, and won Asad considerable good will internationally. For every newspaper denouncing the drama as a "slimy form of international politics,"[7] ten foreign ministers express "gratitude and appreciation."[8]

Keeping and Breaking Promises

"We always mean what we say and we fulfill our promises."[9] That's what Asad says, but you don't have to take his word; the Syrian strongman has such a good reputation for keeping his promises that even his Israeli adversaries acknowledge his probity. Ehud Barak finds that Asad has consistently lived up to his word.[10] A head of Israeli military intelligence, Uri Sagi, asserted that "if and when he signs an agreement, [Asad] will keep his word."[11] Yitzhak Rabin flatly declared that "the Syrians keep their commitments."[12] Shimon Peres concurred: "with the Syrians it is very hard to reach an agreement but the agreement will stand."[13] Abba Eban reached the same conclusion and the press also agrees: Israeli columnist Yoel Marcus writes that "an accord with Asad is enshrined in concrete and steel," while *The New York Times* opines that his regime "has compiled a record of abiding by agreements it does sign."[14]

But these assessments ignore the many agreements Asad has broken with several governments, including those of Israel, Lebanon, and Turkey. Let's look at the particulars of several cases.

(1) *Agreements to leave Lebanon*. On three occasions, the Syrian authorities concurred with decisions made by other bodies that Syrian troops should leave Lebanon; to this day, of course, tens of thousands of them yet remain. Damascus first agreed to leave in October 1976 as part of the Riyadh–Cairo accords.[15] In September 1982, it signed the Fez Declaration that committed it to "start negotiations" with the Lebanese government about "an end to the mission of the Arab deterrent forces in Lebanon [i.e., the Syria troops]."[16]

In October 1989, to win Lebanese Christian support for a revision of the Lebanese government structure (the Ta'if Accord), Asad accepted a provision that Syrian troops would be redeployed from their positions in Beirut to the Biqa' valley two years after four conditions had been met.[17] Those conditions were indeed fulfilled in September 1990; but September 1992 came and went without any change. (Indeed, arrive by plane in Beirut and you'll encounter Syrian troops right in the airport.) Theodor Hanf, a German authority on Lebanon, dubs this a "blatant violation" of the Ta'if Agreement.[18]

The Syrians broke other promises to the Lebanese. For example, an 1989 report of the Arab League agreed, presented by the "troika" dealing with the Lebanon crisis stated: "In spite of their promise to use their influence to open traffic routes and communications, the Syrians have done nothing in this regard; on the contrary, the sea blockade was maintained and violent actions increased."[19] More generally, as Netanyahu rightly notes, "in Lebanon the Syrians broke just about every agreement they signed."[20]

(2) *PKK anti-Turkish activities.* In 1987 and 1992, Damascus signed security protocols with Turkey promising to shut installations used by the PKK, the anti-Turkish group of Kurds. In addition, the Syrians time and again assured Turkish officials that the PKK would cause them no more problems. But year after year little changed on the ground. A base would ostentatiously close down, only to reopen quietly somewhere else. According to a second-hand report, the Turkish Prime Minister's staff counts eighteen agreements that Asad signed with Ankara and subsequently broke. A Turkish press report in late 1993 summer up the problem: "Syria does everything to meet the PKK's losses in terms of men, arms, and cash."[21]

(3) *The "red line" understanding.* In April 1976, the Israelis acquiesced to Syrian forces entering Lebanon in return for several reassurances, dubbed "red lines," brokered by King Husayn and American officials. These unwritten agreements were to circumscribe the Syrian use of force in Lebanon. While not made public, Asad reportedly agreed (among other things) not to deploy aircraft in Lebanon, surface-to-air missiles or more than a single brigade of soldiers; or to place any soldiers in southern Lebanon.

Damascus eventually breached all four of these provisions. In 1981, it ferried troops by helicopter and deployed surface-to-air missiles in the Zahle area of Lebanon. Israelis knew full well about these offenses. Itamar Rabinovich (Israel's subsequent ambassador to the United States) termed them, respectively, an "infringement" and an "unequivocal violation" of the 1976 agreement. Nor were these merely technical issues, he says; the Syrian missiles amounted to "a serious threat" against Israeli interests.[22]

Asad ignored the prohibition on aircraft a second time in October 1990, this time with decisive results. His air force first buzzed the Presidential Palace at Ba'abda, waiting to see whether the Israelis would respond. When they did not, the Syrians understood that the red line in the air "seemed to have disappeared,"[23] so they returned later that day and for the next two days to bomb the palace and actively help Syrian forces conquer Beirut. Fida Nasrallah of the Center for Lebanese Studies in Oxford deems this action a "clear breach" of the red line agreement.[24]

Asad violated the red line agreement more profoundly by sending far more than one brigade into Lebanon; over the years some ten brigades have regularly been stationed there. In short, Asad sought not just to tip the balance of power in Lebanon but to control the whole country. Yair Evron of Tel Aviv University writes that Damascus thereby "overstepped" and "transgress [ed]" its 1976 understanding.[25]

Worst of all, Asad has on occasion denied the very existence of the red line agreement, and so his future obligation to maintain them. To a Lebanese group he once said, "Do not concern yourselves with the 'red line', which the Americans and the Israelis are talking about. It does not exist, [and] in any event I cannot see it."[26]

(4) *Operation Accountability*. After a rocket assault on Israel in July 1993, followed by a massive Israeli military response (Operation Accountability), Asad reached an agreement with Secretary of State Christopher whereby he would in the future prevent any forces in southern Lebanon from launching rocket attacks on Israel. This Syrian–US agreement on the rules of behavior in southern Lebanon was then systematically violated: four times in 1994 the rockets fell and five times in just the first half of 1995. To make matters worse, Damascene sources in June 1994 denied the very existence of a deal with Israel ("Syria has not agreed with the Israelis to stop the firing of Katyushas on northern Israel"),[27] though on other occasions (e.g., March 1995) Damascus apparently acknowledged violations.[28]

Israeli leaders condemned Asad's actions with strong language. Prime Minister Rabin accused the Syrians in March 1995 of a "total violation" of the agreement.[29] A few months later, even as he complained to the US government about the violations, he publicly excused the Syrians' infractions: "They don't always keep to it, we don't always keep to it."[30] Amiram Levin, the commander of Israel's Northern Command, put it more toughly: Katyusha rocket attacks on the western Galilee in June 1995 "grossly violated" the July 1993 understanding.[31] The August 1993 agreement finally fell apart completely in April 1996, and Prime Minister Shimon Peres launched Operation Grapes of Wrath to punish the Lebanese and Syrians for the attacks. Remarkably, even after Asad had so completely breached his 1993 agreement, Peres still spoke of him as someone who keeps his word: "it is very difficult to reach an agreement with Asad. But once he agreed . . . he respects it."[32]

(5) *Syrian Jews*. Asad had long refused to let more than a few of Syria's 4,000 Jews emigrate (usually arguing that they didn't want to leave but sometimes saying that "Jews are essential to the Syrian economy").[33] Then, in April 1992, he announced their release in the course of a telephone conversation with George Bush. Representative Stephen Solarz called the event "an extraordinary development"[34] and all those concerned expected the entire community of Syrian Jews to be free to leave. Indeed, three-quarters of the Jewish population did receive passports and exit visas by mid-October 1992. Then the process stopped and almost nothing happened for over a year. Only after Secretary

Christopher applied new pressure did Asad reopen the doors for 200 more Jews to leave the country in December 1993; President Clinton won another thousand a month later. It was not until October 1994 that the Syrian government allowed any Jew to leave the country. (By then, 3,670 had left and 230 chose to remain in Damascus, Qamishli, and Aleppo, usually because they held property in Syria.)

(6) *Peace process negotiations.* In June 1995, Asad promised Warren Christopher that he would engage in a two-stage negotiation with Israel: a meeting of the chief of staffs in Washington, followed by a break, then a resumption of the military track at a somewhat lower rank. So pleased was the secretary of state with this agreement that he abandoned his habitual reticence and instead declared that "there is a tremendous opportunity to move now toward a goal of a comprehensive peace, perhaps a better opportunity than at any time during the two and a half years that I have been in office."[35]

The chiefs of staff did meet in late June, but then Asad backtracked on his promise to send a lower-ranking military team, requiring instead that the Israelis first agree not to demand early warning stations on the Golan Heights. The Israelis objected vehemently to this new precondition. Prime Minister Rabin asserted he would not permit the Syrians to "renege on an understanding" and pointed to the larger significance of this incident: "If the Syrians do not keep to what they agreed to with the Americans, who will guarantee that they will stick to the assurances they make to Israel?"[36]

(7) *Golan Heights disengagement.* Asad's reputation for trustworthiness rests most especially on his having maintained for twenty-five years a promise he gave in the May 1974 Separation of Forces Agreement with Israel to "scrupulously observe the cease-fire on land, sea and air" and "refrain from all military action." All sides agree on his having fulfilled this promise. Richard Murphy, a former American assistant secretary of Near Eastern Affairs, states that agreement was "scrupulously observed."[37] Ze'ev Schiff, the doyen of Israeli military correspondents, writes that "Both sides have adhered to the Separation of Forces Agreement since it was first reached, and violations have been negligible."[38] "With the exception of several permanent and negligible violations," the head of Israeli military intelligence noted two years ago, Asad "has been keeping the disengagement agreement in letter and in spirit."[39] Even Benjamin Netanyahu concurred, using almost the same words: "Syria has kept to both the letter and the spirit of its disengagement agreement."[40]

But Asad did not exactly fulfill his 1974 agreement with Israel, although he did prevent all violence across the Syrian–Israeli border, thereby making the Golan Heights not just a quiet place but perhaps the safest in the Middle East. At the same time, Damascus did not fulfill all its obligations. First, Asad reassured Jerusalem of his non-belligerent intentions by promising that "Syrian civilians will return" to the territory evacuated by Israeli forces. In fact, civilians have not moved into the area, which remains a military zone. Second, Damascus did in the first years of the agreement allow some terrorist operations, including an attack on Ramat Magshimim in 1975.[41]

Third, the Syrians in 1992 moved commandos into Quneitra and heavy artillery elsewhere into the demilitarized zone agreed to in the 1974 agreement. They illegally placed 21 surface-to-air missiles and eight missile launchers within 25 kilometers of the border, the "thin-out" strip. Oddly, Prime Minister Rabin chose not to make public these violations reported by the United Nations observer force.[42]

Fourth, Rabin acknowledged in September 1994 that the Syrian government had for four years engaged in "limited violations" (not further specified; these could be the same missiles and missile launchers just noted) of the Separation of Forces Agreement. He also disclosed that Jerusalem had complained repeatedly about these to the United Nations, "without any response from the Syrians"; only in mid-1994 had they indicated a willingness to rectify these violations.[43]

Asad's pattern of behavior establishes that he regularly breaks his promises. Typical of a despot, he keeps his word when it's convenient and breaks it when not; more subtly, he wins credit for keeping it when he does not. Asad can get not just ambassadors to keep quiet but also the prime minister of Israel. That he gets away with this points to an important benefit of the double game.

Obstructing and Accepting the Peace Process

"We were surprised by the Palestinian-Israeli agreement and then by the Jordanian-Israeli agreement," Asad publicly acknowledged.[44] And while the Syrian leader made clear his disapproval of these steps, he both tried to stop them and did not.

Israel–PLO agreements. Asad reacted two ways at once to the Oslo Accords, rejecting them and having groups under his influence snipe at them, yet not making a concerted effort to sabotage them. Symbolic of this double policy, he had a Syrian representative at the first Israel–PLO signing ceremony (the Declaration of Principles of September 1993, at the White House) but not the second (for the Cairo agreement, in May 1994). Asad disdained the Declaration of Principles (DoP) of September

1993 ("there is nothing good in it"),[45] on the grounds that it gave the Israelis too much and won too little in return. Asad's minister of information put it more pungently: the DoP means, "the Palestinian people will be in a large jail."[46] Syrian media argued that promised PLO changes to its charter (eliminating references to the destruction of Israel) "means cancellation of the entire charter."[47]

To make the ten rejectionist Palestinian groups based on Syrian-controlled territory more effective at obstructing the peace process, Asad induced them to put together a formal alliance which met after the White House signing specifically to plot ways to subvert the DoP. Its member organizations staged rallies, ceremonies, sit-ins, and strikes in Syria during which, monitored by hundreds of Syrian police officers, they fervently denounced the DoP and called for the arrest of Yasir ʻArafat. They did more than demonstrate: Asad had groups under his influence attempt to sabotage the DoP by repeatedly murdering Israelis and pro-ʻArafat Palestinians. For example, according to Israeli sources,[48] Muhammad Diff, a Hamas leader living in Damascus authorized terrorist attacks on Israelis, killing ten.

The Syrian press then celebrated these efforts. When Hamas operatives seized an Israeli soldier as a hostage, Syrian radio lauded them as "the heroic Palestinian resistance men," "brave soldiers," and "righteous martyrs."[49] That event and the massacre of Israelis on a Tel Aviv bus prompted a clandestine station based in Damascus to exult at the killing of Israeli citizens and crow about "a week of success."[50] The radio justified terrorism against Israelis as "valiant," a "just punishment" and a "heroic operation."[51]

The rejectionist Palestinian groups did Asad's dirty work and took the blame, thereby permitting Asad to maintain an air of schoolboy innocence. The foreign minister denied knowing anything about them: "Syria has not observed preparations by the Palestinian Rejectionist Front operating from its soil for violent opposition to the Israeli–PLO accord."[52] The Israelis were not fooled. Rabin noted that Damascus "provides all facilities to all types of attack on Israel, whether from Lebanon or other places."[53]

And if the Syrians did not engage in an all-out effort to block the PLO's deal with Israel, they did so for the wrong reason. Asad claimed to see the DoP as an inconsequential step, not worthy of his notice. "I did not consider it a significant event. Nor do I think it will have great effect."[54] Why not? Because it will probably fail. "We have not obstructed them [the PLO]. Thus far, we feel their political moves have not posed a real threat. We do not think they will lead to the happy ending expected by some people. In any case, we are watching, and we will wait and see."[55] If, by chance, the DoP does not fail, Asad unambiguously says he can scuttle it. "Had we wanted to obstruct it, we would have foiled it. If it becomes clear to us that its harm is great, we will do so."[56]

Israel–Jordan agreements. King Husayn found himself getting locked out by the Israel–PLO agreement; worse, he received a severe warning from Prime Minister Rabin (at a clandestine meeting on May 19, 1994) that unless he took action soon, the Palestinians could take over in Jordan. Accordingly, the king did something quite out of character and wholly unexpected: declaring that "It is high time Jordan looked to its own interests,"[57] he took four dramatic steps toward Israel during a fifty-day period from June 7, 1994. On that day, Jordanian and Israeli negotiators reached a set of understandings on border, water, and security issues; and the Jordanians committed to work out relations with Israel without reference to other Arab parties (namely Syria). Then, in three quick rounds during July, the negotiating teams met in a tent at their mutual border; Peres publicly visited Jordan; and King Husayn met Rabin in Washington where they called off the state of war between them and pledged to work toward a peace treaty.

Of course, Asad disapproved of all these steps and he communicated his displeasure in a number of small ways – muttering threats, canceling a visit by his prime minister to Amman, and deploying media vituperation for the first time since the Kuwait war. His press condemned the Husayn–Rabin accord as "a violation" of the Madrid rules, which would lead to "an incomplete and distorted peace with Israel."[58] Its signing at the White House marked "a black day in the history of Jordan,"[59] a day which eight Jordanian opposition movements based in Damascus announced they would henceforth memorialize with national mourning. The same groups also condemned the "handshakes and huggings" and called on the "masses" to oppose such gestures.[60] A newspaper threatened that carrying through these understandings with Israel would "isolate Jordan from the Arab world and tamper with its national unity," while Defense Minister Mustafa Talas unsubtly observed that the king's separate deal with Israel means "his fragile entity could fall apart."[61] Hafiz al-Asad ostentatiously met with a delegation of Jordanian opposition leaders. For months, the two governments had no ambassadors in the other country.

Yet these were secondary mechanisms for expressing Syrian displeasure. King Husayn publicly stated a month after the Washington meeting that Asad "has not shown any opposition so far" to his initiatives.[62] He had not heard protests directly from Asad nor had Damascus taken serious steps to obstruct. Indeed, on learning from Bill Clinton about the forthcoming Husayn–Rabin meeting, Asad reportedly told the

American president that "he was not happy about it, but that he accepted it."[63] Less than a week after the meeting, Asad delivered a speech to commemorate Army Day and went explicitly out of his way to avoid the whole subject ("I do not want to speak today about the position of the Arab sides in the peace process"), contenting himself with an abstract threat (Arab leaders who break ranks will "be held accountable by their people and all the Arab masses").[64] A Syrian minister of state declared that "No separate agreement between Jordan and Israel would affect the Syrian position."[65] Indeed, trade between Syria and Jordan continued without interruption, people moved to and from the two countries, and joint companies operated smoothly.

Shimon Peres accurately summed up Damascus' response to Jordanian moves as "moderate and restrained" and "less than what might have been expected."[66] Jordan's Prime Minister referred to a "cloud currently hanging over" the two countries' relations,[67] but it was apparently a cloud of much moisture but little rain.

The same pattern recurred in October 1994, when the Jordanian and Israeli governments signed a peace treaty. Asad again responded negatively but not actively. He vehemently denounced the provision by which Israel would for twenty-five years lease back land turned over to Jordan, correctly fearing that the Israelis would seek to apply this approach to the Golan Heights. "Our land is ours," Asad declared. "We consider it apostasy (*kufr*) for any country to lease its land to another country." But, while noting that "we can cause obstructions," he promised not to block the treaty. Asad quoted himself saying to the Jordanians:

> We do not support you. You have made a big mistake, but we will not make a fuss or fight you on this issue. Even though we believe you have done something wrong and have damaged [Arab] collective action, we wish you good luck. We will not support you but we will not take practical steps to obstruct you.[68]

What does all this contradictory activity amount to? A fog of paradox around the negotiating process that preserves Asad's room to maneuver and permits him to move toward or away peace with Israel.

Making Peace and Not with Israel

Between his agreement to negotiate with Israel in July 1991 and the fall of the Labor government in May 1996, Asad took a flurry of contradictory steps, moving both toward and away from Israel. As Rabin put it, "One [Syrian] hand is as if extended in peace. The other hand opens fire on you."[69] Here are some items in this audacious double game:

Positive signs. Asad reportedly told a closed meeting of Ba'th party leaders in 1993 of a decision in principle to make peace with Israel, and that only the details needed to be worked out. As noted above, the Syrians indicated willingness in July 1994 to correct their violations of their Separation of Forces Agreement with Israel. Civilian infrastructure in the Syrian region by the border with Israel has been newly improved and expanded with houses renovated, mosques put up, water reservoirs built, and windmills installed (for electricity).

Media coverage of Israel no longer showed unremitting hostility. The regime took modest but real steps to prepare Syrians for accord with Israel: "peace" and its synonyms replaced "steadfastness" and "confrontation" as the leitmotifs of public discourse about Israel. The Syrian press raised such scenarios as land-for-peace and noted the benefits of peace with Israel.[70] Most dramatically, Syrian television covered the first public meeting of King Husayn and Yitzhak Rabin, at the White House, live and in full, including Rabin's prayer in Hebrew then rebroadcast it a second time. Syrian newspapers featured front-page pictures of the two together. A few days later, it broadcast King Husayn's unprecedented fly-over across Israel. More generally, the Syria media covered the Jordanian–Israeli story straight, without falsehoods or distorting commentary. Damascus ended four years of jamming Jordanian television in August 1994 and about the same time permitted *The Jerusalem Report* to be sold at the Meridien Hotel in Damascus.

Contacts in third countries between Syrians and Israelis proliferated. Syrian diplomats in Berlin publicly greeted their Israel counterparts. The minister of the economy and foreign trade gave an on-the-record interview to an Israeli newspaper and an administrative attaché at the Syrian Embassy in London told another Tel Aviv newspaper that Israelis who travel on non-Israeli passports are welcome in his country.[71] Syrian academics met their Israel counterparts at a private meeting in Oslo in October 1993, presumably with Asad's permission. Also at that time, representatives of Syrian tourism companies made contact with Israel diplomats and tourist organizations about cooperation. In July 1994, the Syrian chargé d'affaires attended the Husayn–Rabin meeting in Washington and shook hands with Rabin. During a visit to Washington, Foreign Minister Shar' twice submitted to questions by Israel journalists and met with leaders from such American Jewish organizations as the American Israel Public Affairs Committee, the American Jewish Congress, and B'nai B'rith.

Travel between Syria and Israel picked up. An Israeli journalist was let into Syria on a *laisser passer*. Several dozen Syrian Druze reached

Israel via Lebanon to attend the funeral of the Druze spiritual leader in October 1993. A group of Arab Syrians visited their relatives in northern Israel in December 1994. Traveling in the other direction, a delegation of fifty-seven Israeli Arab notables led by a member of the Israeli parliament visited Damascus (but via Cairo and not traveling on their Israeli passports) to extend their condolences to Hafiz al-Asad on the death of his son Basil. At the trip's end, Shar' portrayed the visit as "an opening for additional visits to Syria by Israelis" – conditional, of course, on full withdrawal from the Golan Heights.[72]

Even trade increased. A Tel Aviv newspaper reported that, from early 1994, an Israeli state-owned firm bought raw materials directly from Syria; although it used the cover of third-country companies for cover, it did so with "the full knowledge and approval of the most senior levels in the Syrian government."[73]

Negative signs. A long list of troublesome steps pointed to an intent by Asad to keep the conflict with Israel going. Asad's bargaining position called for Israel to give up all its assets and promises almost nothing in return. Further, his cramped diplomatic style – using passive constructions, and indirectness of speech – pointed to a deep reluctance to come to terms with Israel; it may also have indicate an intent not to let go of the rejectionist option. Writing before he became Israel's chief negotiator with Syria, Itamar Rabinovich noted that:

> Nearly a year after Syria's decision to attend the Madrid conference, there were no signs either of agitation among the public or of any effort by the regime to prepare public opinion for a radical shift in position and policy toward Israel.[74]

A handbook for Syrian teachers issued in 1994 instructed them to present to their students the "liberation of the land occupied in 1967 as an intermediate goal"[75] (implying that the full goal is the destruction of Israel). Syrian diplomats negotiating across the table with Israelis long treated them with artificial coolness. Damascus chose to boycott half the peace process, namely the multilateral talks, and instructed its Lebanese satrapy to do likewise. Evidence suggests that Ron Arad, a captured Israeli aviator, remains in the hands of the Syrians or their allies.

In an extraordinary twist of the double game, Asad has condemned his own diplomacy with Israel. He sent diplomats to Washington for official, direct meetings with Israelis; but when the United Nations General Assembly in December of 1993–95 passed resolutions that identically expressed "full support for the achievements of the peace process thus far" and stressed "the need for achieving rapid progress on the other tracks of the Arab-Israeli negotiations" – a reference to the talks with Syria and Lebanon – Asad all three times voted in the negative!

Syria officials and media continue to bristle with hostility on the subject of Israel, using such terms as "the enemy," "the Zionist enemy," "occupied Palestine," "occupied Jerusalem," and "the Zionist entity."[76] A Syrian radio station called a suicide bombing against Israelis a "martyrdom operation."[77] It also brings up old calumnies, raising in 1995 the August 1969 episode of Michael Dennis Rohan, a deranged Australian Christian who set fire to the Mosque of Al-Aqsa in Jerusalem. It gratuitously claimed that Rohan "is an Israeli Jew even though Israel tried to prove that he is not," that the Israeli authorities "did nothing" to put the fire out," and that Rohan lived under house arrest in a "luxurious Israeli tourist resort."[78]

Even more bizarrely, on the eve of Secretary of State Christopher's arrival in Damascus (along with a large entourage of reporters) in May 1994, the English-language *Syrian Times* ran an article which claimed that American Jews are legally excused from paying US taxes and that "30 percent of Protestant bishops in the US are originally Jews who did not quit Judaism."[79] In response to the ensuing uproar, the Syrian authorities a few days later weakly "expressed regret about the content and tone" of the article.

Asad's extremely ambitious military build-up appeared to be primarily directed against Israel. His regime publicly supported anti-'Arafat Palestinian groups (for example, Vice President Khaddam confirmed its support for George Habash's group in November 1994)[80] and privately backed their violence against Israelis. The same went for Syrian-backed forces in Lebanon; their attacks on the South Lebanese Army (SLA) in the first half of 1995 numbered 55 percent higher than in 1994. At an Europe-Middle East diplomatic meeting on July 24, 1995, the day of a terrorist attack on a bus in Ramat Gan, Israel, killing six, Syria's head of delegation urged all states to support "national liberation movements" against Israel.

Damascus went out of its way to obstruct Israel's budding relations with other Arab states. The Lebanese government charged Lebanon's beauty queen, Ghada al-Turk, with collaborating with the enemy when she posed in a joint picture with Miss Israel. The Syrian press lambasted Oman for hosting an Israeli delegation to the multilateral peace talks and criticized the United Arab Emirates for dropping its anti-Semitic textbooks. In May 1994, Damascus launched an effort to keep the economic boycott of Israel in place until Israeli forces withdrew from all the territories occupied in 1967, then complained bitterly when Tunisia and the GCC states repealed the boycott. Israeli officials blamed Asad for Tunisia's cancellation of a naval exercise that included Israeli vessels, as they did Oman's decision to delay the establishment of interest offices.

Mixed signals. As the peace process began in 1991, a large statue of Salah al-Din on horseback, dragging behind him two Crusader soldiers, went up in a central Damascus square with the inscription "Jerusalem: Lost in 1099, Recaptured in 1187." Then, during the summer of 1994, peace billboards appeared on the main road to the Damascus international airport. None of them, however, mentioned Israel by name but rather (Soviet-style) proclaimed abstract peace to be the goal: "We love peace," "We believe and work for peace," "Peace can allow Syria to invest its full efforts in the people's welfare." These contradictory signals brought the double game to the streets of the capital.

Rumors about personnel changes also sent a double signal. When Asad dropped such mainstays of his regime as 'Ali Haydar, Shafiq Fayyadh, and Majid Sa'id in August and November 1994, observers speculated[81] that Asad rid himself of unsavory and compromised old warriors as a step toward preparing for peace with Israel. But then, why, according to other rumors, did he in late 1994 appoint as chief of the Syrian air force none other than Muhammad al-Khuli, the man implicated in the 1986 attempted bombing of an El Al plane in London?

An obscure incident symbolized the unstable, unclear state of affairs. In a case of unlikely nerviness, two or three Syrian travel agencies ignored their government's policy of boycotting the multilateral talks with Israel and participated, along with Israeli firms, in a tourism conference in Cairo in September 1994. For this transgression, the Ministry of Tourism first expelled the offending firms from Syria's national tourism association, then closed them down.[82] Did this sequence of events signal that some Syrians perceived a new openness in their country? Or was it a provocation planned by the authorities to show their disdain for the peace process? An outsider can only guess.

Generalizing, it appears that the Syrian authorities have adopted an increasingly accommodating position on the official level but have kept things relatively unchanged at the popular level. As Rabin explained, "The Syrians usually are more soft spoken outside their country than they are in speeches for domestic consumption."[83]

The double game in the peace process consisted of Damascus simultaneously pursuing political and military options *vis-à-vis* Israel, offering both friendly and antagonistic faces. Asad took part in American-sponsored negotiations but also talked like an Arab nationalist. He tried, in the words of Israel's chief negotiator with Syria, to "prove to the Arab public that while it might advance in the peace process, it has not abandoned its principles"[84] – not an easy task. Yes, Asad reached out to the West by joining the peace process, but he did not give up his long-established stance as an enemy of Israel. He kept options open: even while pleasing the United States by talking to Israel, he signaled hard-core anti-Zionists that his heart remained with them. He hinted at readiness to make peace with Israel, if need be, while also indicating that, if possible, he would rather make war on it.

Conclusions

Who would deny that Asad has developed the double game, a common pattern of Middle Eastern politics, into a fine art? He maintains both good and bad relations with foreign leaders. He has Western hostages captured, then has them released. He keeps promises and breaks them. He formally engages in negotiations with Israel and publicly condemns them. Today's policy can be reversed tomorrow; it can be contradicted today; or it may not even exist.

The double game is truly Hafiz al-Asad's crowning achievement as a subtle and highly sophisticated political operative. He ranks as one of his era's virtuoso political technicians. Other tyrants could learn something from Asad; one day, perhaps, a Machiavelli will record and analyze his stratagems as a model for others to imitate.

Whence comes the double game? In part, it may result from Asad's 'Alawi origins. As the epigraph to this chapter suggests, 'Alawis have a long tradition of religious dissimulation (*taqiyya*), honed over the centuries by the need to pretend to be Muslim. 'Alawis lived double lives, maintaining an Islamic exterior but in the privacy of their villages cursing Muslims. In part too, the double game reflects Asad's cautious personality. He avoids risk whenever possible ("If out of a 100 percent chance for success there is a 5 percent chance of failure, he will not take the risk")[85] and it allows him to take the fewest chances.

The double game also derives from the nature of despotism; here Asad fits into a long and dishonorable tradition. Stalin, for example, was also a master of this art. During the Moscow show-trial of August 1937, when a group of leading Bolsheviks were accused of trying to sabotage the Soviet state on behalf of Leon Trotsky and the Nazi government, Stalin was simultaneously building links to Berlin. This put him in a dilemma: He evidently wanted to brand the accused as fascist-like and hence to portray the trial and the mass terror it heralded as an anti-fascist undertaking, but to do this without unduly ruffling the high-placed men in Berlin with whom he was continuing to deal and hoped to reach an accord. This was no easy task, but he managed it. To make up for the very public assault on fascism taking place in his courtroom and his underlings' blatant lies about the accused men's links to Germany, Stalin adopted several strategies. He timed a diplomatic approach to the Germans so that it took place even as the brief trial was in session. He had aides point out that 13 of the 18 on trial (two of them in *absentia*) were Jews, including the very three whom Nazi publications had singled out as the "Jewish element in the leadership of Bolshevism."[86] He even had his diplomats suggest that "Trotsky could have been lying" when Trotsky supposedly told a defendant in the show-trial about working for Berlin.[87]

The double game brings a number of benefits. An air of mystery enhances Asad's reputation and causes enemies to fear him. Words only vaguely point to what he thinks; and actions only suggest what he actually intends. Asad is truly inscrutable – "the sphinx of Damascus" as his biographer Moshe Ma'oz calls him. Or, in Milton Viorst's felicitous phrase, he is a ruler for whom "an air of enigma is an instrument of state."[88]

Second, Asad prefers to move slowly in making major shifts in policy, and the double game wins him time.

Third, he much prefers things the way they used to be when the Soviet Union was around and the double game permits him to make the fewest adjustments necessary. It offers a half-way house to someone nostalgic for an international Soviet network and anti-American ideologies but having to deal with new realities.

Fourth, while Asad's game fools neither Syrians nor foreigners, it offers great flexibility of action. It lets him avoid choosing between stark alternatives, instead he can take two or more roads at once. Open Syria or keep it isolated? The double game would have Asad open it up slightly, at the margins, while making no basic changes. Peace with Israel or war? By simultaneously negotiating with Israel and building up his military machine against it, Asad assures himself the possibility to "move in any direction."[89] Join the Western camp or oppose it? The double game permits him not to foreclose options; he finds a third way, remaining a rogue state, retaining his non-Western ties, yet inching far enough in the West's direction to win its forbearance and even goodwill. Creative ambiguity leaves enemies and friends alike unsure, winning maximum room to maneuver without making fundamental changes in policy. Asad can make concessions where necessary and exploit opportunities where possible.

Notes

This chapter was completed in May 1996.

1 Sulayman Efendi al-Adhani, *Kitab al-Bakura al-Sulaymaniyya fi Kashf Asrar al-Diyana al-Nusayriyya*. Summary and Arabic extracts in Edward E. Salisbury, "The Book of Sulaiman's First Ripe Fruit: Disclosing the Mysteries of the Nusairian Religion," *Journal of the American Oriental Society*, Vol. 8 (1866), p. 298.
2 Anwar al-Sadat, *Those I Have Known* (London, 1984), p. 101.
3 *The Jerusalem Post*, December 2, 1994.
4 Michel Aoun, "If Lebanon Fails, So Does the Middle East," *Middle East Quarterly*, Vol. II, No. 4 (December 1995), p. 59.
5 Deputy Defense Minister Mordechai Gur, *La Repubblica,* August 24, 1993. *The Jerusalem Post* argues (October 23, 1994) that Washington's criticism of Damascus for "not doing enough" to make Hizballah stop shelling Israel with Katyushas "is like suggesting that the US is not doing enough to rein in the marines."
6 Qol Yisra'el, April 19, 1994.
7 *The Wall Street Journal*, November 19, 1991.
8 James Baker, quoted on Damascus Television, April 30, 1990.
9 Syrian Arab Television, September 10, 1994.
10 *The Washington Post*, March 7, 1995.
11 *Yedi'ot Aharonot*, March 25, 1994.
12 *Jewish Exponent* (Philadelphia), July 14, 1995. He explained more fully in 1991 to the American Secretary of State that Asad is "very tough, but if you do a deal with him, he'll stick absolutely with the letter of the deal. Don't assume there will be any spirit, but what he agrees to, you can count on." Quoted in James A. Baker III, with Thomas M. DeFrank, *Politics of Diplomacy: Revolution, War and Peace, 1989–1992* (New York, 1995), pp. 425–26.
13 Israel Defense Forces Radio, May 19, 1994.
14 *Ha'aretz* (Tel Aviv), September 30, 1994; *The New York Times*, October 26,1994.
15 Specifically, Damascus agreed to "the withdrawal of armed elements to the places they occupied before April 13, 1975, and to remove all armed manifestations." For the text of the document in English, see: Subcommittee on Europe and the Middle East, Committee on Foreign Affairs, US House of Representatives, *The Search for Peace in the Middle East: Documents and Statements, 1967–79* (Washington, D.C.: US Government Printing Office, 1979), pp. 336–37.
16 For the text of the declaration in English, see: John Norton Moore (ed.), *The Arab-Israeli Conflict*, Vol. 4, *The Difficult Search for Peace* (1975–1988), Part 2, pp. 1154–56.
17 For the text of the accord in English, see: Dilip Hiro, *Lebanon Fire and Embers: A History of the Lebanese Civil War* (New York, 1993), pp. 231–40.
18 Theodor Hanf, *Coexistence in Wartime Lebanon: Decline of a State and Rise of a Nation*, trans. from German by John Richardson (London, 1993), p. 636 [hereafter: Hanf, *Coexistence in Wartime Lebanon*].

19 Quoted in *ibid.*, p. 579. The troika consisted of the kings of Saudi Arabia and Morocco, plus the president of Algeria.
20 *The Star* (Amman), July 21–26, 1994.
21 *Sabah* (Istanbul), November 7, 1993. I have dealt at length with this case in chapter 5 of *Syria Beyond the Peace Process* (Washington, D.C.: Washington Institute for Near East Policy, 1996).
22 Itamar Rabinovich, *The War for Lebanon, 1970–1983* (Ithaca, N.Y., 1984), pp. 117, 118, 122.
23 Hanf, *Coexistence in Wartime Lebanon*, p. 611.
24 Fida Nasrallah, "The Treaty of Brotherhood, Co-operation and Co-ordination: An Assessment," in Youssef M. Choueiri (ed.), *State and Society in Syria and Lebanon* (New York, 1993), p. 107; idem., "Syria after Ta'if: Lebanon and the Lebanese in Syrian Politics," in Eberhard Kienle (ed.), *Contemporary Syria: Liberalization between Cold War and Cold Peace* (London and New York, 1994), p. 135.
25 Yair Evron, *War and Intervention in Lebanon: The Israeli–Syrian Deterrence Dialogue* (Baltimore, 1987), p. 97.
26 Karim Pakradouni, *Stillborn Peace: The Mandate of Elias Sarkis, 1976–1982* (Beirut: Editions FMA, 1985), p. 72.
27 *Al-Hayat* (London), June 6, 1994.
28 Israel Defense Forces Radio, April 2, 1995.
29 Qol Yisra'el, April 1, 1995.
30 *Jewish Exponent* (Philadelphia), July 14, 1995.
31 Israel Defense Forces Radio, June 16, 1995.
32 Speech to the Washington Institute for Near East Policy, April 29, 1996, as transcribed by the Federal News Service.
33 Asad off the record to an unnamed "senior European diplomat," quoted in *Ma'ariv* (Tel Aviv), August 6, 1991.
34 *The New York Times*, April 28, 1992.
35 *Jewish Exponent* (Philadelphia), June 16, 1995.
36 *Ha'aretz*, July 16, 1995, Qol Yisra'el, July 17, 1995.
37 Richard Murphy, "Syria's Foreign Policy: Looking Beyond the Gulf Crisis; the Prospects for Sustaining Improved Relations with the West," unpublished paper, June 1991, p. 3.
38 Ze'ev Schiff, *Peace With Security: Israel's Minimal Security Requirements in Negotiations with Syria* (Washington, D. C.: Washington Institute for Near East Policy, 1993), p. 23 [hereafter: Schiff, *Peace With Security*].
39 *Yedi'ot Aharonot*, November 10, 1994.
40 *The Star*, July 21–26, 1994. After the partial publication by this author of the materials in this section in a *Jerusalem Post* article on August 19, 1994, some Israeli observers – including Netanyahu – changed their minds about Asad. For example, Arye Der'i, leader of the Shas party, said that "Almost all [Syrian–Israeli] agreements have been violated" by Asad (Israel Defense Forces Radio, July 25, 1995). In a notable exchange, Ya'acov 'Ami-Dror, the head of Israel's Military Intelligence research division, said that "Asad keeps an agreement only when it suits him" (*Davar*, November 9, 1994); to which, Rabin retorted: "This is not the first time the intelligence branch has made mistakes in its assessments" (*The Jerusalem Post International Edition*, November 19, 1994).
41 Just exactly when the last of those attacks took place is hard to place from

inconsistent Israeli public statements. Rabin stated on May 26, 1995 that "For seventeen years we have not had an incident along the border with Syria" (Israeli Television Channel One) and on June 8, 1995 that "there have been no border incidents for nineteen years, no infiltrations" (Qol Yisra'el).

42 *Hadashot* (Tel Aviv), November 11, 1992. David Wurmser kindly made this news report available to me.
43 *The Jerusalem Post*, September 5, 1994.
44 Syrian Arab Television, September 10, 1994.
45 Syrian Arab Television, October 2, 1993.
46 Muhammad Salman on Radio Monte Carlo, April 15, 1994.
47 *Tishrin* (Damascus), August 22, 1994.
48 Cited in *The New York Times*, August 24, 1995.
49 Syrian Arab Republic Radio, October 15, 1994.
50 Al-Quds Palestinian Arab Radio (Damascus), October 20, 1994.
51 Exulting: Syrian Arab Republic Radio, May 26, 1994; "valiant": *ibid.*, November 28, 1994; "just punishment": *ibid.*, August 29, 1994; "heroic action": al-Quds Radio, November 20, 1994.
52 As reported by Great Britain's Foreign Minister Douglas Hurd, *Yedi'ot Aharonot*, October 29, 1993.
53 *Al-Musawwar* (Cairo), April 22, 1994.
54 Syrian Arab Television, October 2, 1993.
55 *Al-Qabas* (Kuwait), December 9, 1989.
56 *Al-Akhbar* (Cairo), September 20, 1993.
57 *As-Safir* (Beirut), July 9, 1994.
58 *Al-Ba'th* (Damascus), July 29, 1994.
59 *Tishrin*, July 28, 1994.
60 Syrian Arab Republic Radio, August 8, 1994.
61 *Tishrin*, June 8, 1994; Mustafa Talas, "Syria and the Future of the Peace Process," *Jane's Intelligence Review*, September 1994.
62 *Der Spiegel* (Hamburg), August 22, 1994.
63 *The Jerusalem Post International Edition*, July 30, 1994.
64 Syrian Arab Republic Radio, August 1, 1994. Avoiding discussion of the PLO and Jordanian accords with Israel became a oddly regular feature of official Syrian discourse. For example, a curt "We do not want to discuss what they achieved" was all Prime Minister Zu'bi said about them in the course of an exceedingly long policy review (Syrian Arab Television, November 14, 1994).
65 Nabil al-Malla, *al-Hayat*, June 18, 1994.
66 Qol Yisra'el, July 28, 1994; Israel Defense Forces Radio, July 30, 1994.
67 *Al-Ra'y* (Amman), August 31, 1994.
68 Syrian Arab News Agency, October 18, 1994. Most media accounts have inaccurately translated the term *kufr* as "blasphemy." To this, King Husayn held firm, insisting that the Jordanian-Israeli treaty "could be a precedent for moving in the right direction" (*al-Ra'y*, February 20, 1995).
69 *The New York Times*, September 16, 1994.
70 Eyal Zisser, "Asad Inches toward Peace," *Middle East Quarterly*, Vol. I, No. 3 (September 1994), pp. 37–44.
71 *Yedi'ot Aharonot*, September 26, 1993; *Ha'aretz*, November 18, 1993.
72 Qol Yisra'el, March 11, 1994. Foreign Minister Shimon Peres sent a condolence letter to Asad via an intermediary in England.

73 *Ha'aretz*, April 7, 1995.
74 Itamar Rabinovich, "Stability and Change in Syria," in Robert B. Satloff (ed.), *The Politics of Change in the Middle East* (Boulder, Colo., 1993), pp. 26–27.
75 Nukhba min al-Mudarrisin, *Al-Mawjiz fil-Tarbiya al-Qawmiyya al-Ishtirakiyya li-Tullab al-Shihadatayn* (n.p., n.d.), p. 13.
76 Mustafa Talas, on Radio Lebanon, August 2, 1995; Syrian Arab Republic Radio, August 7, 1994, April 29, 1993, July 16, 1994, August 29, 1994.
77 Syrian Arab Republic Radio, July 24, 1995.
78 Syrian Arab Republic Radio, August 22, 1995.
79 *Syrian Times* (Damascus), May 14, 1994.
80 Reuter, November 17, 1994.
81 Lamis Andoni, "Assad Nudges Syria Closer to Peace Deal with Israel," *The Christian Science Monitor*, August 31, 1994; James Bruce in *Jane's Defence Weekly*, November 26, 1994.
82 Radio Monte Carlo, September 28, 1994; Agence France Presse, October 3, 1994; *al-Wasat* (London), October 31, 1994.
83 *Davar* (Tel Aviv), September 14, 1994.
84 Itamar Rabinovich, Qol Yisra'el, August 27, 1993.
85 Jacob Goldberg, "Syria and the Palestinians: The Change is Real," *New Outlook*, Vol. 35 (January–February 1992), p. 23.
86 Robert C. Tucker, *Stalin in Power: The Revolution from Above, 1928–1941* (New York, 1990), p. 371.
87 Quoted in Tucker, *Stalin in Power*, p. 412. In the process, Stalin's aides acknowledged the mendacity of the trial's whole premise.
88 Milton Viorst, *Sandcastles: The Arabs in Search of the Modern World* (New York, 1994), p. 123.
89 Schiff, *Peace With Security*, p. 85.

Contributors

Ş. Tufan Buzpınar, Ph.D. (University of Manchester, 1991). The President of the TDV (Türkiye Diyanet Vakfı), Center for Islamic Studies, Istanbul, and a member of the Editorial Board of the *Turkish Journal of Islamic Studies*. His major fields of specialization are the European penetration into the Middle East, Jewish immigration into Palestine from the 1880s onward, and Ottoman rule in Syria and the Hijaz during the nineteenth century. Prof. Buzpinar's publications include: *Ottoman Rule in Syria and the Hijaz, 1877–1882* (Istanbul, 1999).

Moshe Efrat, Ph.D. (London School of Economics and Political Science, University of London, 1981). Senior Lecturer in the College of Management, Tel Aviv and formerly Senior Research Fellow at the London School of Economics and Political Science (1983–90), and at the Israeli International Institute for Applied Economic Policy Review, Tel Aviv (1991–95). His major fields of specialization are defense economics and Middle Eastern economy. Dr. Efrat's publications include: *Economics of Soviet Arms* (co-author, London, 1985); *The Palestinian Refugees: The Dynamic of Economic Integration in the Host Countries* (Tel Aviv, 1993); and *Superpowers and Client States in the Middle East: The Imbalance of Influence* (co-editor, London and New York, 1991).

Michael Eppel, Ph.D. (Tel Aviv University, 1991). Senior Lecturer in the Department of Middle Eastern History at the University of Haifa. His major fields of specialization are the modern history of Iraq and Syria, the Israeli-Arab conflict, and the Soviet and Russian involvement in the Middle East. Dr. Eppel's publications include: *The Palestine Conflict in the History of Modern Iraq* (London, 1994); and "The Elite, the Effendiyya, and the Growth of Nationalization and Pan-Arabism in Hashemite Iraq, 1921–1958," *IJMES*, Vol. 30 (1998), pp. 227–50.

Joseph Ginat, Ph.D. (University of Utah, 1975). Professor of social and cultural anthropology at the Department of Land of Israel Studies at the University of Haifa. Prof. Ginat has held several academic positions, including the head of the Jewish–Arab Center at the University of Haifa, and the head of the Israeli Academic Center in Cairo. He also served as adviser to the cabinet and the Prime Minister on Arab affairs and as personal adviser to Moshe Dayan. His major fields of specialization are Middle Eastern anthropology with a special emphasis on Bedouin tribes and Muslim rural societies in Egypt, Jordan and Israel. Prof. Ginat's publications include: *Women in Muslim Rural Society: Status and Role in Family and Community* (New Brunswick, 1982); *Blood Revenge: Family Honor, Mediation and Outcasting* (Brighton, 1996) and *Polygamous Families in Contemporary Society, Coping with Challenging Life Style* (co-author, Cambridge, 1996).

Mordechai Kedar, Ph.D. (Bar-Ilan University, 1998), is Lecturer in the Department of Arabic at Bar-Ilan University. His major field of specialization is in the interdisiplinary approach to Arabic political discourse from both the linguistic and socio-political points of view. His research concentrates on governmental political messages conveyed by the mass-media in contemporary Arab countries. Dr. Kedar's publications include: "Islam in the Syrian Press: Political Messages Relating to Islamic Holidays," *Hamizrah Hehadash* [The New East], Vol. 38 (1996), pp. 183–96 (in Hebrew); and "Arabism in the Syrian Media: Political Messages and Their Language," *International Journal of the Sociology of Language*, No. 137 (1999), pp. 141–46.

David Kushner, Ph.D. (University of California at Los Angeles, 1968). Professor in the Department of Middle Eastern History at the University of Haifa. Prof. Kushner has held several positions at the University of Haifa, including Chairman of the Department of Middle Eastern History and the Jewish-Arab Center, Dean of the Faculty of Humanities, and the Academic Head of Jezreel Valley College. His major fields of specialization are late Ottoman history, the history of Palestine during the late Ottoman period, and ideological and political trends in modern Turkey. Prof. Kushner's publications include: *The Rise of Turkish Nationalism, 1876–1908* (London, 1977); *A Governor City in Jerusalem: The City and Province in the Eyes of Ali Ekrem Bey, 1906–1908* (Jerusalem, 1995, in Hebrew); and *Palestine During the Late Ottoman Period: Political, Social and Economic Transformation* (editor, Jerusalem and Leiden, 1986).

David W. Lesch, Ph.D. (Harvard University, 1990). Professor in the Department of History at Trinity University, San Antonio, Texas. His major fields of specialization are the history of modern Syria, the US policy in the Middle East, and the promotion of business in the Arab world. Prof. Lesch's publications include: *Syria and the United States: Eisenhower's Cold War in the Middle East* (Boulder, Colo., 1992); *The Middle East and United States: A Historical and Political Reassessment* (Boulder, Colo., 1996, second edition, 1999).

Moshe Ma'oz, Ph.D. (Oxford University, 1966). Professor in the Department of Islamic and Middle Eastern Studies at the Hebrew University of Jerusalem, and the former Director of the Harry S. Truman Research Institute for the Advancement of Peace. Prof. Ma'oz also served as deputy advisor to the Prime Minister on Arab Affairs and as advisor to the Minister of Defense, Ezer Weizman. His major fields of specialization are modern Syria, the Palestinian history and politics, and Arab-Israeli relations. Prof. Ma'oz publications include: *Ottoman Reform in Syria and Palestine, 1840–61* (Oxford, 1968); *Palestinian Leadership on the West Bank* (London, 1984); *Asad – The Sphinx of Damascus: A Political Biography* (London and New York, 1988); and *Syria and Israel: From War to Peace-Making* (Oxford, 1995).

Daniel Pipes, Ph.D. (Harvard University, 1978). The editor of the *Middle East Quarterly* and Senior Lecturer at the University of Pennsylvania. Prof. Pipes has also taught at the University of Chicago, Harvard University and the US Naval War College. For seven years, from 1986 to 1993, Prof. Pipes was the Director of the Foreign Policy Research Institute. He also served in the US Departments of State and Defense. His major fields of specialization are the modern history and politics of the Middle East, particularly Syria, and Islam in politics. Prof. Pipes' publications include: *Greater Syria: The History of an Ambition* (Oxford and New York, 1990); and *Syria Beyond the Peace Process* (The Washington Institute for Near East Policy, 1996).

Yoram Shalit, Ph.D. (Friedrich-Alexander Universität, Erlangen–Nürnberg, 1995). Lecturer in the Department of Islamic and Middle Eastern Studies at the Hebrew University of Jerusalem. His major fields of specialization are the minorities in the Middle East and the history of the Syrian region during the Ottoman period. Dr. Shalit's publications include: *Nicht Muslime und Fremde in Aleppo und Damaskus im 18 und in der Ersten Halfte des 19 Jahrhunderts* [Non-Muslims and

Foreigners in Aleppo and Damascus During the 18th and the First Half of the 19th Centuries] (Berlin, 1996).

Moshe Shemesh, Ph.D. (London School of Economics and Political Science, 1983). Senior Lecturer in the Department of Middle East Studies at Ben-Gurion University of the Negev, Be'er-Sheva, and a Senior Research associate at Ben-Gurion Research Center, Sede-Boker. In 1988–89, he was Visiting Fellow at St Antony's College, Oxford University. His major fields of specialization are Palestinian politics and the PLO, the Arab-Israeli conflict, the Lebanon crisis, and Egypt and inter-Arab relations. Dr. Shemesh's Publications include: *The Palestinian Entity 1959–1974: Arab Politics and the PLO* (London, 1988 and revised edition, 1996); and *The Suez–Sinai Crisis 1956: Retrospective and Reappraisal* (co-editor, London, 1990).

Onn Winckler, Ph.D. (University of Haifa, 1994). Lecturer in the Department of Middle Eastern History, University of Haifa. His major fields of specialization are the demographic and economic history of the modern Middle East. Dr. Winckler's publications include: *Population Growth and Migration in Jordan, 1950–1994* (Brighton, 1997); *Demographic Developments and Population Policies in Ba'thist Syria* (Brighton and Portland, 1999); and *The Jordanian-Palestinian-Israeli Triangle: Smoothing the Path to Peace* (co-editor, Brighton and Portland, 1998).

Meir Zamir, Ph.D. (London School of Economics and Political Science, 1980). Professor in the Departments of Middle East Studies and Business Administration at Ben-Gurion University of the Negev, Be'er-Sheva, and Business Administration at the Ben-Gurion Research Center, Sede-Boker. His major fields of specialization are the social and political history of the modern Middle East, particularly Lebanon, and cross-cultural management with special emphasis on the Middle East. Prof. Zamir's publications include: *The Formation of Modern Lebanon, 1918–1926* (London, 1985); and *Lebanon's Quest: The Road to Statehood, 1926–1939* (London, 1997).

Eyal Zisser, Ph.D. (Tel Aviv University, 1992). Research Fellow at the Moshe Dayan Center and Lecturer in the Department of Middle Eastern and African History at Tel Aviv University. His major fields of specialization are the history and politics of Syria and Lebanon. Dr. Zisser's publications include: *Assad's Syria – at a Crossroads* (Tel Aviv, 1999, in Hebrew).

Index

'Abd al-Ilah, 215
'Abd al-Malek, 142
'Abd al-Qader al-Jazairi, 135, 138–40, 146
'Abd al-Qader Efendi, 142
'Abdallah, King, 214, 257
Abdulhamid II, Sultan, 140, 142–6
Abu al-Hasan, 22
Abu Talib, Muhammad, 142
Abu-Ghudda, 'Abd al-Fatah, 36
ACDA (US), 88–9, 90, 92, 93
'Aflaq, Michel, 11*n*, 18, 20, 218
age pyramid, 7, 110–12, 127
Agrarian Reform law (1958), 4
Agricultural Cooperatives, 7
agricultural sector
  cultivated land, 112
  droughts, 63
  employment, 86
  foreign trade, 100–1
  GDP, 81, 82, 86
  job creation, 87
  private sector, 85, 107
  public investments, 84
Aharoni, Reuben, 171, 182*n*
al-Ahdab, Khair al-Din, 201, 202
al-Ahmar, 'Abdallah, 38
aid *see* foreign aid
'Ajlun, 136, 137
Akka, 138
Alaiye, 137
Alanya, 137
'Alawi region, 191, 195, 197, 198, 200, 202
'Alawis
  army, 3, 4, 5, 10*n*, 41, 43–4
  and Asad, 49–50
  French Mandate, 2
  and Islam, 22–3, 67, 287
  Ottoman Rule, 1
  public sector, 104
  state domination, 66–7
  and Sunni-Muslims, 20
Aleppo
  Algerian immigrants, 138
  attitude toward foreigners, 150–65
Alexandretta, 2, 200, 201, 228
Alfayez, M., 173
Algeria, 63
Algerian immigrants, 135–47
'Ali Agha, 160
al-'Ali Ilahiyah, 22
Ali (son of 'Abd al-Qader), 142, 146
'Ali-Salam, Salim, 199
Aman, 153
American Israel Public Affairs Committee, 283
American Jewish Congress, 283
'Ami-Dror, Ya'acov, 290*n*
Amir, Ali, 250, 253
Amman Conference, 71
Anatolia, 137
'Aneze federation, 172
Annan, Kofi, 224
Antalya, 137
Arab al-'Aramshah tribe, 170–81
Arab League, 125, 203, 234, 246, 248, 275–6
Arab Liberation Front, 273
Arab nationalism, 109, 257
  see also pan-Arabism
Arab Summit Conference (1978), 113
Arad, Ron, 284
'Arafat, Yasir, 32*n*, 125, 263, 273, 280
Arida, Pierre Antoine, 193, 194, 195, 196, 198, 203
Armenian Secret Army for the Liberation of Armenia, 235
army
  'Alawis, 3, 4, 5, 10*n*, 41, 43–4
  appointments system, 6

Druze, 4, 10*n*
senior military–security echelons, 35, 37, 44–50
Artin Pasha, 144, 146
al-Asad, Bashar, 35, 37, 40–4, 46, 47–8, 50, 69–70
senior military–security echelons, 45, 46, 48, 50
al-Asad, Basil, 26–7, 39–40, 41–2, 69
al-Asad, Hafiz, 3, 5–9, 62, 229
1973 war, 258
'Alawi coalition, 49–50
announcement of Ramadan, 24–5
Arab unity, 259–60
and 'Arafat, 263, 273
art of the double game, 272–88
Ba'th Revolution (1963), 4
Corrective Movement, 6, 62–3
death of son, 26–7, 40
debt to Russia, 75*n*, 93
economic policies, 62–3, 64, 66–7
and Egypt, 62, 260–1, 266–7
Golan Heights, 62, 72, 258, 260
Greater Syria Union, 259, 262–3
heart attack, 38, 70
Hizballah, 178, 273–4
holiday blessings, 25–6
holiday sermon references, 25
and Iran, 78*n*, 259, 265–6, 269, 273
and Iraq, 79, 218, 224, 258, 261–2, 273
Islamic Conference, 29
Islamic image in Syrian official press, 17–30
and Israel, 62, 71, 72, 73, 78*n*, 257–70, 278, 282–7
Israel-Jordan agreements, 281–2, 283
Israel-PLO agreements, 279–81
and Jordan, 273
Lebanon, 177–8, 203, 259, 262, 263–4, 273, 275–7
neo-Ba'th period, 5
oath of allegiance (*Bay'ah*), 27, 28
Operation Accountability, 277
Palestinian state, 264
personal qualities, 5, 38
PKK activities, 276
presentation of Qur'an, 28
promotion of Bashar as successor, 35, 37, 40–4, 46, 47–8, 50, 69–70
in public prayer, 24
questioning of leadership qualities, 68
red line agreement, 276–7
regional strategy, 257–70
and Sadam Husayn, 109, 224–5, 261, 262, 265
senior military–security echelons, 46
Separation of Forces Agreement, 278–9, 283
strategic balance policy, 109–10, 116–18, 259, 260, 264–6
succession issue, 34–5, 37–44, 50, 69–70
Syrian Jews, 277–8
al-Asad, Na'isa, 38
al-Asad, Rif'at, 28, 38–9, 43, 44, 46, 50, 70
Asad of Syria: The Struggle for the Middle East, 51
ASALA, 235
Ashkenazi, T., 172
Ashraf, 160, 161
Asi River, 233–4, 237
al-'Askari, 'Ali ben Mohhamad, 22
Aslan, 'Ali, 43
al-'Asli, Sabri, 213, 214, 215–16, 226*n*
al-Atasi, Hashim
elected President, 215
as Foreign Minister, 216
Franco-Syrian treaty negotiations, 191, 192, 195, 197, 200, 204–7
restored to Presidency, 215
Syrian–Iraqi federation, 213, 215, 216
Ataturk Dam, 234
Athanasius, 162
'Awn, Michel, 220, 272, 273
A'yan, 159
'Aziz, Tariq, 222, 223

Ba'albak, 192, 193
Bab al-Janub, 158
Bab Tuma, 162
Babil, 223
al-Badri tribe, 170
Baghdad Pact, 4, 216, 231
al-Bakr, Hassan, 219, 262
balance of payments, 95–7
Bani Sakhir, 173
Banias Springs, 250
banking sector, 107, 122
Banque Syrie-Liban, 203
Barak, Ehud, 270, 275
Barakat, Subhi, 192
Barker, John, 155, 163
Barret, John, 154
Barth, F., 176
al-Barudi, Fakhri, 192, 193, 194
al-Ba'th, 27
Ba'th Party Conference, 51
Ba'th party, Iraqi, 211, 217–20, 225*n*
Ba'th party, Syrian, 3–4, 61, 211

Index

Declaration of Principles, 18–19
expanded ranks of, 6–7
historical slogan, 34
Jordan River diversion, 247–9, 254
Ba'th regime (1963–1970), 4–5
Bay'ah, 27, 28
Bayhum, Omar, 199
Beck, L., 173
Bedouins, 170–81
Begin, Menachem, 72
Beilin, Yossi, 177
Beirut, 138, 192, 193, 196, 199, 200
Beit She'an Valley, 173
Bennike, Major-General, 245–6
Biqa' valley, 192, 196, 237
bid proposals, 57–9, 74*n*
Bilad al-Sham, 1
birth rate, 34
Bisar, 'Abd al-Latif, 199, 201
bish'a, 183*n*
al-Bitar, Salah al-Din, 11*n*, 218
Black-Michaud J., 173, 176
Blum, Léon, 195, 196
B'nai B'rith, 283
B'not-Ya'acov Bridge, 245
Bonapartist state, 61–2, 67, 73
bonds, 59
Boutros-Ghali, Boutros, 125
Bowen, Harold, 154
Britain, 47, 171, 197, 213, 214
Bugeaud, Thomas-Robert, 135
Bulgarian Turks, 232
Buq'ata, 28
Burckhardt, John Lewis, 159
Bush, George, 267, 277
Buzo, 'Ali, 216

Cairo economic summit, 72
Caix, Robert de, 192–3
Camp David accord, 109, 265
capital movement, 97–100
Capitulations, 153–4
Capucins, 161
Carter, Jimmy, 264–5, 272
Casablanca Conference, 71
Ceaucesçu, Nicolae, 35, 40
Chaboceau, 161–2
China, 73
Christians
Ottoman Rule, 1, 2
see also Maronites
Christopher, Warren, 277, 278, 285
Circassians, 172, 173
Clinton, Bill, 26, 177–8, 278, 281–2
Colbert, Jean-Baptiste, 154
Common Interests, 197, 203
Communism, collapse of, 118
Communist party, 3–4
Conference of Islamic States, 29
construction sector, 81, 82, 84, 86
contraception, 118
Corrective Movement, 6, 62–3
corruption, 58, 65
Cyprus, 232
Cyrillus, 162

al-Dabagh, Murad, 171–2, 174
Damascus
Algerian immigrants, 138
attitude toward foreigners, 150–65
bus bomb (1996), 52*n*
explosions (1996), 33
Damascus International Fair, 223
Dan River, 251
Da'wa, 221
Dayan, Moshe, 246
debt *see* foreign debt
Defense Companies Division, 39
defense costs, 75–6*n*, 79, 88–95, 104, 110, 115–16, 117
Delbos, Yvon, 196, 202
Demirel, Süleyman, 232, 234, 240
democratization, 124
demographics *see* population
Deng Xiaoping, 73
Der'i, Arye, 290*n*
development programs, 7
dhaif, 183*n*
Dhimmi, 153
Diff, Muhammad, 280
diwan, 176, 183*n*
droughts, 63
Druze
army, 4, 10*n*
French Mandate, 2
independent Syria, 3
neo-Ba'th period, 5
Ottoman Rule, 1
renewal of the *Bay'ah*, 28
revolt (1954), 3
Duba, 'Ali, 43, 45
Dyresse Pasha, 144

East Jerusalem, 264, 267
Eban, Abba, 275
economic crisis of 1980s, 63–6, 113–18
economic development policies, 79–107
economic growth, 62–3, 80–2, 113–14, 120, 126
economic liberalization *see* private sector

Eddé, Emile, 192, 194, 196, 198–9, 200, 201, 202–3
education, 7, 18, 92, 95
Egypt
  1973 war, 258, 261
  Asad's peace proposals, 264
  Asad's regional strategy, 62, 260–1, 266–7
  assistance to Syria, 210
  economic liberalization, 124
  federation of Arab Republics, 260
  foreign exchange reserves, 63
  Free Officers Movement, 61
  industrialization, 76*n*
  Iraqi unity, 222
  ISI policies, 63, 120
  Jordan River diversion, 245, 246–9, 253
  normalization of relations with Syria, 220, 267
  peace treaty with Israel, 71, 72, 78*n*, 109, 125, 218, 261
  Syria under al-Quwatli, 214
  Syrian *coup d'état* (1949), 214–15
  Syrian–Iraqi federation, 215, 216
  Syrian–Turkish relations, 240
  United Arab Republic, 4, 216–17, 226*n*, 229, 246–8, 257–8
  and the West, 64
Egyptians, 2
Eickelman, D. F., 176
Ein Hamoud, 254
Ein Sufeira, 254
Eitan, Michael, 177
electricity network, 7
Emin Bey, 144
employment, 87–8
Encümen-i Hususi-i Vükelâ, 143
English, in Aleppo and Damascus, 150–65
Erbakan, Necmettin, 239–40
Erlich, R., 176
Eshkol, Levi, 246
Euphrates waters, 225, 233–5, 237
European Union, 99, 101, 123
Evron, Yair, 276
exchange rate, 91, 107, 122

Fadlallah, *Shaykh* 'Abbas Muhsayn 'Ali, 178
Fahd, King of Saudi Arabia, 26
fallahin, 171, 175, 182*n*
family planning, 118
Faranjiyya, Sulayman Tony, 41
Faranjiyya, Sulayman (President of Lebanon), 41
Farsoun, S. K., 176
fascism, 61
Fata al-Arab, 199
Fatah, 255
Faysal I, King of Iraq, 257
Faysal, King, 2
Fayyadh, Shafiq, 43, 45, 46, 48, 286
Fermanel, M. de, 161
Fez Declaration, 275
financial sector, 81, 82, 85, 86, 107, 122
five-percenters, 58, 65
foreign aid, 36, 105–6
  Gulf oil-exporting countries (GCC), 62, 63, 65, 80, 105, 113, 119, 126
foreign currency law, 64
foreign debt, 83, 99, 104–5, 123
  to USSR/Russia, 75*n*, 93–4, 95
foreign exchange reserves, 63
foreign grants, 95–7, 104, 105
foreign investments, 36, 64–6, 83–7, 104, 120–2
foreign trade, 100–4
Forster, Richard, 154
France
  Algeria, 135
  Algerian immigrants in Syria, 139–47
  al-'Aramshah tribe, 171
  capitulation agreement, 153–4
  Lebanese Mandate and independence, 191–207
  mandates, 171
  Syrian debt, 123
  Syrian Mandate, 2–3, 60–1, 74–5*n*, 213
  Syrian treaty negotiations, 191–207
  Syrian–Iraqi federation, 215
Free Officers Movement, 61
French, in Aleppo and Damascus, 150–65
Friendship and Cooperation agreement (1991), 264

Gabay, Moshe, 170
Galilee, 140
GAP Project, 233–5
Gaza Strip, 175, 264, 267
Gazit, Shlomo, 177
GCC countries *see* Gulf oil-exporting countries
GDP, 81–2, 86, 120, 121
Gellner, E., 176
General Federation of Trade Unions, 76*n*
Germany, 123
GFCF, 83, 120
GFTU, 76*n*
Gibb, Hamilton, 154
Ginat, Joseph, 176
Glasnost, 73

GNP, 113, 115
Golan Heights
  and Asad, 62, 72, 258, 260
  Separation of Forces Agreement (1974), 278–9
  Syrian military threat, 269–70
  Syrian–Israeli peace process, 71, 266, 267–8, 269–70
  US pressure on Israel, 222
Gorbachev, Mikhail, 73, 220, 266
Granqvist, H., 174
grants, 95–7, 104, 105
Greece, 238
Greeks, 1
Gross Domestic Product (GDP), 81–2, 86, 120, 121
Gross Fixed Capital Formation (GFCF), 83, 120
Gross National Product (GNP), 113, 115
Guerin, Victor, 171
Gulf crisis (1990–91), 35, 63, 65, 119, 125, 220–1, 231, 267
Gulf oil-exporting countries aid to Jordan, 125
  aid to Palestinians, 125
  aid to Syria, 62, 63, 65, 80, 105, 113, 119, 126
  Israeli economic boycott, 286
  Syrian worker's remittances, 122
  see also Kuwait; Saudi Arabia
Gulliver, P., 176
Güney Dogu Anadolu Projesi (GAP), 233–5
Gur, Mordechai, 289*n*

Ha'aretz, 177, 178
Habash, George, 285
Habib, 'Ali, 46
Haddadin tribe, 53*n*
al-Haib tribe, 174
Haifa, 138, 199
Hajj pilgrimage, 23, 150, 158, 161, 165
al-Hal, Ahmad, 25
Halefoğlu, Vahit, 231
Hama, 8, 17, 21, 45, 46, 67, 264
Hamas, 70, 269, 280
Hamdi Pasha, 138–41
Hamdun, Nizar, 223
Hammam, 156, 159
hamula, 183*n*
Handoussa, Heba, 125
Hanf, Theodor, 275
al-Harakat al-Tashihiyya, 6, 62–3
Harman, Tamar, 178
Hasan, 'Adnan Badr, 43
Hasan, 'Ali, 41
al-Hasani, Taj al-Din, 192
Hasbaya, 192
Hashim (son of 'Abd al-Qader), 141, 142, 146
Hatay, 228, 232, 238, 241
Haydar, 'Ali, 45, 46–7, 50, 53*n*, 286
health sector, 7, 92, 95
Hegel, G. W. F., 61
Hijri new year, 24
Hilan, Rizkallah, 109
Hindawi affair, 45, 47
al-Hinnawi, Sami, 215
Hinnebusch, Raymond A., 3, 65, 118
Hizb al-Sha'b, 213
Hizballah, 176, 177, 178–9, 180, 269
  and Asad, 178, 273–4
  attacks on Israel, 70, 77*n*
Hof, F. C., 171
holiday rituals, 25
Houran, 141, 143
Hourani, Akram, 247
Huntziger, General, 202
Husayn, King of Jordan, 263, 273, 276, 281, 283, 291*n*
Husayn, Saddam and Asad, 109, 224–5, 261, 262, 265
  Gulf crisis, 221, 231
  Iran–Iraq war, 265
  and Jordan, 263
  opposition organizations, 221–2
  takeover of Iraq, 218–19
  threat to Syria, 220

Ibrahim Pasha, 2
'Id al-Adha, 20, 24, 25
'Id al-Fitr, 20, 23, 24–5, 26
IDF *see* Israeli Defense Forces (IDF)
Ilian, Michail, 214
illiteracy rate, 7
al-Imadi, Muhammad, 223
Imbert, 141–2
IMF, 59, 64, 91, 114, 123
immigrants, Algerian, 135–47
Import-Substituting Industrialization, 63, 120
Imtiyazat (Capitulations), 153
Infitah, 62, 64
inflation, 114
International Institute for Strategic Studies, 116
Intifada, 175
Investment Law No. 10 (May 1991), 7, 65, 74, 85–7, 120–2
investments, 36, 64–6, 83–7, 104, 120–2

Iran, 22, 31*n*, 222
  industrialization, 76*n*
  Syrian alliance, 78*n*, 238, 259, 265–6, 269, 273
  Syrian–Turkish relations, 239, 240
  threat to Iraq, 212
Iran–Iraq war, 75*n*, 76*n*, 109–10, 113, 219, 262, 265–6
Iraq
  Ba'th regime, 211, 217–20, 225*n*
  economic sanctions, 125
  Euphrates waters, 233
  Gulf crisis, 35, 63, 65, 119, 125, 220–1, 231, 267
  Hashemite rule, 212–17
  involvement in Lebanon, 220, 224
  Iran–Iraq war, 75*n*, 76*n*, 109–10, 113, 219, 262, 265–6
  and Jordan, 263
  Kurdish problem, 219, 222, 231, 239, 273
  oil sector, 99, 105
  oil transit dues to Syria, 113
  opposition organizations, 221–2
  and Palestine, 212
  Shi'is, 198, 219, 222, 273
  and Syria, 4, 77–8*n*, 79, 210–25, 231, 258, 261–2, 273
  turbulence in 1957 and 1958, 229
  and Turkey, 212, 214, 222
Iraqi Petroleum Company, 192
Irons, W., 173
Irtas, 174
Islam
  and the Syrian government, 17–30
Islamic Conference, 29
Islamic Movement, 33, 36
Islamic opposition, 8–9, 17
Israel, 213
  1973 war, 258, 261
  agreement with PLO, 263, 279–81
  Arab al-'Aramshah tribe, 170–81
  Asad's regional strategy, 62, 71, 72, 73, 78*n*, 257–70, 278, 282–7
  border incidents (1967), 19
  creation of, 61
  Golan Heights, 71, 222, 266, 267–8, 269–70, 278–9
  Grapes of Wrath operation, 70–1, 72, 77*n*, 269, 277
  Hizballah attacks, 70, 77*n*
  and Jordan, 71, 78*n*, 110, 125, 281–2, 283
  Jordan River diversion, 245–55
  and Lebanon, 115, 176–8, 263
  Madrid peace process, 63, 70, 73, 177, 267–70
  Operation Accountability, 277
  Palestine War (1948), 214
  and Palestinians, 125–6
  peace treaty with Egypt, 71, 72, 78*n*, 109, 125, 218, 261
  red line agreement, 276–7
  Separation of Forces Agreement, 278–9, 283
  Syrian strategic balance policy, 109–10, 115, 116–18, 259, 260, 264–6
  threat to Syria, 4, 34, 35
  and Turkey, 72, 77*n*, 222, 223, 224, 225, 229, 238–9, 269
  see also Syrian–Israeli peace process
Israeli Defense Forces (IDF), 175, 176–7, 178–9, 251–2, 253, 254
Issawi, Charles, 61

Jabal Druze, 191, 195, 197, 198, 200
Jaber 'Ali, 170, 172, 173–4
al-Jabiri, Sa'adallah, 192, 199, 200–1, 202–3
al-Jabur al-Waie tribe, 170
Jadid, Salah, 5, 8, 218, 229
Ja'far Shuwayhat Group, 52*n*
Jaffa, 138
Jama'a, 6
al-Jamali, Fadhil, 215
Janissaries, 158, 159, 160–1
Japan, 123
Jazira, 2
Jadid, Salah, 62
The Jerusalem Post, 178, 283
Jesuits, 161
Jiang Zemin, 73
Johnston, Eric, 246
Jordan, 213
  assistance to Syria, 210
  close relations with Israel, 110
  economy, 125
  Greater Syria Union, 259, 262–3
  and Iraq, 263
  labor migration policy, 119, 120
  Palestine War (1948), 214
  peace treaty with Israel, 71, 78*n*, 125, 281–2, 283
  and Syria, 34, 260, 273
  Syrian worker's remittances, 113, 122
  turbulence in 1957 and 1958, 229
  Yarmuck Plan, 254
Jordan River, 245–55
Jouvenel, Henry de, 192–3
al-Judr tribe, 170

Jurdie, 171

Kaftaru, *Shaykh* Ahmad, 23
Kamil Pasha, 143–5
Karameh, 'Abd al-Hamid, 199, 201
al-Kasm, Ra'uf, 38
Kazim Bey, 143
Khaddam, 'Abd al-Halim, 6, 38, 41, 42–3, 285
Khalas, Ibrahim, 19
Khalidi, Walid, 172
khans, 158
Khayrbak, Muhammad Nasif, 42
Khazanov, A. M., 173
Khirbet Idmit, 171, 182*n*
Khirbet 'Irribin, 171
Khirbet Jurdie, 171–2
Khirbet Nawqir, 171
al-Khuli, Muhammad, 43, 45, 47–8, 286
Khuri, 'Ali, 42
al-Khuri, Beshara, 193, 194, 198–9, 203
al-Khuri, Fares, 213, 216
Kiernan, Peter, 124
al-Kihya, Rushdi, 213
Kim Il Sung, 40
Kirkuk, 212
Kramer, Martin, 20, 22
Kurds
  Iraq, 219, 222, 231, 239, 273
  Turkey, 33, 235–7, 238, 239, 240, 276
al-Kutla al-Wataniyya see National Bloc
Kuwait, 265
  financial aid, 62
  Gulf crisis, 35, 63, 65, 119, 125, 220–1, 231, 267
  Jordanian workers, 125
  and Syria, 260

labor force participation, 110, 127
labor migration policy, 119–20
labor unions, 65, 76*n*
Ladhiqiya, 138, 160
Lancaster, Fidelity, 172, 173
Lancaster, William, 172, 173, 176, 183*n*
land reform, 61
land shortages, 34
Layard, H., 139
Lebanese National Army (LNA), 179–80
Lebanon, 260
  Arab al-'Aramshah tribe, 170–81
  Bashar given responsibility, 41
  Civil War, 263
  factor in Syrian–Israeli peace negotiations, 126
  French Mandate, 2
  Grapes of Wrath operation, 70–1, 72, 77*n*, 269, 277
  Greater Syria Union, 259, 262–3
  independence question, 191–207
  Iraqi involvement, 220, 224
  Israeli presence, 115, 176–8, 263
  Jordan River diversion, 253, 254
  Madrid peace process, 267, 268
  red line agreement, 276–7
  Shi'i Supreme Council, 21
  Syrian agreements to leave, 275–6
  Syrian dominance, 203, 259, 262, 263–4, 273, 275–7
  Syrian worker's remittances, 113, 122
  terrorist training, 235, 236
  tobacco monopoly crisis, 193–4
  turbulence in 1957 and 1958, 229
  see also Hizballah
Lenin, Vladimir Ilyich, 61
Levant Company, 154, 156, 164
Levin, Amiram, 277
liberalization policy *see* private sector
Libya, 31*n*, 113, 260
Likud party, 69
Locke, John, 61
Lubrani, Uri, 274

madhafa, 183*n*
Madrid peace process, 63, 70, 73, 177, 267–70
Makhluf, 'Adnan, 41
Malamat, A., 173
Mamluk family, 182*n*
Mandela, Nelson, 26
manufacturing sector, 81, 82, 84, 85, 86, 87–8, 100, 107
Ma'oz, Moshe, 21, 22–3, 176, 184*n*, 288
Marcus, Yoel, 275
Mardam, Jamil, 192, 193, 195, 199, 200–1, 202–3
Maronites, 191, 195, 200, 263
  Biqa' valley annexation proposal, 192
  Syrian press criticism of, 196, 199
  Tripoli, 193
Martel, Damien de, 191, 193–5, 198–200, 201, 204–6
Marx, E., 176
Marx, Karl, 61
Meclis-i Vâlâ-yı Ahkâm-ı Adliyye, 137
mediation, 58, 176
MEED, 114
Megheis *Khams*, 170
Menderes, Adnan, 231
Middle East International Business Associates, Inc., 57

Midianites, 173
Mill, John Stuart, 61
mining sector, 81, 82, 84, 85, 86
Mishmar ha-Yarden, 252
missionaries, 161
Montebello, 142, 143–4, 145–6
Morocco, 7, 63, 260
mosques, 9, 21
Mosul, 212, 231
Mubarak, Hosni, 64, 177
Mubarak, Ignatius, 196
Mubash'a, 183*n*
Muhammad 'Ali, 163, 165
Muhammad Pasha, 140, 142
Muhyi al-Din, b. Mustafa, 142
Muhyi al-Din Pasha, 140, 141, 142–3
al-Mujahidin Palace, 6
multi-national corporations, 68
al-Murabit Mosque, 23
Murphy, Richard, 278
Musil, A., 172, 183*n*
Muslim Brotherhood, 8–9, 44
  on 'Alawi sect, 22
  Hama rebellion, 8, 17, 21, 45, 46, 67
  reconciliation policy, 36
Must'amin, 153

al-Nadhir, 21
al-Nahar, 22
al-Najjar, Bashir, 41–2
Nami, Ahmad, 192
Namik, Mehmed, 136
Nashid Pasha, Rashid, 141
Nasrallah, Fida, 276
al-Nasser, Gamal 'Abd, 216, 217, 258
  Jordan River diversion, 245, 247, 248, 250, 253
National Bloc, 191, 193–6, 197–9, 200–2, 212–13
National Party, 214, 215, 226*n*
National Progressive Front, 6, 36
nationalization, 4
Nawaquir, 171
Nazi Germany, 61
neo-Ba'th period, 5
Netanyahu, Benjamin
  Golan Heights disengagement, 278
  IDF withdrawal from Lebanon, 178
  "Lebanon first" plan, 72, 177
  Syrian agreement to leave Lebanon, 276
  Syrian–Israeli peace process, 69, 71, 269
The New York Times, 114, 178, 275
Nietzsche, Friedrich Wilhelm, 61
North Korea, 40
al-Numayri, Muhammad b. Nusayr, 22
Nusayris ('Alawis), 22

Öcalan, Abdullah, xv, 236, 240–1
oil sector, Iraqi, 99, 105
oil sector, Syrian, 81, 88, 105
  balance of trade, 100–1
  decline in prices, 63, 126
  exports, 122
  increased revenues, 36, 95, 113, 119
Oman, 119, 285, 286
'Omar (grandson of 'Abd al-Qader), 146
Order of the Knights of the Salt Valley, 156
Oslo Accords (1993), 263, 279–81
Ottoman Empire
  Algeria, 135
  foreigners in Syria, 150–65
  Syria, 1–2, 60, 135–47
Owen, Roger, 60
Özal, Turgut, 232, 233, 236, 237

Palestine
  Asad's proposals, 264
  and Iraq, 212
  partition of, 197
Palestine Exploration Fund, 171
Palestine War (1948), 214
Palestinian Authority, 34
Palestinian Rejectionist Front, 280
Palestinians, 125–6, 175
Pan Am plane bombing, 35
pan-Arabism, 210–11, 212, 213, 219–20, 260
Paton, A. B., 159
patronage, 62
Peace Water Project, 234
Peled, Yossie, 177
People's Assembly, 3, 5–6, 9, 36–37, 44
People's Council, 27
People's Party, 213, 214, 215, 229
Peres, Shimon
  Asad's peace tactics, 78*n*
  Golan Heights, 71
  Grapes of Wrath operation, 72, 269, 277
  and Jordan, 281, 282
  Middle Eastern common market, 77*n*
  suspension of talks with Syria, 268–9
  Syrian agreements, 275
Perestroika, 73
Permanent Constitution (1973), 5, 8
Permanent Mandates Commission, 196, 199, 201–2
Persians, 1
Perthes, Volker, 64, 77*n*, 124

Peters, E. L., 174
Phalanges, 200
Picot, Georges, 171
Pipes, Daniel, 19
PKK Kurdish movement, 33, 235–7, 238, 240, 276
PLO, 78*n*, 125, 259, 262, 263, 279–81
Pococke, Richard, 155
Ponsot, Henri, 192
population
  age pyramid, 7, 110–12, 127
  growth rate, 36, 66, 110–12
Primakov, Yvegeny, 75*n*
private sector, 7–8, 63–4, 67, 68–9, 80, 118, 123–4
  financial sector, 107
  foreign trade, 102–4
  Investment Law No. 10 (1991), 7, 65, 74, 85–7, 120–2
  investment sector, 83, 85, 107, 120–2
  trade sector, 107
professional unions, 7
public sector, 7, 67, 79, 80
  economic performance, 118
  effects of liberalization, 64
  financial sector, 107
  foreign trade, 102–4
  investment, 83–5
  support for ruling regime, 61

al-Qadr night prayers, 24
Qalbiyya tribe, 40
al-Qassem, ʻAbd al-Rauf, 231–2
Qassem, ʻAbd al-Karim, 217
Qatar, 119
Qatar economic summit, 72
Qubat Qarʻa, 253, 254
al-Qudsi, ʻAdnan, 223
al-Qudsi, Nazim, 213, 217
Qulitat tribe, 172, 174
al-Qomi, Saʻad al-Din, 22
Quneitra, 146, 279
Qur'an, 27–8
Qur'anic schools, 9
al-Quwatli, Shukri, 192, 195, 200, 214

Rabin, Yitzhak
  assassination, 72
  border incidents, 291*n*
  Golan Heights, 71, 268, 279
  and Jordan, 281, 283
  rocket attacks on Israel, 277, 280
  Syrian agreements, 275, 290*n*
  Syrian peace negotiations, 278
  Syrian–Israeli peace process, 282–3, 286
Rabinovich, Itamar, 276, 284
Rabinovich, Danny, 178
Rafeq, Abdul Karim, 163
Ramadan, 20, 24–5, 26–7
Ramat Gan, 286
Ramat Magshimim, 279
Rashaya, 192
Rashid, Amir Muhammad, 223, 224
Rashid, Mehmet, 136, 137
Rashid Pasha, Mustafa, 137
red line agreement, 276–7
Republican Guards, 39, 41
Riyadh–Cairo accords, 275
Rıza, Hüseyın, 141, 142
Robins, Philip, 241
Rohan, Michael Dennis, 285
Romania, 35, 40
Romans, 1
Russia, 69, 75*n*, 95, 269
Rwala tribe, 172, 173, 183*n*

Saʻdi, ʻAli Salih, 218
Sabbagh, Suha, 175
Sadat, Anwar
  1973 war, 258, 269
  economic policies, 62
  peace treaty with Israel, 125, 218, 261, 264, 265
  Syria, 264, 272
  and the West, 64
al-Sadr, Musa, 8, 21–2
Safi, Ibrahim, 43, 45, 46, 48
Safveti Pasha, 136
Sagi, Uri, 275
al-Sahaf, Muhammad, 223, 224
Saʻid, Majid, 286
al-Saʻid, Nuri, 214, 215, 257
Salah al-Din, 286
Salamé, Ghassan, 68
Salih, Muhammad Mahdi, 223
Salim, Ahmad b., 135, 136, 137
Salman, Muhammad, 34
Salzman, P. C., 173
San-Remo Conference, 2
Sarai, 160
Saudi Arabia
  aid to Syria, 80, 119
  Asad's regional strategy, 62, 260, 265, 266
  assistance to Syria, 210
  co-optation policy, 67
  Iraqi unity, 222
  Syria under al-Quwatli, 214
  Syrian *coup d'état* (1949), 214–15
  Syrian–Iraqi federation, 215

savings, 83–5
Sayda, 138
al-Sayyed, 'Abd al-Sattar, 27–8
al-Sayyid, *Shaykh* Tawfiq, 25
Schiff, Ze'ev, 278
school enrolment ratio, 7
Schumacher, G., 172
Seale, Patrick, 5, 6, 47, 51, 262
security forces, appointments system, 6
service sector, 81, 82, 84, 85, 86, 87
Shafik, Nemat, 125
Shalit, Yoram, 151, 152
Shamir, Yitzhak, 268, 269
al-Shar', Faruq, 222, 223, 283–4
Shari'a, 24–5, 153
al-Shatiji, 'Abdallah, 162
Shatt al-'Arab, 212
Shihab, President of Lebanon, 253
Shehadeh, Lamia Rustum, 183*n*
Shihabi, Hikmat, 38, 42, 47
Shi'i Supreme Council, 21
Shi'is, in Iraq, 198, 219, 222, 273
Shishakli, Adib, 3, 4, 215
al-Shufi, Hamud, 218
Shukour, Yusuf, 249
Sidon, 196, 197
Simmel, George, 176
SIPRI, 88–9, 90, 92, 93
SLA *see* South Lebanese Army (SLA)
Socialist Decrees (1961), 4
Solarz, Stephen, 277
South Lebanese Army (SLA), 175, 176, 177, 178–9, 285
Soviet Union
  arms supply to Syria, 93–4
  change in Cold War policies, 220
  change in policy towards Syria, 80, 259, 266
  collapse of, 34, 50, 230, 259
  Glasnost, 73
  support for Syria, 35, 63, 230
  Syrian debt, 75*n*, 93–4, 95
  Syrian strategic balance policy, 116–18
  withdrawal from world politics, 118
Stalin, Joseph, 287–8
state capitalism, 60–2, 66–9
Stock exchange, 122–3
Stockholm Peace Research Institute (SIPRI), 88–9, 90, 92, 93
The Struggle for Syria, 51
Sublime Porte, 136–7, 139, 141, 142, 153
Suez Canal, 60
al-Sulh, Afif, 199
al-Sulh, Riad, 193, 194, 199, 200
Sunni-Muslims
  and 'Alawis, 20
  French Mandate, 2
  government bureaucracy, 6
  independent Syria, 3, 36
  Islamic opposition, 8–9, 17
  Ottoman Rule, 1
Sunni Arabs, Iraq, 212
Supreme Council of Investment, 87
Surat al-Fatiha, 27
Sweet, Louise, 173
Sykes, Sir Mark, 171
Syrian Computer Association, 41
Syrian Constitution, 8
Syrian Family Planning Association, 118
Syrian Jews, 277–8
Syrian National party, 3–4
Syrian Times, 285
Syrian-Arab national movement, 2
Syrian–Israeli peace process, 50, 68, 124–6, 278, 282–73
  Golan Heights, 71, 266, 267–8, 269–70
  Madrid talks, 63, 70, 73, 177, 267–70
  stagnation of, 69, 70–3, 222, 223, 225
  Syrian military–security echelons opposition, 45

al-Tabbakh, Muhammad, 161
Ta'if agreement (1989), 264, 275
al-Takhtajiyah, 22
Talas, Mustafa, 6, 38, 281
Tanzimat regime, 2
Tapper, R., 173
Tarablus, 138
Teke, 137
Tel-Dan, 251–2
tender proposals, 57–9, 74*n*
Teonge, Henry, 156
Terra Santa missionaries, 161
al-Thawra
  Asad in holiday sermons, 25
  Asad in public prayer, 24
  Asad's *'Umra* pilgrimage, 23
  death of Asad's son, 27
  foreign holiday greetings to Asad, 26
  Islamic Conference, 29
  oath of allegiance to Asad, 28
Third World Debt, 63
Tiberias, 138, 146
Tigris River, 233, 237
Torcy, Louis de, 139
tourism industry, 122
trade sector, 81, 82, 85, 86
transport and communications sector, 81, 82, 84, 85, 86

Treaty of Brotherhood Cooperation and Coordination (1991), 203
Tripoli
autonomy, 198
demonstrations, 196, 199, 200
English business operations, 154
return to Syria, 192–3, 196, 197, 201–2
Trotsky, Leon, 287–8
Troupes Spéciales du Levant, 2
Tunisia, 7, 31*n*, 63, 285–6
al-Turk, Ghada, 285
Turkey, 213
annexation of Alexandretta, 201
Euphrates waters, 225, 233–5, 237
industrialization, 76*n*
and Iraq, 212, 214, 222
and Israel, 72, 77*n*, 222, 223, 224, 225, 229, 238–9, 269
Kurdish problem, 33, 235–7, 238, 239, 240, 276
Palestine War (1948), 214
and Syria, 4, 33, 68, 228–41
Syrian support for terrorists, 235–8, 240, 276

'ulama, 1, 158, 159
'Umar Ridha Kahala, 170
Umayya Mosque, 30, 158
'Umra, 8, 23
UNDP, 7
unemployment, 114, 126
United Arab Emirates (UAE), 285
United Arab Republic (UAR), 4, 216–17, 226*n*, 229, 246–8, 257–8
United Nations (UN), 223–4, 246
United States (US)
Asad's peace proposals, 264
Asad's regional strategy, 266, 267
cooling of relations with, 33–4
Israeli withdrawal from Golan Heights, 222, 258
Jordan River diversion, 246
Operation Accountability, 277
planned military strikes against Iraq, 224
relations with Syria, 37, 45, 47, 71, 118, 220, 221, 230
support for Netanyahu, 72
Syrian–Iraqi relations, 224
threat to Syria, 35
'Uqla, 'Adnan, 36
urbanization, 34
US Arms Control and Disarmament Agency (ACDA), 88–9, 90, 92, 93
utilities, 81, 82, 84, 85, 86

Viénot, Pierre, 191, 196, 198, 200, 202, 207
Viorst, Milton, 288
Volney, Constantine, 155
Voltaire, Françoise Marie Arouet de, 61

Wahabiyya ideology, 162
Wal-Mart, 68
waqfs, 26
wasam, 171, 182*n*
wasta, 58, 176
water shortages, 34
Weizman, Ezer, 125
Welfare Party (Turkey), 239
West Bank, 175, 264, 267–8
Wilson, Rodney, 76–7*n*
women's unions, 7
worker's remittances, 62, 63, 113, 122
World Bank, 59, 64, 85, 94, 99, 123

Yaar, Ephraim, 178
Yadin, Yigal, 125
Yarmuck Plan, 254
Yeltsin, Boris, 73
Yemen, 119, 120
Yılmaz, Mesut, 238, 240
Yizrael Valley, 173
youth organizations, 7

Zahirah, 171, 172, 180
Zahle, 276
al-Za'im, Husni, 214, 229
Zittrain Eisenberg, Laura, 177
al-Zu'bi, Mahmud, 38, 115, 291*n*